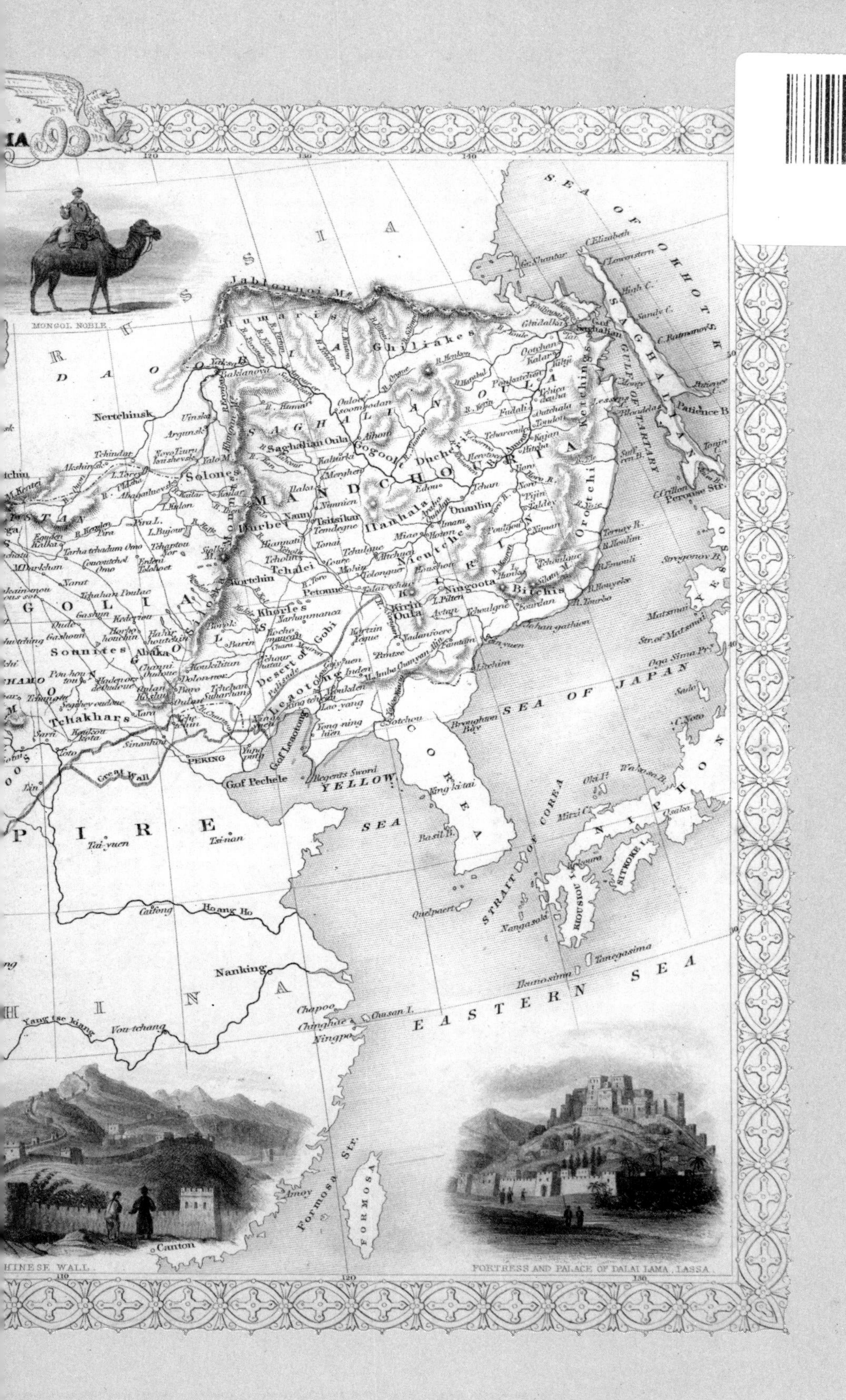

MONGOL NOBLE

CHINESE WALL

FORTRESS AND PALACE OF DALAI LAMA, LASSA

This Grand Beyond

This Grand Beyond

The Travels of Isabella Bird Bishop

Selected By Cicely Palser Havely

CENTURY PUBLISHING
LONDON

A Note On The Text

Victorian travel narratives were generally packed with facts and details that would weary a modern reader. They were designed to inform as well as entertain. But my purpose is to show the response of a Victorian gentlewoman to remote cultures and regions of the world then barely explored. Consequently I have pruned away some of the duller factual passages and left only enough to give the authentic instructive flavour. I have also cut out passages where what was familiar to Mrs Bishop's contemporaries is lost to us. And I have frequently boiled down quite ruthlessly her leisurely discursiveness to make a good rich stock—a process of which I hope such an admirer of the virtues of Liebig's Essence of Beef would approve. Consequently, at one stage in the compilation of this selection, I found that passages of the text were suffused with ellipses to indicate omissions. These proved so intrusive to all who read that draft that I decided to go against the approved scholarly practices and to leave out the ellipses. My intention is to spare the reader, not to give a false impression of Mrs Bishop's character or writing.

I have tried to supply all necessary extra information in the brief headnotes to each section which are also intended to provide the briefest possible framework and connecting thread. A fuller examination of Mrs Bishop's life and the qualities of her work is to be found in the Introduction. Her lavish use of quotation marks and fragments of hymns and usually now obscure poetry is typically Victorian and it would be pointless to try and identify all of them. Her frequent use of Scottish words and phrases testifies to her deep affection for the Western Isles and to the fact that her first five books were based on letters sent home to her sister in Edinburgh and Tobermory; this also accounts for the British topographical references. Mrs Bishop hardly ever paused to give details of other European travellers, missionaries, settlers or diplomatic personages; and neither have I.

Contents

Introduction

Climbing the Peh-teo-shan spur by a long series of rocky, broken zigzags, cut on its side through a hazel wood, and reaching an altitude of about 9270 feet in advance of my men, I felt the joy of a 'born traveller' as I watched the mules with their picturesque Man-tze muleteer, the eleven men no longer staggering under burdens, but jumping, laughing and singing, some of them with leaves of an artemisia stuffed into their nostrils to prevent the bleeding from the nose which had troubled them since leaving Weichou, the two soldiers in their rags, and myself the worst ragamuffin of all. There were many such Elysian moments in this grand 'Beyond'.

When she wrote this, Mrs Bishop was 65 years old and had suffered from heart disease for four years. But illness was nothing new to her. She had been a frail child whose friends would have guessed her born for a life of ladylike invalidism, not for travelling. Yet in the second half of her life she travelled tirelessly in Canada and the United States, in the Pacific, in Japan, Korea, and the Malay States, in India and Tibet, Persia, Turkey, and North Africa; and the nine books she wrote about her experiences made her famous. In the last years of her life (she died in 1904) she seemed to be an embodiment of Britain's confident moral superiority. She was unstoppable: neither floods nor man-eating tigers, corrupt officials nor incompetent servants, extremes of climate, fleas, nor the hostility of local populations ever prevented her from going where she wanted to go and seeing what she wanted to see. There was apparently nowhere in the world where such a dauntless representative of the British will could ever be thwarted. Not the least useful of her attributes was that she presented the same short, stout, upright figure as Queen Victoria herself.

As a figurehead of Empire, Isabella Bird Bishop is now only a historical curiosity. But she is still exemplary because she never let notions of what a woman ought or ought not to do stand in her way. We tend to think that few Victorian women achieved much in any kind of extra-domestic activity. In fact research in almost any area of Victorian life tends to turn up names of once distinguished but now almost forgotten women who deserve bringing to light again. The personality and achievements of Isabella Bird Bishop merit an honourable place in this renaissance of interest.

Isabella Lucy Bird was born at Boroughbridge in North Yorkshire on 15 October 1831. Her father came from what used to be called 'an Indian family'. He had been educated for the legal profession in India, but in Calcutta cholera had killed his first wife and their young son and had broken his own health. He returned to England and entered the Church—a decision reinforced by another strong family tradition, the moral enthusiasm derived from his mother's close connection with the Wilberforce family.

According to Anne Stoddart, who was Isabella's first biographer (or hagiographer), the ladies of the family took no sugar in their tea as 'a sacred protest against slave-grown products', and continued in their sacrifice long after the slaves were freed.

Isabella's mother was the highly educated daughter of another clergyman, and the sister of two Members of Parliament, for which office, Stoddart tersely adds, another sister, 'the more brilliant Barbara was unhappily disqualified'. So Isabella was closely related to at least one woman whose sex barred her from what she might have achieved.

For eight years of Isabella's childhood her father held the rural living of Tattenhall in Cheshire. On account of her frailty, a local doctor suggested that her father should take her with him on the front of his saddle when he went about his parish business. Not only did she thus learn to ride at an early age, but she later attributed all her habits of careful observation to her father's keen interest in everything he saw and shared with his daughter as they rode together.

Miss Stoddart looked for a strictly moral motivation for her subject's travels and found one in Isabella's early devotion to the traditional duties of a clergy daughter, first assumed when the family moved in her eleventh year to a busy urban parish in Birmingham. They were there for six years, and when the Rev. Edward Bird's health began to fail they moved back to a quieter rural parish, this time at Wyton near Olney and Houghton, then in Huntingdonshire. It was there at the age of 18 that Isabella developed what Stoddart called a 'fibrous tumour' of the spine which was surgically removed. She suffered from severe back pain for the rest of her life.

Boroughbridge Hall, Yorkshire, where
Isabella Lucy Bird was born.

Only travelling brought her any significant relief. Her earliest journeys were undertaken specifically for her health's sake, and the later ones continued to relieve her of much pain, even when her increasing age brought about its inevitable general stiffening. She felt less pain on a mud floor or in a wet tent, riding on a horse, a mule, an elephant, a yak, or even a cow than she did on any padded Victorian sofa.

This brings to mind Elizabeth Barrett's famous quitting of her couch at Robert

Mrs Edward Bird, Mrs Bishop's mother.

The Rev. Edward Bird, Mrs Bishop's father.

Browning's call, and Florence Nightingale's almost equally famous taking to hers once the Crimean War was over.

In all three, as in so many other famous and mysterious Victorian illnesses, there is an obvious psychosomatic element, and in Isabella Bird's case there seems to have been some kind of equation between what was lacking in her life in England and Scotland and what she found in so many of the remote places that the goods and values of nineteenth-century Europe had hardly touched.

Convalescent visits to relations, excursions to bracing seaside resorts, and family holidays in the Western Isles of Scotland failed to set her up. She wrote and published a few articles, studied chemistry, and sewed, 'all of which were possible in a semi-recumbent position'. A long sea voyage was prescribed, and eventually in 1854 a suitable opportunity was found for her to travel to Nova Scotia, Canada, and the United States with some distant cousins.

One of the most useful functions of the medical practitioner is to give the patient permission to do what he or she wants to do. *The Englishwoman in America*, the book resulting from her trip, is clearly the work of a young person delighted by her own independence. She shows no signs of convalescent weakness. Beside her narrative the better-known American travels of Mrs Trollope (*The Domestic Manners of the Americans*, 1832) and Charles Dickens (*American Notes*, 1842) seem obviously touched by the querulousness and languor of those who are not quite their best selves.

Mrs Trollope, for example, was appalled by the Americans' hasty, unceremonious eating habits, their constant segregation of the sexes, their over-protective etiquette—and above all by their disregard of old social distinctions. Her work is a far more reliable guide to part of the British inner landscape than it is to the manners and morals of the Americans.

Miss Bird's travels in the area of the St Lawrence and the Great Lakes were in most respects no more than an extended tourist jaunt which hardly ever took her beyond the limits of well-established public transport systems. What was remarkable about the trip was the way this young woman threw herself into the experience. She quite simply *enjoyed* America, which was something many of her compatriots were unwilling to do. Not even an unusually noxious hotel in Chicago (the first of so many grim hostelries that she took in her stride) could damp her spirits. She never let the unpleasant aspects of a journey (and there were to be far lousier beds, far more nauseating meals, among other more serious hardships) spoil the experience of the whole. A tourist's holiday can be wrecked by a bad hotel, but the traveller's journey is enriched by anything that is unusual, whether on the good or bad side of the normal. It was the instincts of a traveller that made her not at all sorry for the opportunity 'of seeing something of American society in its lowest grade'. What she saw of course was still safely some way above the very 'lowest grade', but such an inn and the proximity of the colourful and possibly lawless characters on the westbound train were new experiences for a gently raised young woman—even one who had done her duty as a clergyman's daughter in an industrial parish. The prissy, ladylike reservations of her upbringing can still be detected in her careful generalizations about bad language in America and the deference shown to women.

The Englishwoman in America was published by John Murray in 1856. The title was not of her choosing and quite at odds with her commendable reluctance to make too many chauvinistic judgements on what she saw. Indeed her most rounded pronouncements on national characteristics tend to be about the former inhabitants of the British Isles. In her account of Cincinnati she notes that 'the Irish are still the willing and ignorant tools of an ambitious and despotic priesthood'; that the English and Scots are unemployable in the furniture factories 'on account of their intemperance'; and that English spades and axes are unsaleable because they 'won't stand two days' hard work'.

It would be wrong, however, to claim that she was entirely free of that sense of their own moral superiority which some English men and women still retained to an extraordinary degree. On certain themes Miss Bird expatiated with a preposterous but charming gravity:

> The facility with which English books are reprinted in America, and the immense circulation which they attain in consequence of their cheapness, greatly increases the responsibility which rests upon our authors as to the direction which they give, whether for good or evil, to the intelligent and enquiring mind of the youth of America—minds ceaselessly occupied, both in religion and politics, in investigation and enquiry—in overturning old systems before they have devised new ones.

There was no question of a bashful young lady being cajoled reluctantly into print; Isabella Bird had already published several articles and seems to have set out with every intention of writing a book about her travels. A professional life like that of the modern freelance journalist was as open to women then as it is now, and the number of publications by women and their success compare quite favourably with the situation today. The procedure she followed with all her books, until death deprived her of the right kind of recipients, was to write long, detailed letters back to her family, and make separate notes about the more inert statistics of her travels. The letters, tidied up and freed from anything that was for family consumption only, then provided the basis of the published narrative.

The Birds were a fairly well-to-do family, but Isabella was not short of a use for the 'substantial cheques' she received from her publisher. Like many well-heeled visitors to western Scotland, she had been shocked by the plight of the local people. Large areas of the then over-populated Western Isles had been devastated by potato blight during the 1840s, and the resulting enforced emigration, which was partly necessary but simultaneously convenient for the landowners, continued through the 1850s. These clearances were appallingly brutal, and it was to the alleviation of the ensuing distress that Isabella Bird devoted the considerable royalties from *The Englishwoman in America* and some of her subsequent books. She not only contributed money for the purchase of deep-sea fishing boats, for equipment for tweed manufacture, and for kitting out emigrant families (who all too often were dumped on the shores of the New World with no more than the clothes on their backs), but over many years lent her very considerable organizing abilities to these projects as well. The pattern which developed later in her life suggests that her arduous charitable work was not only funded in a very real sense by her travels but fuelled by them in a more emotional sense as well. A relatively brief period of travelling, devoted to the achievement of intense personal satisfaction, seemed to charge her up for years of laborious and often tedious work on behalf of others in Britain until the onset of illness once again allowed her to set off on her own. The economic relationship between the two sides of her life—the hardworking, charitable, conventional Victorian woman and the adventurer—is very strong: each side paid for the other.

In some ways *The Englishwoman in America* was a false start. It was nearly twenty years before she began the journeys she was born for. During that time her father died and she moved with her mother and her sister Henrietta to Edinburgh, where her mother also died. The sisters continued to live together, mostly in Edinburgh and at Tobermory on the island of Mull. Isabella travelled to North America and around Britain in pursuit of her work for the Highlanders and other charitable causes. She led the busy, organized, and useful life of a well-educated, devout Victorian lady of independent status and means with no particular profession. Throughout this time her health was vaguely poor, and from Anna Stoddart's description she seems to have suffered periods of withdrawal and depression. Eventually the customary sea voyage was once again prescribed and she left for a trip to New York and the Mediterranean. It did no good. The dose was increased. She set off round the world in an easterly direction. About neither Australia nor New Zealand could she find a good word to say: Australia combined the worst of Britain with a fretful climate and in New Zealand everyone was drunk. But as they reached Honolulu her health began to improve, and it was during 1873 in Hawaii and later in Colorado that her life came to a late and splendid spring. It was her forty-second year.

At first she spent her time conventionally enough, collecting ferns, gossiping with the missionaries and other white settlers, and inspecting the recently and not very profoundly converted native Hawaiians. The high point of the first part of her stay in what were then called the Sandwich Islands was an easy jaunt to the active crater of the volcano Kilauea. The mountain is just over 4000 feet high, the tracks were clearly marked, and the inn at the crater was well established and much used by tourists of whom the American Miss Karpe, Miss Bird's companion on this trip, was probably a fair example.

But it was the most strenuous trip she had ever undertaken, and her letters to Henrietta play up its drama to the full. It was her first ride astride, and her first use for the travelling dress that became so famous that she agreed to its display at the National Health Exhibition in 1884, 'at the request of the Committee'. She refers to

Mrs Bishop in her travelling dress in Armenia, 1890.

this garment frequently in her writings, but not in the kind of detail that makes either its construction or its virtues plain to the modern reader. It consisted of baggy bloomers gathered into frills around the ankles and topped with a long skirt cut in such a way as to fall either side of the saddle and conceal the bloomers. When she dismounted, the garment fell into instant, skirtlike respectability.

Once she had acquired the taste for adventure, all kinds of caution were thrown to the winds. She never did anything indecorous—she was a lady to the bone—but she seems to have learnt in an instant how to be unconventional without embarrassment. Reflecting that her riding dress was 'really not unlike a fashionable Newport bathing suit', she waded up to her neck along a river to admire a remote waterfall: 'a gruesome den, but well worth a visit', she comments drily in the immemorial manner of guidebooks. If she made too much of a fuss about the rigours of her trip up Kilauea, she probably took too little account of the very real dangers of her ride recorded in the second extract from *Six Months in the Sandwich Islands* with only two very young Hawaiians for company along the northeastern coast of Hawaii from Hilo to Waipio. Part of this coast is scored with deep ravines (*palis*), and the rivers that flow down them run dangerously fast after heavy tropical storms. Even allowing for a certain amount of excusable bravado, her account of this ride suggests that it was not a very sensible undertaking: 'a white man . . . or an experienced native' would never have allowed it.

Miss Bird had put so much into her letters about her first volcano that she had few resources left to make a proper climax out of her account of her second, which was a much more unusual achievement. Mauna Loa is over 14,000 feet and its remote summit was accessible only after a long and arduous ride. Few people had ever visited it, and it seems remarkable that Mr W. L. Green, 'a gentleman of wide scientific and literary culture', should ask for the company of a middle-aged Englishwoman who had only so recently shown any evidence of the hardihood the expedition called for and who had no particular expertise to contribute. But Isabella Bird was a woman of spirit. She made up her mind that 'he should never have any bother in consequence of his kindness in taking me with him', and kept her upper lip stiff even when it proved impossible to brew tea in their summit camp.

However it was not just temperament that was to enable her to undertake journeys far more strenuous than this, but a combination of temperament and a lucky constitution. Her ability to bear cold (another characteristic she shared with Queen Victoria) was later attributed to 'a physically large heart'. The altitude of Mauna Loa's summit did not trouble her, and later she was unaffected by Himalayan altitudes of over 17,000 feet, at which even many of the local people were liable to fail. Perhaps her most fortunate attribute was her 'superb digestion' which, Anna Stoddart says with transparent admiration, 'conquered strange food and endured its lack'. Yet it was partly for her health's sake that Isabella went next to a region noted for killing, if it did not cure, the consumptives who ventured there: the Front Range of the Rocky Mountains near Denver.

Indeed Miss Stoddart euphemistically refers to the rough-and-ready dude ranch where Isabella stayed in Estes Park as a 'sanatorium'.

It was in what is now the Rocky Mountain National Park that I first came across Isabella Bird, and her third travel book, *A Lady's Life in the Rocky Mountains*. It is a work of great charm, and unlike her other works, contains not a single passage that time has dulled. Happily it has now been reprinted in its entirety by Virago. The choice of excerpts here was particularly difficult and yet inevitable, because any anthology that could claim to represent the range of its author's personality has to include the great romance of her life: James Nugent, known as 'Rocky Mountain Jim'.

The story of the opening up of the West is studded with characters like Jim, the black sheep of good European families in whom the tattered remnants of their education combined with a swashbuckling contempt for civilization. Twenty years earlier Isabella Bird had ingenuously noted 'that there is no country in the world where the presence of a lady is such a restraint upon manners and conversation' as America, and so at first she felt able to enjoy quite unguardedly the company of a man who could have had no place in her circle at home. However, the relationship deepened into something much more than mountain camaraderie, as even the published version of the story shows. Some unpublished passages in the original letters to her sister Henrietta help us to read with a fuller understanding the discreet hints which were all that Isabella Bird could allow herself to print.

It had become her habit to write at the top of her letters 'Nothing annoying in this', so that Henrietta would know immediately she opened one of her sister's densely written packages that Isabella was still unscathed, emotionally as well as physically, by her adventures. But Isabella was obliged to begin a long letter started at Estes Park on 18 November 1873 with the words 'I cannot say there is nothing annoying in it', for she had to relate that Jim had 'admitted he was attached' to her and it was killing him. It began on Long's Peak, he said. It made me shake all over and even cry. He is a man who any woman might love, but who no sane woman would marry.' Isabella was shocked, but not really surprised: 'For 5 minutes at the camping ground on Long's Peak his manner was such that for a moment I thought this possible, but I put it away as egregious vanity impardonable in a woman of 40.' And although she told him firmly that she 'would not dare to trust [her] happiness to him because of whisky', she admitted to Henrietta that her feelings for him were painfully strong: 'I could not bear to think of him that night out in the snow neither eating nor sleeping, mad, lost, hopeless, wretched . . . I miss him very much . . . it takes peace away.'

Her subconscious mind disclosed her passion even more vividly: 'I dreamt last night that as we were sitting by the fire, Mr Nugent came in with his revolver in his hand and shot me.' The violence of the conflict between her instincts and her sense of what was proper or wise is plain in passages she could not print. For how could a respectable clergy daughter reveal that she had fallen in love with a drunken desperado? 'He looked so ill . . . going to his dark lonely lair and I felt that I had stabbed him and not made sufficient allowances for him . . . I wished him goodbye wishing I could bring him here and make him warm tea and be nice to him rather than kill him as I had done.' In the book she finds an acceptable way of giving some expression to these simple, painful feelings by suggesting an earnest desire to bring Jim to a Christian repentance. For though it was impossible to tell the public the real story of her relationship with 'poor dear Jim', it was equally impossible to leave out of her narrative altogether what had made her months in Colorado so important.

Her desire to tell the truth but keep it veiled is suggested by a curious violent ornament she adds to the narrative of her reckless excursion to Longmont for her letters in dangerous weather. In the published version Jim suddenly appears out of the freezing mist 'and at the same moment there was the flash of a pistol close to my ear'. But in the original letter she 'nearly rode over him' before he made himself known, and there is no pistol shot. The shot is a private acknowledgement of the force of her dream.

Jim seems to have been the first—and perhaps the only—man she ever loved passionately. But he was not the first man who had fallen in love with her. In Hawaii a 'fine pleasant backwoodsman' confessed that she made him feel 'strange all over' the first time she spoke to him, and a little later he persuaded a friend to propose to her on his behalf. He admitted 'he had been what women called very wild. And what this means in Waimea, it is fearful to think of!' She declined, of course, but cheerfully and uninhibitedly admitted that she enjoyed his company: His frank jovial manners and handsome fresh-looking face are such a pleasant contrast to the icy bloodless Americans . . . In that style of life and country there is a seemliness about a nice Garibaldi [i.e. red] shirt especially when worn by handsome men. In every way she was coming into her own. In the next thirty years there were to be further instances of men seeking her company in some of the more comfortless places of the world.

Estes Park is now the name of a prosperous small resort about seventy miles from Denver, but the name used to denote a high and then remote valley area of parklike scenery among the highest mountains of northern Colorado. There was no white settlement in the area before the 1860s, but by the end of the decade it was quite regularly visited by tourists and hunters. Griff Evans, with whom Isabella Bird stayed, had settled there in 1867 and made his living raising cattle and running a kind of dude ranch for visitors. Other settlers in other valleys of the still only thinly populated region took in travellers, and Isabella Bird had been riding alone and staying where she might for several weeks before she came to Estes Park. Her vivid record of that time is a valuable contribution to the history of the early settlement of the West, but the more personal parts of her narrative have to be taken with a pinch of salt.

The two 'students' who accompanied her and Mountain Jim in their climb, or rather haul, up Long's Peak were a future judge of Boulder and a future mayor of Denver. Mayor Rogers later recorded his own version of the trip which was included in a collection of local reminiscences (*Early Estes Park* by Enos A. Mills, 1911). When they were asked if a lady might accompany them, they consoled themselves 'with the hope that she would prove young, beautiful and vivacious. Our hopes were dispelled when Miss Bird appeared, wearing bloomers, riding cowboy fashion, with a face and figure not corresponding to our ideals. The rest of his brief account is characterized by a rather dreary grass-roots rationalism, doubtless intended as a corrective to Miss Bird's famous high-flown romanticism. Rogers says that Miss Bird was taken in by Jim, who was no better than a braggart and a drunk and not even a very reliable guide to the mountain they were climbing. Miss Bird herself readily admitted that the climb was almost too much for her (even today, over excellent National Park trails, it is a 12- to 15-hour hike for the very fit), but Rogers suggests that her will to make the climb was so far in excess of her actual strength that the expedition was a dangerous folly. Later, her ride to Longmont seems to have been undertaken in equally reckless defiance of the weather and the terrain. She was still very much a greenhorn in the back country. The two young men do not come very well out of Miss Bird's story and no doubt Mayor Rogers felt he had to set the record straight. From his and other contemporary accounts of the young but thriving tourist industry in Estes Park it is clear that *A Lady's Life in the Rocky Mountains* is not quite the way it really was, but life a little more highly coloured, a little exaggerated, enriched, romanticized, and generally adjusted to make a better story.

And this is probably true of all her narratives—and indeed of most travellers' tales. When she was in Hawaii her sister Henrietta gently suggested that if life there was as agreeable as Isabella's letters made out, she might join her. Isabella's immediate negative was incongruously fierce. To some extent she was living out a fantasy when she travelled, a fantasy that could not have survived the scrutiny of someone whose presence would have transformed Hawaii into another Edinburgh. There is nothing really reprehensible about her usually quite moderate self-glamorization; she never positively lied about what she did, though sometimes her stories are a little tall. On one Colorado ride she claimed she had satisfied her hunger by cracking the cherry-stones she found in the stomach of a dead bear! She had all the instincts of an astute self-publicist, and was fortunate enough to appeal to a public who unsceptically took her at her own estimation. Later, for example, a story appeared in all the early accounts of her life which seems to have been concocted to plump out the formative years of a future heroine. Anna Stoddart gives a circumstantial version.

> She had taken a cab from the railway station, and while driving out of the gate received on her lap a small parcel of advertisements, which, as was usual then, were thrown in at the open window. Putting it on the seat in front of her, she noticed another parcel lying, evidently left by the former 'fare'. She opened it, and found papers inside giving details of a plot to assassinate a member of the Cabinet at the approaching funeral of the Duke of Wellington. She had scarcely put them into her pocket, when she heard a voice stopping the cab and a dark-coloured foreign-looking man addressed her at the window. He asked if a parcel had been found in the carriage. At once she handed him the little bundle of advertisements, and after a minute's progress bade the driver hasten to the Home Office where she insisted upon seeing the Minister, in whose hands she placed the papers. So serious did the matter appear to the Home Office that,

> while she remained in London a detective was posted there to guard her against the vengeance of those whose plans she had frustrated.

No government department that I have approached has any records to indicate a grain of truth in that unlikely story.

In many respects Isabella Bird—and so many others like her—was the equivalent of the maker of spectacular television documentaries today. Though she travelled for her own pleasure, in her books she was doing other people's travelling for them. She both raised an appetite for faraway places and adventure and half, but only half, satisfied it. A television documentary about a remote corner of the world follows very similar conventions. It makes the most of both the pleasures and the dangers of the experience and excludes the tedious and the routine. It creates an illusion of great intimacy with the land and the local people which for the most part depends upon an elaborate pretence that there is no intervening technology and no intervening foreign sensibility. It was only later that Isabella Bird took a camera on her journeys, but she inevitably took with her the mental attitudes of a Victorian gentlewoman, and she could no more become an integrated inhabitant of the places she visited than a maker of a modern television documentary can become a sherpa. She remained a traveller, a passer-through, and her naive delight at the spectacle of herself in outlandish places and among exotic characters is very charming. 'It was so new, and so odd, to be the only white woman among eleven natives in a lonely house, and yet to be as secure from danger and annoyance as in our own home.' Television conventions, on the other hand, usually require an unexcited, neutral attitude in the presenter and an assumption that his or her own presence on the scene is a normal, even humdrum occurrence. Where Isabella Bird exactly duplicates the function of the documentary film maker is in the instructive and descriptive aspects of her work. I have for example drastically abbreviated her careful record of the vegetation she found around the crater of Kilauea so that only a flavour remains of passages that a modern reader would find pedantic. But television companies are able to count on very large audiences for films about almost any branch of natural history, and they know well enough that the substance of even a simplified commentary will not actually be absorbed by the audience, which nevertheless expects and enjoys it.

Elaborate description of the kind Miss Bird wrote so impressively has been so totally superseded by photography that a modern reader can find it difficult. It often seems too high-coloured and high-flown, but we must remember that she had to create her kind of powerful visual impressions by words alone, and, of its kind, what she does is very well done. It is not easy to describe the simplest pastoral landscape, let alone an erupting volcano or the remote heights of the Rocky Mountains, in words that not only convey the emotional impact of the sight but give the reader some precise information about it at the same time. Miss Bird does not simply rave about Nature: her description of the 'huge coiled hawsers' of lava is both vivid and accurate, and her account of the behaviour of molten lava within the crater suggests an impressively disciplined eye: 'At times . . . bits of the lake skinned over with a skin of a wonderful silvery, satiny sheen, to be immediately devoured; and as the lurid billows broke, they were mingled with misplaced patches as if of bright moonlight.' This is not fanciful flimflam; it is popular science.

Her aim was the venerable combination of pleasure with instruction, and

Dr John Bishop.

religious and moral instruction were quite inseparable from her purpose. Like so many other Victorians, she read Nature with a moralist's eye: 'Last night I thought the Southern Cross out of place; tonight it seems essential, as Calvary over against Sinai. For Halemaumau involuntarily typifies the wrath which shall consume all evil: and the constellation, pale against its lurid light, the great love and yearning of the Father.' I am more inclined than Miss Bird to suspect Mountain Jim of humbug when he 'involuntarily and reverently uncovered his head, and exclaimed "I believe there is a God" ' at the sight of dawn on Long's Peak, but very few of her contemporaries were ever embarrassed by such a display of religious excitement.

Six Months in the Sandwich Islands and a serialization of her Rocky Mountain letters in *The Leisure Hour* were immediately successful, and Isabella Bird became famous. For the next four years she studied and devoted herself to the erection of a shelter and coffee house for cabmen in Princes' Street, Edinburgh, and to the raising of funds to commemorate David Livingstone. She corresponded with Jim Nugent until his death, shot in a quarrel with Griff Evans. She claimed that at the moment of his death she saw a vision of him in the Swiss hotel where she was taking a holiday. When her sister's physician, Dr John Bishop, proposed marriage she declined. At the end of 1877 another physician ordered her to travel again and she turned to Japan.

Unbeaten Tracks in Japan is the work of a professional traveller, whose first concern was to set down a conscientious record of a remote country that had only very recently become open to Western visitors. Her previous works had been fairly haphazard accounts of whatever chanced to happen to her; but this journey was a systematic undertaking. She was impressed by Japan, but despite what was obviously exotic in the people, the landscape, and the buildings, too much was too like Britain to satisfy her: she felt oppressed by the efficient and ubiquitous Japanese bureaucracy and the well-organized commercial life of the towns. Japan was not wild or primitive enough for her, but Hokkaido (then called Yezo) was quite unlike the more southerly islands. Its aboriginal inhabitants, the Ainu or 'hairy Aino' (so called to distinguish them from the smooth-faced Japanese), were a subject race, despised by the Japanese. Their culture was still almost uncontaminated by foreign influence and only two or three Europeans are known to have visited the interior of Hokkaido before Isabella Bird. I have omitted most of her careful and detailed account of the Ainu way of life (though it is still of value to geographers and anthropologists) because for the majority of readers it is the more subjectively coloured parts of the narrative that are most interesting.

She was accompanied only by Ito, her Japanese servant and interpreter, so no elaborate retinue or cumbersome mass of travelling gear cut her off from the people she was visiting. Indeed it was Ito, the uneasy representative of the ruling race, who found it more difficult to adapt to the experience and took with him much of his own food and accoutrements to ensure that his contact with the Ainu should be as superficial as possible. Isabella Bird took with her a 'cold fowl and potatoes'. She never really 'went native' but she was aware of her bias and moderate in her expression of her prejudices. Though such a devout Christian, she was glad not accidentally to have desecrated a god that was 'a stick with festoons of shavings hanging from it'. She naturally found nakedness and sexual frankness rather startling, but she quickly learned to take such things in her stride, though the delicacy of her readers had to be protected. The Ainu women 'asked . . . a number of questions regarding their own sex among ourselves, but few of these would bear repetition, and they answered a number of mine'.

Even on the subject of drink, a theme that could make a dragon out of a temperance dove, she did her best to record what she saw without too much praise or censure: 'Drinking, their great vice, is not, as among us, in antagonism to their religion, but is actually a part of it, and as such would be exceptionally difficult to eradicate.' On Hawaii she had seen the bigoted policies of so many missionaries who tried to eradicate everything they saw as vicious or immoral from the native culture without any attempt to understand the lives they intended to reform. In comparison her own views on drink were decidedly progressive, though she felt it necessary to stress that it was only because there was no tea on the summit of Mauna Loa that she made 'a great tin of brandy toddy' to accompany the tinned salmon and doughnuts. Her character is most transparently revealed in the summary of her impressions of the Ainu, when she stands back a little from the thrill she felt at being a lone white woman among savages. She saw the poverty of their lives clearly enough, but realized that the value of the experience to her was not just a moral education but a sensory delight. The pleasure she takes in describing the Ainu around their fire is as fervent as the tone of her message to any readers too complacent in their British certainties: 'they are uncivilizable and altogether irreclaimable savages, yet they are attractive, and in some ways fascinating, and I hope I shall never forget the music of their low, sweet voices.' *Unbeaten Tracks in Japan* established her reputation as a serious geographer. Its reputation was, as she said in a letter to her publisher, 'a triumph for a lady traveller', and she added,

Mrs Bishop's straw cloak.

Trackers preparing to meet Mrs Bishop at a Chinese inn, 1895.

Bridge and inn of Shan-rang-sar, China, 1896.

'It vindicates the right of a woman to do anything which she can do well.'

On her way home she visited Hong Kong, China, and the Malay States, and recorded her experiences in *The Golden Chersonese*, eventually published in 1883. The first extract from this book is a chilling description of the prison and execution site in Canton. To us it seems quite remarkable that anyone would want to visit such a place or that the local authorities should allow it. I have cut out of Miss Bird's account almost everything that was not her direct experience, but I have kept in Mr Bulkeley Johnson of Shanghai, who 'saw one hundred heads fall in one morning', as representative of the large numbers of European residents and visitors who made excursions to this dreadful place. Nor did they observe the proceedings from a discreet distance; at the tribunal Isabella Bird stood so close to the prisoners being interrogated that 'the dress of one touched my feet'. Later, wandering among the blood and fragments of corpses at the place of execution, she picked up as a souvenir the tag that had fallen from the neck of a decapitated prisoner with the same composure with which she had recorded that the street leading to the site was noted for 'the manufacture from palm leaves of very serviceable rain cloaks'. The serious traveller was in search of experience, not holiday pleasures. Yet of course there was pleasure of a kind even in an experience such as this. Isabella Bird ingenuously reveals a transparent pride in her ability to face this horror squarely, and her patriotic heart was clearly so touched by hearing the Cantonese prisoners cry 'Good, good is the prison of your Queen' that she seems not to have suspected their motives, nor to have made any connection between her party's resistance to their appeals for baksheesh and the 'execrations' that followed their departure.

The Malay States afforded her first sustained experience of the business of Empire. The region was returning to an uneasy stability after a period of guerrilla war; there was tension between the various racial groups as well as between them all and the British, and enough planters and administrators were still coming to a bloody end to give a spice of danger to the expeditions that Miss Bird made to the interior. She scoffed at the danger, and was far more disconcerted by the unwelcome company of two young ladies, whom politeness to the Governor obliged her to take on an up-river trip, than she was by tigers, poisonous snakes, or hostile inhabitants.

> We are apparently stuck fast, the chief cause for anxiety and embarrassment being that the youngest Miss Shaw is lying huddled up and shivering on one of the beds, completely prostrated by a violent, sick headache . . . brought on by the heat of the sun in the launch. She declares that she cannot move; but our experienced escort, who much fears bilious fever for her, is resolved that she shall as soon as any means of transit can be procured. Heretofore I have always travelled 'without encumbrance'. Is it treasonable to feel at this moment that these fair girls are one?

The insects were nearly as great a pest, and because her ankles were so swollen 'stockings have been an impossibility, and I have had to sew up my feet daily in linen'. But a tropical jungle was not cause enough for modifying her sturdy British tweeds, and she several times comments briskly on the 'most healthy climate of the region'. Really it was the moral climate that she approved so heartily. In pirate-infested waters she was moved to the following patriotic outburst:

> Our wretched little launch, moored to a cocoa palm, flies a blue ensign, and the Malay policemen wear an Imperial crown upon their caps,—both representing somewhat touchingly in this equatorial jungle the might of the small island lying far off amidst the fogs of the northern seas, and in this instance at least not her might only, but the security and justice of her rule.

Miss Bird's stay with the eccentric solitary, Mr Low, a 'model administrator', suited her so well because it combined the freedom to do as she pleased with the satisfying sense of British duty being done.

No one ever seems to have told Miss Bird that what she wanted to do was too dangerous for a woman. Nor, of course, was she the sole example of her kind. We think of middle-class Victorian women as living in a kind of purdah, but some of those who managed to escape were able to enjoy an enviable degree of freedom which may in part have been due to the very notions of sexual propriety that tended to keep the majority respectably at home. No one seems to have thought it odd that Mr Green should take Miss Bird camping on the edge of a volcano, or that she should stay unchaperoned in the residence of Mr Low, or accompany Captain Walker on a 'shooting excursion to a lotus lake'. Her relationship with Rocky Mountain Jim was clearly of a rather different kind, but still her contemporaries apparently accepted her account and did not feel compelled to look beyond the generalized romantic excitement for any specifically sexual encounter. Rare though it then was, Isabella Bird's freedom to share with men companionably the pursuits traditionally reserved for men alone became for decades after her time not less but far more difficult for a woman to achieve.

The excursion with Captain Walker turned out to be the last such jaunt for seven years. She arrived home weakened by a bout of typhoid contracted in Egypt, and generally debilitated and depressed. Her sister Henrietta's death in June 1880 thoroughly prostrated her. At the end of the year she rather joylessly agreed to marry Dr John Bishop, with whom she had shared the nursing of Henrietta and who had several times before asked for her hand. They were married in March 1881. He was 40, she 50. The bride wore deep mourning and, if one reads between Stoddart's over-sweet lines, seems to have been grimly determined to radiate grief rather than nuptial ecstasy. Perhaps it was dread of being tied by children that made her postpone marriage for so long, and perhaps what she was mourning at a less conscious level was the precious freedom of which marriage, even at 50, might deprive her. Dr Bishop himself was conscious of this, and according to Stoddart would say rather sadly, 'I have only one formidable rival in Isabella's heart, and that is the high Table Land of Central Asia.'

After such an inauspicious start their brief marriage seems, however, to have become genuinely affectionate. But within a year Dr Bishop contracted an infection during his work in the erysipelas ward at the Edinburgh Infirmary and although he lived until March 1886, he was never well again. His wife also suffered several severe recurrences of her old spinal disorder and various other lowering ailments. Despite these problems they were happy enough, and after his death she mourned him deeply. She spent a year recuperating, writing and busy with all her old occupations in the Western Isles, then went to London to take an intensive three-month nursing course at St Mary's Hospital in Paddington. In fact, Central Asia was calling. Dr Bishop had been an advocate of medical missions, and his widow's intention was to endow a hospital in his memory.

Among the Tibetans is the record of the journey she undertook after establishing such a hospital for women and children (the first of several such enterprises) near Srinagar in the Himalayan foothills. Like *Unbeaten Tracks in Japan*, this much briefer book remains valuable for the account it gives of a culture still barely touched by Western influences.

Although she was becoming increasingly devout, she was still genuinely tolerant of other beliefs, and her uncensorious attitude to not just the religion of the Tibetans but also their 'terribly faulty' morals is one of the pleasures of the work. The sexual insouciance of the Tibetans must have been startling, but she simply observed with her customary briskness that many of the sacred texts were 'nothing better than . . . stories of doubtful morality' and felt no need for sanctimonious horror when the abbot of a lamasery opined for his part that the Gospel of St Matthew was 'very laughable reading'. And despite the exclamation marks that ornament her account of Tibetan polyandry she recognizes its merits as well as its outlandishness. She exulted once more in being able to meet the challenges of a physically arduous journey. Triumphantly she recalls that she did not suffer from a climate and altitude that rendered 'water-colour sketching nearly impossible' and tea 'flavourless and flat'. Her considerable talent for describing such wild country and the physical hardships that such journeys involve was enhanced by her usual sense of personal drama. This trait, however, did not detract from her growing reputation as a geographer and the general esteem in which her opinion on a wide variety of subjects was held. If she had not been quite well known and so highly regarded it is doubtful whether she would have been allowed to go on her next journeys, with Major Sawyer's 'military-geographical' mission, through what was then Persia. Her travels with him in 1890 were no picnic to a lotus lake.

Then, as now, Iran was a source of much international tension, only at that time the super-powers were Russia and Britain, not Russia and the USA. The Shah's rule was tyrannical and yet unstable because the tribes of the remoter regions were fiercely independent, the government was corrupt, and the people impoverished. The country was ripe for intervention. Major Herbert Sawyer was an intelligence agent of the British Army, and Mrs Bishop records in an unpublished note that 'because of military necessity' she was not allowed to write

Believe me
Yours very sincerely
Isabella L Bishop

Mrs Bishop in later life.

or lecture about everything she saw on the two momentous journeys that she undertook with his party. 'An objection was raised even to my mentioning the garden plants of the region'. She was forbidden to take photographs of the terrain. It was not, of course, an entirely secret mission. They travelled with too large a party to be inconspicuous. Normally Mrs Bishop liked to travel with the smallest possible encumbrance, but the status of women in Muslim countries made such a procedure unwise, and politically it would have been disastrous to have risked anything that might have provoked an 'incident'.

The first journey was from Baghdad to Teheran in the depths of winter, but it was really neither the weather nor the terrain, harsh and dangerous though both were, that appalled Mrs Bishop. What shocked her was the desperate poverty of the people. In a letter quoted by Stoddart she wrote:

> I have learnt two things . . . I think [Islam] the most blighting, withering, degrading influence of any of the false creeds. The second thing takes a very short time to learn, i.e. that if there is a more venal, devastating, and diabolical oppression on earth than that of the Turk it is that of the Shah. This is a ruined, played-out country, perishing for want of people, of water, of fuel, and above all for want of security, crushed by the most grinding exactions to which there is no limit but the total ruin of those on whom they press, without a middle class, and without hope.

Everywhere the party stopped her medical skills were in demand—indeed it was probably because of those skills and the respectable 'cover' she provided that Major Sawyer agreed to take her along. She was never warm and never dry, and she was touched by the well-meaning attentions of the women who had to live all their lives in such conditions.

Since Hokkaido she had become increasingly aware of how most societies favour their males. In a lecture called *Heathen Claims and Christian Duty*, given to mark the Gleaners' Union anniversary, before a large audience in Exeter Hall on 1 November 1893, she spoke with particular passion about the plight of women.

> These false faiths . . . degrade women with an infinite degradation. I have lived in zenanas, and harems, and have seen the daily life of the secluded women, and I can speak from bitter experience of what their lives are—the intellect dwarfed . . . while all the worst passions of human nature are stimulated and developed in a dreadful degree; jealousy, envy, murderous hate, intrigue . . . It follows necessarily that there is also an infinite degradation of men.

Like so many successful Victorian women, she was not herself a feminist and her growing sympathy for women in primitive or non-Christian societies did not extend to women of her own kind who failed to live up to her high standards of achievement. She believed for example that only well-trained medical missionaries, equipped to be of immediate service to a local population, had any chance of practical or spiritual success. She had little patience with educated women who lacked her talent for thriving in adversity.

Mrs Bishop's reflections on all kinds of religious topics in her later life were not the romantic raptures of her earlier journeys. The caravanserais or inns of the journey to Teheran were abominable: up to four hundred beasts with their burdens and the men who accompanied them would be crowded together on a floor 'deep with the manure of ages'. The travellers' cooking fires were insufficient to lessen the cold or keep out the damp. As she tried to find a tolerably private corner amid the noise and stench, Mrs Bishop reflected that 'Such must have been the inn at Bethlehem, and surely the first step to the humiliation of "the death of the Cross" must have been the birth amidst the crowd and horrors of such a stable.'

Mrs Bishop's second journey with Major Sawyer took her through the mountain regions of Luristan. This time the danger was not the weather but warring tribes. On a couple of occasions the party was fired on, and they were under constant threat of being robbed and—a refinement particularly favoured in this region—stripped to the skin. The full route had never been traversed by Europeans before, and the few who knew even part of it agreed that it was 'impossible for a lady'. Such an injunction seems to have made the prospect even more attractive to Mrs Bishop, and indeed for some of the journey she was not the only woman in the party. She was now 59. A photograph taken on this expedition shows her in striking contrast to two other Europeans: a man and a slim woman, the latter wearing a plain but conventional floor-length dress. Mrs Bishop is small, very stout, and obviously uncorseted. Over her mid-calf-length skirt she wears an enormous jerkin of some shaggy fur, and beneath the skirt can be seen the famous baggy bloomers of the Hawaiian riding dress.

She had learnt to travel lightly as regards personal needs, and besides preserved meat, milk, and jam her food consisted of 'a quantity of Edwards' Desiccated Soup, portable and excellent, and twelve pounds of tea'. Flour and rice were to be obtained on the march. Other items were more important than food or personal comfort.

> Presents for the 'savages' are also essential, and I have succeeded in getting 100 thimbles, many gross of small china buttons which, it is said, they like to sew on children's caps, 1000 needles, a quantity of Russian thread, a number of boxes with mirror tops, two dozen double-bladed knives, and the same number of strong scissors, Kashmir *kamarbands*, gay handkerchiefs for women's heads, Isfahan printed 'table-cloths', dozens of bead bracelets and necklaces, leather purses and tobacco pouches, and many other things. The remaining portion of my outfit . . . consists of a beautiful medicine chest of the most compact and portable make, most kindly given to me by Messrs Burroughes and Wellcome, containing fifty small bottles of their invaluable 'tabloids', a hypodermic syringe, and surgical instruments for simple cases. To these I have added a quantity of quinine, and Dr Odling at Tihran gave me some valuable remedies. A quantity of bandages, lint, absorbent cotton, etc., completes this essential equipment. Among the many uncertainties of the future this appears certain, that the Bakhtiaris will be clamorous for European medicine.

This turned out to be an understatement. At every village, under a scorching sun, scores, sometimes hundreds, of men, women, and children demanded treatment hour after hour for all kinds of ailments, particularly eye and skin diseases and neglected bullet wounds.

It was not just human cases that were presented for her attention. The precious mare belonging to one of the most important of their local guides was brought to her with 'an enormous swelling from knee to shoulder', which its owner begged her to open. Reluctantly she made an incision, and 'very gradual pressure at the back of the leg brought out a black solid mass weighing fully a pound. "God is great," exclaimed the bystanders.' Mrs Bishop must have echoed their sentiments because as she well knew her medical knowledge was very limited, relief through her remedies was very uncertain, and failure could have had serious consequences.

The last part of her journey, after parting with Major Sawyer, took her through northwestern Iran, Syria, and Armenia to Trebizond (Trabzon) on the Black Sea coast. During these four months she was very much moved by the endurance of small pockets of long-established Christians under constant Muslim harassment. From then on, says Stoddart, 'Mrs Bishop's attitude towards Christian mission work was one of uncompromising and unflinching support [although there] had been a time when she would make a detour of twenty miles to avoid a mission station, being not only apathetic about its work, but in some degree averse to its interference with native creeds and its too frequent political indiscretions.' Now, Stoddart continues, 'The spirit of Christ inspired her to a deep, instant, urgent yearning to bring the whole world to a knowledge of Him.' This reported evangelical zeal cannot quite be squared with the evidence of Mrs Bishop's major writings. It may be that her lectures and her conversations gave her contemporaries a view of her that her writings alone cannot give. In her last years she worked tirelessly to raise interest in and money for the Church's medical missions; but there were then no secular relief agencies and, even if there had been, a Christian would not have subscribed to them. Yet it was the distress of the people among whom she travelled, not their heathenism, that roused her. It was, she said in her address to the Gleaners' Union, 'the desperate needs of the non-Christianized world' that aroused her. She was far from blind to the needs of the Christian world: the difference as she saw it was that only a Christian society did *anything* to alleviate the sufferings of the poor, the sick, the criminal, and the politically oppressed.

Her lectures, articles, and the book *Journeys in Persia and Kurdistan* won her very great respect from missionary societies, geographers, and politicians. She was elected a Fellow of the Royal Scottish Geographical Society and in 1893 was one of the first women to become a Fellow of the Royal Geographical Society. A few other lady travellers were distinguished in the same way, but then the Society decided that enough was enough, and in May 1893 a meeting was called to 'ensure the removal of all Lady Fellows from the Society'. This was, said Mrs Bishop, 'a dastardly injustice to women'. Her health now was indifferent, but she still felt obliged to organize cookery classes for the not very responsive poor in Tobermory and give improving lectures to the YWCA on such themes as 'I'll do it tomorrow' and 'How to make home happy'.

Despite a diagnosis of heart and lung malfunction she set off for Japan once more in 1894, via Canada and the Pacific. From Japan she went to Korea, where at first she found the people to be 'indolent, cunning, limp and unmanly'. The roads and inns were dreadful, and man-eating tigers a very real danger. However, at the beginning of her first Persian journey she had written that there was in her dirty, cold, and depressing circumstances 'that amount of general unpropitiousness which is highly stimulating and inspiring', and once again before long her interest was so deeply engaged that most discomforts lost their importance. Only one thing perturbed her: the insatiable curiosity of people who had never seen a European woman before.

> The women and children sat on my bed in heaps, examined my clothing, took out my hairpins and pulled down my hair, took off my slippers, drew my sleeves up to the elbow and pinched my arms to see if they were of the same flesh and blood as their own; they investigated my few possessions minutely, trying on my hat and gloves, and after being turned out by Wong [her servant] three times, returned in fuller force,

Mrs Bishop about to photograph a group of Chinese at Swatow, 1895.

Mrs Bishop (right) with her tent in Persia, 1890.

Mrs Bishop's sampan on the Han River, Korea, 1894.

accompanied by unmarried youths . . . Wong cleared the room a fourth time, and suggested that when they forced their way in again, they should find me sitting on the bed cleaning my revolver, a suggestion I accepted.

Korea had been ruled by China for centuries and had only been open to Western travellers for about a decade, so once again Mrs Bishop's account is valuable in recording an ancient cultural tradition before the impact of Westernization. It was Japan, however, that was the source of the most imminent danger to Korea. Mrs Bishop had several audiences with the Korean king and his queen shortly before the rebellion in which the latter was assassinated, partly because of their introduction of 'Western' reforms. The Japanese took advantage of the upheaval and invaded, effectively taking Korea out of China's power, and Mrs Bishop had to leave with no more than the clothes she stood up in for Chefoo (Yantai) in China. She did not even have enough money for a rickshaw, and presented herself hot, dishevelled, and somewhat nervously at the British Consulate. 'I experienced something of the anxiety and timidity which are the everyday lot of thousands, and I have felt a far tenderer sympathy with the penniless, especially the educated penniless, ever since.' But of course she was soon fitted out and on her way to Mukden (Shenyang) in southern Manchuria.

The two extracts selected from *Korea and her Neighbours* show the contrasting forces in Mrs Bishop's character still operating. She visited the Buddhist monasteries of the Diamond Mountain in Korea because both as a traveller and as a supporter of missionary work she had a professional interest in the religious practices of different countries. But it was really the journey through difficult, beautiful country that aroused her spirits, and the primitive excitement she so clearly felt when a young monk made the valley vibrate with the 'unforgettable music' of the temple bells comes across more forcefully than her general criticisms of the community's devotional shortcomings. For her journey up the flooded River Liau to Mukden there seems to have been no social or religious motive whatsoever, only a compulsion to undertake a difficult journey that only one foreigner had ever made before. It turned out to be such an uncomfortable and hazardous excursion

Left Mrs Bishop's trackers at dinner.

Right Mrs Bishop's boat.

that one would have expected her to decide to travel more comfortably in future (she was 64). But the excitements of Eastern travel outweighed any amount of cold, wet, dirt, and hunger, and though her final book, *The Yangtze Valley and Beyond*, indicates that she had lost some of her elasticity of spirit, she was still game for most things.

Her last long journey took her up the Yangtze, over the Chengtu plain, and through the mountains bordering on Tibet. Away from the principal routes, however, China was a place of serious danger for Europeans. The only European residents were a brave, often pathetic, scattering of missionaries who lived beleaguered lives in their isolated compounds and were not infrequently molested and sometimes killed for their pains. But Mrs Bishop had always got through before, and this time she took some rather foolish risks. She rode in an open chair and wore a distinctive Japanese hat. Inevitably she was set upon. Most female missionaries rode in a closed chair, and men adopted an inconspicuous Chinese costume. But Mrs Bishop was too stubborn to learn from their example, and on an expedition which took place shortly after the second extract included here, she was lucky to escape with her life. The missionary who was with her at the time told her that a Chinese 'reason talker' held back the crowd by warning them that if anything happened to her, 'foreign soldiers would come and burn their houses and destroy their crops, and worse'. (And that, of course, was one of the secrets of Mrs Bishop's success: if anything had happened to her, a gunboat would have been sent to investigate—or might have been—and the very possibility gave her a cloak of invincibility as valuable as a robust digestion.) And so, despite the attempts of Chinese officials to thwart her, she abandoned her dutiful tour of the mission stations, and rode out of the unexciting landscape of the Chengtu plain, up into the mountains to the west. Once again she barely survived a blizzard in the high passes. But if such danger and discomfort were the price that had to be paid for the high excitement she craved, it was worth it. The passage that stands at the head of this Introduction comes from that journey. It records an unabashed pleasure in an entirely selfish achievement.

Mrs Bishop set up three hospitals in China and a small orphanage in Tokyo and left them in the care of local medical missionaries, before returning to Europe after a three-year absence. There she resumed the less than joyful round of raising funds and enlisting indignation for the many causes which she had vested with her conscience, but not her whole heart. She would occasionally indicate her longings for the East by wearing rather elaborate, loose-fitting Chinese garments. From photographs (see Frontispiece) one may guess that a prime advantage of such a costume was that it enabled her to dispense with corsets—a form of constraint she had come to feel was the equivalent in the West of foot-binding in China. She was old and distinguished enough to be as eccentric and comfortable as she pleased.

The Yangtze Valley and Beyond was her last book, but not her last journey. To end my selection from her writings with something of her best form, rather than with the tetchiness to which only a violent Chinese mob ever brought her, I include some brief extracts from letters written on her last journey through North Africa. It was a new continent for her. She had always decided against Africa because she felt that the climate would disagree with her—though what possible meteorological variation that she had not successfully surmounted elsewhere it is difficult to imagine. But really she had not been to Africa before because the East was her magnet. America and Hawaii were the holiday destinations of her late youth. It was Asia, from the Black Sea to Japan, that she had been born for.

She returned from Morocco in her seventieth year, and knew that she could not live long. Since her husband's death she had never been able to settle happily in England or Scotland, and her last three years were mostly spent with friends, in rented rooms, and latterly in different nursing homes. She died in Edinburgh in 1904. Stored in London were trunks that had been packed for one more journey to China. What she achieved can partly be summed up in her own words to her publisher following the gratifying success of *Unbeaten Tracks in Japan*: like that work, her whole life 'vindicates the right of a woman to do anything which she can do well'. Such a claim was immodest enough. What Isabella Bird Bishop could never quite bring herself to express was that her life vindicated the right of a woman to do what she wants to do.

Mrs Bishop in Tangier, 1901, on her last trip abroad: 'I am taking for rest photography, embroidery and water-colours.'

Chapter One

The Englishwoman in America, 1856

Isabella Bird's first journey was undertaken for her health's sake. The English have always been ready to set down their impressions of America with a complacency that exasperates the Americans, but Miss Bird responded to the vigorous expansiveness of North America with a hearty delight that pleased her American as well as her British readers. Her journey took her through Nova Scotia, up the St Lawrence, through the eastern part of the Great Lakes area, as far south as Cincinnati and Kentucky—where, true to her Wilberforce blood, she responded indignantly to her first sight of slavery. Her expedition across the prairies to Chicago (the extract here) marked her furthest westward point—still then beyond the frontier. Afterwards she returned east to Canada again and New York.

Extensive districts of Ohio are still without inhabitants, yet its energetic people have constructed within a period of five years half as many miles of railroad as the whole of Great Britain contains; they are a *'great people'*, these Yankees. We were going ahead, and in a few hours arrived at Forest, the junction of the Clyde, Mad River, and Indiana lines.

Away with all English ideas which may be conjured up by the word *junction*— the labyrinth of iron rails, the smart policeman at the points, the handsome station, and elegant refreshment-rooms. Here was a dense forest, with merely a clearing round the rails, a small shanty for the man who cuts wood for the engine, and two sidings for the trains coming in different directions. There was not even a platform for passengers, who, to the number of two or three hundred, were standing on the clearing, resting against the stumps of trees. And yet for a few minutes every day the bustle of life pervades this lonely spot, for here meet travellers from east, west, and south; the

careworn merchant from the Atlantic cities, and the hardy trapper from the western prairies. We here changed cars for those of the Indianapolis line, and, nearly at the same time with three other trains, plunged into the depths of the forest.

We travelled the whole of that night, our fellow-passengers becoming more extravagant in appearance at every station, and morning found us on the prairies. Cooper influences our youthful imaginations by telling us of the prairies—Mayne Reid makes us long to cross them; botanists tell us of their flowers, sportsmen of their buffaloes—but without seeing them few people can form a correct idea of what they are really like.

The sun rose over a monotonous plain covered with grass, rank, high, and silky-looking, blown before the breeze into long, shiny waves. The sky was blue above, and the grass a brownish green beneath; wild pigeons and turkeys flew over our heads; the horizontal line had not a single inequality; all was hot, unsuggestive, silent, and monotonous. This was the grass prairie.

A belt of low timber would bound the expanse, and on the other side of it a green sea would open before us, stretching as far as the eye could reach — stationary billows of earth, covered with short green grass, which, waving beneath the wind, completed the oceanic illusion. This was the rolling prairie.

Again a belt of timber, and a flat surface covered with flowers, brilliant even at this season of the year; though, of the most gorgeous, nothing remained but the withered stalks. The ground was enamelled with lilies, the helianthus and cineraria flourished, and the deep-green leaves and blue blossom of the lupin contrasted with the prickly stem and scarlet flower of the euphorbia. For what purpose was 'the wilderness made so gay where for years no eye sees it', but to show forth his goodness who does what he will with his own? This was the weed prairie, more fitly termed 'the Garden of God'.

These three kinds of prairie were continually alternating with belts of timber and small lakes; but few signs of population were apparent during that long day's journey. We occasionally stopped for water at shanties on the prairies, and took in two or three men; but this vast expanse of fertile soil still must remain for many years a field for the enterprise of the European races.

Towards evening we changed cars again, and took in stores of refreshment for our night's journey, as little could be procured along the route. What strange people now crammed the cars! Traders, merchants, hunters, diggers, trappers, and adventurers from every land, most of them armed to the teeth, and not without good reason; for within the last few months, Indians, enraged at the aggressions of the white men, have taken a terrible revenge upon western travellers. Some of their rifles were of most costly

workmanship, and were nursed with paternal care by their possessors. On the seat in front of me were two 'prairie- men'; tall, handsome, broad-chested, and athletic, with aquiline noses, piercing grey eyes, and brown curling hair and beards. They wore leathern jackets, slashed and embroidered, leather smallclothes, large boots with embroidered tops, silver spurs, and caps of scarlet cloth, worked with somewhat tarnished gold thread, doubtless the gifts of some fair ones enamoured of the handsome physiognomies and reckless bearing of the hunters. Dullness fled from their presence; they could tell stories, whistle melodies, and sing comic songs without weariness or cessation: fortunate were those near enough to be enlivened by their drolleries during the tedium of a night detention. Each of them wore a leathern belt—with two pistols stuck into it—gold earrings, and costly rings. Blithe, cheerful souls they were, telling racy stories of Western life, chivalrous in their manners, and free as the winds.

There were Californians dressed for the diggings, with leather pouches for the gold-dust; Mormons on their way to Utah; and restless spirits seeking for that excitement and variety which they had sought for in vain in civilized life! And conveying this motley assortment of human beings, the cars dashed along, none of their inmates heeding each other, or perhaps Him

——who heeds and holds them all
In his large love and boundless thought.

At eleven we came to an abrupt pause upon the prairie. After waiting quietly for some time without seeing any vestiges of a station, my friends got out to inquire the cause of the detention, when we found that a freight-train had broken down in front, and that we might be *détenus* for some time, a mark for Indian bullets! Refreshments were produced and clubbed together; the 'prairie-men' told stories; the hunters looked to their rifles, and polished their already resplendent chasing;

some Mexicans sang Spanish songs, a New Englander 'Yankee Doodle'; some *guessed*, others *calculated*, till at last all grew sleepy: the trappers exhausted their stories, the singers their songs, and a Mormon, who had been setting forth the peculiar advantages of his creed, the patience of his auditors—till at length sonorous sounds, emitted by numerous nasal organs, proving infectious, I fell asleep to dream confusedly of 'Yankee Doodle', pistols, and pickpockets.

In due time I awoke; we were stopping still, and there was a light on our right. 'We're at Rock Island, I suppose?' I asked sleepily. A laugh from my friends and the hunters followed the question; after which they informed me in the most polite tones that we were where we had been for the last five hours, namely stationary on the prairie. The intense cold and heavy dew which accompany an American dawn made me yet more amazed at the characteristic patience with which the Americans submit to an unavoidable necessity, however disagreeable. It is true that there were complaints of cold, and heavy sighs, but no blame was imputed to any one, and the quiescence of my companions made me quite ashamed of my English impatience. In England we should have had a perfect chorus of complaints, varied by 'rowing' the conductor, abuse of the company, and resolutions to write to *The Times*, or bring up the subject of railway mismanagement in the House of Commons. These people sat quietly, ate, slept, and smoked, and were thankful when the cars at last moved off to their destination.

On we flew to the West, the land of Wild Indians and buffaloes, on the narrow rims of metal with which this 'great people' is girdling the earth. Evening succeeded noon, and twilight to the blaze of a summer day; the yellow sun sank cloudless behind the waves of the rolling prairie, yet still we hurried on, only stopping our headlong course to take in wood and water at some nameless stations. When the sun set, it set behind the prairie waves. I was oblivious of any changes during the night, and at rosy dawn an ocean of long green grass encircled us round. Still on—belts of timber diversify the prospect—we rush into a thick wood, and, emerging from it, arrive at Rock Island, an unfinished-looking settlement, which might bear the name of the Desert City, situated at the confluence of the Rock River and Mississippi. We stop at a little wharf, where waits a little steamer of uncouth construction; we step in, a steam-whistle breaks the silence of that dewy dawn, and at a very rapid rate we run between high wooded bluffs, down a turbid stream, whirling in rapid eddies.

We steam for three miles, and land at a clearing containing the small settlement of Davenport. We had come down the Mississippi, mightiest of rivers! half a mile wide seventeen hundred miles from its mouth, and were in the *far West*. Wagons with white tilts, thick-hided oxen with heavy yokes, mettlesome steeds with high peaked saddles, picketed to stumps of trees, lashing away the flies with their tails; emigrants on blue boxes, wondering if this were the El Dorado of their dreams; arms, accoutrements, and baggage surrounded the house or shed where we were to breakfast. Most of our companions were bound for Nebraska, Oregon, and Utah, the most distant districts of which they would scarcely reach with their slow-paced animals for four months; exposed in the meantime to the attacks of the Sioux, Comanches, and Blackfeet.

There, in a long wooden shed with blackened rafters and an earthen floor, we breakfasted, at seven o'clock, on johnny-cake, squirrels, buffalo-hump, dampers, and buckwheat, tea and corn spirit, with a crowd of emigrants, hunters, and adventurers; and soon after re-embarked for Rock Island, our little steamer with difficulty stemming the mighty tide of the Father of Rivers. The machinery, such as it was, was very visible, the boiler patched in several places, and steam escaped in different directions. I asked the captain if he were not in the habit of 'sitting upon the safety-valve', but he stoutly denied the charge. At eight we left Rock Island, and, turning my unwilling steps eastward from the land of adventure and romance, we entered the cars for Chicago.

The inn was a large brick building at the corner of a street, with nothing very unprepossessing in its external appearance. The wooden stairs were dirty enough, and, on ascending them to the so-called 'ladies' parlour', I found a large, meanly furnished apartment, garnished with six spittoons, which, however, to my disgust, did not prevent the floor from receiving a large quantity of tobacco-juice.

There were two rifles, a pistol, and powder-flask on the table; two Irish emigrant women were seated on the floor (which swarmed with black beetles and ants), undressing a screaming child; a woman evidently in a fever was tossing restlessly on the sofa; two females in tarnished Bloomer habiliments were looking out of the window; and other extraordinary-looking human beings filled the room. I asked for accommodation for the night, hoping that I should find a room where I could sit quietly. A dirty chambermaid took me to a room or dormitory containing four beds. In one part of it three women were affectionately and assiduously nursing a sick child; in another, two were combing tangled black hair; upon which I declared that I must have a room to myself.

The chambermaid then took me down a long, darkish passage, and showed me a small room without a fireplace, and only lighted by a pane of glass in the door; consequently, it was nearly dark. There was a small bed with a dirty buffalo-skin upon it; I took it up, and swarms of living creatures fell out of it, and the floor was literally alive with them. The sight of such a room made me feel quite ill, and it was with the greatest reluctance that I deposited my bonnet and shawl in it.

Outside the door were some medicine-bottles and other suspicious signs of illness, and, after making some cautious inquiries, we found that there was a case of typhus fever in the house, also one of Asiatic cholera, and three of ague! My friends were extremely shocked with the aspect of affairs. I believe that they were annoyed that I should see such a specimen of an hotel in their country, and they decided, that I could not possibly remain there for the night. Though I certainly felt rather out of my element in this place, I was not at all sorry for the opportunity, thus accidentally given me, of seeing something of American society in its lowest grade.

We went down to dinner, and only the fact of not having tasted food for many hours could have made me touch it in such a room. We were in a long apartment, with one table down the middle, with plates laid for one hundred people. Every seat was occupied, these seats being benches of somewhat uncouth workmanship. The floor had recently been washed, and emitted a damp fetid odour. At one side was a large fireplace, where, in spite of the heat of the day, sundry manipulations were going on, coming under the general name of cookery. At the end of the room was a long leaden trough or sink, where three greasy scullery-boys without shoes, were perpetually engaged in washing plates, which they wiped upon their aprons. The plates, however, were not washed, only superficially rinsed. There were four brigand-looking waiters with prodigious beards and moustachios.

There was no great variety at table. There were eight boiled legs of mutton, nearly raw; six antiquated fowls, whose legs were of the consistence of guitar-strings; baked pork with 'onion fixings', the meat swimming in grease; and for vegetables, yams, corn-cobs, and squash. A cup of stewed tea, sweetened with molasses, stood by each plate, and no fermented liquor of any description was consumed by the company. There were no carving-knives, so each person *hacked* the joints with his own, and some of those present carved them dexterously with bowie-knives taken out of their belts. Neither were there salt-spoons, so everybody dipped his greasy knife into the little pewter pot containing salt. Dinner began, and after satisfying my own hunger with the least objectionable dish, namely 'pork with onion fixings', I had leisure to look round me.

Every quarter of the globe had contributed to swell that motley array, even China. Motives of interest or adventure had drawn them all together to this extraordinary outpost of civilization, and soon would disperse them among lands where civilization is unknown.

As far as I could judge, we were the only representatives of England. There were Scots, for Scots are always to be found where there is any hope of honest gain—there were Irish emigrants, speaking with a rich brogue—French traders from St Louis—Mexicans from Santa Fé—Californians fitting out, and Californians coming home with fortunes made—keen-eyed speculators from New England—packmen from Canada—'Prairie-men', trappers, hunters, and adventurers of all descriptions. Many of these wore bowie-knives or pistols in their belts. The costumes were very varied and picturesque. Two Bloomers in very poor green habiliments sat opposite to me, and did not appear to attract any attention, though Bloomerism is happily defunct in the States.

There had been three duels at Chicago in the morning, and one of the duellists, a swarthy, dark-browed villain, sat next but one to me. The quarrel originated in a gambling-house, and this Mexican's opponent was mortally wounded, and there he sat, with the guilt of human blood upon his hands, describing to his *vis-à-vis* the way in which he had taken aim at his adversary, and no one seemed to think anything about it. From what I heard, I fear duelling must have become very common in the West, and no wonder, from the number of lawless spirits who congregate where they can be comparatively unfettered.

The second course consisted exclusively of pumpkin-pies; but when the waiters changed the plates, their way of cleaning the knives and forks was so peculiarly disgusting, that I did not attempt to eat anything. But I must remark that

in this motley assembly there was nothing of coarseness, and not a word of bad language—indeed, nothing which could offend the most fastidious ears. I must in this respect bear very favourable testimony to the Americans; for, in the course of my somewhat extensive travels in the United States, and mixing as I did very frequently with the lower classes, I never heard any of that language which so frequently offends the ear in England. I must not be misunderstood here. Profane language is only too notoriously common in the States, but custom, which in America is frequently stronger than law, totally prohibits its use before ladies. I suppose that there is no country in the world where the presence of a lady is such a restraint upon manners and conversation. A female, whatever her age or rank may be, is invariably treated with deferential respect; and if this deference may occasionally trespass upon the limits of absurdity, or if the extinct chivalry of the past ages of Europe meets with a partial revival upon the shores of America, this extreme is vastly preferable to the *brusquerie*, if not incivility, which ladies, as I have heard, too often meet with in England.

The apparently temperate habits in the United States form another very pleasing feature to dwell upon. It is to be feared that there is a considerable amount of drunkenness among the English, Irish, and Germans, who form a large portion of the American population; but the temperate, tea-drinking, water-drinking habits of the native Americans are most remarkable. In fact, I only saw one intoxicated person in the States, and he was a Scotch fiddler. In the West, I never saw wine, beer, or spirits upon the table; and the spectacle gratified me exceedingly, of seeing fierce-looking, armed, and bearded men, drinking frequently in the day of that cup 'which cheers, but not inebriates'. Water is a beverage which I never enjoyed in purity and perfection before I visited America. It is provided in abundance in the cars, the hotels, the waiting-rooms, the steamers, and even the stores, in crystal jugs or stone filters, and it is always iced. This may be either the result or the cause of the temperance of the people.

After dinner, being only too glad to escape from a house where pestilence was rife, we went out into Chicago. It is a wonderful place, and tells more forcibly of the astonishing energy and progress of the Americans than anything I saw. Forty years ago the whole ground on which the town stands could have been bought for six hundred dollars; now, a person would give ten thousand for the site of a single store. The city has sprung up rapidly, and is supplied with all the accessories of a high state of civilization. Chicago, in everything that contributes to *real use and comfort*, will compare favourably with any city in the world. In 1830 it was a mere trading-post, situated in the theatre of the Black Hawk war.

It is regularly laid out with wide airy streets. The wooden houses are fast giving place to lofty substantial structures of brick, or a stone similar in appearance to white marble, and are often six storeys high. These houses, as in all business streets in the American cities, are disfigured, up to the third storey, by large glaring sign-boards containing the names and occupations of their residents. The side-walks are of wood, and, wherever they are made of this unsubstantial material, one frequently finds oneself stepping into a hole, or upon the end of a board which tilts up under one's feet. The houses are always let in flats, so that there are generally three stores one above another. These stores are very handsome, those of the outfitters particularly so, though the quantity of goods displayed in the streets gives them rather a barbaric appearance. The side-walks are literally encumbered with bales of scarlet flannel, and every other article of an emigrant's outfit. At the outfitters' stores you can buy anything, from a cart-nail to a revolver; from a suit of oilskin to a paper of needles. The streets present an extraordinary spectacle. Everything reminds that one is standing on the very verge of western civilization.

The roads are crowded to an inconvenient extent with carriages of curious construction, wagons, carts, and men on horseback, and the side-walks with eager foot-passengers. By the side of a carriage drawn by two or three handsome horses, a creaking wagon with a white tilt, drawn by four heavy oxen, may be seen—Mexicans and hunters dash down the crowded streets at full gallop on mettlesome steeds, with bits so powerful as to throw their horses on their haunches when they meet with any obstacle. They ride animals that look too proud to touch the earth, on high-peaked saddles, with pistols in the holsters, short stirrups, and long, cruel-looking Spanish spurs. They wear scarlet caps or palmetto hats, and high jack-boots. Knives are stuck into their belts, and light rifles are slung behind them.

We returned to tea at the hotel, and found our viands and companions just the same as at dinner. It is impossible to give an idea of the 'Western men' to anyone who has not seen one at least as a specimen. They are the men before whom the Indians melt away as grass before the scythe. They shoot them down on the smallest provocation, and speak of 'head of Indian', as we do in England of head of game. Their bearing is bold, reckless, and independent in the extreme; they are as ready to fight a foe as to wait upon women and children with tender assiduity; their very appearance says to you, 'Stranger, I belong to the greatest, most enlightened, and most progressive nation on earth; I may be the President or a millionaire next year; I don't care a straw for you or anyone else.'

Chapter Two

Six Months in the Sandwich Islands, 1875

It was nearly twenty years after her first journey to North America that Isabella Bird began the series of travels that were to make her famous. Her experiences in the Sandwich Islands (Hawaii) and the Rocky Mountains were part of a trip around the world, once again undertaken on doctor's orders. Although the ride to the crater of Kilauea (with its tutelary deity Pelé) was quite commonly done by the more intrepid tourists, like Miss Karpe, it was crucial to Isabella Bird's career because it was her first ride astride. The adoption of an unladylike saddle made possible all her later more adventurous journeys, and, having taken to breeches of sorts herself, the disapproval of bloomers that she had expressed in Chicago quite disappeared. Victorian England and Scotland would never quite satisfy her again.

In the second episode Isabella, emboldened by success, explores on her own with only two young Hawaiians, Deborah and Kaluna, as guides on what turned out to be a hazardous ride through the precipitous *palis* (gulches) of Hawaii's north coast. Later, while staying on another island, she got news that Hawaii's largest volcano, Mauna Loa, was showing signs of activity after a long period of dormancy. Full of the discovery that she thrived on roughing it, she had no hesitation in setting off for its crater—a far more arduous expedition than before and well beyond the scope of the normal tourist. On the way she revisited Kilauea, this time a stepping-stone on the way to the higher volcano. As it turned out, the larger crater was the less fiery of the two, as activity in Kilauea had increased dramatically since her previous visit. But this did not diminish her sense of achievement in reaching a summit nearly 10,000 feet higher than the modest altitude of Kilauea.

As it was getting dark we passed through a forest strip, where tree-ferns from 12 to 18 feet in height, and with fronds from 5 to 7 feet long, were the most attractive novelties. As we emerged, 'with one stride came the dark', a great darkness, a cloudy night, with neither moon nor stars. There were five miles of this, and I was so dead from fatigue and want of food, that I would willingly have lain down in the bush in the rain. I most heartlessly wished that Miss Karpe were

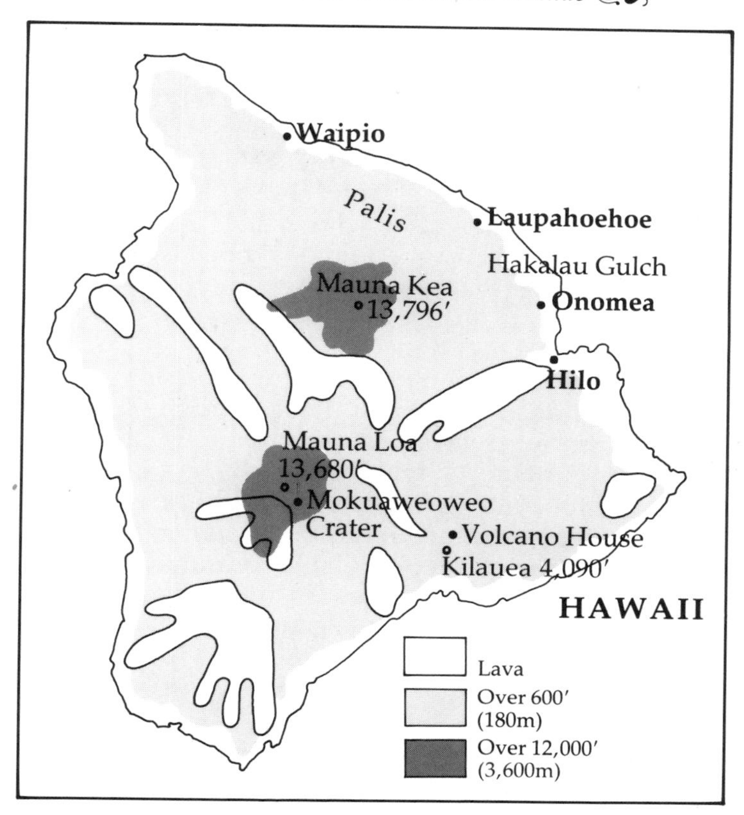

tired too, for her voice, which seemed tireless as she rode ahead in the dark, rasped upon my ears. I could only keep on my saddle by leaning on the horn, and my clothes were soaked with the heavy rain. 'A dreadful ride', one and another had said, and I then believed them. It seemed an awful solitude full of mystery. Often, I only knew that my companions were ahead by the sparks struck from their horses' shoes.

It became a darkness which could be felt.

'Is that possibly a pool of blood?' I thought in horror, as a rain puddle glowed crimson on the track. Not that indeed! A glare brighter and redder than that from any furnace suddenly lightened the whole sky, and from that moment brightened our path. There sat Miss Karpe under her dripping umbrella as provokingly erect as when she left Hilo. There Upa jogged along, huddled up in his poncho, and his canteen shone red. There the *ohia* trees were relieved blackly against the sky. The scene started out from the darkness with the suddenness of a revelation. We felt the pungency of sulphurous fumes in the still night air. A sound as of the sea broke on our ears, rising and falling as if breaking on the shore, but the ocean was thirty miles away. The heavens became redder and brighter, and when we reached the crater-house at eight, clouds of red vapour mixed with flame were curling ceaselessly out of a huge invisible pit of blackness, and Kilauea was in all its fiery glory. We had reached the largest active volcano in the world, the 'place of everlasting burnings'.

Rarely was light more welcome than that which twinkled from under the verandah of the lonely crater-house into the rainy night. The hospitable landlord of this unique dwelling lifted me from my horse, and carried me into a pleasant room thoroughly warmed by a large wood fire, and I hastily retired to bed to spend much of the bitterly cold night in watching the fiery vapours rolling up out of the infinite darkness, and in dreading the descent into the crater.

We were accompanied into the crater by a comical native guide, who mimicked us constantly, our Hilo guide, who 'makes up' a little English, a native woman from Kona, who speaks imperfect English poetically, and her brother who speaks none. I was conscious that we foreign women with our stout staffs and grotesque dress looked like caricatures, and the natives, who have a keen sense of the ludicrous, did not conceal that they thought us so.

The first descent down the terminal wall of the crater is very precipitous, but it and the slope which extends to the second descent are thickly covered with *ohias*, *ohelos* (a species of whortleberry), sadlerias, polypodiums, silver grass, and a great variety of bulbous plants many of which bore clusters of berries of a brilliant turquoise blue. The 'beyond' looked terrible. I could not help clinging to these vestiges of the kindlier mood of nature in which she sought to cover the horrors she had wrought. The next descent is over rough blocks and ridges of broken lava, and appears to form part of a break which extends irregularly round the whole crater, and which probably marks a tremendous subsidence of its floor. Here the last apparent vegetation was left behind, and the familiar earth. We were in a new Plutonic region of blackness and awful desolation, the accustomed sights and sounds of nature all gone. Terraces, cliffs, lakes, ridges, rivers, mountain sides, whirlpools, chasms of lava surrounded us, solid, black, and shining, as if vitrified, or an ashen-grey, stained yellow with sulphur here and there, or white with alum. The lava was fissured and upheaved everywhere by earthquakes, hot underneath, and emitting a hot breath.

After more than an hour of very difficult climbing we reached the lowest level of the crater, pretty nearly a mile across, presenting from above the appearance of a sea at rest, but on crossing it we found it to be an expanse of waves and convolutions of ashy-coloured lava, with huge cracks filled up with black iridescent rolls of lava, only a few weeks old. Parts of it are very rough and ridgy, jammed together like field ice, or compacted by rolls of lava which may have swelled up from beneath, but the largest part of the area presents the appearance of huge coiled hawsers, the ropy formation of the lava rendering the illusion almost perfect. These are riven by deep cracks which emit hot sulphurous vapours.

Strange to say, in one of these, deep down in that black and awful region, three slender metamorphosed ferns were growing, three exquisite forms, the fragile heralds of the great forest of vegetation, which probably in coming years will clothe this pit with beauty. Truly they seemed to speak of the love of God.

As we ascended, the flow became hotter under our feet, as well as more porous and glistening. It was so hot that a shower of rain hissed as it fell upon it. The crust became increasingly insecure, and necessitated our walking in single file with the guide in front, to test the security of the footing. I fell through several times, and always into holes full of sulphurous steam, so malignantly acid that my strong dog-skin gloves were burned through as I raised myself on my hands.

Suddenly, just above, and in front of us, gory drops were tossed in air, and springing forwards we stood on the brink of Halemaumau, which was about 35 feet below us. I think we all screamed, I know we all wept, but we were speechless, for a new glory and terror had been added to the earth. It is the most unutterable of wonderful things. The words of common speech are quite useless. It is unimaginable, indescribable, a sight to remember for ever, a sight which at once took possession of every faculty of sense and soul, removing one altogether out of the range of ordinary life. Here was the real 'bottomless pit'—the 'fire which is not quenched'—'the place of hell'—'the lake which burneth with fire and brimstone'—the 'everlasting burnings'—the fiery sea whose waves are never weary. There were groanings, rumblings, and detonations, rushings, hissings, and splashings, and the crashing sound of breakers on the coast, but it was the surging of fiery waves upon a fiery shore.

Since writing the above I have been looking over the 'Volcano Book', which contains the observations and impressions of people from all parts of the world. Some of these are painstaking and valuable as showing the extent and rapidity of the changes which take place in the crater, but there is an immense quantity of flippant rubbish, and would-be wit. Some of the entries are brief and absurd, 'Not much of a fizz', 'a grand splutter', 'Madam Pelé in the dumps', and so forth. These generally have English signatures. The American wit is far racier, but depends mainly on the profane use of certain passages of scripture, a species of wit which is at once easy and disgusting.

This inn is a unique and interesting place. Its existence is strikingly precarious, for the whole region is in a state of perpetual throb from earthquakes, and the sights and sounds are gruesome and awful both by day and night. The surrounding country steams and smokes from cracks and pits, and a smell of sulphur fills the air. They cook in a steam apparatus of nature's own work just behind the house, and every drop of water is from a distillery similarly provided. Mr Gilman, our host, is a fine picturesque-looking man.

A party of native travellers rainbound are here, and the native women are sitting on the floor stringing flowers and berries for *leis*. One very attractive-looking young woman, refined by consumption, is lying on some blankets, and three native men are smoking by the fire. Upa attempts conversation with us in broken English, and the others laugh and talk incessantly. My inkstand, pen, and small handwriting amuse them very much. Miss Karpe, the typical American travelling lady, who is encountered everywhere from the Andes to the Pyramids, tireless, with an indomitable energy, Spartan endurance, and a genius for attaining everything, and myself, a limp, ragged, shoeless wretch, complete the group, and our heaps of saddles, blankets, spurs, and gear tell of real travelling, past and future. It is a most picturesque sight by the light of the flickering fire, and the fire which is unquenchable burns without.

About 300 yards off there is a sulphur steam vapour-bath, highly recommended by the host as a panacea for the woeful aches, pains, and stiffness produced by the six-mile scramble through the crater, and I groaned and limped down to it: but it is a truly spasmodic arrangement, singularly independent of human control, and I have not the slightest doubt that the reason why Mr Gilman obligingly remained in the vicinity was, lest I should be scalded or blown to atoms by a sudden freak of Kilauea, though I don't see that he was capable of preventing either catastrophe! A slight grass shed has been built over a sulphur steam crack, and within this there is a deep box with a sliding lid and a hole for the throat, and the victim is supposed to sit in this and be steamed. But on this occasion the temperature was so high, that my hand, which I unwisely experimented upon, was immediately

peeled. In order not to wound Mr Gilman's feelings, which are evidently sensitive on the subject of this irresponsible contrivance, I remained the prescribed time within the shed, and then managed to limp a little less.

It is such a complete novelty to take a five days' ride alone with natives. Deborah is a very nice native girl of 17, who speaks English tolerably. She was lately married to a white man. Our equipment was a matter for some consideration, as I had no waterproof; but eventually I wore my flannel riding dress, and carried my plaid in front of the saddle. My saddle-bags, which were behind, contained besides our changes of clothes, a jar of Liebig's essence of beef, some potted beef, a tin of butter, a tin of biscuits, a tin of sardines, a small loaf, and some roast yams. Deborah looked very *piquante* in a bloomer dress of dark blue, with masses of shining hair in natural ringlets falling over the collar, mixing with her *lei* of red rose-buds.

We were shortly joined by Kaluna, Deborah's cousin, on an old, big, wall-eyed, bare-tailed, raw-boned horse. He is a very handsome youth of 16, with eyes which are remarkable, even in this land of splendid eyes, a straight nose, a very fine mouth, and beautiful teeth, a mass of wavy, almost curly hair, and a complexion not so brown as to conceal the mantling of the bright southern blood in his cheeks. His figure is lithe, athletic, and as pliable as if he were an invertebrate animal, capable of unlimited doublings up and contortions, to which his thin white shirt and blue cotton trousers are no impediment. He is almost a complete savage; his movements are impulsive and uncontrolled, and his handsome face looks as if it belonged to a half-tamed creature out of the woods. He talks loud, laughs incessantly, croons a monotonous chant, which sounds almost as heathenish as tom-toms, throws himself out of his saddle, hanging on by one foot, lingers behind to gather fruits, and then comes tearing up, beating his horse over the ears and nose, with a fearful yell and a prolonged sound like *har-r-r-ouche*, striking my mule and threatening to overturn me as he passes me on the narrow track. He is the most thoroughly careless and irresponsible being I ever saw, reckless about the horses, reckless about himself, without any manners or any obvious sense of right and propriety. In his mouth this musical tongue becomes as harsh as the speech of a cockatoo or parrot. His manner is familiar. He rides up to me, pokes his head under my hat, and says, interrogatively, 'Cold!' by which I understand that the poor boy is shivering himself. In eating he plunges his hand into my bowl of fowl, or snatches half my biscuit. Yet I daresay he means well, and I am thoroughly amused with him, except when he maltreats his horse.

After breakfast, we three left for the waterfall, though the natives tried to dissuade us by saying that stones came down, and it was dangerous; also that people could not go in their clothes, there was so much wading. In deference to this last opinion, Deborah rode without boots, and I without stockings. We rode through the beautiful valley till we reached a deep gorge turning off from it, which opens out into a nearly circular chasm with walls 2000 feet in height, where we tethered our horses. A short time after leaving them, Deborah said, 'We can't go further in our clothes,' but when the natives saw me plunge boldly into the river in my riding dress, which is really not unlike a fashionable Newport bathing suit, they thought better of it. It was a thoroughly rough tramp, wading ten times through the river, which was sometimes up to our knees, and sometimes to our waists, and besides the fighting among slippery rocks in rushing water, we had to crawl and slide up and down wet, mossy masses of dislodged rock, to push with eyes shut through wet jungles of Indian shot, guava, and a thorny vine, and sometimes to climb from tree to tree at a considerable height. When, after an hour's fighting we arrived in sight of the cascade, but not of the basin into which it falls,

our pretty guide declined to go further, saying that the wind was rising, and that stones would fall and kill us, but being incredulous on this point, I left them, and with great difficulty and many bruises, got up the river to its exit from the basin, and there, being unable to climb the rocks on either side, stood up to my throat in the still tepid water till the scene became real to me.

I do not care for any waterfall but Niagara, nor do I care in itself for this one, for though its first leap is 200 feet and its second 1600, it is so frittered away and dissipated in spray, owing to the very magnitude of its descent, that there is no volume of water within sight to create mass or sound. But no words can paint the majesty of the surroundings, the caverned, precipitous walls of rock coming down in one black plunge from the blue sky above to the dark abyss of water below, the sullen shuddering sound with which pieces of rock came hurtling down among the trees, the thin tinkle of the water as it falls, the full rush of the river, the feathery growth of ferns, gigantic below, but so diminished by the height above, as only to show their presence by the green tinge upon the rocks, while in addition to the gloom produced by the stupendous height of the cliffs, there is a cool, green darkness of dense forest, and mighty trees of strange tropical forms glass themselves in the black mirror of the basin. For one moment a ray of sunshine turned the upper part of the spray into a rainbow, and never to my eyes had the bow of promise looked so heavenly as when it spanned the black, solemn, tree-shadowed abyss, whose deep, still waters only catch a sunbeam on five days of the year.

I found the natives regaling themselves on papaya, and on live fresh-water shrimps, which they find in great numbers in the river. I remembered that white people at home calling themselves civilized, eat live, or at least raw, oysters, but the sight of these active, squirming shrimps struggling between the white teeth of my associates was yet more repulsive.

We finished our adventurous expedition with limbs much bruised, as well as torn and scratched, and before we emerged from the chasm saw a rock dislodged, which came crashing down not far from us, carrying away an *ohia*. It is a gruesome den, but well worth a visit.

When I woke the next morning a strong breeze was blowing, the surf was roaring so loud as almost to drown human voices, and rolling up in gigantic surges, and to judge from appearances, the rain which was falling in torrents had been falling for some hours. The sides of the great gulch rose like prison walls, cascades which had no existence the previous night hurled themselves from the summit of the cliffs directly into the sea, the rain, which fell in sheets, not drops, covered the ground to the depth of 2 or 3 inches, and dripped from the wretched, shivering horses, which stood huddled together with their tails between their legs. My thin flannel suit was wet through even before we mounted. I dispensed with stockings, as I was told that wearing them in rain chills and stiffens the limbs. Deborah, about whom I was anxious, as well as about the mule, had a really waterproof cloak, and I am glad to say has quite lost the cough from which she suffered before our expedition. She does not care about rain any more than I do.

We soon reached the top of the worst and dizziest of all the *palis*, and then splashed on mile after mile, down sliding banks, and along rocky tracks, from which the soil had been completely carried, the rain falling all the time. In some places several feet of soil had been carried away, and we passed through water-rents, the sides of which were as high as our horses' heads, where the ground had been level a few days before. By noon the aspect of things became so bad that I wished we had a white man with us, as I was uneasy about some of the deepest gulches. Four hours' journey from Onomea, Kaluna's horse broke down, and he left us to get another.

Deborah then said that the next gulch was rather a bad one, and that we must not wait for Kaluna, but ride fast, and try to get through it. She got safely across, but when she was near the opposite side her large horse plunged, slipped, and scrambled in a most unpleasant way, and she screamed something to me which I could not hear. Then I went in, and

> At the first plunge the horse sank low,
> And the water broke o'er the saddle bow:

but the brave animal struggled through, with the water up to the top of her back, till she reached the place where Deborah's horse had looked so insecure. In another moment she and I rolled backwards into deep water, as if she had slipped from a submerged rock. I saw her fore-feet pawing the air, and then only her head was above water. I struck her hard with my spurs, she snorted, clawed, made a desperate struggle, regained her footing, got into shallow water, and landed safely. It was a small but not an agreeable adventure.

We went on again, the track now really dangerous from denudation and slipperiness. The rain came down, if possible, yet more heavily, and coursed fiercely down each *pali* track. Hundreds of cascades leapt from the cliffs, bringing down stones with a sharp rattling sound. We crossed a bridge over one gulch, where the water was thundering down in such volume that it seemed as if it must rend the hard basalt of the *palis*. Then we reached the lofty top of the great Hakalau gulch, the largest of all, with the double river, and the ocean close to the ford.

The dense foliage, and the exigencies of the steep track, which had become very difficult, owing to the washing away of the soil, prevented me from seeing anything till I got down. I found Deborah speaking to a native, who was gesticulating very emphatically, and pointing up the river. The roar was deafening, and the sight terrific. Where there were two shallow streams a week ago, with a house and good-sized piece of ground above their confluence, there was now one spinning, rushing, chafing, foaming river, twice as wide as the Clyde at Glasgow, the land was submerged, and, if I remember correctly, the house only stood above the flood. And, most fearful to look upon, the ocean, in three huge breakers, had come quite in, and its mountains of white surge looked fearfully near the only possible crossing. I entreated Deborah not to go on. She said we could not go back, that the last gulch was already impassable, that between the two there was no house in which we could sleep, that the river had a good bottom, that the man thought if our horses were strong we could cross now, but not later, etc.

Deborah's horse I knew was strong, and shod, but my unshod and untried mare, what of her? My soul and senses literally reeled among the dizzy horrors of the wide, wild tide, but with an effort I regained sense and self-possession, for we were in, and there was no turning. Deborah, ahead, screeched to me what I could not hear; she said afterwards it was 'Spur, spur, and keep up the river'; the native was shrieking in Hawaiian from the hinder shore, and waving to the right, but the torrents of rain, the crash of the breakers, and the rush and hurry of the river confused both sight and hearing. I saw Deborah's great horse carried off his legs,

my mare, too, was swimming, and shortly afterwards, between swimming, struggling, and floundering, we reached what had been the junction of the two rivers, where there was foothold, and the water was only up to the seat of the saddles. I attempted to shift my saddle-bags upon her powerful horse, but being full of water and under water, the attempt failed, and as we spoke both our horses were carried off their vantage ground into deep water.

With wilder fury the river rushed by, its waters whirled dizzily, and, in spite of spurring and lifting with the rein, the horses were swept seawards. It was a very fearful sight. I saw Deborah's horse spin round, and thought woefully of the possible fate of the bright young wife, almost a bride; only the horses' heads and our own heads and shoulders were above water; the surf was thundering on our left, and we were drifting towards it 'broadside on'. When I saw the young girl's face of horror I felt increased presence of mind, and raising my voice to a shriek, and telling her to do as I did, I lifted and turned my mare with the rein, so that her chest and not her side should receive the force of the river, and the brave animal, as if seeing what she should do, struck out desperately. It was a horrible suspense. Were we stemming the torrent, or was it sweeping us back that very short distance which lay between us and the mountainous breakers? I constantly spurred my mare, guiding her slightly to the left, the side grew nearer, and after exhausting struggles, Deborah's horse touched ground, and her voice came faintly towards me like a voice in a dream, still calling 'Spur, spur'. My mare touched ground twice, and was carried off again before she fairly got to land some yards nearer the sea than the bridle track.

When our tired horses were taking breath I felt as if my heart stopped, and I trembled all over, for we had narrowly escaped death. I then put our saddle-bags on Deborah's horse. It was one of the worst and steepest of the *palis* that we had to ascend; but I can't remember anything about the road except that we had to leap some place which we could not cross otherwise. Deborah, then thoroughly alive to a sense of risk, said that there was only one more bad gulch to cross before we reached Onomea, but it was the most dangerous of all, and we could not get across, she feared, but we might go and look at it. I only remember the extreme solitude of the region, and scrambling and sliding down a most precipitous *pali*, hearing a roar like cataract upon cataract, and coming suddenly down upon a sublime and picturesque scene, with only standing room, and that knee-deep in water, between a savage torrent and the cliff. This gulch, called the Scotchman's gulch, I am told, because a Scotchman was drowned there, must be at its crossing three-quarters of a mile inland, and 300 feet above the sea. In going to Waipio, on noticing the deep holes and enormous boulders, some of them higher than a man on horseback, I had thought what a fearful place it would be if it were ever full; but my imagination had

not reached the reality. One huge compressed impetuous torrent, leaping in creamy foam, boiling in creamy eddies, rioting in deep black chasms, roared and thundered over the whole in rapids of the most tempestuous kind, leaping down to the ocean in three grand broad cataracts, the nearest of them not more than 40 feet from the crossing. Imagine the Moriston at the Falls, four times as wide and fifty times as furious, walled in by precipices, and with a miniature Niagara above and below, and you have a feeble illustration of it.

Portions of two or three rocks only could be seen, and on one of these, about 12 feet from the shore, a nude native, beautifully tattooed, with a lasso in his hands, was standing nearly up to his knees in foam; and about a third of the way from the other side, another native in deeper water, steadying himself by a pole. A young woman on horseback, whose near relative was dangerously ill at Hilo, was jammed under the cliff, and the men were going to get her across. Deborah, to my dismay, said that if she got safely over we would go too, as these natives were very skilful. I asked if she thought her husband would let her cross, and she said 'No'. I asked her if she were frightened, and she said 'Yes'; but she wished so to get home, and her face was as pale as a brown face can be. I only hope the man will prove worthy of her affectionate devotion.

Here, though people say it is a most perilous gulch, I was not afraid for her life or mine, with the amphibious natives to help us; but I was sorely afraid of being bruised, and scarred, and of breaking the horses' legs, and I said I would not cross, but would sleep among the trees; but the tumult drowned our voices, though the Hawaiians by screeching could make themselves understood. The nearest man then approached the shore, put the lasso round the nose of the woman's horse, and dragged it into the torrent; and it was exciting to see a horse creeping from rock to rock in a cataract with alarming possibilities in every direction. But beasts may well be bold, as they have not 'the foreknowledge of death'. When the nearest native had got the horse as far as he could, he threw the lasso to the man who was steadying himself with the pole, and urged the horse on. There was a deep chasm between the two into which the animal fell, as he tried to leap from one rock to another. I saw for a moment only a woman's head and shoulders, a horse's head, a commotion of foam, a native tugging at the lasso, and then a violent scramble on to a rock, and a plunging and floundering through deep water to shore.

Then Deborah said she would go, that her horse was a better and stronger one; and the same process was repeated with the same slip into the chasm, only with the variation that for a second she went out of sight altogether. It was a terribly interesting and exciting spectacle with sublime accompaniments. Though I had no fear of absolute danger, yet my mare was tired, and I had made up my mind to remain on that side till the flood abated; but I could not make the natives understand that I wished to turn, and while I was screaming 'No, no', and trying to withdraw my stiffened limbs from the stirrups, the noose was put round the mare's nose, and she went in. It was horrible to know that into the chasm as the others went I too must go, and in the mare went with a blind plunge. With violent plunging and struggling she got her fore-feet on the rock, but just as she was jumping up to it altogether she slipped back snorting into the hole, and the water went over my eyes. I struck her with my spurs, the men screeched and shouted, the hinder man jumped in, they both tugged at the lasso, and slipping and struggling, the animal gained the rock, and plunged through deep water to shore.

Kaluna came up just after we had crossed, undressed, made his clothes into a bundle, and got over amphibiously, leaping, swimming, and diving, looking like a water-god, with the horse and mule after him. His dexterity was a beautiful sight; but on looking back I wondered how human beings ever devised to cross such a flood. We got over just in time. Some travellers who reached Laupahoehoe shortly after we left, more experienced than we were, suffered a two days' detention rather than incur a similar risk.

Shortly after this, Deborah uttered a delighted exclamation, and her pretty face lighted up, and I saw her husband, spurring along the top of the next *pali*, and he presently joined us, and I exchanged my tired mare for his fresh, powerful horse. He knew that a freshet was imminent, and believing that we should never leave Laupahoehoe, he was setting off, provided with tackle for getting himself across, intending to join us, and remain with us till the rivers fell. The presence of a responsible white man seemed a rest at once. We had several more gulches to cross, but none of them were dangerous; and we rode the last seven miles at a great pace, though the mire and water were often up to the horses' knees, and came up to Onomea at full gallop, with spirit and strength enough for riding other twenty miles. Dry clothing, hot baths, and good tea followed delightfully upon our drowning ride. I remained over Sunday at Onomea, and yesterday rode here with a native in heavy rain, and received a warm welcome. Our adventures are a nine days' wonder, and every one says that if we had had a white man or an experienced native with us, we should never have been allowed to attempt the perilous ride. Had I been on a side-saddle, and encumbered with a riding-habit, I should have been drowned. I feel able now to ride anywhere and any distance, while Miss Karpe, who began by being much stronger than I was, has never recovered from the volcano ride, and seems quite ill.

I was unpacking, and in the midst of a floor littered with ferns, photographs, books, and clothes, when Mrs Whipple rushed in to say that the steamer was just reaching the landing below, and that there was scarcely the barest hope of catching her. Hopeless as the case seemed, we crushed most of my things promiscuously into a carpet-bag, Mr Whipple rode off with it, a horse was imperfectly saddled for me, and I mounted him, with my bag, straps, spurs, and a package of ferns in one hand, and my plaid over the saddle, while Mrs Whipple stuffed the rest of my possessions into a clothes-bag, and the Chinaman ran away frantically to catch a horse on which to ride down with them.

I galloped off after Mr Whipple, though people called to me that I could not catch the boat, and that my horse would fall on the steep broken descent. My saddle slipped over his neck, but he still sped down the hill with the rapid 'racking' movement of a Narraganset pacer. First a new veil blew away, next my plaid was missing, then I passed my trunk on the ox-cart which should have been at the landing; but still though the heat was fierce, and the glare from the black lava blinding, I dashed heedlessly down, and in twenty minutes had ridden three miles down a descent of 2000 feet, to find the *Kilauea* puffing and smoking with her anchor up; but I was in time, for her friendly clerk, knowing that I was coming, detained the scow. You will not wonder at my desperation when I tell you that half-way down, a person called to me, 'Mauna Loa is in action!'

As I find that a lady can travel alone with perfect safety, I have many projects in view, but whatever I do or plan to do, I find my eyes always turning to the light on the top of Mauna Loa. I know that the ascent is not feasible for me, and that so far as I am concerned the mystery must remain unsolved; but that glory, nearly 14,000 feet aloft, rising, falling, 'a pillar of cloud by day and a pillar of fire by night', uplifted in its awful loneliness above all human interests, has an intolerable fascination. As the twilight deepens, the light intensifies, and often as I watch it in the night, it seems to flare up and take the form of a fiery palm-tree. No one has ascended the mountain since the activity began a month ago; but the fire is believed to be in 'the old traditional crater of Mokuaweoweo, in a region rarely visited by man'.

A few days ago I was so fortunate as to make the acquaintance of Mr W. L. Green (now Minister of the Interior), an English resident in Honolulu, a gentleman

of wide scientific and literary culture, one of whose objects in visiting Hawaii is the investigation of certain volcanic phenomena.

This morning early, Mr Green came in, on his way to Kilauea, to which I was to accompany him, and on my casually remarking that I envied him his further journey, he at once asked me to join him, and I joyfully accepted the invitation! For, indeed, my heart has been secretly set on going, and I have had to repeat to myself fifty times a day, 'No, I must not think of it, for it is *impossible.*'

Mr Green is going up well equipped with a tent, horses, a baggage mule, and a servant, and is confident of being able to get a guide and additional mules fifty miles from Hilo. I had to go to the Union School examination where the Hilo world was gathered, but I could think of nothing but the future; and I can hardly write sense, the prospect of the next week is so exciting, and the time for making preparations is so short. It is an adventurous trip anyhow, and the sufferings which our predecessors have undergone make me anxious not to omit any precaution. I have hunted all the beach stores through for such essentials as will pack into small compass. Among the friends of my hosts all sorts of useful articles were produced, a camp kettle, a camping blanket, a huge Mexican poncho, a cardigan, capacious saddle-bags, etc. The greatest difficulty was about warm clothing, for in this perfect climate, woollen underclothing is not necessary as in many tropical countries, but it is absolutely essential on yonder mountain, and till late in the afternoon the best intentions and the most energetic rummaging in old trunks failed to produce it. At last Mrs—, wife of an old Scotch settler, bestowed upon me the invaluable loan of a stout flannel shirt, and a pair of venerable worsted stockings, much darned, knitted in Fifeshire a quarter of a century ago. When she brought them, the excellent lady exclaimed, 'Oh, what some people will do!' with an obvious personal reference. She fears we shall not get a guide, as the native who went up with Mr Whyte suffered so dreadfully from mountain sickness, that they were obliged to help him down, and he declares that he will not go up again. Mr Whyte tells us that he suffered himself from vomiting and vertigo for fourteen hours, and severely from thirst also, as the water froze in their canteens; but I am almost well now, and as my capacity for 'roughing it' has been severely tested, I hope to 'get on' much better. A party made the ascent nine months ago, and the members of it also suffered severely, but I see no reason why cautious people, who look well to their gear and clothing, and are prudent with regard to taking exercise at the top, should suffer anything worse than the inconveniences which are inseparable from nocturnal cold at a high elevation.

We have been all day in the crater, in fact, I left Mr Green and his native there, and came up with the guide, sore, stiff, bruised, cut, singed, grimy, with my thick gloves shrivelled off by the touch of sulphurous acid, and my boots nearly burned off. But what are cuts, bruises, fatigue, and singed eyelashes, in comparison with the awful sublimities I have witnessed today? The activity of Kilauea on 31 January was as child's play to its activity today: as a display of fireworks compared to the conflagration of a metropolis. *Then*, the sense of awe gave way speedily to that of admiration of the dancing fire fountains of a fiery lake; *now*, it was all terror, horror, and sublimity, blackness, suffocating gases, scorching heat, crashings, surgings, detonations; half-seen fires, hideous, tortured, wallowing waves.

We coasted the north, till we reached the south lake. Here there was comparatively little smoke, and the whole mass of contained lava was ebullient and incandescent, its level marked the whole way round by a shelf or rim of molten lava, which adhered to the side, as ice often adheres to the margin of rapids, when the rest of the water is liberated and in motion. For two or three minutes we kept going to the edge, seeing the spectacle as with a flash, through half-closed eyes, and going back again; but a few trials, in which throats, nostrils, and eyes were irritated to torture by the acid gases, convinced us that it was unsafe to attempt to remain by the lake, as the pain and gasping for breath which followed each inhalation, threatened serious consequences.

With regard to the north lake we were more fortunate, and more persevering, and I regard the three hours we spent by it as containing some of the most solemn, as well as most fascinating, experiences of my life The awful sublimity of what we did see, was enhanced by the knowledge that it was only a thousandth part of what we did not see, mere momentary glimpses of a terror and fearfulness which otherwise could not have been borne.

A ledge, only 3 or 4 feet wide, hung over the lake, and between that and the comparative *terra firma* of the older lava, there was a fissure of unknown depth, emitting hot blasts of pernicious gases. The guide would not venture on the outside ledge, but Mr Green, in his scientific zeal, crossed the crack, telling me not to follow him, but presently, in his absorption with what he saw, called to me to come, and I jumped across, and this remained our perilous standpoint.

Burned, singed, stifled, blinded, only able to stand on one foot at a time, jumping back across the fissure every two or three minutes to escape an unendurable whiff of heat and sulphurous stench, or when splitting sounds below threatened the disruption of the ledge: lured as often back by the fascination of the horrors below; so we spent three hours.

There was every circumstance of awfulness to make the impression of the sight indelible. Sometimes dense volumes of smoke hid everything, and yet, upwards, from out 'their sulphurous canopy' fearful sounds rose, crashings, thunderings, detonations, and we never knew then whether the spray of some hugely uplifted wave might not dash up to where we stood. At other times the smoke partially lifting, but still swirling in strong eddies, revealed a central whirlpool of fire, wallowing at unknown depths, to which the lava, from all parts of the lake, slid centrewards and downwards as into a vortex, where it mingled its waves with indescribable noise and fury, and then, breaking upwards, dashed itself to a great height in fierce, gory, gouts and clots, while hell itself seemed opening at our feet. At times, again, bits of the lake skinned over with a skin of a wonderful silvery, satiny sheen, to be immediately devoured; and as the lurid billows broke, they were mingled with misplaced patches as if of bright moonlight. Always changing, always suggesting force which nothing could repel, agony indescribable, mystery inscrutable, terror unutterable, a thing of eternal dread, revealed only in glimpses!

Last night I thought the Southern Cross out of place; tonight it seems essential, as Calvary over against Sinai. For Halemaumau involuntarily typifies the wrath which shall consume all evil: and the constellation, pale against its lurid light, the great love and yearning of the Father.

We had a great fright last evening. We had been engaging mules, and talking over our plans with our half-Indian host, when he opened the door and exclaimed, 'There's no light on Mauna Loa; the fire's gone out.' We rushed out, and though the night was clear and frosty, the mountain curve rose against the sky without the accustomed wavering glow upon it. 'I'm afraid you'll have your trouble for nothing,' Mr Gilman unsympathizingly remarked; 'anyhow, it's awfully cold up there', and rubbing his hands, reseated himself at the fire. Mr Green and I stayed out till we were half-frozen, and I persuaded myself and him that there was a redder tinge than the moonlight above the summit, but the mountain has given no sign all day, so that I fear that I 'evolved' the light out of my 'inner consciousness'.

Mr Gilman was eloquent on the misfortunes of our predecessors, lent me a pair of woollen socks to put on over my gloves, told me privately that if anyone could succeed in getting a guide it would be Mr Green, and dispatched us at eight this morning with a lurking smile at our 'fool's errand', thinly veiled by warm wishes for our success.

Our expedition, comprising two natives who knew not a word of English, Mr Green who does not know very much more Hawaiian than I do, and myself, started at seven. We had four superb mules, and two good pack-horses, a large tent, and a plentiful supply of camping blankets. I put on all my own warm clothes, as well as most of those which had been lent to me, which gave me the squat, padded look of a puffin or Esquimaux, but all, and more were needed long before we reached the top. The mules were beyond all praise. They went up the most severe ascent I have ever seen, climbing steadily for nine hours, without a touch of the spur, and after twenty-four hours of cold, thirst, and hunger, came down again as actively as cats. The pack-horses too were very good, but from the comparative clumsiness with which they move their feet they were very severely cut.

We soon entered on vast uplands of *pahochoe* which ground away the animals' feet, a horrid waste, extending upwards for 7000 feet. For miles and miles, above and around, great billowy masses, tossed and twisted into an infinity of fantastic shapes, arrest and weary the eye, lava in all its forms, from a compact phonolite, to the lightest pumice stone, the mere froth of the volcano, exceeding in wildness and confusion the most extravagant nightmare ever inflicted on man.

Struggling, slipping, tumbling, jumping, ledge after ledge was surmounted, but still, upheaved against the glittering sky, rose new difficulties to be overcome. Immense bubbles have risen from the confused masses, and bursting, have yawned apart. Swift-running streams of more recent lava have cleft straight furrows through the older congealed surface. Massive flows have fallen in, exposing caverned depths of jagged outlines. Earthquakes have riven the mountain, splitting its sides and opening deep crevasses, which must be leapt or circumvented. Horrid streams of *a-a* have to be cautiously skirted, which after rushing remorselessly over the kindlier lava have heaped rugged pinnacles of brown scoriae into impassable walls. Winding round the bases of tossed up, fissured hummocks of *pahoehoe*, leaping from one broken hummock to another,

clambering up acclivities so steep that the pack-horse rolled backwards once, and my cat-like mule fell twice, moving cautiously over crusts which rang hollow to the tread; stepping over deep cracks, which, perhaps, led down to the burning fathomless sea, traversing hilly lakes ruptured by earthquakes, and split in cooling into a thousand fissures, painfully toiling up the sides of mounds of scoriae frothed with pumice-stone, and again for miles surmounting rolling surfaces of billowy ropy lava—so passed the long day, under the tropic sun, and the deep blue sky.

We tried to eat some food, found that our pulses were beating 100 a minute, bathed our heads, specially our temples, with snow, as we had been advised to do by the oldest mountaineer on Hawaii, and heaped on yet more clothing. In fact, I tied a double woollen scarf over all my face but my eyes, and put on a French soldier's overcoat, with cape and hood, which Mr Green had brought in case of emergency. The cold had become intense. We had not wasted words at any time, and on remounting, preserved as profound a silence as if we were on a forlorn hope, even the natives intermitting their ceaseless gabble.

At half-past four we reached the edge of an *a-a* stream, about as wide as the Ouse at Huntingdon Bridge, and it was obvious that somehow or other we must cross it: indeed, I know not if it be possible to reach the crater without passing through one or another of these obstacles. I should have liked to have left the animals there, but it was represented as impossible to proceed on foot, and though this was a decided misrepresentation, Mr Green plunged in. I had resolved that he should never have any bother in consequence of his kindness in taking me with him, and, indeed, everyone had enough to do in taking care of himself and his own beast, but I never found it harder to repress a cry for help. Not that I was in the least danger, but there was every risk of the beautiful mule being much hurt, or breaking her legs. The fear shown by the animals was pathetic; they shrank back, cowered, trembled, breathed hard and heavily, and stumbled and plunged painfully. It was sickening to see their terror and suffering, the struggling and slipping into cracks, the blood and torture. The mules with their small legs and wonderful agility were more frightened than hurt, but the horses were splashed with blood up to their knees, and their poor eyes looked piteous.

We were then, as we knew, close to the edge of the crater, but the faint smoke wreath had disappeared, and there was nothing but the westering sun hanging like a ball over the black horizon of the desolate summit. We rode as far as a deep fissure filled with frozen snow, with a ledge beyond, threw ourselves from our mules, jumped the fissure, and more than 800 feet below yawned the inaccessible blackness and horror of the crater of Mokuaweoweo, six miles in circumference, and 11,000 feet long by 8000 wide. The mystery was solved, for at one end of the crater, in a deep gorge of its own, above the level of the rest of the area, there was the lonely fire, the reflection of which, for six weeks, has been seen for a hundred miles.

Nearly opposite us, a thing of beauty, a perfect fountain of pure yellow fire, unlike the gory gleam of Kilauea, was regularly playing in several united but independent jets, throwing up its glorious incandescence, to a height, as we afterwards ascertained, of from 150 to 300 feet, and attaining at one time 600! You cannot imagine such a beautiful sight. The sunset gold was not purer than the living fire. The distance which we were from it, divested it of the inevitable horrors which surround it. It was all beauty. For the last two miles of the ascent, we had heard a distant vibrating roar: there, at the crater's edge, it was a glorious sound, the roar of an ocean at dispeace, mingled with the hollow murmur of surf echoing in sea caves, booming on, rising and falling, like the thunder music of windward Hawaii.

We sat on the ledge outside the fissure for some time, and Mr Green actually proposed to pitch the tent there, but I dissuaded him, on the ground that an earthquake might send the whole thing tumbling into the crater; nor was this a whimsical objection, for during the night there were two such falls, and after breakfast, another quite near us.

The natives pitched the tent as near to the crater as was safe, with one pole in a crack, and the other in the great fissure, which was filled to within three feet of the top with snow and ice. I arranged the camping blankets, made my own part of the tent as comfortable as possible by putting my inverted saddle down for a pillow, put on my last reserve of warm clothing, took the food out of the saddle-bags, and then felt how impossible it was to exert myself in the rarified air, or even to upbraid Mr Green for having forgotten the tea, of which I had reminded him as often as was consistent with politeness!

This discovery was not made till after we had boiled the kettle, and my dismay was softened by remembering that as water boils up there at 187°, our tea would have been worthless. In spite of my objection to stimulants, and in defiance of the law against giving liquor to natives, I made a great tin of brandy toddy, of which all partook, along with tinned salmon and dough-nuts. Then the men piled faggots on the fire and began their everlasting chatter, and Mr Green and I, huddled up in blankets, sat on the outer ledge in solemn silence, to devote ourselves to the volcano.

I crowded on everything attainable, two pairs of gloves, with Mr Gilman's socks over them, and a thick plaid muffled up my face. Mr Green and the natives, buried in blankets, occupied the other part of the tent. The phrase, 'sleeping on the brink of a volcano', was literally true, for I fell asleep, and fear I might have been prosaic enough to sleep all night, had it not been for fleas which had come up in the camping blankets. When I woke, it was light enough to see that the three muffled figures were all asleep, instead of spending the night in shiverings and vertigo, as it appears that others have done. Doubtless the bathing of our heads several times with snow and ice-water had been beneficial.

Creeping over the sleeping forms, which never stirred even though I had to kneel upon one of the natives while I untied the flap of the tent, I crept cautiously into the crevasse in which the snow-water was then hard frozen, and out upon the projecting ledge. The four hours in which we had previously watched the volcano had passed like one; but the lonely hours which followed might have been two minutes or a year, for time was obliterated.

Things had changed, as they change hourly in craters. The previous loud detonations were probably connected with the evolutions of some 'blowing cones', which were now very fierce, and throwing up lava at the comparatively dead end of the crater. Lone stars of fire broke out frequently through the blackened crust. The molten river, flowing from the incandescent lake, had advanced and broadened considerably. That lake itself, whose diameter has been estimated at 800 feet, was rose-red and self-illuminated, and the increased noise was owing to the increased force of the fire-fountain, which was playing regularly at a height of 300 feet, with the cross fountains, like wheat-sheaves, at its lower part. These cross-fountains were the colour of a mixture of blood and fire, and the lower part of the perpendicular jets was the same; but as they rose and thinned, this colour passed into a vivid rose-red, and the spray and splashes were as rubies and flame mingled. For ever falling in fiery masses and fiery foam: accompanied by a thunder-music of its own: companioned only by the solemn stars: exhibiting no other token of its glories to man than the reflection of its fires on mist and smoke; it burns for the Creator's eye alone. No foot of mortal can approach it.

Chapter Three

A Lady's Life in the Rocky Mountains, 1879

Isabella Bird went to Colorado in 1873 (when she was 42) before the last remnants of its lawless glamour had quite disappeared. On her way to the already famous beauties of Estes Park (the town is now on the eastern edge of the Rocky Mountain National Park) she met James Nugent—a former scout, a trapper, a drunk, a desperado, but still a gentleman—known locally as 'Rocky Mountain Jim': 'a man for whom there is now no room'.

Like all her books before her marriage, *A Lady's Life in the Rocky Mountains* is based on letters sent home to her less adventurous sister Henrietta. These letters were first published in serial form in *The Leisure Hour*, carefully pruned of certain details about Mr Nugent—as she scrupulously called him—that were for her sister's eyes alone.

A very pretty mare, hobbled, was feeding; a collie dog barked at us, and among the scrub, not far from the track, there was a rude, black log cabin, as rough as it could be to be a shelter at all, with smoke coming out of the roof and window. The big dog lay outside it in a threatening attitude and growled. The mud roof was covered with lynx, beaver, and other furs laid out to dry, beaver paws were pinned out on the logs, a part of the carcass of a deer hung at one end of the cabin, a skinned beaver lay in front of a heap of peltry just within the door, and antlers of deer, old horseshoes, and offal of many animals, lay about the den.

Roused by the growling of the dog, his owner came out, a broad, thickset man, about the middle height, with an old cap on his head, and wearing a grey hunting-suit much the worse for wear (almost falling to pieces, in fact), a digger's scarf knotted round his waist, a knife in his belt, and 'a bosom friend', a revolver, sticking out of the breast-pocket of his coat; his feet, which were very small, were bare, except for some dilapidated moccasins made of horse hide. The marvel was how his clothes hung together, and on him. The scarf round his waist must have had something to do with it. His face was remarkable. He is a man about 45, and must have been strikingly handsome. He has large grey-blue eyes, deeply set, with well-marked eyebrows, a handsome aquiline nose, and a very handsome mouth. His face was smooth shaven except for a dense moustache and imperial. Tawny hair, in thin uncared-for curls, fell from under his hunter's cap and over his collar.

One eye was entirely gone, and the loss made one side of the face repulsive, while the other might have been modelled in marble. 'Desperado' was written in large letters all over him. I almost repented of having sought his acquaintance.

His first impulse was to swear at the dog, but on seeing a lady he contented himself with kicking him, and coming up to me he raised his cap, showing as he did so a magnificently formed brow and head, and in a cultured tone of voice asked if there were anything he could do for me? I asked for some water, and he brought some in a battered tin, gracefully apologizing for not having anything more presentable. We entered into conversation, and as he spoke I forgot both his reputation and appearance, for his manner was that of a chivalrous gentleman, his accent refined, and his language easy and elegant. I inquired about some beavers' paws which were drying, and in a moment they hung on the horn of my saddle.

Apropos of the wild animals of the region, he told me that the loss of his eye was owing to a recent encounter with a grizzly bear, which after giving him a death hug, tearing him all over, breaking his arm and scratching out his eye, had left him for dead. As we rode away, for the sun was sinking, he said, courteously, 'You are not an American. I know from your voice that you are a countrywoman of mine. I hope you will allow me the pleasure of calling on you.'

This man, known through the Territories and beyond them as 'Rocky Mountain Jim', or, more briefly, as 'Mountain Jim', is one of the famous scouts of the Plains, and is the original of some daring portraits in fiction concerning Indian frontier warfare. So far as I have at present heard, he is a man for whom there is now no room, for the time for blows and blood in this part of Colorado is past, and the fame of many daring exploits is sullied by crimes which are not easily forgiven here.

From the ridge at a height of 9000 feet, we saw at last Estes Park, lying 1500 feet below in the glory of the setting sun, an irregular basin, lighted up by the bright waters of the rushing Thompson, guarded by sentinel mountains of fantastic shape and monstrous size, with Long's Peak rising above them all in unapproachable grandeur, while the Snowy Range, with its outlying spurs heavily timbered, come down upon the park slashed by stupendous canyons lying deep in purple gloom.

The rushing river was blood-red, Long's Peak was aflame, the glory of the glowing heaven was given back from earth. The mountain fever seized me, and, giving my tireless horse one encouraging word, he dashed at full gallop over a mile of smooth sward at delirious speed.

But I was hungry, and the air was frosty, and I was wondering what the prospects of food and shelter were in this enchanted region, when we came suddenly upon a small lake, close to which was a very trim-looking log cabin, with a flat mud roof, with four smaller ones; picturesquely dotted about near it, two corrals, a long shed, in front of which a steer was being killed, a log dairy with a waterwheel, some hay piles, and various evidences of comfort; and two men, on serviceable horses, were just bringing in some tolerable cows to be milked. A short, pleasant-looking man ran up to me and shook hands gleefully, which surprised me; but he has since told me that in the evening light he thought I was 'Mountain Jim, dressed up as a woman!' I recognized in him a countryman, and he introduced himself as Griffith Evans, a Welshman from the slate quarries near Llanberis.

When the cabin door was opened I saw a good-sized log room, unchinked, however, with windows of infamous glass, looking two ways; a rough stone fireplace, in which pine logs, half as large as I am, were burning; a boarded floor, a round table, two rocking chairs, a carpet-covered backwoods couch; and skins, Indian bows and arrows, wampum belts, and antlers, fitly decorated the rough walls, and equally fitly, rifles were stuck up in the corners. Seven men, smoking, were lying about on the floor, a sick man lay on the couch, and a middle-aged lady sat at the table writing. I went out again and asked Evans if he could take me in, expecting nothing better than a shakedown; but, to my joy, he told me he could give me a cabin to myself, two minutes' walk from his own. So in this glorious upper world, with the mountain pines behind and the clear lake in front, in the 'blue hollow at the foot of Long's Peak', at a height of 7500 feet, where the hoar frost crisps the grass every night of the year, I have found far more than I ever dared to hope for.

Long's Peak, 14,700 feet high, blocks up one end of Estes Park, and dwarfs all the surrounding mountains. From it on this side rise, snow-born, the bright St Vrain, and the Big and Little Thompson. By sunlight or moonlight its splintered grey crest is the one object which, in spite of wapiti and bighorn, skunk and grizzly, unfailingly arrests the eyes. From it come all storms of snow and wind, and the forked lightnings play round its head like a glory. It is one of the noblest of mountains, but in one's imagination it grows to be much more than a mountain. It becomes invested with a personality. In its caverns and abysses one comes to fancy that it generates and chains the strong winds, to let them loose in its fury. The thunder becomes its voice, and the lightnings do it homage. Other summits blush under the morning kiss of the sun, and turn pale the next moment; but it detains the first sunlight and holds it round its head for an hour at least, till it pleases to change from rosy red to deep blue; and the sunset, as if spell-bound, lingers latest on its crest. The soft winds which hardly rustle the pine needles down here are raging rudely up there round its motionless summit. The mark of fire is upon it; and though it has passed into a grim repose, it tells of fire and upheaval as truly, though not as eloquently, as the living volcanoes of Hawaii. Here under its shadow one learns how naturally nature worship, and the propitiation of the forces of nature, arose in minds which had no better light.

Long's Peak, 'the American Matterhorn', as some call it, was ascended five years ago for the first time. I thought I should like to attempt it, but up to Monday, when Evans left for Denver, cold water was thrown upon the project. It was too late in the season, the winds were likely to be strong, etc.; but just before leaving, Evans said that the weather was looking more settled, and if I did not get farther than the timber line it would be worth going. Soon after he left, 'Mountain Jim' came in, and he would go up as guide, and the two youths who rode here with me from Longmount and I caught at the proposal.

Mrs Edwards at once baked bread for three days, steaks were cut from the steer which hangs up conveniently, and tea, sugar, and butter were benevolently added. Our picnic was not to be a luxurious or 'well-found' one, for, in order to avoid the expense of a pack mule, we limited our luggage to what our saddle horses could carry. Behind my saddle I carried three pair of camping blankets and a quilt, which reached to my shoulders. My own boots were so much worn that it was painful to walk, even about the park, in them, so Evans had lent me a pair of his hunting boots, which hung to the horn of my saddle. The horses of the two young men were equally loaded, for we had to prepare for many degrees of frost. 'Jim' was a shocking figure; he had on an old pair of high boots, with a baggy pair of old trousers made of deer hide, held on by an old scarf tucked into them; a leather shirt, with three or four ragged unbuttoned waistcoats over it; an old smashed wideawake, from under which his tawny, neglected ringlets hung; and with his one eye, his one long spur, his knife in his belt, his revolver in his waistcoat pocket, his saddle covered with an old beaver skin, from which the paws hung down; his camping blankets behind him, his rifle laid across the saddle in front of him, and his axe, canteen, and other gear hanging to the horn, he was as awful-looking a ruffian as one could see. By way of contrast he rode a small Arab mare, of exquisite beauty, skittish, high-spirited, gentle, but altogether too light for him, and he fretted her incessantly to make her display herself.

Heavily loaded as all our horses were, 'Jim' started over the half mile of level grass at a hard gallop, and then throwing his mare on her haunches, pulled up alongside of me, and with a grace of manner which soon made me forget his appearance, entered into a conversation which lasted for more than three hours, in spite of the manifold checks of fording streams, single file, abrupt ascents and descents, and other incidents of mountain travel. The ride was one series of glories and surprises, of 'park' and glade, of lake and stream, of mountains on mountains, culminating in the rent pinnacles of Long's Peak, which looked yet grander and ghastlier as we crossed an attendant mountain 11,000 feet high. The slanting sun added fresh beauty every hour. There were dark pines against a lemon sky, grey peaks reddening and etherealizing, gorges of deep and infinite blue, floods of golden glory pouring through canyons of enormous depth, an atmosphere of absolute purity, an occasional foreground of cotton-wood and

aspen flaunting in red and gold to intensify the blue gloom of the pines, the trickle and murmur of streams fringed with icicles, the strange sough of gusts moving among the pine-tops—sights and sounds not of the lower earth, but of the solitary, beast-haunted, frozen upper altitudes. From the dry, buff grass of Estes Park we turned off up a trail on the side of a pine-hung gorge, up a steep pine-clothed hill, down to a small valley, rich in fine, sun-cured hay about 18 inches high, and enclosed by high mountains whose deep hollow contains a lily-covered lake, fitly named 'The Lake of the Lilies'. Ah, how magical its beauty was, as it slept in silence, while there the dark pines were mirrored motionless in its pale gold, and here the great white lily cups and dark green leaves rested on amethyst-coloured water!

From this we ascended into the purple gloom of great pine forests which clothe the skirts of the mountains up to a height of about 11,000 feet, and from their chill and solitary depths we had glimpses of golden atmosphere and rose-lit summits, glimpses, too, through a broken vista of purple gorges, of the illimitable

Plains lying idealized in the late sunlight, their baked, brown expanse transfigured into the likeness of a sunset sea rolling infinitely in waves of misty gold.

We rode upwards through the gloom on a steep trail blazed through the forest, all my intellect concentrated on avoiding being dragged off my horse by impending branches, or having the blankets badly torn, as those of my companions were, by sharp dead limbs, between which there was hardly room to pass—the horses breathless, and requiring to stop every few yards, though their riders, except myself, were afoot. The gloom of the dense, ancient, silent forest is to me awe-inspiring. On such an evening it is soundless, except for the branches creaking in the soft wind, the frequent snap of decayed timber, and a murmur in the pine tops as of a not distant waterfall, all tending to produce eeriness and a sadness 'hardly akin to pain'. There no lumberer's axe has ever rung. The trees die when they have attained their prime, and stand there, dead and bare, till the fierce mountain winds lay them prostrate. The pines grew smaller and more sparse as we ascended, and the last stragglers wore a tortured, warring look. The timber line was passed, but yet a little higher a slope of mountain meadow dipped to the southwest towards a bright stream trickling under ice and icicles, and there a grove of the beautiful silver spruce marked our camping ground. The trees were in miniature, but so exquisitely arranged that one might well ask what artist's hand had planted them, scattering them here, clumping them there, and training their slim spires towards heaven. Looking east, gorges opened to the distant Plains, then fading into purple grey. Mountains with pine-clothed skirts rose in ranges, or, solitary, uplifted their grey summits, while close behind, but nearly 3000 feet above us, towered the bald white crest of Long's Peak, its huge precipices red with the light of a sun long lost to our eyes. Close to us, in the caverned side of the Peak, was snow that, owing to its position, is eternal. Soon the afterglow came on, and before it faded a big half-moon hung out of the heavens, shining through the silver-blue foliage of the pines on the frigid background of snow, and turning the whole into fairyland.

Unsaddling and picketing the horses securely, making the beds of pine shoots, and dragging up logs for fuel, warmed us all. 'Jim' built up a great fire, and before long we were all sitting around it at supper. It didn't matter much that we had to drink our tea out of the battered meat tins in which it was boiled, and eat strips of beef reeking with pine smoke without plates or forks.

'Treat Jim as a gentleman and you'll find him one,' I had been told; and though

his manner was certainly bolder and freer than that of gentlemen generally, no imaginable fault could be found. He was very agreeable as a man of culture as well as a child of nature; the desperado was altogether out of sight. He was very courteous and even kind to me, which was fortunate, as the young men had little idea of showing even ordinary civilities. That night I made the acquaintance of his dog Ring, said to be the best hunting dog in Colorado, with the body and legs of a collie, but a head approaching that of a mastiff, a noble face with a wistful human expression, and the most truthful eyes I ever saw in an animal. His master loves him if he loves anything, but in his savage moods ill-treats him. Ring's devotion never swerves, and his truthful eyes are rarely taken off his master's face. He is almost human in his intelligence, and, unless he is told to do so, he never takes notice of anyone but 'Jim'. In a tone as if speaking to a human being, his master, pointing to me, said, 'Ring, go to that lady, and don't leave her again tonight.' Ring at once came to me, looked into my face, laid his head on my shoulder, and then lay down beside me with his head on my lap, but never taking his eyes from 'Jim's' face.

The long shadows of the pines lay upon the frosted grass, an aurora leaped fitfully, and the moonlight, though intensely bright, was pale beside the red, leaping flames of our pine logs and their red glow on our gear, ourselves, and Ring's truthful face. One of the young men sang a Latin student's song and two Negro melodies; the other 'Sweet Spirit, hear my Prayer'. 'Jim' sang one of Moore's melodies in a singular falsetto, and all together sang 'The Star-spangled Banner' and 'The Red, White, and Blue'. Then 'Jim' recited a very clever poem of his own composition, and told some fearful Indian stories.

A group of small silver spruces away from the fire was my sleeping place. It was thickly strewn with young pine shoots, and these, when covered with a blanket, with an inverted saddle for a pillow, made a luxurious bed. The mercury at 9 p.m. was 12° below the freezing point. 'Jim', after a last look at the horses, made a huge fire, and stretched himself out beside it, but Ring lay at my back to keep me warm. I could not sleep, but the night passed rapidly. I was anxious about the ascent, for gusts of ominous sound swept through the pines at intervals. Then wild animals howled, and Ring was perturbed in spirit about them. Then it was strange to see the notorious desperado, a red-handed man, sleeping as quietly as innocence sleeps. But, above all, it was exciting to lie there, with no better shelter than a bower of pines, on a mountain 11,000 feet high, in the very heart of the Rocky range, under twelve degrees of frost, hearing sounds of wolves, with shivering stars looking through the fragrant canopy, with arrowy pines for bed-posts, and for a night lamp the red flames of a camp-fire.

Day dawned long before the sun rose, pure and lemon coloured. The rest were looking after the horses, when one of the students came running to tell me that I must come farther down the slope, for 'Jim' said he had never seen such a sunrise. From the chill, grey Peak above, from the everlasting snows, from the silvered pines, down through mountain ranges with their depths of Tyrian purple, we looked to where the Plains lay cold, in blue-grey, like a morning sea against a far horizon. Suddenly, as a dazzling streak at first, but enlarging rapidly into a dazzling sphere, the sun wheeled above the grey line, a light and glory as when it was first created. 'Jim' involuntarily and reverently uncovered his head, and exclaimed, 'I believe there is a God!' I felt as if, Parsee-like, I must worship. The grey of the Plains changed to purple, the sky was all one rose-red flush, on which vermilion cloud-streaks rested; the ghastly peaks gleamed like rubies, the earth and heavens were new created. Surely 'the Most High dwelleth not in temples made with hands!' For a full hour those Plains simulated the ocean, down to whose limitless expanse of purple, cliff, rocks, and promontories swept down.

By seven we had finished breakfast, and passed into the ghastlier solitudes above, I riding as far as what, rightly or wrongly, are called the 'Lava Beds', an expanse of large and small boulders, with snow in their crevices. It was very cold; some water which we crossed was frozen hard enough to bear the horse. 'Jim' had advised me against taking any wraps, and my thin Hawaiian riding-dress, only fit for the tropics, was penetrated by the keen air. The rarefied atmosphere soon began to oppress our breathing, and I found that Evans's boots were so large that I had no foothold. Fortunately, before the real difficulty of the ascent began, we found, under a rock, a pair of small overshoes, probably left by [an earlier] exploring expedition, which just lasted for the day. As we were leaping from rock to rock, 'Jim' said, 'I was thinking in the night about your travelling alone, and wondering where you carried your derringer, for I could see no signs of it.' On my telling him that I travelled unarmed, he could hardly believe it, and adjured me to get a revolver at once.

On arriving at the 'Notch' (a literal gate of rock), we found ourselves absolutely on the knifelike ridge or backbone of Long's Peak, only a few feet wide, covered with colossal boulders and fragments, and on the other side shelving in one precipitous, snow-patched sweep of 3000 feet to a picturesque hollow, containing a lake of pure green water. Other lakes, hidden among dense pine woods, were farther off, while close above us rose the Peak, which, for about 500 feet, is a smooth, gaunt, inaccessible-looking pile of granite. Passing through the 'Notch', we looked along the nearly inaccessible side of the Peak, composed of boulders and debris of all shapes and sizes, through which appeared broad, smooth ribs of reddish-coloured granite, looking as if they upheld the towering rock mass above. I usually dislike bird's-eye and panoramic views, but, though from a mountain, this was not one. Serrated ridges, not much lower than that on which we stood, rose, one beyond another, far as that pure atmosphere could carry the vision, broken into awful chasms deep with ice and snow, rising into pinnacles piercing the heavenly blue with their cold, barren grey, on, on for ever, till the most distant range upbore unsullied snow alone. There were fair lakes mirroring the dark pine woods, canyons dark and blue-black with unbroken expanses of pines, snow-slashed pinnacles, wintry heights frowning upon lovely parks, watered and wooded, lying in the lap of summer; North Park floating off into the blue distance, Middle Park closed till another season, the sunny slopes of Estes Park, and winding down among the mountains the snowy ridge of the Divide, whose bright waters seek both the Atlantic and Pacific Oceans. There, far below, links of diamonds showed where the Grand River takes its rise to seek the mysterious Colorado, with its still unsolved enigma, and lose itself in the waters of the Pacific; and nearer the snow-born Thompson bursts forth from the ice to begin its journey to the Gulf of Mexico. Never-to-be-forgotten glories they were, burnt in upon my memory by six succeeding hours of terror.

You know I have no head and no ankles, and never ought to dream of mountaineering; and had I known that the ascent was a real mountaineering feat I should not have felt the slightest ambition to perform it. As it is, I am only humiliated by my success, for 'Jim' dragged me up, like a bale of goods, by sheer force of muscle. At the 'Notch' the real business of the ascent began. Two thousand feet of solid rock towered above us, 4000 feet of broken rock shelved precipitously below; smooth granite ribs, with barely foothold, stood out here and there; melted snow refrozen several times, presented a more serious obstacle; many of the rocks were loose, and tumbled down when touched. To me it was a time of extreme terror. I was roped to 'Jim', but it was of no use; my feet were paralysed and slipped on the bare rock, and he said it was useless to try to go that way, and we retraced our steps. I wanted to return to the 'Notch', knowing that my incompetence would detain the party, and one of the young men said almost plainly that a woman was a dangerous encumbrance, but the trapper replied shortly that if it were not to take a lady up he would not go up at all. He went on to explore, and reported that further progress on the correct line of ascent was blocked by ice; and then for two hours we descended, lowering ourselves by our hands from rock to rock along a boulder-strewn sweep of 4000 feet, patched with ice and snow, and perilous from rolling stones. My fatigue, giddiness, and pain from bruised ankles, and arms half pulled out of their sockets, were so great that I should never have gone half-way had not 'Jim', *nolens volens*, dragged me along with a patience and skill, and withal a determination that I should ascend the Peak, which never failed. After descending about 2000 feet to avoid the ice, we got into a deep ravine with inaccessible sides, partly filled with ice and snow and partly with large and small fragments of rock, which were constantly giving away, rendering the footing very insecure. That part to me was two hours of painful and unwilling

submission to the inevitable; of trembling, slipping, straining, of smooth ice appearing when it was least expected, and of weak entreaties to be left behind while the others went on. 'Jim' always said that there was no danger, that there was only a short bad bit ahead, and that I should go up even if he carried me!

Slipping, faltering, gasping from the exhausting toil in the rarefied air, with throbbing hearts and panting lungs, we reached the top of the gorge and squeezed ourselves between two gigantic fragments of rock by a passage called the 'Dog's Lift', when I climbed on the shoulders of one man and then was hauled up. This introduced us by an abrupt turn round the southwest angle of the Peak to a narrow shelf of considerable length, rugged, uneven, and so overhung by the cliff in some places that it is necessary to crouch to pass at all. Above, the Peak looks nearly vertical for 400 feet; and below, the most tremendous precipice I have ever seen descends in one unbroken fall. This is usually considered the most dangerous part of the ascent, but it does not seem so to me, for such foothold as there is is secure, and one fancies that it is possible to hold on with the hands. But there, and on the final, and, to my thinking, the worst part of the climb, one slip, and a breathing,

thinking, human being would lie 3000 feet below, a shapeless, bloody heap! Ring refused to traverse the ledge, and remained at the 'Lift' howling piteously.

As we crept from the ledge round a horn of rock I beheld what made me perfectly sick and dizzy to look at—the terminal Peak itself—a smooth, cracked face or wall of pink granite, as nearly perpendicular as anything could well be up which it was possible to climb.

Scaling, not climbing, is the correct term for this last ascent. It took one hour to accomplish 500 feet, pausing for breath every minute or two. The only foothold was in narrow cracks or on minute projections on the granite. To get a toe in these cracks, or here and there on a scarcely obvious projection, while crawling on hands and knees, all the while tortured with thirst and gasping and struggling for breath, this was the climb; but at last the Peak was won. A grand, well-defined mountain top it is, a nearly level acre of boulders, with precipitous sides all round, the one we came up being the only accessible one.

It was not possible to remain long. One of the young men was seriously alarmed by bleeding from the lungs, and the intense dryness of the day and the rarefaction of the air, at a height of nearly 15,000 feet, made respiration very painful. There is always water on the Peak, but it was frozen as hard as a rock, and the sucking of ice and snow increases thirst. We all suffered severely from the want of water, and the gasping for breath made our mouths and tongues so dry that articulation was difficult, and the speech of all unnatural.

From the summit were seen in unrivalled combination all the views which had rejoiced our eyes during the ascent. It was something at last to stand upon the storm-rent crown of this lonely sentinel of the Rocky range, on one of the mightiest of the vertebrae of the backbone of the North American continent, and to see the waters start for both oceans. Uplifted above love and hate and storms of passion, calm amidst the eternal silences, fanned by zephyrs and bathed in living blue, peace rested for that one bright day on the Peak, as if it were some region

Where falls not rain, or hail, or any snow,
Or ever wind blows loudly.

We placed our names, with the date of ascent, in a tin within a crevice, and descended to the ledge, sitting on the smooth granite, getting our feet into cracks and against projections, and letting ourselves down by our hands, 'Jim' going before me, so that I might steady my feet against his powerful shoulders. I was no longer giddy, and faced the precipice of 3500 feet without a shiver. Repassing the ledge and Lift, we accomplished the descent through 1500 feet of ice and snow, with many falls and bruises, but no worse mishap, and there separated, the young men taking the steepest but most direct way to the 'Notch', with the intention of getting ready for the march home, and 'Jim' and I taking what he thought the safer route for me—a descent over boulders for 2000 feet, and then a tremendous ascent to the 'Notch'. I had various falls, and once hung by my frock, which caught on a rock, and 'Jim' severed it with his hunting-knife, upon which I fell into a crevice full of soft snow. We were driven lower down the mountains than he had intended by impassable tracts of ice, and the ascent was tremendous. For the last 200 feet the boulders were of enormous size, and the steepness fearful. Sometimes I drew myself up on hands and knees, sometimes crawled; sometimes 'Jim' pulled me up by my arms or a lariat, and sometimes I stood on his shoulders, or he made steps for me of his feet and hands, but at six we stood on the 'Notch' in the splendour of the sinking sun, all colour deepening, all peaks glorifying, all shadows purpling, all peril past.

'Jim' had parted with his brusquerie when we parted from the students, and was gentle and considerate beyond anything, though I knew that he must be grievously disappointed, both in my courage and strength. Water was an object of earnest desire. My tongue rattled in my mouth, and I could hardly articulate. It is good for one's sympathies to have for once a severe experience of thirst. Truly, there was

Water, water, everywhere,
But not a drop to drink.

Three times its apparent gleam deceived even the mountaineer's practised eye, but we found only a foot of 'glare ice'. At last, in a deep hole, he succeeded in breaking the ice, and by putting one's arm far down one could scoop up a little water in one's hand, but it was tormentingly insufficient. With great difficulty and much assistance I recrossed the 'Lava Beds', was carried to the horse and lifted upon him, and when we reached the camping ground I was lifted off him, and laid on the ground wrapped up in blankets, a humiliating termination of a great exploit. The horses were saddled, and the young men were all ready to start, but 'Jim' quietly said, 'Now, gentlemen, I want a good night's rest, and we shan't stir from here tonight.' I believe they were really glad to have it so, as one of them was quite finished. I retired to my arbour, wrapped myself in a roll of blankets, and was soon asleep.

When I woke, the moon was high shining through the silvery branches, whitening the bald Peak above, and glittering on the great abyss of snow behind, and pine logs were blazing like a bonfire in the cold still air. My feet were so icy cold that I could not sleep again, and getting some blankets to sit in, and making a roll of them for my back, I sat for two hours by the camp-fire. It was weird and gloriously beautiful. The students were asleep not far off in their blankets with their feet towards the fire. Ring lay on one side of me with his fine head on my arm, and his master sat smoking, with the fire lighting up the handsome side of his face, and except for the tones of our voices, and an occasional crackle and splutter as a pine knot blazed up, there was no sound on the mountainside. The beloved stars of my far-off home were overhead, the Plough and Pole Star, with their steady light; the glittering Pleiades, looking larger than I ever saw them, and Orion's studded belt shining gloriously. Once only some wild animals prowled near the camp, when Ring, with one bound, disappeared from my side; and the horses, which were picketed by the stream, broke their lariats, stampeded, and came rushing wildly towards the fire, and it was fully half an hour before they were caught and quiet was restored. 'Jim', or Mr Nugent, as I always scrupulously called him, told stories of his early youth, and of a great sorrow which had led him to embark on a lawless and desperate life. His voice trembled, and tears rolled down his cheek. Was it semi-conscious acting, I wondered, or was his dark soul really stirred to its depths by the silence, the beauty, and the memories of youth?

We reached Estes Park at noon of the following day. A more successful ascent of the Peak was never made.

> Later in her travels in this region a crisis in the financial world and the impossibility of getting ready cash happily compelled Miss Bird to return to Estes Park where the settler Evans owed her money. She made the long ride up from Longmount (now Longmont) at a time when most settlers were coming down to the plains for the winter. M'Ginn's Gulch was actually less elegantly known as Muggins Gulch.

I rode up to 'Mountain Jim's' den, but no light shone through the chinks, and all was silent. So I rode tediously down M'Ginn's Gulch, which was full of cracklings and other strange mountain noises, and was pitch dark, though the stars were bright overhead.

Soon I heard the welcome sound of a barking dog. I supposed it to denote strange hunters, but calling 'Ring' at a venture, the noble dog's large paws and grand head were in a moment on my saddle, and he greeted me with all those inarticulate but perfectly comprehensible noises with which dogs welcome their human friends. Of the two men on horses who accompanied him, one was his master, as I knew by the musical voice and grace of manner, but it was too dark to see anyone, though he struck a light to show me the valuable furs with which one of the horses was loaded. The desperado was heartily glad to see me, and sending the man and fur-laden horse on to his cabin, he turned with me to Evans's; and as the cold was very severe, and Birdie was very tired, we dismounted and walked the remaining three miles.

All my visions of a comfortable reception and good meal after my long ride vanished with his first words. The Edwardses had left for the winter on the previous morning, but had not passed through Longmount; the cabin was dismantled, the stores were low, and two young men, Mr Kavan, a miner, and Mr Buchan, whom I was slightly acquainted with before, were 'baching' there to look after the stock until Evans, who was daily expected, returned. The other settler and his wife had left the park, so there was not a woman within twenty-five miles. A fierce wind had arisen, and the cold was awful, which seemed to make matters darker. I did not care in the least about myself, I could rough it, and enjoy doing so, but I was very sorry for the young men, who, I knew, would be much embarrassed by the sudden appearance of a lady for an indefinite time. But the difficulty had to be faced, and I walked in and took them by surprise as they were sitting smoking by the fire in the living room, which was dismantled, unswept, and wretched-looking.

The young men did not show any annoyance, but exerted themselves to prepare a meal, and courteously made 'Jim' share it. After he had gone, I boldly confessed my impecunious circumstances, and told them that I must stay there till things changed, that I hoped not to inconvenience them in any way, and that by dividing the work among us they would be free to be out hunting. So we agreed to make the best of it.

Sundry practical difficulties had to be faced and overcome. There was one of the common spring mattresses of the country in the little room which opened from the living-room, but nothing upon it. This was remedied by making a large bag and filling it with hay. Then there were neither sheets, towels, nor table-cloths. This was irremediable, and I never missed the first or last. Candles were another loss, and we had only one paraffin lamp. I slept all night in spite of a gale which blew all Sunday and into Monday afternoon, threatening to lift the cabin from the ground, and actually removing part of the roof from the little room between the kitchen and living-room, in which we used to dine. Sunday was brilliant, but nearly a hurricane, and I dared not stir outside the cabin. The parlour was 2 inches deep in the mud from the roof. We nominally divide the cooking. Mr Kavan makes the best bread I ever ate; they bring in wood and water, and wash the supper things, and I do my room and the parlour, wash the breakfast things, and a number of etceteras. My room is easily done, but the parlour is a never-ending business. I have swept shovelfuls of mud out of it three times today. There is nothing to dust it with but a buffalo's tail, and every now and then a gust descends the open chimney and drives the wood ashes all over the room. However, I have found an old shawl which answers for a table-cloth, and have made our parlour look a little more habitable. Jim came in yesterday in a silent mood, and sat looking vacantly into the fire. The young men said that this mood was the usual precursor of an 'ugly fit'.

[A few days later] Mr Nugent came in looking very black, and asked me to ride with him to see the beaver dams on the Black Canyon. No more whistling or singing, or talking to his beautiful mare, or sparkling repartee. His mood was as dark as the sky overhead, which was black with an impending snowstorm. He was quite silent, struck his horse often, started off on a furious gallop, and then throwing his mare on her haunches close to me, said, 'You're the first man or woman who's treated me like a human being for many a year.' 'If you want to know', he continued, 'how nearly a man can become a devil, I'll tell you now.' There was no choice, and we rode up the canyon, and I listened to one of the darkest tales of ruin I have ever heard or read.

Its early features were very simple. He ran away from home, entered the service of the Hudson's Bay Company, and remained in it for several years, only leaving it because he found even that lawless life too strict for him. Then, being as I suppose about 27, he entered the service of the United States Government, and became one of the famous Indian Scouts of the Plains, distinguishing himself by some of the most daring deeds on record, and some of the bloodiest crimes. Some of these tales I have heard before, but never so terribly told. Years must have passed in that service, till he became a character known through all the West, and much dreaded for his readiness to take offence, and his equal readiness with his revolver. Vain, even in his dark mood, he told me that he was idolized by women, and that in his worst hours he was always chivalrous to good women. He described himself as riding through camps in his scout's dress with a red scarf round his waist, and sixteen golden curls, 18 inches long, hanging over his shoulders. The handsome, even superbly handsome, side of his face was towards me as he spoke. As a scout and as an armed escort of emigrant parties he was evidently implicated in all the blood and broil of a lawless region and period, and went from bad to worse, varying his life by drunken sprees, which brought nothing but violence and loss. I suspect, and not without reason, that he joined one or more of those gangs of border ruffians which for so long raided through Kansas. Of course I cannot give details. The story took three hours to tell, and was crowded with terrific illustrations of a desperado's career, told with a rush of wild eloquence that was truly thrilling.

When the snow, which for some time had been falling, compelled him to break off and guide me to a sheltered place from which I could make my own way back again, he stopped his horse and said, 'Now you see a man who has made a devil of himself! Lost! Lost! Lost! I believe in God. . . . I'm afraid to die. You've stirred the better nature in me too late.'

He made me promise to keep one or two things secret whether he were living or dead, and I promised, for I had no choice; but they come between me and the sunshine sometimes, and I wake at night to think of them. I wish I had been spared the regret and excitement of that afternoon. A less ungovernable nature would never have spoken as he did, nor told me what he did; but his proud, fierce soul all poured itself out then, with hatred and self-loathing, blood on his hands and murder in his heart, though even then he could not be altogether other than a gentleman, or altogether divest himself of fascination, even when so tempestuously revealing the darkest points of his character. My soul dissolved in pity for his dark, lost, self-ruined life, as he left me and turned away in the blinding storm to the Snowy Range, where he said he was going to camp out for a fortnight.

On a subsequent visit to 'Jim's' den he read her 'a very able paper on spiritualism which he was writing'. Unpublished passages in the letters reveal that he was really trying to write about spiritualism to resolve his feelings about her—and perhaps raise them to a higher plane. They had been circling gingerly around one another for several weeks. They would part for ever and then contrive to meet by accident on the trails between Muggins Gulch and Evans's ranch. The route to Longmount where she expected to find letters led her past 'Jim's' cabin, and whether she admitted it to herself or not, she must have known that 'Jim' would try to prevent her undertaking such a reckless ride alone in dangerous winter weather. And it was 'Jim' who escorted her when she left Estes Park for the last time.

'Fyking' is a Scottish dialect word that may be translated as 'nagging'.

I had not been up from the park at sunrise before, and it was quite glorious, the purple depths of M'Ginn's Gulch, from which at a height of 9000 feet you look down on the sunlit park 1500 feet below, lying in a real haze, with its pearly needle-shaped peaks, framed by mountain-sides dark with pines—my glorious, solitary, unique mountain home! The purple sun rose in front. Had I known what

made it purple I should certainly have gone no farther. Then clouds, the morning mist as I supposed, lifted themselves up rose-lighted, showing the sun's disc as purple as one of the jars in a chemist's window, and having permitted this glimpse of their king, came down again as a dense mist, the wind chopped round, and the mist began to freeze hard. Soon Birdie and myself were a mass of acidular crystals; it was a true easterly fog. I galloped on, hoping to get through it, unable to see a yard before me; but it thickened, and I was obliged to subside into a jog-trot.

As I rode on, about four miles from the cabin, a human figure, looking gigantic like the spectre of the Brocken, with long hair white as snow, appeared close to me, and at the same moment there was the flash of a pistol close to my ear, and I recognized 'Mountain Jim' frozen from head to foot, looking a century old with his snowy hair. It was 'ugly' altogether certainly, a desperado's grim jest, and it was best to accept it as such, though I had just cause for displeasure. He stormed and scolded, dragged me off the pony—for my hands and feet were numb with cold—took the bridle, and went off at a rapid stride, so that I had to run to keep them in sight in the darkness, for we were off the road in a thicket of scrub, looking like white branch coral, I knew not where. Then we came suddenly on his cabin, and dear old Ring, white like all else; and the ruffian insisted on my going in, and he made a good fire, and heated some coffee, raging all the time. He said everything against my going forward, except that it was dangerous; all he said came true, and here I am safe! Your letters, however, outweighed everything but danger, and I decided on going on, when he said, 'I've seen many foolish people, but never one so foolish as you—you haven't a grain of sense. Why, I, an old mountaineer, wouldn't go down to the Plains today.' I told him he could not, though he would like it very much, for that he had turned his horses loose; on which he laughed heartily, and more heartily still at the stories I told him of young Lyman [an unwelcome guest at Evans's cabin] so that I have still a doubt how much of the dark moods I have lately seen was assumed.

He took me back to the track; and the interview which began with a pistol-shot, ended quite pleasantly. It was an eerie ride, one not to be forgotten, though there was no danger. I could not recognize any localities. Every tree was silvered, and the fir-tree tufts of needles looked like white chrysanthemums. The snow lay a foot deep in the gulches, with its hard, smooth surface marked by the feet of innumerable birds and beasts. Ice bridges had formed across all the streams, and I crossed them without knowing when. Gulches looked fathomless abysses, with clouds boiling up out of them, and shaggy mountain summits, half seen for a moment through the eddies, as quickly vanished. Everything looked vast and indefinite. Then a huge creation, like one of Doré's phantom illustrations, with much breathing of wings, came sailing towards me in a temporary opening in the mist. As with a strange rustle it passed close over my head, I saw, for the first time, the great mountain eagle, carrying a good-sized beast in his talons. It was a noble vision. Then there were ten miles of metamorphosed gulches—silent, awful — many ice bridges, then a frozen drizzle, and then the winds changed from east to northeast. Birdie was covered with exquisite crystals, and her long mane and the long beard which covers her throat were pure white.

I reached the prairie and pushed on. It was simply fearful. It was twilight from the thick snow, and I faced a furious east wind loaded with fine, hard-frozen crystals, which literally made my face bleed. I could only see a very short distance anywhere; the drifts were often two feet deep, and only now and then, through the blinding whirl, I caught a glimpse of snow through which withered sunflowers did not protrude, and then I knew that I was on the track. But reaching a wild place, I lost it, and still cantered on, trusting to the pony's sagacity. It failed for once, for she took me on a lake and we fell through the ice into the water 100 yards from land, and had a hard fight back again. It grew worse and worse. I had wrapped up my face, but the sharp, hard snow beat on my eyes—the only exposed part—bringing tears into them, which froze and closed up my eyelids at once. You cannot imagine what that was. I had to take off one glove to pick one eye open, for as to the other, the storm beat so savagely against it that I left it frozen, and drew over it the double piece of flannel which protected my face. I could hardly keep the other open by picking the ice from it constantly with my numb fingers, in doing which I got the back of my hand slightly frostbitten. It was truly awful at the time. I often thought, 'Suppose I am going south instead of east? Suppose Birdie should fail? Suppose it should grow quite dark?' I was mountaineer enough to shake these fears off and keep up my spirits, but I knew how many had perished on the prairie in similar storms.

Not a quarter of an hour after I had wondered how long I could hold on I saw, to my surprise, close to me, half-smothered in snow, the scattered houses and blessed lights of Longmount, and welcome, indeed, its wide, dreary, lifeless, soundless road looked! When I reached the hotel I was so benumbed that I could not get off, and the worthy host lifted me off and carried me in.

I should not have been able to leave if Mr Nugent had not offered his services. His chivalry to women is so well known, that Evans said I could be safer and better cared for with no one. He added, 'His heart is good and kind, as kind a heart as ever beat. He's a great enemy of his own, but he's been living pretty quietly for the last four years.' At the door of his den I took leave of Birdie, who had been my faithful companion for more than 700 miles of travelling, and of Evans, who had been uniformly kind to me and just in all his dealings, even to paying to me at that moment the very last dollar he owed me. May God bless him and his!

'Jim' shortened the way by repeating a great deal of poetry, and by earnest, reasonable conversation, so that I was quite surprised when it grew dark. He told me that he never lay down to sleep without prayer—prayer chiefly that God would give him a happy death. He had previously promised that he would not hurry or scold, but 'fyking' had not been included in the arrangement, and when in the early darkness we reached the steep hill, at whose foot the rapid deep St Vrain flows, he 'fyked' unreasonably about me, the mare, and the crossing generally, and seemed to think I could not get through, for the ice had been cut with an axe, and we could not see whether glaze had formed since or not.

I was to have slept at the house of a woman farther down the canyon, who never ceases talking, but Miller, the young man whose attractive house and admirable habits I have mentioned before, came out and said his house was 'now fixed for ladies', so we stayed there, and I was made as comfortable as could be. His house is a model. He cleans everything as soon as it is used, so nothing is ever dirty, and his stove and cooking gear in their bright parts look like polished silver. It was amusing to hear the two men talk like two women about various ways of making bread and biscuits, one even writing out a recipe for the other. It was almost grievous that a solitary man should have the power of making a house so comfortable! They heated a stone for my feet, warmed a blanket for me to sleep in, and put logs enough on the fire to burn all night, for the mercury was 11° below zero. The stars were intensely bright, and a well-defined auroral arch, throwing off fantastic coruscations, lighted the whole northern sky.

The next morning, as soon as the sun was well risen, we left for our journey of thirty miles. I did not wish to realize that it was my last ride, and my last association with any of the men of the mountains whom I had learned to trust, and in some respects to admire. No more hunters' tales told while the pine knots crack and blaze; no more thrilling narratives of adventures with Indians and bears; and never again shall I hear that strange talk of Nature and her doings which is the speech of those who live with her and her alone. Already the dismalness of a level land comes over me. All that day we neither saw man, beast, nor bird. 'Jim' was silent mostly. Like all true children of the mountains, he pined even when temporarily absent from them.

At sunset we reached a cluster of houses where, to my dismay, I heard that there was to be a dance at the one little inn to which we were going. I pictured to myself no privacy, no peace, no sleep, drinking, low sounds, and worse than all, 'Jim' getting into a quarrel and using his pistols. He was uncomfortable about it for another reason. He said he had dreamt the night before that there was to be a dance, and that he had to shoot a man for making 'an unpleasant remark!' When we got to the queer little place where they 'keep strangers' at St Louis, they were very civil, and said that after supper we could have the kitchen to ourselves.

The landlady asked, with great eagerness, who the gentleman was who was with me, and said that the men outside were saying that they were sure that it was 'Rocky Mountain Jim', but she was sure it was not. When I told her that the men were right, she exclaimed, 'Do tell! I want to know! that quiet, kind gentleman!' and she said she used to frighten her children when they were naughty by telling them that 'he would get them, for he came down from the mountains every week, and took back a child with him to eat!' She was as proud of having him in her house as if he had been the President, and I gained a reflected importance! All the men in the settlement assembled in the front room, hoping he would go and smoke there, and when he remained in the kitchen they came round the window and into the doorway to look at him. The children got on his knee, and, to my great relief, he kept them good and quiet, and let them play with his curls, to the great delight of the two women, who never took their eyes off him. At last the bad-smelling supper was served, and ten silent men came in and gobbled it up, staring steadily at 'Jim' as they gobbled.

It was a most respectable dance, a fortnightly gathering got up by the neighbouring settlers, most of them young married people, and there was no drinking at all. I wrote to you for some time, while Mr Nugent copied poems which he recited with deep feeling. It was altogether very quiet and peaceful. He repeated to me several poems of great merit which he had composed, and told me much more about his life. I knew that no one else could or would speak to him as I could, and for the last time I urged upon him the necessity of a reformation in his life, beginning with the giving up of whisky, going so far as to tell him that I despised a man of his intellect for being a slave to such a vice. 'Too late! too late!' he always answered, 'for such a change.' Ay, *too late*. He shed tears quietly. 'It might have been once,' he said. Ay, *might* have been. He has excellent sense for every one but himself, and, as I have seen him with a single exception, a gentleness, propriety, and considerateness of manner surprising in any man, but especially so in a man associating only with the rough men of the West. As I looked at him, I felt a pity such as I never before felt for a human being. My thought at the moment was, Will not our Father in heaven, 'who spared not His own Son, but delivered Him up for us all,' be far more pitiful?

Yesterday morning the mercury was 20° below zero. I think I never saw such a brilliant atmosphere. That curious phenomena called frost-fall was occurring, in which, whatever moisture may exist in the air, somehow aggregates into feathers and fern leaves, the loveliest of creations, only seen in rarefied air and intense cold. One breath and they vanish. The air was filled with diamond sparks quite intangible. They seemed just glitter and no more. It was still and cloudless, and the shapes of violet mountains were softened by a veil of the tenderest blue. When the Greeley stage wagon came up, Mr Fodder, whom I met at Lower Canyon, was on it. He had expressed a great wish to go to Estes Park, and to hunt with 'Mountain Jim', if it would be safe to do the latter. He was now dressed in the extreme of English dandyism, and when I introduced them, he put out a small hand cased in a perfectly-fitting lemon-coloured kid glove. As the trapper stood there in his grotesque rags and odds and ends of apparel, his gentlemanliness of deportment brought into relief the innate vulgarity of a rich parvenu. Mr Fodder rattled so amusingly as we drove away that I never realized that my Rocky Mountain life was at an end, not even when I saw 'Mountain Jim', with his golden hair yellow in the sunshine, slowly leading the beautiful mare over the snowy Plains back to Estes Park, equipped with the saddle on which I had ridden 800 miles!

A drive of several hours over the Plains brought us to Greeley, and a few hours later, in the far blue distance, the Rocky Mountains, and all that they enclose, went down below the prairie sea.

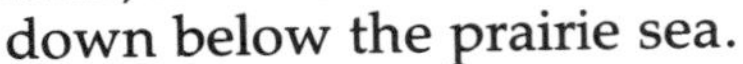

Chapter Four

Unbeaten Tracks in Japan, 1880

Japan had been open to Western travellers for barely twenty years when Isabella Bird visited it in 1878. Though she found much to admire on the mainland, it was too civilized and highly bureaucratized for her taste, and so with Ito, her Japanese interpreter, she went on to the then almost unknown island of Yezo, now Hokkaido, inhabited by the aboriginal 'hairy Ainos' (as distinct from the smooth-faced Japanese), a subject people much despised by their civilized Japanese rulers. On this journey she was no longer a mere 'lady traveller', but a serious student whose observations and opinions would draw respectful attention in Britain.

A *kura* is a fire-proof storehouse, and *séance* is used to mean a 'sitting'.

I am in the lonely Aino land, and I think that the most interesting of my travelling experiences has been the living for three days and two nights in an Aino hut, and seeing and sharing the daily life of complete savages, who go on with their ordinary occupations just as if I were not among them.

Ito is very greedy and self-indulgent, and whimpered very much about coming to Biratori at all—one would have thought he was going to the stake. He actually borrowed for himself a sleeping-mat and *futons*, and has brought a chicken, onions, potatoes, French beans, Japanese sauce, tea, rice, a kettle, a stew-pan, and a rice-pan, while I contented myself with a cold fowl and potatoes.

We took three horses and a mounted Aino guide, and found a beaten track the whole way. It turns into the forest at once on leaving Sarufuto, and goes through forest the entire distance, with an abundance of reedy grass higher than my hat on horseback along it, and as it is only 12 inches broad and much overgrown, the horses were constantly pushing through leafage soaking from a night's rain, and I was soon wet up to my shoulders. The forest trees are almost solely the *Ailanthus glandulosus* and the *Zelkowa keaki*, often matted together with a white-flowered trailer of the Hydrangea genus. The undergrowth is simply hideous, consisting mainly of coarse reedy grass, monstrous docks, the large-leaved *Polygonum cuspidatum*, several umbelliferous plants, and a 'ragweed', which, like most of its gawky fellows, grows from 5 to 6 feet high. The forest is dark and very silent, threaded by this narrow path, and by others as narrow, made by the hunters in

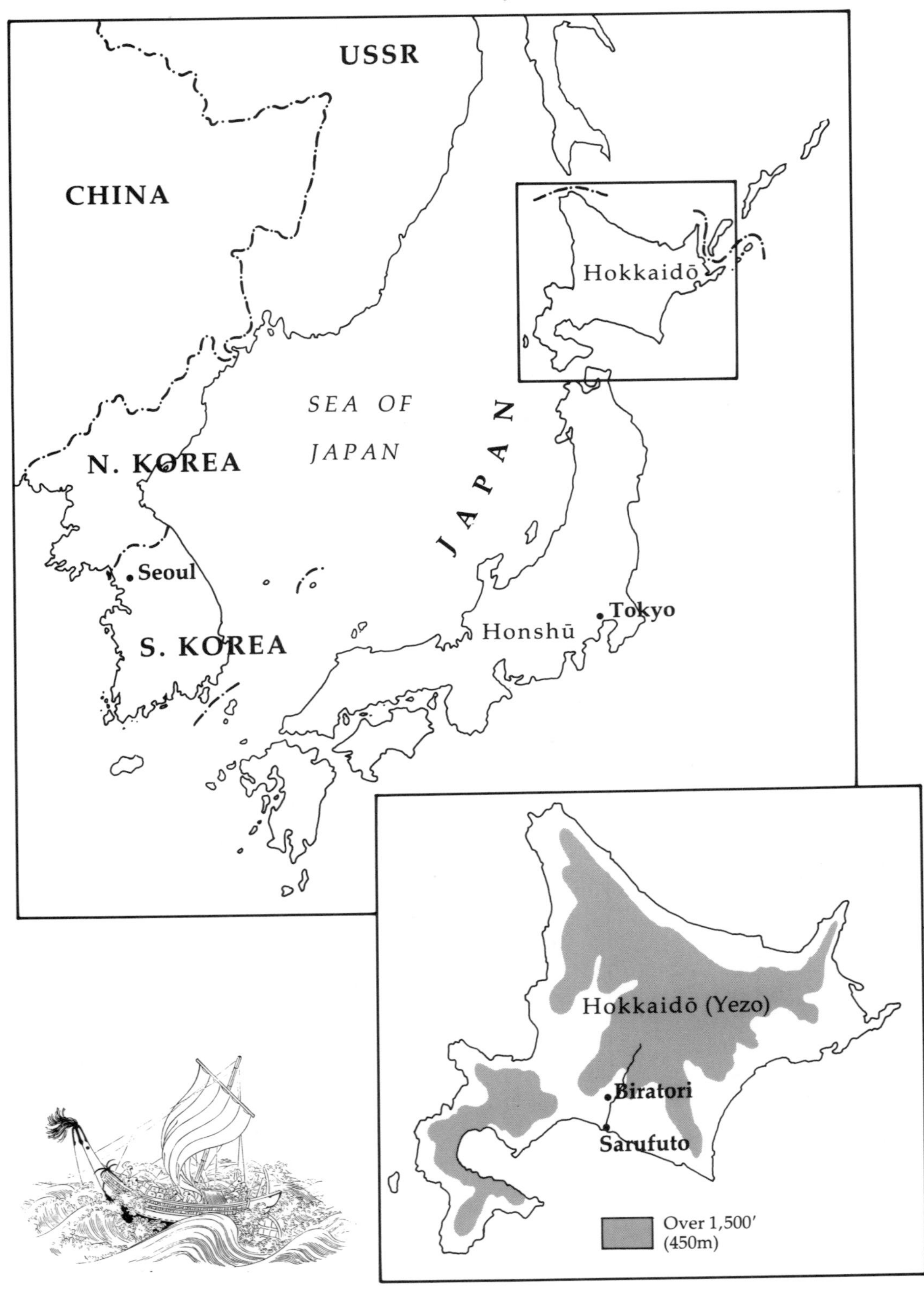
USSR
CHINA
Hokkaidō
SEA OF
JAPAN
JAPAN
N. KOREA
Seoul
S. KOREA
Tokyo
Honshū
Hokkaidō (Yezo)
Biratori
Sarufuto
Over 1,500′
(450m)

search of game. The 'main road' sometimes plunges into deep bogs, at others is roughly corduroyed by the roots of trees, and frequently hangs over the edge of abrupt and much-worn declivities, in going up one of which the baggage-horse rolled down a bank fully 30 feet high, and nearly all the tea was lost. At another the guide's pack-saddle lost its balance, and man, horse, and saddle went over the slope, pots, pans, and packages flying after them. At another time my horse sank up to his chest in a very bad bog, and as he was totally unable to extricate himself, I was obliged to scramble upon his neck and jump to *terra firma* over his ears.

There is something very gloomy in the solitude of this silent land, with its beast-haunted forests, its great patches of pasture, the resort of wild animals which haunt the lower regions in search of food when the snow drives them down from the mountains, and its narrow track, indicating the single file in which the savages

of the interior walk with their bare, noiseless feet. Reaching the Sarufutogawa, a river with a treacherous bottom, I hailed an Aino boy, who took me up the stream in a 'dug-out', and after that we passed through Biroka, Saruba, and Mina, all purely Aino villages, situated among small patches of millet, tobacco, and pumpkins, so choked with weeds that it was doubtful whether they were crops. I was much surprised with the extreme neatness and cleanliness outside the houses; 'model villages' they are in these respects, with no litter lying in sight anywhere, nothing indeed but dog troughs, hollowed out of logs, like 'dug-outs', for the numerous yellow dogs, which are a feature of Aino life. There are neither puddles nor heaps, but the houses, all trim and in good repair, rise clean out of the sandy soil.

Biratori, the largest of the Aino settlements in this region, is very prettily

situated among forests and mountains, on rising ground, with a very sinuous river winding at its feet and a wooded height above. A lonelier place could scarcely be found. As we passed among the houses the yellow dogs barked, the women looked shy and smiled, and the men made their graceful salutation. We stopped at the chief's house, where, of course, we were unexpected guests; but Shinondi, his nephew, and two other men came out, saluted us, and with most hospitable intent helped Ito to unload the horses. Indeed their eager hospitality created quite a commotion, one running hither and the other thither in their anxiety to welcome a stranger. It is a large house, the room being 35 by 25, and the roof 20 feet high; but

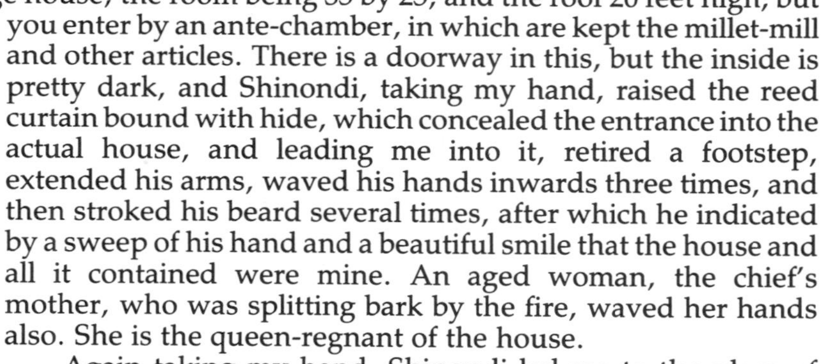

you enter by an ante-chamber, in which are kept the millet-mill and other articles. There is a doorway in this, but the inside is pretty dark, and Shinondi, taking my hand, raised the reed curtain bound with hide, which concealed the entrance into the actual house, and leading me into it, retired a footstep, extended his arms, waved his hands inwards three times, and then stroked his beard several times, after which he indicated by a sweep of his hand and a beautiful smile that the house and all it contained were mine. An aged woman, the chief's mother, who was splitting bark by the fire, waved her hands also. She is the queen-regnant of the house.

Again taking my hand, Shinondi led me to the place of honour at the head of the fire, a rude, movable platform 6 feet long, by 4 broad, and 1 foot high, on which he laid an ornamental mat, apologizing for not having at that moment a bearskin wherewith to cover it. The baggage was speedily brought in by several willing pairs of hands; some reed mats 15 feet long were laid down upon the very coarse ones which covered the whole floor, and when they saw Ito putting up my stretcher they hung a fine mat along the rough wall to conceal it, and suspended another on the beams of the roof for a canopy. The alacrity and instinctive hospitality with which these men rushed about to make things comfortable were very fascinating, though comfort is a word misapplied in an Aino hut. The women only did what the men told them.

They offered food at once, but I told them that I had brought my own, and would only ask leave to cook it on their fire. I need not have brought any cups, for they have many lacquer bowls, and Shinondi brought me on a lacquer tray a bowl full of water from one of their four wells. They said that Benri, the chief, would wish me to make his house my own for as long as I cared to stay, and I must excuse them in all things in which their ways were different from my own. Shinondi and four others in the village speak tolerable Japanese, and this of course is the medium of communication. Ito has exerted himself nobly as an interpreter, and has entered into my wishes with a cordiality and intelligence which have been perfectly invaluable; and though he did growl at injunctions regarding politeness, he has

carried them out to my satisfaction, and even admits that the mountain Ainos are better than he expected; 'but,' he added, 'they have learned their politeness from the Japanese!' They have never seen a foreign woman, and only three foreign men, but there is neither crowding nor staring as among the Japanese, possibly in part from apathy and want of intelligence. For three days they have kept up their graceful and kindly hospitality, going on with their ordinary life and occupations, and though I have lived among them in this room by day and night, there has been nothing which in any way could offend the most fastidious sense of delicacy.

They said they would leave me to eat and rest, and all retired but the chief's mother, a weird, witch-like woman of 80, with shocks of yellow-white hair, and a stern suspiciousness in her wrinkled face. I have come to feel as if she had the evil eye, as she sits there watching, watching always, and for ever knotting the bark thread like one of the Fates, keeping a jealous watch on her son's two wives, and on other young women who come in to weave—neither the dullness nor the repose of old age about her; and her eyes gleam with a greedy light when she sees *saké*, of which she drains a bowl without taking breath. She alone is suspicious of strangers, and she thinks that my visit bodes no good to her tribe. I see her eyes fixed upon me now, and they make me shudder.

I had a good meal seated in my chair on the top of the guest-seat to avoid the fleas, which are truly legion. At dusk Shinondi returned, and soon people began to drop in, till eighteen were assembled, including the sub-chief, and several very grand-looking old men, with full, grey, wavy beards. Age is held in much reverence, and it is etiquette for these old men to do honour to a guest in the chief's absence. As each entered he saluted me several times, and after sitting down turned towards me and saluted again, going through the same ceremony with every other person. They said they had come 'to bid me welcome'. They took their places in rigid order at each side of the fireplace, which is 6 feet long, Benri's mother in the place of honour at the right, then Shinondi, then the sub-chief, and on the other side the old men. Besides these, seven women sat in a row in the background splitting bark. A large iron pan hung over the fire from a blackened arrangement above, and Benri's principal wife cut wild roots, green beans, and seaweed, and shred dried fish and venison among them, adding millet, water, and some strong- smelling fish-oil, and set the whole on to stew for three hours, stirring the 'mess' now and then with a wooden spoon.

Several of the older people smoke, and I handed round some mild tobacco, which they received with waving hands. I told them that I came from a land in the sea, very far away, where they saw the sun go down, so very far away that a horse would have to gallop day and night for five weeks to reach it, and that I had come a long journey to see them, and that I wanted to ask them many questions, so that when I went home I might tell my own people something about them. Shinondi and another man, who understood Japanese, bowed, and (as on every occasion) translated what I said into Aino for the venerable group opposite. Shinondi then said 'that he and Shinrichi, the other Japanese speaker, would tell me all they knew, but they were but young men, and only knew what was told to them. They would speak what they believed to be true, but the chief knew more than they, and when he came back he might tell me differently, and then I should think that they had spoken lies.' I said that no one who looked into their faces could think that they ever told lies. They were very much pleased, and waved their hands and stroked their beards repeatedly. Before they told me anything, they begged and prayed that I would not inform the Japanese Government that they had told me of their customs, or harm might come to them!

For the next two hours, and for two more after supper, I asked them questions

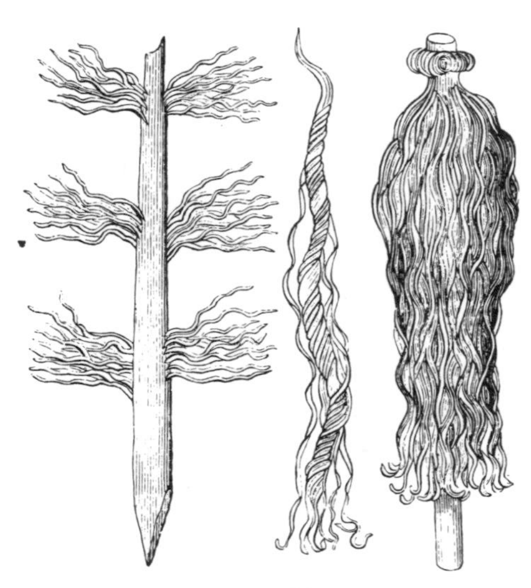

concerning their religion and customs, and again yesterday for a considerable time, and this morning, after Benri's return, I went over the same subjects with him, and have also employed a considerable time in getting about three hundred words from them, which I have spelt phonetically of course, and intend to go over again when I visit the coast Ainos.

The process was slow, as both question and answer had to pass through three languages. There was a very manifest desire to tell the truth, and I think that their statements concerning their few and simple customs may be relied upon.

About nine the stew was ready, and the women ladled it into lacquer bowls with wooden spoons. The men were served first, but all ate together. Afterwards *saké*, their curse, was poured into lacquer bowls, and across each bowl a finely-carved *saké* stick was laid. These sticks are very highly prized. The bowls were waved several times with an inward motion, then each man took his stick and, dipping it into the *saké*, made six libations to the fire, and several to the 'god', a wooden post, with a quantity of spiral white shavings falling from near the top. The Ainos are not affected by *saké* nearly so easily as the Japanese. They took it cold, it is true, but each drank about three times as much as would have made a Japanese foolish, and it had no effect upon them. After two hours more talk one after another got up and went out, making profuse salutations to me and to the others. My candles had been forgotten, and our *séance* was held by the fitful light of the big logs on the fire, aided by a succession of chips of birch bark, with which a woman replenished a cleft stick that was stuck into the fire-hole. I never saw such a strangely picturesque sight as that group of magnificent savages with the fitful firelight on their faces, and for adjuncts the flare of the torch, the strong lights, the blackness of the recesses of the room and of the roof, at one end of which the stars looked in, and the row of savage women in the background—eastern savagery and western civilization met in this hut, savagery giving, and civilization receiving, the yellow-skinned Ito the connecting link between the two, and the representative of a civilization to which our own is but an 'infant of days'.

I found it very exciting, and when all had left crept out into the starlight. The lodges were all dark and silent, and the dogs, mild like their masters, took no notice of me. The only sound was the rustle of a light breeze through the surrounding forest. The verse came into my mind, 'It is not the will of your Father which is in Heaven that one of these little ones should perish.' Surely these simple savages are children, as children to be judged; may we not hope as children to be saved through Him who came 'not to judge the world, but to save the world'?

I crept back again and into my mosquito net, and suffered not from fleas or mosquitoes, but from severe cold. Shinondi conversed with Ito for some time in a low musical voice, having previously asked if it would keep me from sleeping. No Japanese ever intermitted his ceaseless chatter at any hour of the night for a similar reason. Later, the chief's principal wife, Noma, stuck a triply-cleft stick in a fire-hole, put a potsherd with a wick and some fish-oil upon it, and by the dim light of this rude lamp sewed until midnight at a garment of bark cloth which she was ornamenting for her lord with strips of blue cloth, and when I opened my eyes the next morning she was at the window sewing by the earliest daylight. She is the most intelligent-looking of all the women, but looks sad and almost stern, and speaks seldom. Although she is the principal wife of the chief, she is not happy, for she is childless, and I thought that her sad look darkened into something evil as the other wife caressed a fine baby boy. Benri seems to me something of a brute, and the mother-in-law obviously holds the reins of government pretty tight. After sewing till midnight she swept the mats with a bunch of twigs, and then crept into her bed behind a hanging mat. For a moment in the stillness I felt a feeling of panic, as if I were incurring a risk by being alone among savages, but I conquered it, and after watching the fire till it went out, fell asleep till I was awoke by the severe cold of the next day's dawn.

When I crept from under my net, much benumbed with cold, there were about eleven people in the room, who all made their graceful salutation. It did not seem as if they had ever heard of washing, for when water was asked for, Shinondi brought a little in a lacquer bowl, and held it while I bathed my face and hands, supposing the performance to be an act of worship! I was about to throw some cold tea out of the window by my bed, when he arrested me with an anxious face, and I saw what I had not observed before, that there was a god at that window, a stick with festoons of shavings hanging from it, and beside it a dead bird. The Ainos have two meals a day, and their breakfast was a repetition of the previous night's supper. We all ate together, and I gave the children the remains of my rice, and it was most amusing to see little creatures of 3, 4 and 5 years old, with no other clothing than a piece of pewter hanging round their necks, first formally asking leave of the parents before taking the rice, and then waving their hands. The obedience of the children is instantaneous. Their parents are more demonstrative in their affection than the Japanese are, caressing them a good deal, and two of the men are devoted to children who are not their own. These little ones are as grave and dignified as Japanese children, and are very gentle.

I went out soon after five, when the dew was glittering in the sunshine, and the mountain hollow in which Biratori stands was looking its very best, and the silence of the place, even though the people were all astir, was as impressive as that of the night before. What a strange life! Knowing nothing, hoping nothing, fearing

a little, the need for clothes and food the one motive principle, *saké* in abundance the one good! How very few points of contact it is possible to have! I was just thinking so, when Shinondi met me, and took me to his house to see if I could do anything for a child sorely afflicted with skin disease, and his extreme tenderness for this very loathsome object made me feel that human affections were the same among them as with us. He had carried it on his back from a village, five miles distant, that morning, in the hope that it might be cured. As soon as I entered, he laid a fine mat on the floor, and covered the guest-seat with a bearskin. After breakfast he took me to the lodge of the sub-chief, the largest in the village, 45 feet square, and into about twenty others all constructed in the same way, but some of them were not more than 20 feet square. In all, I was received with the same courtesy, but a few of the people asked Shinondi not to take me into their houses, as they did not want me to see how poor they are. In every house there was the low

shelf with more or fewer curios upon it, but besides these, none but the barest necessaries of life, though the skins which they sell or barter every year would enable them to surround themselves with comforts, were it not that their gains represent to them *saké* and nothing else. They are not nomads. On the contrary, they cling tenaciously to the sites on which their fathers have lived and died. But anything more deplorable than the attempts at cultivation which surround their lodges could not be seen. The soil is little better than white sand, on which without manure they attempt to grow millet, which is to them in the place of rice, pumpkins, onions, and tobacco, but the look of their plots is as if they had been cultivated ten years ago, and some chance-sown grain and vegetables had come up among the weeds. When nothing more will grow, they partially clear another bit of forest, and exhaust that in its turn.

In every house the same honour was paid to a guest. This seems a savage virtue which is not strong enough to survive much contact with civilization. Before I entered one lodge, the woman brought several of the finer mats, and arranged them as a pathway for me to walk to the fire upon. They will not accept anything for lodging, or for anything that they give, so I was anxious to help them by buying some of their handiwork, but found even this a difficult matter. They were very anxious to give, but when I desired to buy they said they did not wish to part with their things. I wanted what they had in actual use, such as a tobacco box and pipe-sheath, and knives with carved handles and scabbards, and for three of these I offered 2½ dollars. They said they did not care to sell them, but in the evening they came saying they were not worth more than 1 dollar 10 cents, and they would sell them for that; and I could not get them to take more. They said it was 'not their custom'. I bought a bow and three poisoned arrows, two reed-mats, with a diamond pattern on them in reeds stained red, some knives with sheaths, and a bark cloth dress. I tried to buy the *saké*-sticks with which they make libations to their gods, but they said it was 'not their custom' to part with the *saké*-stick of any living man—however, this morning Shinondi has brought me, as a very valuable present, the stick of a dead man! This morning the man who sold the arrows brought two new ones, to replace two which were imperfect. They wear very large earrings with hoops an inch and a half in diameter, a pair constituting the dowry of an Aino bride, but they would not part with these.

A house was burned down two nights ago, and 'custom' in such a case requires that all the men should work at rebuilding it, so in their absence I got two boys to take me in a 'dug-out' as far as we could go up the Sarufutogawa, a lovely river, which winds tortuously through the forests and mountains in unspeakable loveliness. I had much of the feeling of the ancient mariner—

We were the first
Who ever burst
Into that silent sea.

For certainly no European had ever previously floated on the dark and forest-shrouded waters. I enjoyed those hours thoroughly, for the silence was profound, and the faint blue of the autumn sky, and the soft blue veil which 'spiritualized' the distances, were so exquisitely like the Indian summer.

The evening was spent like the previous one, but the hearts of the savages were sad, for there was no more *saké* in Biratori, so they could not 'drink to the god', and the fire and the post with the shavings had to go without libations. There was no more oil, so after the strangers retired the hut was in complete darkness.

Yesterday morning we all breakfasted soon after daylight, and the able-bodied men went away to hunt. Hunting and fishing are their occupations, and for 'indoor recreation' they carve tobacco-boxes, knife-sheaths, *saké*-sticks, and shuttles. It is quite unnecessary for them to do anything; they are quite contented to sit by the fire, and smoke occasionally, and eat and sleep, this apathy being varied by spasms of activity when there is no more dried flesh in the *kuras*, and when skins must be taken to Sarufuto to pay for *saké*. The women seem never to have an idle moment. They rise early to sew, weave, and split bark, for they not only clothe themselves and their husbands in this nearly indestructible cloth, but weave it for barter, and the lower class of Japanese are constantly to be seen wearing the product of Aino industry. They do all the hard work, such as drawing water, chopping wood, grinding millet, and cultivating the soil, after their fashion; but to do the men justice, I often see them trudging along, carrying one and even two children. The women take the exclusive charge of the *kuras*, which are never entered by men.

I was left for some hours alone with the women, of whom there were seven in the hut, with a few children. On the one side of the fire the chief's mother sat like a Fate, for ever splitting and knotting bark, and petrifying me by her cold, fateful eyes. Her thick, grey hair hangs in shocks, the tattooing round her mouth has nearly faded, and no longer disguises her really handsome features. She is dressed in a much ornamented bark-cloth dress, and wears two silver beads tied round her neck by a piece of blue cotton, in addition to very large earrings. She has much sway in the house, sitting on the men's side of the fire, drinking plenty of *saké*, and occasionally chiding her grandson Shinondi for telling me too much, saying that it will bring harm to her people. Though her expression is so severe and forbidding, she is certainly very handsome, and it is a European, not an Asiatic, beauty.

The younger women were all at work; two were seated on the floor weaving without a loom, and the others were making and mending the bark coats which are worn by both sexes. Noma, the chief's principal wife, sat apart, seldom speaking. Two of the youngest women are very pretty—as fair as ourselves, and their comeliness is of the rosy, peasant kind. It turns out that two of them, though they would not divulge it before men, speak Japanese, and they prattled to Ito with great vivacity and merriment; the ancient Fate scowling at them the while from under her shaggy eyebrows. I got a number of words from them, and they laughed heartily at my erroneous pronunciation. They even asked me a number of questions regarding their own sex among ourselves, but few of these would bear repetition, and they answered a number of mine. As the merriment increased the old woman looked increasingly angry and restless, and at last rated them sharply, as I have heard since, telling them that, if they spoke another word, she should tell their husbands that they had been talking to strangers. After this not another word was spoken, and Noma, who is an industrious housewife, boiled some millet into a mash for a midday lunch.

During the afternoon a very handsome young Aino, with a washed, richly-coloured skin and fine clear eyes, came up from the coast, where he had been working at the fishing. He saluted the old woman and Benri's wife on entering, and presented the former with a gourd of *saké*, bringing a greedy light into her eyes as she took a long draught, after which, saluting me, he threw himself down in the place of honour by the fire, with the easy grace of a staghound, a savage all over. His name is Pipichari, and he is the chief's adopted son. He had cut his foot badly with a root, and asked me to cure it, and I stipulated that it should be bathed for some time in warm water before anything more was done, after which I bandaged it with lint. He said 'he did not like me to touch his foot, it was not clean enough, my hands were too white,' etc.; but when I had dressed it, and the pain was much relieved, he bowed very low and then kissed my hand! He was the only one among them all who showed the slightest curiosity regarding my things. He looked at my scissors, touched my boots, and watched me, as I wrote, with the simple curiosity of a child. He could speak a little Japanese, but he said he was 'too young to tell me anything, the older men would know'. He is a 'total abstainer' from *saké*, and he says that there are four such besides himself among the large number of Ainos who are just now at the fishing at Mombets, and that the others keep separate from them, because they think that the gods will be angry with them for not drinking.

Several 'patients', mostly children, were brought in during the afternoon. Ito was much disgusted by my interest in these people, who, he repeated, 'are just dogs'; referring to their legendary origin, of which they are not ashamed. His assertion that they have learned politeness from the

Japanese, is simply baseless. Their politeness, though of quite another and more manly stamp, is savage, not civilized. The men came back at dark, the meal was prepared, and we sat round the fire as before; but there was no *saké*, except in the possession of the old woman; and again the hearts of the savages were sad. I could multiply instances of their politeness. As we were talking, Pipichari, who is a very 'untutored' savage, dropped his coat from one shoulder, and at once Shinondi signed to him to put it on again. Again, a woman was sent to a distant village for some oil, as soon as they heard that I usually burned a light all night. Little acts of courtesy were constantly being performed; but I really appreciated nothing more than the quiet way in which they went on with the routine of their ordinary lives.

The glamour which at first disguises the inherent barrenness of savage life has had time to pass away, and I see it in all its nakedness as a life not much raised above the

necessities of animal existence, timid, monotonous, barren of good, dark, dull, 'without hope, and without God in the world'; though at its lowest and worst considerably higher and better than that of many other aboriginal races, and, must I say it? considerably higher and better than that of thousands of the lapsed masses of our own great cities, who are baptized into Christ's name, and are laid at last in holy ground, inasmuch as the Ainos are truthful, and, on the whole, chaste, hospitable, honest, reverent, and kind to the aged. Drinking, their great vice, is not, as among us, in antagonism to their religion, but is actually a part of it, and as such would be exceptionally difficult to eradicate.

The early darkness has once again come on, and once again the elders have assembled round the fire in two long lines, with the younger men at the ends, Pipichari, who yesterday sat in the place of honour, and was helped to food first as the newest arrival, taking his place as the youngest at the end of the right-hand row. The birch-bark chips beam with fitful glare, the evening *saké* bowls are filled, the fire-god and the garlanded god receive their libations, the ancient woman, still sitting like a Fate, splits bark, and the younger women knot it, and the log-fire lights up as magnificent a set of venerable heads as painter or sculptor would desire to see—heads, full of—what? They have no history, their traditions are scarcely worthy the name, they claim descent from a dog, their houses and persons swarm with vermin, they are sunk in the grossest ignorance, they have no letters, or any numbers above a thousand, they are clothed in the bark of trees and the untanned skins of beasts, they worship the bear, the sun, moon, fire, water, and I know not what, they are uncivilizable and altogether irreclaimable savages, yet they are attractive, and in some ways fascinating, and I hope I shall never forget the music of their low, sweet voices, the soft light of their mild, brown eyes, and the wonderful sweetness of their smile.

Chapter Five

The Golden Chersonese, 1883

Among the more extraordinary habits of the serious Victorian traveller was the compulsion to visit prisons and places of execution. Isabella Bird visited Canton (Guangzhou) on her way from Japan to the Malay States in 1879, and neither the misery nor the stench of the Yamun (both tribunal and prison) deterred her from a sometimes Gradgrindian compilation of facts.

Both sides of the road which leads into the courtyard of the Yamun were crowded with unshaven, ragged, forlorn, dirty wretches, heavily fettered round their ankles, and with long heavy chains padlocked round their necks, attached, some to large stones with holes in the centre, others to short thick bars of iron. Two or three, into whose legs the ankle fetters had cut deep raw grooves, were lying in a heap on a ragged mat in the corner; some were sitting on stones, but most were standing, or shifting their position uneasily, dragging their weighty fetters about, making a jarring and dismal clank with every movement. These unfortunates are daily exposed thus to the scorn and contempt of the passers-by as a punishment for small thefts. Of those who were seated on stones or who were kneeling attempting to support themselves on their hands, most wore square wooden collars of considerable size, weighing thirty pounds each, round their necks. These *cangues* are so constructed that it is impossible for their wearers to raise their hands to their mouths for the purpose of feeding themselves, and it seemed to be a choice pastime for small boys to tantalize these criminals by placing food tied to the ends of sticks just within reach of their mouths, and then suddenly withdrawing them.

Two of the gaolers were lying on their beds smoking opium. There we met the head gaoler, of all Chinamen that I have seen the most repulsive in appearance, manner, and dress; for his long costume of frayed and patched brown silk looked as if it had not been taken off for a year; the lean, brown hands which clutched the prison keys with an instinctive grip were dirty, and the nails long and hooked like claws, and the face, worse I thought than that of any of the criminal horde, and scored with lines of grip and greed, was saturated with opium smoke. This wretch pays for his place, and in a few years will retire with a fortune, gains arising from bribes wrung from prisoners and their friends by threats and torture, and by

defrauding them daily of a part of their allowance of rice.

This gaoler, this fiend, made such by the customs of his country, took us down a passage, and unlocking a wooden grating turned us into a roughly paved courtyard about 50 feet long by 24 broad, and remained standing in the doorway jangling his keys.

This ward is divided into four 'apartments', each one having a high wall at the back. The sides next to the court are formed of a double row of strong wooden bars, black from age and dirt, which reach from the floor to the roof, and let in light and air through the chinks between them. The interiors of these cribs or cattle-pens are roughly paved with slabs of granite, slimy with accumulations of dirt. In the middle and round the sides are stout platforms of laths, forming a coarse, black gridiron, on which the prisoners sit and sleep. In each ward there is a shrine of a deity who is supposed to have the power of melting the wicked into contrition, and to this accursed mockery, on his birthday, the prisoners are compelled to give a feast, which is provided by the gaoler out of his peculations from their daily allowances. No water is allowed for washing, and the tubs containing the allowance of foul drinking water are placed close to those which are provided for the accumulation of night soil, etc., the contents of which are only removed once a fortnight. Two pounds of rice is the daily allowance of each prisoner, but this is reduced to about one by the greed of the gaoler.

As we entered the yard, fifty or sixty men swarmed out from the dark doorways which led into their dens, all heavily chained, with long, coarse, matted hair hanging in wisps, or standing on end round their death-like faces, in filthy rags, with emaciated forms caked with dirt, and bearing marks of the torture; and nearly all with sore eyes, swelled and bleeding lips, skin diseases, and putrefying sores. These surrounded us closely, and as, not without a shudder, I passed through them and entered one of their dens, they pressed upon us, blocking out the light, uttering discordant cries, and clamouring with one voice, *kum-sha, i.e.*, backsheesh, looking more like demons than living men, as abject and depraved as crime, despair, and cruelty can make them.

On earth can there be seen a spectacle more hideous than that of these abject wretches, with their heavy fetters eating into the flesh of their necks and ankles (if on their wasted skeletons, covered with vermin and running sores, there is any flesh left), their thick, matted, bristly, black hair—contrasting with the shaven heads of the free—the long, broken claws on their fingers and toes, the hungry look in their emaciated faces, and their clamorous cry, *kum-sha! kum-sha!* They thronged round us clattering their chains, one man saying that they had so little rice that they

had to 'drink the foul water to fill themselves'; another shrieked, 'Would I were in your prison in Hongkong', and this was chorused by many voices saying, 'In your prison at Hongkong they have fish and vegetables, and more rice than they can eat, and baths, and beds to sleep on; good, good is the prison of your Queen!' but higher swelled the cry of *kum-sha*, and as we could not give alms among several hundred, we eluded them, though with difficulty, and, as we squeezed through the narrow door, execrations followed us, and high above the heavy clank of the fetters and the general din rose the cry, 'Foreign Devils' (Fan-Kwai), as we passed out into sunshine and liberty, and the key was turned upon them and their misery.

From the prison it is only a short distance to the judgement-seat, a square hall, open at one end, with a roof supported on three columns. In a high-backed, ebony arm-chair, such as might be seen in any English hall, sat the man who has the awful power of life and death in his hands. A look of singular coldness and hauteur sat permanently on his face, over which a flush of indescribable impatience sometimes passed. He is not of the people, this lordly magistrate. He is one of the privileged *literati*. He used the mandarin tongue, and whether cognisant of the dialect of the prisoners or not, he put all his questions through an interpreter, who stood at his left, a handsomely dressed old man, who wore a gold chain with a dependent ivory comb, with which while he spoke he frequently combed a small and scanty grey moustache.

Notaries, attendants with scarlet-crowned hats, and a rabble of men and boys, in front of whom we placed ourselves, stood down each side. The open hall, though lofty, is shabby and extremely dirty, with an unswept broken pavement, littered at one side with potsherds, and disfigured by a number of more or less broken black pots as well as other rubbish, making it look rather like a shed in an untidy nursery garden than an imperial judgement-hall. On the pillars there are certain classical inscriptions, one of which is said to be an exhortation to mercy. Pieces of bamboo of different sizes are ranged against the south wall. These are used for the bastinado, and there were various instruments ranged against the same wall, at which I could only look fitfully and with a shudder, for they are used in 'The Question by Torture', which rapid method of gaining a desired end appears to be practised on witnesses as well as criminals.

The yard or uncovered part of this place has a pavement in the middle, and on one side of this the most loathsome trench I ever beheld, such a one as I think could not be found in the foulest slum of the dirtiest city in Europe, not only loathsome to the eye, but emitting a stench which even on that cool day might produce vertigo, and this under the very eye of the magistrate, and not more than 30 feet from the judgement-seat.

More than an hour and a half had passed since we entered, and for two hours before that the four chained prisoners had been undergoing the torture of kneeling on a coarsely sanded stone in an immovable and unsupported position. I was standing so close to them that the dress of one touched my feet. I could hear their breathing, which had been heavy at first, become a series of gasps, and cool as the afternoon was, the sweat of pain fell from their brows upon the dusty floor, and they were so emaciated that, even through their clothing, I could see the outlines of their bones. There were no counsel, and no witnesses, and the judge asked but one question as he beat his foot impatiently on the floor, 'Are you guilty?'

From such a system one is compelled to fall back upon the righteousness of the Judge of all the earth; and as I stood in that hideous judgement-hall beside the tortured wretches, I could not shut out of my heart a trembling hope that for these and the legion of these, a worthier than an earthly intercessor pleads before a mightier than an earthly judge.

Passing along a street the speciality of which is the manufacture from palm leaves of very serviceable rain cloaks, we arrived at the Ma T'au, the place of execution, on which more than one hundred heads at times fall in a morning. It is simply a pottery yard, and at the hours when space is required for the executioner's purposes more or fewer pots are cleared out of the way, according to the number of the condemned. The spectacle is open to the street and to all passers-by. Against the south wall are five crosses, which are used for the crucifixion of malefactors. At the base of the east wall are four large earthenware vessels full of quicklime, into which heads which are afterwards to be exposed on poles are cast, until the flesh has been destroyed. From this bald sketch it may be surmised that few accessories of solemnity or even propriety consecrate the last tragedy of justice. It is not an uncommon thing, under ordinary circumstances, for fifteen, twenty, or thirty-five wretches to suffer the penalty of death in this spot; and this number swells to very large dimensions at a gaol delivery, or during a rebellion, or when crews of pirates are captured in the act of piracy. My friend Mr Bulkeley Johnson of Shanghai saw one hundred heads fall in one morning.

We had not gone far into this aceldema when we came to a space cleared from pots, and to a great pool of blood and dust mingled, blackening in the sun, then another and another, till there were five of them almost close together, with splashes of blood upon the adjacent pots, and blood trodden into the thirsty ground. Against the wall opposite, a rudely constructed cross was resting, dark here and there with patches of blood. Among the rubbish at the base of the wall there were some human fragments partly covered with matting; a little farther some jaw-bones with the teeth in them, then four more crosses, and some human heads lying at the foot of the wall, from which it was evident that dogs had partially gnawed off the matting in which they had been tied up. The dead stare of one

human eye amidst the heap haunts me still. A blood-splashed wooden ticket, with a human name on one side and that of the Naam-Hoi prison on the other, was lying near one of the pools of blood, and I picked it up as a memento; as the stroke which had severed its string had also severed at the same time the culprit's neck. The place was ghastly and smelt of blood.

The strangest and most thrilling sight of all was the cross in this unholy spot, not a symbol of victory and hope, but of the lowest infamy and degradation, of the vilest death which the vilest men can die.

These facts do not require to be dressed out with words. They are most effective when most baldly stated. I left the execution ground as I left the prison—with the prayer, which has gained a new significance, 'For all prisoners and captives we beseech Thee to hear us, good Lord'; but though our hands are nationally clean now as regards the administration of justice and the treatment of criminals, we need not hold them up in holy horror as if the Chinese were guilty above all other men, for the framers of the Litany were familiar with dungeons perhaps worse than the prison of the Naam-Hoi magistrate, and with forms of torture which spared not even women, and the judges' and gaolers' palms were intimate with the gold of accused persons. It is simply that heathenism in Canton is practising at this day what Christianity in Europe looked upon with indifference for centuries.

In the Malay States Miss Bird penetrated a tropical rain-forest for the first time, still wearing her usual tweeds. It was no country for horses, and riding an elephant turned out to be far less glamorous than it sounded. Though she continued to record much that was merely edifying, the later chapters of *The Golden Chersonese and the Way Thither* (a title taken from *Paradise Lost* xi 392) show her enjoying herself quite unselfconsciously once again. This was neither the first nor the last time that she found herself without a female companion, alone with men, and miles from civilization. The rules of propriety had to be waived in the wild places of the earth; and that no doubt was partly why Miss Bird visited them.

I waited for the elephant in a rambling empty house, and Malays brought pierced coconuts, buffalo milk, and a great bouquet of lotus blossoms and seed-vessels, out of which they took the seeds, and presented them on the grand lotus leaf itself. Each seed is in appearance and taste like a hazel-nut, but in the centre, in an oval slit, the future lotus plant is folded up, the one vivid green seed leaf being folded over a shoot, and this is intensely bitter.

The elephant at last came up and was brought below the porch. They are truly hideous beasts, with their grey, wrinkled, hairless hides, the huge ragged 'flappers' which cover their ears, and with which they fan themselves ceaselessly, the small mean eyes, the hideous proboscis which coils itself snakishly round everything; the formless legs, so like trunks of trees; the piggish back, with the steep slope down to the mean, bare tail, and the general unlikeness to all familiar and friendly beasts. I can hardly write, for a little *wah-wah*, the most delightful of apes, is hanging with one long, lean arm round my throat, while with its disengaged hand it keeps taking my pen, dipping it in the ink, and scrawling over my letter. It is the most winsome of creatures, but if I were to oppose it there is no knowing what it might do, so I will take another pen. The same is true of an elephant. I am without knowledge of what it may be capable of!

Before I came I dreamt of howdahs and cloth of gold trappings, but my elephant had neither. In fact there was nothing grand about him but his ugliness. His back was covered with a piece of raw hide, over which were several mats, and on either side of the ridgy backbone a shallow basket, filled with fresh leaves and twigs, and held in place by ropes of rattan. I dropped into one of these baskets from the porch, a young Malay lad into the other, and my bag was tied on behind with rattan. A noose of the same with a stirrup served for the driver to mount. He was a Malay, wearing only a handkerchief and sarong, a gossiping careless fellow, who jumped off whenever he had a chance of a talk, and left us to ourselves. He drove with a stick with a curved spike at the end of it, which, when the elephant was bad, was hooked into the membranous 'flapper', always evoking the uprearing and brandishing of the proboscis, and a sound of ungentle expostulation, which could be heard a mile off. He sat on the head of the beast, sometimes cross-legged, and sometimes with his legs behind the huge ear covers. Mr Maxwell assured me that he would not send me into a region without a European unless it were perfectly safe, which I fully believed, any doubts as to my safety, if I had any, being closely connected with my steed.

This mode of riding is not comfortable. One sits facing forwards with the feet dangling over the edge of the basket. This edge soon produces a sharp ache or cramp, and when one tries to get relief by leaning back on anything, the awkward, rolling motion is so painful, that one reverts to the former position till it again becomes intolerable. Then the elephant had not been loaded 'with brains', and his pack was as troublesome as the straw shoes of the Japanese horses. It was always slipping forwards or backwards, and as I was heavier than the Malay lad, I was always slipping down and trying to wriggle myself up on the great ridge which was the creature's backbone, and always failing, and the mahout was always stopping and pulling the rattan ropes which bound the whole arrangement together, but never succeeding in improving it.

Before we had travelled two hours, the great bulk of the elephant without any warning gently subsided behind, and then as gently in front, the huge, ugly legs being extended in front of him, and the man signed to me to get off, which I did by getting on his head and letting myself down by a rattan rope upon the driver, who made a step of his back, for even when 'kneeling', as this queer attitude is called, a good ladder is needed for comfortable getting off and on. While the whole arrangement of baskets was being re-rigged, I clambered into a Malay dwelling of the poorer class, and was courteously received and regaled with bananas and buffalo milk.

The furniture consists entirely of mats, which cover a part of the floor, and are used both for sitting on and sleeping on, and a few small, hard, circular bolsters with embroidered ends. A musket, a spear, some fishing-rods, and a buffalo yoke hung against the wall of the reception-room. In the back room, the province of the women and children, there were an iron pot, a cluster of bananas, and two calabashes. The women wore only sarongs, and the children nothing. The men, who were not much clothed, were lounging on the mats.

The Malays are passionately fond of pets, and are said to have much skill in taming birds and animals. Doubtless their low voices and gentle, supple movements never shock the timid sensitiveness of brutes. Besides this, Malay children yield a very ready obedience to their elders, and are encouraged to invite the confidence of birds and beasts, rather than to torment them. They catch birds by means of bird-lime made of gutta, by horse-hair nooses, and by imitating their call. In this small house there were bamboo cages containing twenty birds, most of them talking minas and green-feathered small pigeons. They came out of their cages when called, and perched in rows on the arms of the men. The children catch small grasshoppers for their birds with a shovel-shaped instrument of open rattan work. When I add that there were some homely domestic fowls and a nearly tailless cat, I think I have catalogued the visible possessions of this family, with the exception of a bamboo cradle with a small brown inmate hanging from the rafters, and a small shed, used, I believe, for storing rice.

The open floor, while it gives air and ventilation, has also its disadvantages, for solid and liquid refuse is thrown through it so conveniently that the ground under the house is apt to contain stagnant pools and heaps of decomposing matter, and men lying asleep on mats on these gridirons have sometimes been stabbed with a *kris* inserted between the bars from below by an enemy seeking revenge.

I must not, however, give the impression that the Malays are a dirty people. They wash their clothes frequently, and bathe as often as is possible. They try to build their houses near water, and use small bathing-sheds.

I went into another house, rather poorer than the former, and, with a touching hospitality, they made signs to me to know if I would like a coconut. I hinted that I would, and the man at once got up and called to him an ape or monkey about 3 feet high, which was playing with a child, and the animal went out with him, and in no time was at the top of a tall coconut tree. His master said something to him, and he moved about examining the nuts till he decided upon a green one, which he wrung off, using teeth and hands for the operation. The slightly acid milk was refreshing, but its 'meat', which was of the consistency and nearly the tastelessness of the white of an egg boiled for five minutes, was not so good as that of the riper nuts.

I had walked on for some distance, and I had to walk back again before I found

my elephant. I had been poking about in the scrub in search of some acid fruits, and when I got back to the road, was much surprised to find that my boots were filled with blood, and on looking for the cause I found five small brown leeches, beautifully striped with yellow, firmly attached to my ankles. I had not heard that these were pests in Perak, and feared that they were something worse; but the elephant driver, seeing my plight, made some tobacco juice and squirted it over the creatures, when they recoiled in great disgust. Owing to the exercise I was obliged to take, the bites bled for several hours.

I am making my narrative as slow as my journey, but the things I write of will be as new to you as they were to me. New it was certainly to stand upon a carpet of the Sensitive Plant at noon, with the rays of a nearly vertical sun streaming down from a cloudless, steely blue sky, watching the jungle monster meekly kneeling on the ground, with two Malays who do not know a word of English as my companions, and myself unarmed and unescorted in the heart of a region so lately the scene of war, about which seven blue books have been written, and about the lawlessness and violence of which so many stories have been industriously circulated.

When the pack was adjusted, the mahout jumped on the back, and giving me his hands hauled me up over the head, after which the creature rose gently from the ground, and we went on our journey. Soon the driver jumped off for a gossip and a smoke, leaving the elephant to 'gang his ain gates' for a mile or more, and he turned into the jungle, where he began to rend and tear the trees, and then going to a mud-hole he drew all the water out of it, squirted it with a loud noise over himself and his riders, soaking my clothes, and when he turned back to the road again, he several times stopped and seemed to stand on his head by stiffening his proboscis and leaning upon it, and when I hit him with my umbrella he uttered the loudest roar I ever heard. I hung on with difficulty, wondering what other possible contingencies could occur, always expecting that the beast would lift me off and deposit me in a mud-hole.

On the driver's return I had to dismount again, and this time the elephant was allowed to go and take a proper bath in a river. He threw quantities of water over himself, and took up plenty more with which to cool his sides as he went along. Thick as the wrinkled hide of an elephant looks, a very small insect can draw blood from it, and when left to himself he sagaciously plasters himself with mud to protect himself like the water buffalo. Mounting again, I rode for another two hours, but he crawled about a mile an hour, and seemed to have a steady purpose to lie down. He roared whenever he was asked to go faster, sometimes in plaintive remonstrance. The driver got off and walked behind him, and then he stopped altogether. Then the man tried to pull him along by putting a hooked stick in his huge 'flapper', but this produced no other effect than a series of howls; then he got on his head again, after which the brute made a succession of huge stumbles, each one of which threatened to be a fall, and then the driver with a look of despair got off again. Then I made signs that I would get off, but the elephant refused to lie down, and I let myself down his unshapely shoulder by a rattan rope till I could use the mahout's shoulders as steps. The baskets were taken off and left at a house, the elephant was turned loose in the jungle; I walked the remaining miles to Kwala Kangsa, and the driver carried my portmanteau! Such was the comical end of my first elephant ride. I think that altogether I walked about eight miles, and as I was not knocked up, this says a great deal for the climate of Perak. The Malay who came with me told the people here that it was 'a wicked elephant', but I have since been told that it was 'very sick and tired to death', which I hope is the true version of its most obnoxious conduct.

I have said nothing about the magnificence of the scenery for a part of the way, where the road goes through a grand mountain pass, where all the vegetable glories of the tropics seem assembled, and one gets a new idea of what scenery can be; while beneath superb tree-ferns and untattered bananas, and palms, and bright flowered lianas, and graceful trailers, and vermilion-coloured orchids, and under sunbirds and humming-birds and the most splendid butterflies I ever saw, a torrent, as clear as crystal, dashes over the rocks, and adds the music of tumbling water to the enchantment of a scene whose loveliness no words can give any idea of. The pass of Bukit Berapit, seen in solitude on a glorious morning, is almost worth a journey round the world.

At the end of ten hours travelling, as I was tramping along alone, I began to meet Malays, then I met nine elephants in groups of three, with men, women, and children on their backs, apparently taking 'an airing'.

When the sun was low I looked down upon a broad and beautiful river, with hills and mountains on its farther side, a village on the shores of a promontory, and above that a grassy hill with a bungalow under coco-palms at its top, which I knew must be the Residency, from the scarlet uniforms at the door.

My valise had not arrived, and I had been obliged to re-dress myself in my mud-splashed tweed dress, therefore I was much annoyed to find the table set for three, and I hung about unwillingly in the veranda, fully expecting two Government clerks in faultless evening dress to appear, and I was vexed to think that my dream of solitude was not to be realized, when Assam more emphatically assured me that the meal was 'served', and I sat down, much mystified, at the well-appointed table, when he led in a large ape, and the Malay servant brought in a small one, and a Sikh brought in a large retriever and tied him to my chair! This was all done with the most profound solemnity. The circle being then complete, dinner proceeded with great stateliness. The apes had their curry, chutney, pineapple, eggs, and bananas on porcelain plates, and so had I. The chief difference was that, whereas I waited to be helped, the big ape was impolite enough occasionally to snatch something from a dish as the butler passed round the table, and that the small one before very long migrated from his chair to the table, and sitting by my plate, helped himself daintily from it. What a grotesque dinner party! What a delightful one! My 'next of kin' were so reasonably silent; they required no conversational efforts; they were most interesting companions. 'Silence is golden,' I felt; shall I ever enjoy a dinner party so much again?

That first night tigers came very near the house, roaring discontentedly. At 4 a.m. I was awoke by a loud noise, and looking out saw a wonderful scene. The superb plumes of the coconut trees were motionless against a sky blazing with stars. Four large elephants, part of the regalia of the deposed Sultan, one of them the Royal Elephant, a beast of prodigious size, were standing at the door, looking

majestic; mahouts were flitting about with torches; Sikhs, whose great stature was exaggerated by the fitful light—some in their undress white robes, and others in scarlet uniforms and blue turbans—were grouped as onlookers, the torchlight glinted on peripatetic bayonets, and the greenish, undulating lamps of countless fireflies moved gently in the shadow.

I have now been for three nights the sole inhabitant of this bungalow! I have taken five meals in the society of apes only, who make me laugh with genuine laughter. The sentries are absolutely silent, and I hardly hear a human voice. It is so good to be away for a time from the 'wearing world', from all clatter, chatter, and 'strife of tongues', in the unsophisticated society of apes and elephants. When drum beat and bugle blast, and the turning out of the Sikh guard, indicated that the Resident was in sight, I felt a little reluctant to relinquish the society of animals, and my 'solitary reign'.

This is a curious life. Mr Low sits at one end of the veranda at his business table with Eblis looking like his familiar spirit, beside him. I sit at a table at the other end, and during the long working hours we never exchange one word. Mahmoud [the larger ape] sometimes executes wonderful capers, the strange, wild, half-human face of the siamang peers down from the roof with a half-trustful, half-suspicious expression; the retriever lies on the floor with his head on his paws, sleeping with one eye open, always on the watch for a coveted word of recognition from his

master, or a yet more coveted opportunity of going out with him; tiffin and dinner are silently served in the veranda recess at long intervals; the sentries at the door are so silently changed that one fancies that the motionless blue turbans and scarlet coats contain always the same men; in the foreground the river flows silently, and the soft airs which alternate are too feeble to stir the overshadowing palm-fronds or rustle the *attap* of the roof. It is hot, silent, tropical. The sound of Mr Low's busy pen alone breaks the stillness during much of the day; so silent is it that the first heavy drops of the daily tropical shower on the roof have a startling effect.

Mr Low is greatly esteemed, and is regarded in the official circles of the Settlements as a model administrator. He understands the Malays and likes them, and has not a vestige of contempt for a dark skin, a prejudice which is apt to create an impassable gulf between the British official and the Asiatics under his sway. I am inclined to think that Mr Low is happier among the Malays and among his apes and other pets than he would be among civilized Europeans!

He is working fourteen hours out of the twenty-four. I think that work is his passion, and a change of work his sole recreation. He devotes himself to the promotion of the interests of the State, and his evident desire is to train the native rajahs to rule the people equitably. He seems to grudge every dollar spent superfluously on the English establishment, and contents himself with this small and old-fashioned bungalow. In this once disaffected region he goes about unarmed, and in the day-time the sentries only carry canes. His manner is as quiet and unpretending as can possibly be, and he speaks to Malays as respectfully as to Europeans, neither lowering thereby his own dignity nor theirs. Apparently they have free access to him during all hours of daylight, and as I sit writing to you or reading, a Malay shadow constantly falls across my paper, and a Malay, with silent, cat-like tread glides up the steps and appears unannounced in the veranda, on which Mr Low at once lays aside whatever he is doing, and quietly gives himself to the business in hand. The reigning prince, the Rajah Muda Yusuf, and Rajah Dris, are daily visitors; the former brings a troop of followers with him, and they remain outside, their red sarongs and picturesque attitudes as they lounge in the shade giving to the place that 'native' air which everywhere I love, at least where 'natives' are treated as I think that they ought to be, and my requirements are pretty severe!

> This companionable silence was ended by the arrival of more conventional visitors. Captain Walker is another in the long list of gentlemen whose apparently quite unreserved requests for the pleasure of Miss Bird's company in unlikely places say much about her character.

Captain Walker was going on a shooting excursion to a lotus lake at some distance, and invited me to join him. So we started after tiffin with two Malays, crossed the Perak in a 'dug-out', and walked for a mile over a sandy, grassy shore, which there lies between the bright water and the forest, then turned into the jungle, and waded through a stream which was up to my knees as we went, and up to my waist as we returned. Then a tremendous shower came on, and we were asked to climb into a largish Malay house, of which the floor was a perilously open gridiron. At least three families were in it, and there were some very big men, but the women hid themselves behind a screen of matting. It looked forlorn. A young baboon was chained to the floor, and walked up and down restlessly like a wild beast in a menagerie; there were many birds in cages, and under the house was much rubbish, among which numerous fowls were picking.

When the rain ceased we got through the timber belt into a forlorn swamp of wet paddy, where the water was a foot deep, and in some places so unintelligibly hot that it was unpleasant to put one's feet into it. It was truly a dismal swamp, and looked as if the paddy were coming up by accident among the reeds and weeds. Indeed, I should have thought that it was a rice fallow, but for a number of grotesque scarecrows, some mere bundles of tatters, but others wearing the aspect of big birds, big dolls, or cats. I could not think how it was that these things made spasmodic jerking movements, as there was not a breath of air, and they were all soaked by the shower, till I saw that they were attached by long strings to a little grass hut raised on poles, in which a girl or boy sat 'bird-scaring'. The sparrows rob the rice-fields, and so do the beautiful paddy-birds, of which we saw great numbers.

Ah, that swamp is a doleful region! One cannot tell where it ends and where the jungle begins, and dark, heavy, ominous-looking clouds generally concealed the forest-covered hills which are not far off. I almost felt the redundancy of vegetation to be oppressive, and the redundancy of insect and reptile life certainly was so; swarms of living creatures leapt in and out of the water, bigger ones hidden from view splashed heavily, and a few blackish, slug-like looking reptiles which drew blood, and hung on for an hour or two, attached themselves to my ankles. I was amused when Captain Walker congratulated himself on the absence of leeches, for these blood-suckers were at least their next-of-kin. I fell down into the water twice from the submerged ridge that I tried to walk upon, but there is no risk of cold from a hot bath in a stove.

Then we came to a smothered, reedy, ditch-like stream, in which was an old 'dug-out' half full of water, in which we managed to stow ourselves, and by careful balancing contrived to keep its edge just above the water. Our impeded progress down this ditch started myriads of whirring, splashing creatures. The ditch opened into a reedy swamp where hideous, pink, water buffaloes were wallowing and enjoying themselves, but on the report of a gun they all plunged into deep water and swam away, except for their big horns looking more like hippopotami than bovine quadrupeds. They are nearly as ugly as a rhinoceros; all albino animals are ugly, and when these are wet their hides are a bright salmon pink.

The swamp merged itself into a lotus lake, covered over much of its extent with thousands of noble leaves and rose-pink blossoms. It seemed almost sacrilege to tear and bruise and break them and push rudely through them in our canoe. A sadder and lonelier scene could not be. I have seldom been more powerfully affected by nature. The lake lying in hot mist under dark clouds, with the swamp and jungle on one side and an absolutely impenetrable wall of entangled trees and trailers on the other, so dense and matted that before putting one's feet on shore space would have to be cut for them with a parang, seemed as if it must be a hundred miles from the abodes of men, and as if nobody had ever been there before or ever would be there again. The heavy mist lifted, showing mountains, range beyond range, forest-covered, extending back into the heart of the peninsula, and from something in the grey, sad atmosphere, they looked fully 10,000 feet high.

Captain Walker climbed into a low tree which overhung the lake to look out for teal and widgeon which were perfectly innumerable, while the Malays, never uttering a word, silently poled the boat over the dreary lake in the dreary evening to put up the birds. There they went high over our heads in long flights, and every time there was the report of a gun there were screams and shrieks and squawks, and myriads of birds rose out of their reedy covers, and fish splashed, and the smoke lay heavily on the water, and then all was silent again. To and fro, up and down, we poled over the tragic waters till I actually felt a terror far beyond eeriness taking possession of me.

It grew greyer and darker, and we went back for Captain Walker, who, with the absorption of a true sportsman, had hardly noticed the falling shadows. It was a relief to hear the human voice once more. It broke the worst spell I was ever bound by. As he came out on the branch to get into the canoe it gave way, and he fell into the water up to his chin. Then the boat pole broke, so that when we got back to the padi it was obvious that 'the dark' was coming 'at one stride', and I suggested that, as we had two miles to walk and a river to cross at night, and we should certainly be very late for dinner, Mr Low might become uneasy about us, as we were both strangers and unable to speak the language, but Captain Walker thought differently.

There had been so much rain that it was heavy wading through the paddy, and it was quite dark when we reached the jungle, in which the rain had made the footing very precarious, and in darkness we forded the swollen stream, and stumbled along the shore of the Perak, where fireflies in thousands were flashing

among the bushes, a beautiful sight. When we reached the bank of the river where we had left the canoe we found several Malays, who laughed and seemed singularly pleased to see us. It was very difficult to get down the steep, slippery bank, into a precarious canoe which I could not see, and so thick was the darkness that I sat down in the water between the two gridirons, and had to remain there during the crossing, which took a long time, being against the stream.

When we landed a Sikh sergeant met us, very much excited. He spoke Malayan, and I guessed from a few words that I knew that there was a hue and cry at the Residency. You know how all pleasure is at once spoilt when, after you have been enjoying yourself very much, you find that people at home have been restless and uneasy about you, and as it is one of my travelling principles to avoid being a bother to people, I was very sorry. We found a general state of perturbation. Major Swinburne, who was leaning over the veranda, received us with some very pungent objurgations, and told us that Mr Low was out and very anxious. I was covered with mire, and wet from head to foot, and disappeared, but when we sat down to the long-delayed dinner I saw from Mr Low's silence and gloomy manner that he had been really much annoyed; however, he recovered himself, and we had a very lively evening of conversation and discussion, though I had a good deal of pain from the inflamed bites of the bloodsuckers in the swamp. Malay scouting parties had been sent in various directions. Rajah Dris was away with one, and the Sikh police were all ready to do nobody knows what, as there were no dogs. Major Swinburne said that his fears did not travel further than the river, which he thinks is dangerous to cross at night in a 'dug-out'; but Mr Low had before him the possibility of our having been assailed by bad characters, or of our having encountered a tiger in the jungle, and of my having been carried off from my inability to climb a tree!

Chapter Six

Among the Tibetans, 1894

Before they were married Isabella's future husband, Dr John Bishop, said, 'I have only one formidable rival in Isabella's heart, and that is the high tableland of Central Asia.' And three years after his death, in 1886, Mrs Bishop set out from northern India, where she had founded a hospital in his memory at Srinagar, for Leh—now in Kashmir, then the capital of Lesser Tibet. In the company of one of the Moravian missionaries who lived there, she rode deeper into the Himalayas to the foot of the Karakoram Pass.

Mrs Bishop's transliteration of Tibetan words does not quite correspond with the preferred usage of modern scholars. A *chod-ten* is one of the huge bell-shaped reliquaries found throughout the Tibetan region; a *mani* is a stone carved with the sacred words *Aum mani padne hun* (O jewel in the lotus); a *gonpo* is a hermitage; a *gopa* a district headman; and a *zho* is a cross between a yak and a cow. The name of Mrs Bishop's horse Gyalpo is the Tibetan word for 'king'. A *zemindar* is a land-holder, and a *jemadar* is an Indian official equal in rank to a lieutenant.

The Tibetans [are] truthful, independent, and friendly, one of the pleasantest of peoples. I took to them at once at Shergol, and terribly faulty though their morals are in some respects, I found no reason to change my good opinion of them in the succeeding four months.

The marches to Leh, the capital of Lesser Tibet, were full of fascination and novelty. Everywhere the Tibetans were friendly and cordial. In each village I was invited to the headman's house, and taken by him to visit the chief inhabitants; every traveller, lay and clerical, passed by with the cheerful salutation *Tzu*, asked me where I came from and whither I was going, wished me a good journey, admired Gyalpo, and when he scaled rock ladders and scrambled gamely through difficult torrents, cheered him like Englishmen, the general jollity and cordiality of manners contrasting cheerily with the chilling aloofness of Muslims.

Passing along faces of precipices and over water-

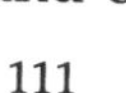

less plateaux of blazing red gravel—'waste places', truly—the journey was cheered by the meeting of red and yellow lamas in companies, each lama twirling his prayer-cylinder, abbots, and *skushoks* (the latter believed to be incarnations of Buddha) with many retainers, or gay groups of priestly students, intoning in harsh

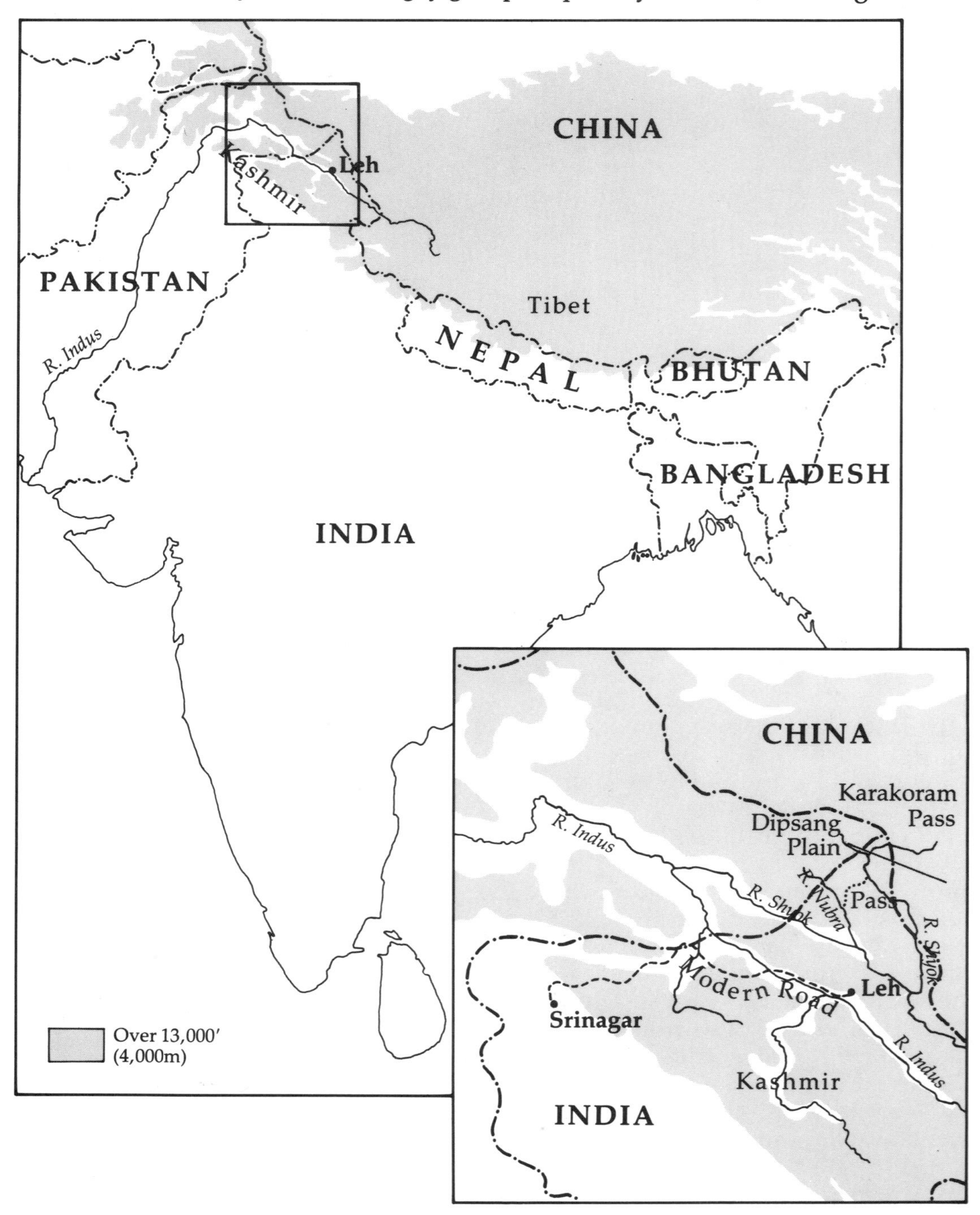

and high-pitched monotones, *Aum mani padne hun.* And so past fascinating monastic buildings, through crystal torrents rushing over red rock, through flaming ravines, on rock ledges by scaffolded paths, camping in the afternoons near friendly villages on oases of irrigated alluvium, and down the Wanla water by the steepest and narrowest cleft ever used for traffic, I reached the Indus, crossed it by a wooden bridge where its broad, fierce current is narrowed by rocks to a width of 65 feet, and entered Ladakh proper. A picturesque fort guards the bridge, and there travellers inscribe their names and are reported to Leh. I camped at Khalsi, a mile higher, but returned to the bridge in the evening to sketch, if I could, the grim nudity and repulsive horror of the surrounding mountains, attended only by Usman Shah. A few months earlier, this ruffian was sent down from Leh with six other soldiers and an officer to guard the fort, where they became the terror of all who crossed the bridge by their outrageous levies of blackmail. My swashbuckler quarrelled with the officer over a disreputable affair, and one night stabbed him mortally, induced his six comrades to plunge their knives into the body, sewed it up in a blanket, and threw it into the Indus, which disgorged it a little lower down. The men were all arrested and marched to Srinagar, where Usman turned 'king's evidence'.

The remaining marches were alongside of the tremendous granite ranges which divide the Indus from its great tributary, the Shayok. Colossal scenery, desperate aridity, tremendous solar heat, and an atmosphere highly rarefied and of nearly intolerable dryness, were the chief characteristics. At these Tibetan altitudes, where the valleys exceed 11,000 feet, the sun's rays are even more powerful than on the 'burning plains of India'. The day wind, rising at 9 a.m., and only falling near sunset, blows with great heat and force. The solar heat at noon was from 120° to 130°, and at night the mercury frequently fell below the freezing point. I did not suffer from the climate, but in the case of most Europeans the air passages become irritated, the skin cracks, and after a time the action of the heart is

affected. The hair when released stands out from the head, leather shrivels and splits, horn combs break to pieces, food dries up, rapid evaporation renders water-colour sketching nearly impossible, and tea made with water from 15° to 20° below the boiling-point of 212°, is flavourless and flat.

After a delightful journey of twenty-five days I camped at Spitak, among the *chod-tens* and *manis* which cluster round the base of a lofty and isolated rock, crowned with one of the most striking monasteries in Ladakh, and very early the next morning, under a sun of terrific fierceness, rode up a five-mile slope of blazing gravel to the goal of my long march. Even at a short distance off, the Tibetan capital can scarcely be distinguished from the bare, ribbed, scored, jagged, vermilion and rose-red mountains which nearly surround it, were it not for the palace of the former kings or Gyalpos of Ladakh, a huge building attaining ten storeys in height, with massive walls sloping inwards, while long balconies and galleries, carved projections of brown wood, and prominent windows, give it a singular picturesqueness. It can be seen for many miles, and dwarfs the little Central Asian town which clusters round its base.

Long lines of *chod-tens* and *manis* mark the approach to Leh. Then come barley fields and poplar and willow plantations, bright streams are crossed, and a small gateway, within which is a colony of very poor Baltis, gives access to the city. In consequence of 'the vigilance of the guard at the bridge of Khalsi', I was expected, and was met at the gate by the wazir's *jemadar*, or head of police, in artistic attire, with *spahis* in apricot turbans, violet *chogas*, and green leggings, who cleared the way with spears, Gyalpo frolicking as merrily and as ready to bite, and the Afghan striding in front as firmly as though they had not marched for twenty-five days through the rugged passes of the Himalayas. In such wise I was escorted to a shady bungalow of three rooms, in the grounds of HBM's Joint Commissioner, who lives at Leh during the four months of the 'caravan season', to assist in regulating the traffic and to guard the interests of the numerous British subjects who pass through Leh with merchandise. For their benefit also, the Indian Government aids in the support of a small hospital, open, however, to all, which, with a largely attended dispensary, is under the charge of a Moravian medical missionary.

Just outside the Commissioner's grounds are two very humble whitewashed dwellings, with small gardens brilliant with European flowers; and in these the two Moravian missionaries, the only permanent European residents in Leh, were

living, Mr Redslob and Dr Karl Marx, with their wives. Dr Marx was at his gate to welcome me.

To these two men, especially the former, I owe a debt of gratitude which in no shape, not even by the hearty acknowledgement of it, can ever be repaid, for they died within a few days of each other, of an epidemic, last year, Dr Marx and a newborn son being buried in one grave.

I had scarcely finished breakfast when [Mr Redslob] called; a man of great height and strong voice, with a cheery manner, a face beaming with kindness, and speaking excellent English. Leh was the goal of my journey, but Mr Redslob came with a proposal to escort me over the great passes to the northward for a three weeks' journey to Nubra, a district formed of the combined valleys of the Shayok and Nubra rivers, tributaries of the Indus, and abounding in interest. Of course I at once accepted an offer so full of advantages, and the performance was better even than the promise.

Leh is one of the centres of Central Asian commerce. There all traders from India, Kashmir, and Afgh there also merchants from the mysterious city of Lhasa do a great business in brick tea and in Lhasa wares, chiefly ecclesiastical. . . Great caravans *en route* for Khotan, Yarkand, and even Chinese Tibet arrived daily from Kashmir, the Punjab, and Afghanistan, and stacked their bales of goods in the *place*; the Lhasa traders opened shops in which the specialities were brick tea and instruments of worship; merchants from Amritsar, Kabul, Bokhara, and Yarkand, stately in costume and gait, thronged the bazaar and opened bales of costly goods in tantalizing fashion; mules, asses, horses, and yaks kicked, squealed, and bellowed; the dissonance of bargaining tongues rose high; there were mendicant monks, Indian fakirs, Muslim dervishes, Mecca pilgrims, itinerant musicians, and Buddhist ballad howlers; bold-faced women with creels on their backs brought in lucerne; Ladakhis, Baltis, and Lahulis tended the beasts, and the wazir's *jemadar* and gay *spahis* moved about among the throngs. In the midst of this picturesque confusion, the short, square-built, Lhasa traders, who face the blazing sun in heavy winter clothing, exchange their expensive tea for Nubra and Baltistan dried apricots, Kashmir saffron, and rich stuffs from India; and merchants from Yarkand on big Turkestan horses offer hemp, which is smoked as opium, and Russian trifles and dress goods, under cloudless skies. With the huge Kailas range as a background, this great rendezvous of Central Asian traffic has a great fascination, even though moral shadows of the darkest kind abound.

On the second morning, while I was taking [a] sketch of Usman Shah, he was recognized both by the Joint Commissioner and the chief of police as a mutineer and murderer, and was marched out of Leh. I was asked to look over my baggage, but did not. I had trusted him, he had been faithful in his way, and later I found that nothing was missing. He was a brutal ruffian, one of a band of irregulars sent by the Maharajah of Kashmir to garrison the fort at Leh. From it they used to descend on the town, plunder the bazaar, insult the women, take all they wanted without payment, and when one of their number was being tried for some offence, they dragged the judge out of court and beat him! After holding Leh in terror for some time the British Commissioner obtained their removal. It was, however, at the fort at the Indus bridge, as related before, that the crime of murder was committed. Still there was something almost grand in the defiant attitude of the fantastic

swashbuckler, as, standing outside the bungalow, he faced the British Commissioner, to him the embodiment of all earthly power, and the chief of police, and defied them. Not an inch would he stir till the wazir gave him a coolie to carry his baggage. He had been acquitted of the murder, he said, 'And though I killed the man, it was according to the custom of my country—he gave me an insult which could only be wiped out in blood!' The guard dared not touch him, and he went to the wazir, demanded a coolie, and got one!

Our party left Leh early on a glorious morning, travelling light, Mr Redslob, a very learned Lhasa monk named Gergan, Mr Redslob's servant, my three, and four

baggage horses, with two drivers engaged for the journey. The great Kailas range was to be crossed, and the first day's march up long, barren, stony valleys, without interest, took us to a piece of level ground, with a small semi-subterranean refuge on which there was barely room for two tents, at the altitude of the summit of Mont Blanc. For two hours before we reached it the men and animals showed great distress. Gyalpo stopped every few yards, gasping, with blood trickling from his nostrils, and turned his head so as to look at me, with the question in his eyes, What does this mean? Hassan Khan was reeling from vertigo, but would not give in; the *seis*, a creature without pluck, was carried in a blanket slung on my tent poles, and even the Tibetans suffered. I felt no inconvenience, but as I unsaddled Gyalpo I was glad that there was no more work to do! This 'mountain-sickness', called by the natives *ladug*, or 'pass-poison', is supposed by them to be the result of the odour or pollen of certain plants which grow on the passes. Horses and mules

are unable to carry their loads, and men suffer from vertigo, vomiting, violent headache and bleeding from the nose, mouth, and ears, as well as prostration of strength, sometimes complete, and occasionally ending fatally.

After a bitterly cold night I was awakened at dawn by novel sounds, gruntings, and low, resonant bellowing round my tent, and the grey light revealed several yaks (the *Bos grunniens*, the Tibetan ox), the pride of the Tibetan highlands. This magnificent animal only flourishes at altitudes exceeding 12,000 feet. Even after generations of semi-domestication he is very wild, and can only be managed by being led with a rope attached to a ring in the nostrils. He disdains the plough, but condescends to carry burdens, and numbers of the Ladakh and Nubra people get their living by carrying goods for the traders on his broad back over the great passes. His legs are very short, and he has a sensible way of measuring distance with his eyes and planting his feet, which enables him to carry loads where it might be supposed that only a goat could climb. He picks up a living anyhow, in that respect resembling the camel.

He has an uncertain temper, and is not favourably disposed towards his rider. Indeed, my experience was that just as one was about to mount him he usually made a lunge at one with his horns. Some of my yak steeds shied, plunged, kicked, executed fantastic movements on the ledges of precipices, knocked down their leaders, bellowed defiance, and rushed madly down mountain sides, leaping from boulder to boulder, till they landed me among their fellows. The rush of a herd of bellowing yaks at a wild gallop, waving their huge tails, is a grand sight.

My first yak was fairly quiet, and looked a noble steed, with my Mexican saddle and gay blanket among rather than upon his thick black locks. His back seemed as broad as that of an elephant, and with his slow, sure, resolute step, he was like a mountain in motion. We took five hours for the ascent of the Digar Pass, our loads and some of us on yaks, some walking, and those who suffered most from the 'pass-poison' and could not sit on yaks were carried. A number of Tibetans went up with us. It was a new thing for a European lady to travel in Nubra, and they took a friendly interest in my getting through all right. The dreary stretches of the ascent, though at first white with edelweiss, of which the people make their tinder, are surmounted for the most part by steep, short zigzags of broken stone. The heavens were dark with snow-showers, the wind was high and the cold severe, and gasping horses, and men prostrate on their faces unable to move, suggested a considerable amount of suffering; but all safely reached the summit, 17,930 feet, where in a snow-storm the guides huzzaed, praised their gods, and tucked rag streamers into a cairn. The loads were replaced on the horses, and over wastes of ice, across snowfields margined by broad splashes of rose-red primulas, down desert valleys and along irrigated hillsides, we descended 3700 feet to the village of Digar in Nubra, where under a cloudless sky the mercury stood at 90°!

Upper and Lower Nubra consist of the valleys of the Nubra and Shayok rivers. These are deep, fierce, variable streams, which have buried the lower levels under great stretches of shingle, patched with jungles of *hippophaë* and tamarisk, affording cover for innumerable wolves. Great lateral torrents descend to these rivers, and on alluvial ridges formed at the junctions are the villages with their pleasant surroundings of barley, lucerne, wheat, with poplar and fruit trees, and their picturesque *gonpos* crowning spurs of rock above them. The first view of Nubra is not beautiful. Yellow, absolutely barren mountains, cleft by yellow gorges, and apparently formed of yellow gravel, the huge rifts in their sides alone showing their substructure of rock, look as if they had never been finished, or had been finished so long that they had returned to chaos. These hem in a valley of grey sand and shingle, threaded by a greyish stream. From the second viewpoint mountains are seen descending on a pleasanter part of the Shayok valley in grey, yellow, or vermilion masses of naked rock, 7000 and 8000 feet in height, above which rise snow-capped peaks sending out fantastic spurs and buttresses, while the colossal walls of rock are cleft by rifts as colossal. The central ridge between the Nubra and Upper Shayok valleys is 20,000 feet in altitude, and on this are superimposed five peaks of rock, ascertained by survey to be from 24,000 to 25,000 feet in height, while at one point the eye takes in a nearly vertical height of 14,000 feet from the level of the Shayok River! The Shayok and Nubra valleys are only five and four miles in width respectively at their widest parts. The early winter traffic chiefly follows along river beds, then nearly dry, while summer caravans have to

labour along difficult tracks at great heights, where mud and snow avalanches are common, to climb dangerous rock ladders, and to cross glaciers and the risky fords of the Shayok. Nubra is similar in character to Ladakh, but it is hotter and more fertile, the mountains are loftier, the *gonpos* are more numerous, and the people are simpler, more religious, and more purely Tibetan. Mr Redslob loved Nubra, and as love begets love he received a hearty welcome at Digar and everywhere else.

The descent to the Shayok river gave us a most severe day of twelve hours. The river had covered the usual track, and we had to take to torrent beds and precipice ledges, I on one yak, and my tent on another. In years of travel I have never seen such difficulties. Eventually at dusk Mr Redslob, Gergan, the servants, and I descended on a broad shingle bed by the rushing Shayok; but it was not till dawn on the following day that, by means of our two yaks and the muleteers, our baggage and food arrived, the baggage horses being brought down unloaded, with men holding the head and tail of each. Our saddle horses, which we led with us, were much cut by falls. Gyalpo fell fully 20 feet, and got his side laid open. The baggage horses, according to their owners, had all gone over one precipice, which delayed them five hours.

A halt for Sunday in an apricot grove in the pleasant village of Sati refreshed us all for the long marches which followed, by which we crossed the Sasir Pass, full of difficulties from snow and glaciers, which extend for many miles, to the Dipsang Plain, the bleakest and dreariest of Central Asian wastes, from which the gentle ascent of the Karakorum Pass rises, and returned, varying our route slightly, to the pleasant villages of the Nubra valley. Everywhere Mr Redslob's Tibetan scholarship, his old-world courtesy, his kindness and adaptability, and his medical skill, ensured us a welcome the heartiness of which I cannot describe. The headmen and elders of the villages came to meet us when we arrived, and escorted us when we left; the monasteries and houses with the best they contained were thrown open to us; the men sat round our camp-fires at night, telling stories and local gossip, and asking questions, everything being translated to me by my kind guide, and so we actually lived 'among the Tibetans'.

In order to visit Lower Nubra and return to Leh we were obliged to cross the great fords of the Shayok at the most dangerous season of the year. Mr Redslob questioned every man we met on the subject, solemn and noisy conclaves were held upon it round the camp-fires; it was said that the 'European woman' and her 'spider- legged horse' could never get across, and for days before we reached the stream, the *chupas*, or government water- guides, made nightly reports to the village headmen of the state of the waters, which were steadily rising, the final verdict being that they were only just practicable for strong horses. To delay till the waters fell was impossible. Mr Redslob had engagements in Leh, and I was already somewhat late for the passage of the lofty passes between Tibet and British

India before the winter, so we decided on crossing with every precaution which experience could suggest.

At Lagshung, the evening before, the Tibetans made prayers and offerings for a day cloudy enough to keep the water down, but in the morning from a cloudless sky a scintillating sun blazed down like a magnesium light, and every glacier and snowfield sent its tribute torrent to the Shayok. In crossing a stretch of white sand the solar heat was so fierce that our European skins were blistered through our clothing. We halted at Lagshung, at the house of a friendly *zemindar*, who pressed upon me the loan of a big Yarkand horse for the ford, a kindness which nearly proved fatal; and then by shingle paths through lacerating thickets of the horrid *Hippophaë rhamnoides*, we reached a *chod-ten* on the shingly bank of the river, where the Tibetans renewed their prayers and offerings, and the final orders for the crossing were issued. We had twelve horses, carrying only quarter loads each, all led; the servants were mounted, 'water-guides' with 10-foot poles sounded the river ahead, one led Mr Redslob's horse (the rider being bare-legged) in front of mine with a long rope, and two more led mine, while the *gopas* of three villages and the *zemindar* steadied my horse against the stream. The water- guides only wore girdles, and with elf-locks and pig-tails streaming from their heads, and their uncouth yells and wild gesticulations, they looked true river-demons.

The Shayok presented an expanse of eight branches and a main stream, divided by shallows and shingle banks, the whole a mile and a half in width. On the brink the *chupas* made us all drink good draughts of the turbid river water, 'to prevent giddiness', they said, and they added that I must not think them rude if they dashed water at my face frequently with the same object. Hassan Khan, and Mando, who was livid with fright, wore dark-green goggles, that they might not see the rapids. In the second branch the water reached the horses' bodies, and my animal tottered and swerved. There were bursts of wild laughter, not merriment but excitement, accompanied by yells as the streams grew fiercer, a loud chorus of *Kabadar! Sharbaz!* ('Caution!' 'Well done!') was yelled to encourage the horses, and the boom and hiss of the Shayok made a wild accompaniment. Gyalpo, for whose legs of steel I longed, frolicked as usual, making mirthful lunges at his leader when the pair halted. Hassan Khan, in the deepest branch, shakily said to me, 'I not afraid, Mem Sahib.' During the hour spent in crossing the eight branches, I thought that the risk had been exaggerated, and that giddiness was the chief peril.

But when we halted, cold and dripping, on the shingle bank of the main stream I changed my mind. A deep, fierce, swirling rapid, with a calmer depth below its farther bank, and fully a quarter of a mile wide, was yet to be crossed. The business was serious. All the *chupas* went up and down, sounding, long before they found a possible passage. All loads were raised higher, the men roped their soaked clothing on their shoulders, water was dashed repeatedly at our faces, girths were tightened, and then, with shouts and yells, the whole caravan plunged into deep water, strong, and almost ice-cold. Half an hour was spent in that devious ford, without any apparent progress, for in the dizzy swirl the horses simply seemed treading the water backwards. Louder grew the yells as the torrent raged more hoarsely, the chorus of *kabadar* grew frantic, the water was up to the men's armpits and the seat of my saddle, my horse tottered and swerved several times, the nearing shore presented an abrupt bank underscooped by the stream. There was a deeper plunge, an encouraging shout, and Mr Redslob's strong horse leapt the bank. The *gopas* encouraged mine; he made a desperate effort, but fell short and rolled over backwards into the Shayok with his rider under him. A struggle, a moment of suffocation, and I was extricated by strong arms, to be knocked down again by the rush of the water, to be again dragged up and hauled and hoisted up the crumbling bank. I escaped with a broken rib and some severe bruises, but the horse was drowned. Mr Redslob, who had thought that my life could not be saved, and the Tibetans were so distressed by the accident that I made very light of it, and only took one day of rest. The following morning some men and

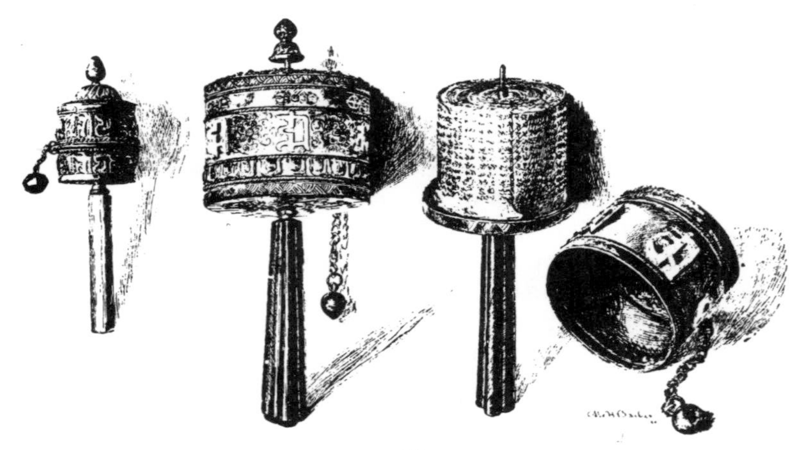

animals were carried away, and afterwards the ford was impassable for a fortnight. Such risks are among the amenities of the great trade route from India into Central Asia!

At Hundar, a superbly situated village, we were received at the house of Gergan the monk, who had accompanied us throughout. He is a *zemindar*, and the large house in which he made us welcome stands in his own patrimony. Everything was prepared for us. The mud floors were swept, cotton quilts were laid down on the balconies, blue cornflowers and marigolds, cultivated for religious ornament, were in all the rooms, and the women were in gala dress and loaded with coarse jewellery. Right hearty was the welcome.

So at Hundar, as everywhere else, the elders came out to meet us and cut the apricot branches away on our road, and the silver horns of the *gonpo* above brayed a dissonant welcome. Along the Indus valley the servants of Englishmen beat the Tibetans, in the Shayok and Nubra valleys the Yarkand traders beat and cheat them, and the women are shy with strangers, but at Hundar they were frank and friendly with me, saying, as many others had said, 'We will trust any one who comes with the missionary.'

Our food in this hospitable house was simple: apricots, fresh, or dried and stewed with honey; *zho's* milk, curds and cheese, sour cream, peas, beans, balls of barley dough, barley porridge, and 'broth of abominable things'. *Chang*, a dirty-looking beer made from barley, was offered with each meal, and tea frequently, but I took my own 'on the sly'. I have mentioned a churn as part of the 'plenishings' of the living- room. In Tibet the churn is used for making tea! I give the recipe. 'For six persons. Boil a teacupful of tea in three pints of water for ten minutes with a heaped dessert-spoonful of soda. Put the infusion into the churn with one pound of butter and a small tablespoonful of salt. Churn until as thick as cream.' Tea made after this fashion holds the second place to *chang* in Tibetan affections. The butter according to our thinking is always rancid, the mode of making it is uncleanly, and it always has a rank flavour from the goatskin in which it was kept. Its value is enhanced by age. I saw skins of it 40, 50, and even 60 years old, which were very highly prized, and would only be opened at some special family festival or funeral.

During the three days of our visits to Hundar both men and women wore their festival dresses, and apparently abandoned most of their ordinary occupations in our honour. The men were very anxious that I should be 'amused', and made many

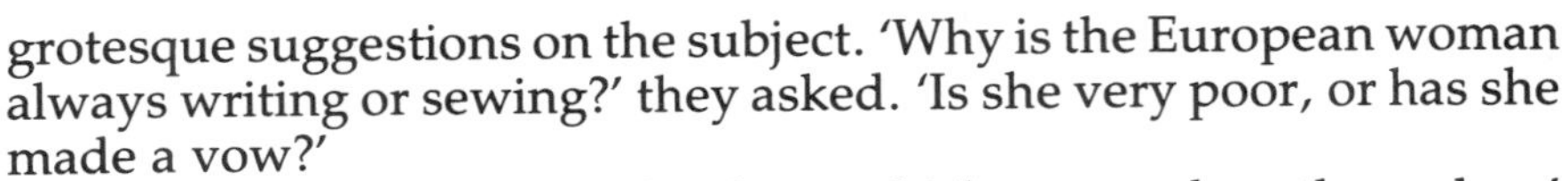

grotesque suggestions on the subject. 'Why is the European woman always writing or sewing?' they asked. 'Is she very poor, or has she made a vow?'

The monastery of Deskyid, to which we made a three days' expedition, is from its size and the picturesque situation the most imposing in Nubra. Built on a majestic spur of rock rising on one side 2000 feet perpendicularly from a torrent, the spur itself having an altitude of 11,000 feet, with red peaks, snow-capped, rising to a height of over 20,000 feet behind the vast irregular pile of red, white, and yellow temples, towers, storehouses, cloisters, galleries, and balconies, rising for 300 feet one above another, hanging over chasms, built out on wooden buttresses, and surmounted with flags, tridents, and yaks' tails, a central tower or keep dominating the whole, it is perhaps the most picturesque object I have ever seen, well worth the crossing of the Shayok fords, my painful accident, and much besides. It looks inaccessible, but in fact can be attained by rude zigzags of a thousand steps of rock, some natural, others roughly hewn, getting worse and worse as they rise higher, till the later zigzags suggest the difficulties of the ascent of the Great Pyramid. The day was fearfully hot, 99° in the shade, and the naked, shining surfaces of purple rock with a metallic lustre radiated heat. My 'gallant grey' took me up half-way—a great feat—and the Tibetans cheered and shouted '*Sharbaz!*' ('Well done!') as he pluckily leapt up the great slippery rock ledges. After I dismounted, any number of willing hands hauled and helped me up the remaining horrible ascent, the rugged rudeness of which is quite indescribable. The inner entrance is a gateway decorated with a yak's head and many Buddhist emblems. High above, on a rude gallery, fifty monks were gathered with their musical instruments. As soon as the *Kan-po* or abbot, Punt-sog-sogman (the most perfect Merit), received us at the gate, the monkish orchestra broke forth in a tornado of sound of a most tremendous and thrilling quality, which was all but overwhelming, as the mountain echoes took up and prolonged the sound of fearful blasts on 6-foot silver horns, the bellowing thunder of 6-foot drums, the clash of cymbals, and the dissonance of a number of monster gongs. It was not music, but it was sublime. The blasts on the horns are to welcome a great personage, and such to the monks who despised his teaching was the devout and learned German missionary, Mr Redslob. We mounted to a corridor full of lamas in ragged red dresses, yellow girdles, and yellow caps, where we were presented with plates of apricots, and the door of the lowest of the seven temples heavily grated backwards.

The first view, and indeed the whole view of this temple of *Wrath* or *Justice*, was suggestive of a frightful *Inferno*, with its rows of demon gods, hideous beyond Western conception, engaged in torturing writhing and bleeding specimens of humanity. Demon masks of ancient lacquer hung from the pillars, naked swords gleamed in motionless hands, and in a deep recess whose 'darkness' was rendered 'visible' by one lamp, was that indescribable horror, the executioner of the Lord of Hell, his many brandished arms holding instruments of torture, and before him the bell, the thunderbolt and sceptre,

the holy water, and the baptismal flagon. Our joss-sticks fumed on the still air, monks waved censers, and blasts of dissonant music woke the semi- subterranean echoes. In this temple of Justice the younger lamas spend some hours daily in the supposed contemplation of the torments reserved for the unholy. In the highest temple, that of Peace, the summer sunshine fell on Shakya Thubba and the Buddhist triad seated in endless serenity. The walls were covered with frescoes of great lamas, and a series of alcoves, each with an image representing an incarnation of Buddha, ran round the temple. In a chapel full of monstrous images and piles of medallions made of the ashes of 'holy' men, the sub-abbot was discoursing to the acolytes on the religious classics. In the chapel of meditations, among lighted incense sticks, monks seated before images were telling their beads with the object of working themselves into a state of ecstatic contemplation (somewhat resembling a certain hypnotic trance), for there are undoubtedly devout lamas, though the majority are idle and unholy. It must be understood that all Tibetan literature is 'sacred', though some of the volumes of exquisite calligraphy on parchment, which for our benefit were divested of their silken and brocaded wrappings, contain nothing better than fairy tales and stories of doubtful morality, which are recited by the lamas to the accompaniment of incessant cups of *chang*, as a religious duty when they visit their 'flocks' in the winter.

We remained long on the blazing roof of the highest tower

of the *gonpo*, while good Mr Redslob disputed with the abbot 'concerning the things pertaining to the kingdom of God'. The monks standing round laughed sneeringly. They had shown a little interest, Mr Redslob said, on his earlier visits. The abbot accepted a copy of the Gospel of St John. 'St Matthew,' he observed, 'is very laughable reading.' Blasts of wild music and the braying of colossal horns honoured our departure, and our difficult descent to the apricot groves of Deskyid. On our return to Hundar the grain was ripe on Gergan's fields. The first ripe ears were cut off, offered to the family divinity, and were then bound to the pillars of the house. In the comparatively fertile Nubra valley the wheat and barley are cut, not rooted up. While they cut the grain the men chant, 'May it increase, We will give to the poor, we will give to the lamas,' with every stroke. They believe that it can be made to multiply both under the sickle and in the threshing, and perform many religious rites for its increase while it is in sheaves. After eight days the corn is trodden out by oxen on a threshing-floor renewed every year. After winnowing with wooden forks, they make the grain into a pyramid, insert a sacred symbol, and pile upon it the threshing instruments and sacks, erecting an axe on the apex with its blade turned to the west, as that is the quarter from which demons are supposed to come. In the afternoon they feast round it, always giving a portion to the axe, saying, 'It is yours, it belongs not to me.' At dusk they pour it into the sacks again, chanting, 'May it increase.' But these are not removed to the granary until late at night, at an hour when the hands of the demons are too much benumbed by the nightly frost to diminish the store. At the beginning of every one of these operations the presence of lamas is essential, to announce the auspicious moment, and conduct religious ceremonies. They receive fees, and are regaled with abundant *chang* and the fat of the land.

Family life presents some curious features. In the disposal in marriage of a girl, her eldest brother has more 'say' than the parents. The eldest son brings home the bride to his father's house, but at a given age the old people are 'shelved', i.e. they retire to a small house, which may be termed a 'jointure house', and the eldest son assumes the patrimony and the rule of affairs. I have not met with a similar custom anywhere in the East. It is difficult to speak of Tibetan life, with all its affection and jollity, as 'family life', for Buddhism, which enjoins monastic life, and usually celibacy along with it, on eleven thousand out of a total population of a hundred and twenty thousand, further restrains the increase of population within the limits of sustenance by inculcating and rigidly upholding the system of polyandry, permitting marriage only to the eldest son, the heir of the land, while the bride accepts all his brothers as inferior or subordinate husbands, thus attaching the whole family to the soil and family roof-tree, the children being regarded legally as the property of the eldest son, who is addressed by them as 'Big Father', his brothers receiving the title of 'Little Father'. The resolute determination, on economic as well as religious grounds, not to abandon this ancient custom, is the most formidable obstacle in the way of the reception of Christianity by the Tibetans. The women cling to it. They say, 'We have three or four men to help us instead of one', and sneer at the dullness and monotony of European monogamous life! A woman said to me, 'If I had only one husband, and he died, I should be a widow; if I have two or three I am never a widow!' The word 'widow' is with them a term of reproach, and is applied abusively to animals and men. Children are brought up to be very obedient to fathers and mother, and to take great care of little ones and cattle. Parental affection is strong. Husbands and wives beat each other, but separation usually follows a violent outbreak of this kind. It is the custom for the men and women of a village to assemble when a bride enters the house of her husbands, each of them presenting her with three rupees. The Tibetan wife, far from spending these gifts on personal adornment, looks ahead, contemplating possible contingencies, and immediately hires a field, the produce of which is her own, and which accumulates year after year in a separate granary, so that she may not be portionless in case she leaves her husband!

It was impossible not to become attached to the Nubra people, we lived so completely among them, and met with such unbounded goodwill. Feasts were given in our honour, every *gonpo* was open to us, monkish blasts on colossal horns brayed out welcomes, and while nothing could exceed the helpfulness and alacrity of kindness shown by all, there was not a thought or suggestion of baksheesh. The men of the villages always sat by our camp-fires at night, friendly and jolly, but never obtrusive, telling stories, discussing local news and the oppressions exercised by the Kashmiri officials, the designs of Russia, the advance of the Central Asian Railway, and what they consider as the weakness of the Indian Government in not annexing the provinces of the northern frontier. Many of their ideas and feelings are akin to ours, and a mutual understanding is not only possible, but inevitable.

It was not an easy matter to get back to Leh. The rise of the Shayok made it impossible to reach and return by the Digar Pass, and the alternative route over the Kharzong glacier continued for some time impracticable—that is, it was perfectly smooth ice. At length the news came that a fall of snow had roughened its surface.

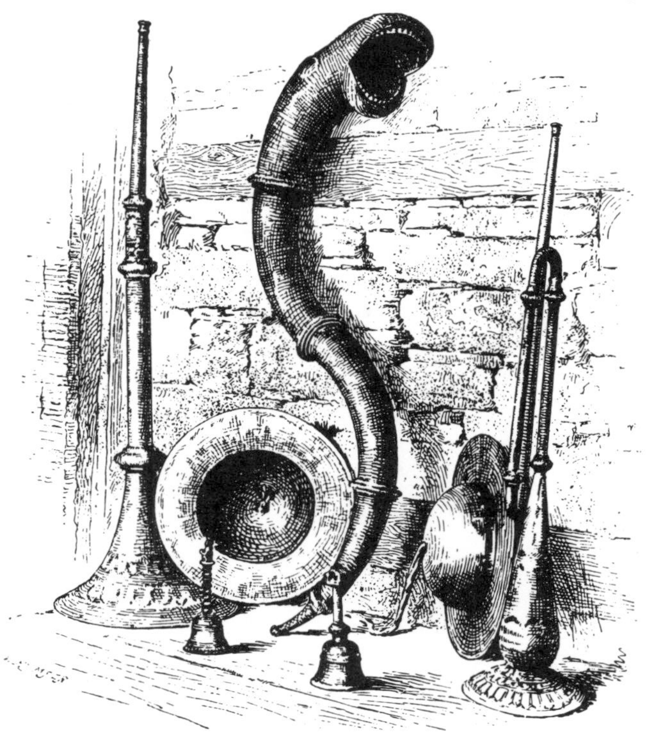

A number of men worked for two days at scaffolding a path, and with great difficulty, and the loss of one yak from a falling rock, a fruitful source of fatalities in Tibet, we reached Khalsar, where with great regret we parted with *Tse- ring-don-drub* (Life's purpose fulfilled), the *gopa* of Sati, whose friendship had been a real pleasure, and to whose courage and promptitude, in Mr Redslob's opinion, I owed my rescue from drowning. Two days of very severe marching and long and steep ascents brought us to the wretched hamlet of Kharzong Lar-sa, in a snowstorm, at an altitude higher than the summit of Mont Blanc. The servants were all ill of 'pass-poison', and crept into a cave along with a number of big Tibetan mastiffs, where they enjoyed the comfort of semi- suffocation till the next morning, Mr Redslob and I, with some willing Tibetan helpers, pitching our own tents. The wind was strong and keen, and with the mercury down at 15° Fahrenheit it was impossible to do anything but to go to bed in the early afternoon, and stay there till the next day. Mr Redslob took a severe chill, which produced an alarming attack of pleurisy, from the effects of which he never fully recovered.

We started on a grim snowy morning, with six yaks carrying our baggage or ridden by ourselves, four led horses, and a number of Tibetans, several more having been sent on in advance to cut steps in the glacier and roughen them with gravel. Within certain limits the ground grows greener as one ascends, and we passed upwards among primulas, asters, a large blue myosotis, gentians, potentillas, and great sheets of edelweiss. At the glacier foot we skirted a deep green lake on snow with a glorious view of the Kharzong glacier and the pass, a nearly perpendicular wall of rock, bearing up a steep glacier and a snowfield of great width and depth, above which tower pinnacles of naked rock. It presented to all appearance an impassable barrier rising 2500 feet above the lake, grand and awful in the dazzling whiteness of the new-fallen snow. Thanks to the ice steps our yaks took us over in four hours without a false step, and from the summit, a sharp ridge 17,500 feet in altitude, we looked our last on grimness, blackness, and snow, and southward for many a weary mile to the Indus valley lying in sunshine and summer. Fully two dozen carcases of horses newly dead lay in cavities of the glacier. Our animals were ill of 'pass- poison', and nearly blind, and I was obliged to ride my yak into Leh, a severe march of thirteen hours, down miles of crumbling zigzags, and then among villages of irrigated terraces, till the grand view of the Gyalpo's palace, with its air- hung *gonpo* and clustering *chod-tens*, and of the desert city itself, burst suddenly upon us, and our benumbed and stiffened limbs thawed in the hot sunshine. I pitched my tent in a poplar grove for a fortnight, near the Moravian compounds and close to the travellers' bungalow, in which is a British Postal Agency, with a Tibetan postmaster who speaks English.

Chapter Seven

Journeys in Persia and Kurdistan, 1891

Although this book was published before *Among the Tibetans*, the journeys it records were made later (in 1890). At Simla, on her way back from Tibet, Mrs Bishop met Major Herbert Sawyer who, according to her first biographer, was 'charged with a military-geographical mission to Persia', a country then as now the subject of much international tension. Mrs Bishop arranged to travel with Major Sawyer on two journeys. The first (from which the following extracts are taken) was from Baghdad to Teheran in bitter winter weather across the northern ranges of the Zagros Mountains and the Dasht-i-Kavir or Great Salt Desert, at that season a sea of mud. A second journey together in high summer was to take them from Isfahan through the mountains of Luristan.

Although an armed escort was necessary on both journeys, the encumbrances of a large party were never to Mrs Bishop's taste, and whenever possible she would ride apart from the main body of the expedition. The benefits of the arrangement were not one-sided, however. Her medical training, though rudimentary, was invaluable to the members of the expedition and to the local population, and her skill, patience and tolerance eased their progress when in the later stages of their travels Major Sawyer's increasing contempt for the tribespeople threatened to hinder them. In an unpublished note she records with some asperity the Sahib's distressing habit of addressing local dignitaries as 'old cock'.

A *sowar* is a cavalry soldier; a *chadar* the all-covering garment worn by women in the Middle East; a *duffadar* is equivalent in rank to a corporal, and a *hakim* is a doctor or sage.

Horses are very good and cheap here. . . . A muleteer, remarkable in appearance and beauty, and twelve fine mules have been engaged. The *sowar* and several other men have applied to me for medicine, having fearful coughs, etc., but I have not been fortunate enough to cure them, as their maladies chiefly require good feeding, warm bedding, and poultices, which are unattainable. It is pitiable to see the poor shivering in their thin cotton clothes in such weather. The men make shift with the seamless felt coats—more cloaks than coats, with long bag-like sleeves tapering to the size of a glove but with a slit midway, through which the hands can

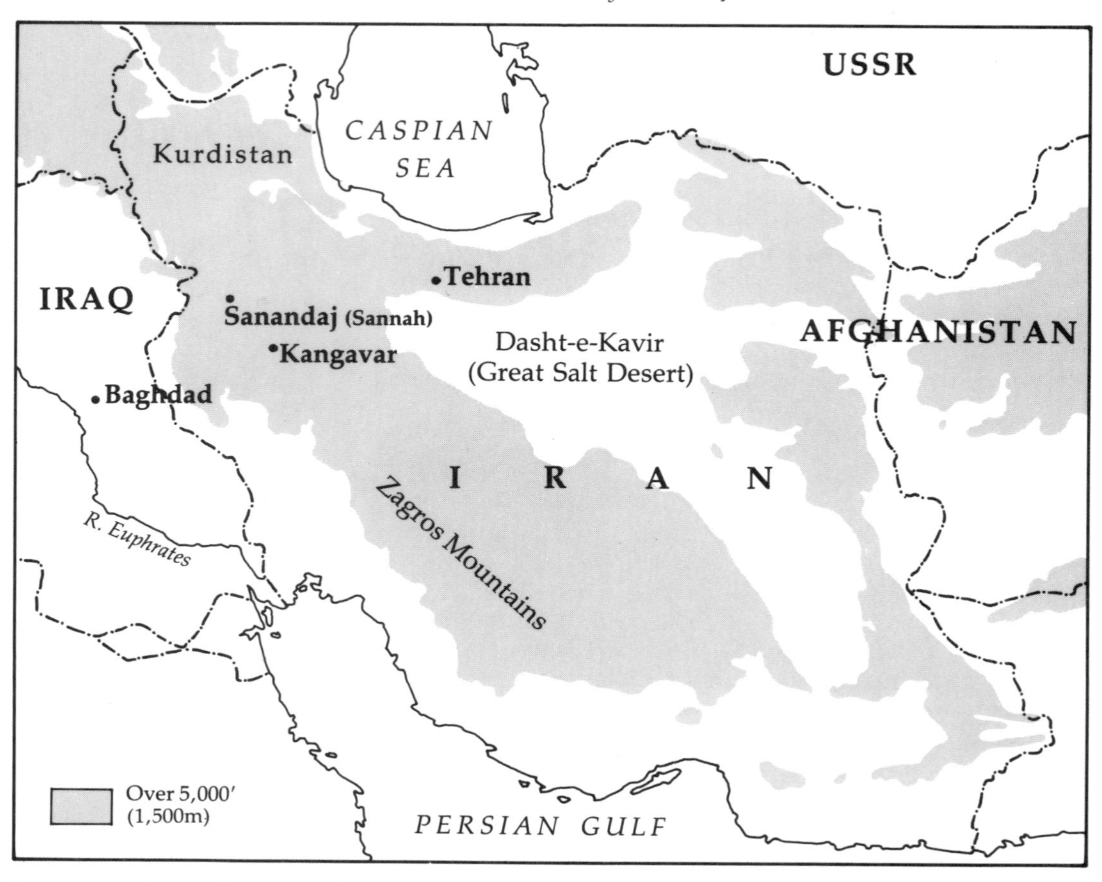

be protruded when need arises. The women have no outer garment but the thin cotton *chadar*.

After much noise the caravan got under way, but it was soon evident that the fine mules we had engaged had been changed for a poor, sore-backed set, and that the fine saddle-mule I was to have had was metamorphosed into a poor weak creature, which . . . lost no opportunity of tumbling down, and I felt myself a barbarian for urging him on. Hills and mountains glistened in all directions. The only exception to the general whiteness was Piru, the great rock mass of Besitun, which ever loomed blackly overhead through clouds and darkness, and never seemed any nearer. It was very solitary. I met only a caravan of carpets, and a few men struggling along with laden asses.

It was the most artistic day of the whole journey, much cloud flying about, mountains in indigo gloom, or in grey, with storm clouds round their heads, or pure white, with shadows touched in with cobalt, while peaks and ridges, sun-kissed, gleamed here and there above indigo and grey. Not a tree or even bush, on them or on the plain, broke the monotony after a summer palace of the Shah, surrounded by poplars, was passed. There is plenty of water everywhere.

As the sun was stormily tinging with pink the rolling snow-clouds here and there, I halted on the brow of a slope under the imposing rock front of Besitun to wait for orders. It was wildly magnificent: the huge precipice of Piru, rising 1700 feet from the level, the mountains on both sides of the valley approaching each other, and behind Piru a craggy ravine, glorified here and there by touches of amber and pink upon the clouds which boiled furiously out of its depths. In the foreground were a huge caravanserai with a noble portal, a solitary thing upon the snow, not a dwelling, but offering its frigid hospitality to all comers; a river with many windings, and the ruinous hovels of Besitun huddled in the mud behind. An appalling view in the wild twilight of a winter evening; and as the pink died out, a desolate ghastliness fell upon it. As I waited, all but worn out by the long march, the tumbling mule, and the icy wind, I thought I should like never to hear the deep chimes of a Persian caravan, or see the huge portal of a Persian caravanserai any more. These are cowardly emotions which are dispelled by warmth and food, but at that moment there was not much prospect of either.

Through seas of mud and by mounds of filth we entered Besitun, a most wretched village of eighteen hovels, chiefly ruinous, where we dismounted in the mixed snow and mud of a yard at a hovel of three rooms vacated by a family. . . . Hadji said he was ill of fever, and seemed like an idiot; but the orderly said that the illness was shammed and the stupidity assumed in order not to work. I told him to put the mattress on the bed; 'Pour water on the mattress,' he replied. I repeated, 'Put—the—mattress—on—the—bed,' to which he replied, 'Put the mattress into water!' I said if he felt too ill for his work he might go to bed. 'God knows,' he answered. 'Yes, knows that you are a lazy, good-for-nothing, humbugging brute'—a well-timed objurgation from Major Sawyer which elicited a prolonged '*Ya Allah*!' but produced no effect, as the tea and chapaties were not relatively but absolutely cold the next morning.

It has been a severe day. I rode a big mule not used to the bit, very troublesome and mulish at first, but broken in an hour. The others had to make several halts, so I left the 'light division' and rode on alone. It became dark and wild, and presently the

surface of the snow began to move and to drift furiously for about a foot above the ground. The wind rose to a gale. I held my hat on with one half-frozen hand. My mackintosh cape blew inside out, and struck me such a heavy blow on the eyes that for some time I could not see and had to trust to the mule. The wind rose higher; it was furious, and the drift, not only from the valley but from the mountain sides, was higher than my head, stinging and hissing as it raced by. It was a blizzard, a brutal snow-laden northeaster, carrying fine, sharp, hard-frozen snow crystals, which beat on my eyes and blinded them.

After a short experience of it my mule 'turned tail' and needed a spurring to make him face it. I fought on for an hour, crossed what appeared to be a bridge, where there were a few mud hovels, and pressed on down a narrower valley. The blizzard became frightful; from every ravine gusts of storm came down, sweeping the powdery snow from the hillsides into the valley; the mountains were blotted out, the depression in the snow which erewhile had marked the path was gone, I could not even see the mule's neck, and he was floundering in deep snow up to the girths; the hiss of the drift had increased to a roar, the violence of the storm produced breathlessness and the intense cold numbness. It was dangerous for a solitary traveller, and thinking that Major Sawyer would be bothered by missing one of the party under such circumstances, I turned and waited under the lee of a ruinous mud hovel for a long, long time till the others came up—two of the men having been unhorsed in a drift.

In those hovels there were neither accommodation nor supplies, and we decided to push on. Through all this region thistles grow to a height of 4 feet, and the only way of finding the track was to look out for a space on which no withered thistle-blooms appeared above the snow. There is a large caravanserai at the entrance to Sannah . . . After nearly nine hours of a crawling pace and exposure to violent weather, I suffered from intense pain in my joints, and was dragged and lifted in and put into a chair. I write 'put', for I was nearly helpless, and had to take a teaspoonful of whisky in warm milk. While the fire was being made two women, with a gentle kindliness which won my heart, chafed my trembling, nearly frozen hands with their own, with kindly womanly looks, which supplied the place of speech.

I lay down under a heap of good blankets, sorry to see them in thin cotton clothes, and when I was less frozen observed my room and its grotesquely miserable aspect. There are no windows, and the divided door does not shut by 3 inches. A low hole leads into the granary, which is also the fowl-house, but the fowls have no idea of keeping to their own apartment. Two sheep with injured legs lie in a corner with some fodder beside them. A heap of faggots, the bed placed diagonally to avoid the firehole in the floor, a splashed tarpaulin on which Hadji threw down the saddle and bridle plastered with mud, and all my travelling gear, a puddle of frozen water, a plough, and some ox yokes, an occasional gust of ashes covering everything, and clouds of smoke from wood which refuses to do anything but smoke, are the luxuries of the halt. The house is full of people, and the women come in and out without scruple, and I am really glad to see them, though it is difficult to rouse Hadji from his opium pipe and coffee, and his comfortable lounge by a good fire, to interpret for them. But tired and benumbed as I am, I much prefer a march with excitements and difficulties to the monotony of splashing through mud in warm rain.

The next morning opened cloudless, with the mercury at 18°, which was hardly an excuse for tea and chapaties being quite cold. I was ready much too early, and the servants having given out that I am a *Hakīm*, my room was crowded with women and children, all suffering from eye diseases and scrofula, five women not nearly in middle life with cataract advanced in both eyes, and many with incurved eyelids, the result of wood smoke. It was most painful to see their disappointment when I told them that it would need time to cure some of them, and that for others I could do nothing. Could I not stay? they pleaded. I could have that room and milk and eggs—the best they had. 'And they lifted up their voices and wept.' I felt like a brute for leaving them. The people there showed much interest in our movements, crowding on the roofs to see our gear, and the start.

To write that we all survived the march of that day is strange, when the same pitiless blast or 'demon wind', blowing from 'the roof of the world'—the Pamir desert—made corpses of five men who started with a caravan ahead of us that morning.

A sun without heat glared and scintillated like an electric light, white and unsympathetic, out of a pitiless sky without a cloud. As soon as we emerged from Sannah the 'demon wind' seized on us—a steady, blighting, searching, merciless blast, no rise or fall, no lull, no hope. Steadily and strongly it swept, at a temperature of 9°, across the glittering ascent—swept mountain-sides bare; enveloped us at times in glittering swirls of powdery snow, which after biting and stinging careered over the slopes in twisted columns; screeched down gorges and whistled like the demon it was, as it drifted the light frozen snow in layers, in ripples, in waves, a cruel, benumbing, blinding, withering invisibility!

The six woollen layers of my mask, my three pairs of gloves, my sheepskin coat, fur cloak, and mackintosh piled on over a swaddling mass of woollen clothing, were as nothing before that awful blast. It was not a question of comfort or discomfort, or of suffering more or less severe, but of life or death, as the corpses a few miles ahead of us show. I am certain that if it had lasted another half-hour I too should have perished. The torture of my limbs down to my feet, of my temples and cheekbones, the anguish and uselessness of my hands, from which the reins had dropped, were of small consequence compared with a chill which crept round my heart, threatening a cessation of work.

There were groans behind me; the cook and Hadji had rolled off into the snow, where Hadji was calling on Him 'who is not far from every one of us'. Major Sawyer was on foot. His mask was frozen hard. He was using a scientific instrument, and told his orderly, an Afghan, a smart little *duffadar* of a crack Indian corps, to fasten a strap. The man replied sadly, 'I can't, Sahib.' His arms and hands were useless. My

mask was frozen to my lips. The tears extorted from my eyes were frozen. I was so helpless, and in such torture, that I would gladly have lain down to die in the snow. The mercury fell to 4°.

After fighting the elements for three hours and a half, we crossed the crest of the pass at an altitude of 7000 feet, to look down upon a snow world stretched out everywhere, pure, glistering, awful; mountains rolling in snowy ranges, valleys without a trace of man, a world of horror, glittering under a mocking sun.

Hadji, with many pious ejaculations, gasped out that he was dying (in fact, for some time all speech had been reduced to a gasp); but when we got over the crest there was no more wind, and all the benumbed limbs resumed sensation, through an experience of anguish.

The road to Kangawar lies through a broad valley, which has many streams. We had been promised good accommodation there but Abbas Khan had chosen something very wretched. Crumbling, difficult stairs at each end of a crumbling mud house led to rooms which barely afforded a shelter. A man shovelled most of the snow out of my room, and tried to make a fire but failed, as neither he nor I could stand the smoke produced by the attempt. But one is always hungry and sleepy, and the hibernation of the insects makes up for any minor discomforts. It was so cold that some water in a cup froze before I could drink it, and the blanket over my face was hard frozen.

At night the muleteers were beseeching on their knees. They said that they could not go on, that the caravan which had attempted to leave Kangawar in the morning had put back with three corpses, and that they and their mules would perish. In the morning it was for some time doubtful whether they could be induced or bribed to proceed. The day was fine and still, but they said that the snow was not broken. At last they agreed to start if we would promise to return at the first breath of wind!

Every resource against cold was brought out and put on. One eye was all that was visible of the servants' faces. The *charvadars* relied on their felt coats and raw sheepskins, with the fur inside, roped round their legs. There is danger of frost-bite even with all precautions. In addition to double woollen underclothing I put on a pair of thick Chitral socks over two pairs of woollen stockings, and over these a pair of long, loose Afghan boots, made of sheepskin with the fur inside. Over my riding dress, which is of flannel lined with heavy homespun, I had a long homespun jacket, an Afghan sheepskin coat, a heavy fur cloak over my knees, and a stout 'regulation' waterproof to keep out the wind. Add to this a cork helmet, a fisherman's hood, a 'six-ply' mask, two pairs of woollen gloves with mittens and double gauntlets, and the difficulty of mounting and dismounting for a person thus *swaddled* may be imagined! The Persians are all in cotton clothes.

Ere long we came on solemn traces of the struggle and defeat of the day before: every now and then a load of chopped straw thrown away, then the deep snow much trampled, then the snow dug away and piled round a small space, in which the *charvadars* had tried to shelter themselves from the wind as the shadows of

death fell, then more straw, and a grave under a high mound of snow; farther on some men busy burying one of the bodies. The air was still, and the sun shone as it had shone the day before on baffled struggles, exhaustion, and death. The trampling of the snow near the track marked the place where the caravan had turned, taking three out of the five bodies back to Kangawar. The fury with which the wind had swept over the plain was shown by the absolute level to which it had reduced the snow, the deep watercourses being filled up with the drifts.

Except for the crossing of a pass with an altitude of 7500 feet, the next day's route was monotonous, across plains, among mountains, all pure white, the only incidents being that my chair was broken by the fall of a mule, and that my mule and I went over our heads in a snow-drift. The track was very little broken, and I was four hours in doing ten miles.

I have a house, i.e. a mud room, to myself. These two days I have had rather a severe chill, after getting in, including a shivering lasting about two hours, perhaps owing to the severe fatigue; and I was lying down with the blankets over my face and was just getting warm when I heard much buzzing about me, and looking up saw the room thronged with men, women, and children, just such a crowd as constantly besieged our blessed Lord when the toilsome day full of 'the contradiction of sinners against Himself' was done, most of them ill of 'divers diseases and torments', smallpox, rheumatism, ulcers on the cornea, abortive and shortened limbs, decay of the bones of the nose, palate, and cheek, tumours, cancers, skin maladies, ophthalmia, opaque films over the eyes, wounds, and many ailments too obscure for my elementary knowledge. Nothing is more painful than to be obliged to say that one cannot do anything for them.

I had to get up, and for nearly two hours was hearing their tales of suffering, interpreted by Hadji with brutal frankness; and they crowded my room again this morning. All I could do was to make various ointments, taking tallow as the basis, drop lotion into some eyes, give a few simple medicines, and send the majority sadly away. The *sowar*, Abbas Khan, is responsible for spreading my fame as a *Hakīm*. He is being cured of a severe cough, and comes to my room for medicine (in which I have no faith) every evening, a lean man with a lean face, lighted with a rapacious astuteness, with a kaftan streaming from his brow, except where it is roped round his shaven skull, a zouave jacket, a skirt something like a kilt, but which stands out like a ballet dancer's dress, all sorts of wrappings round his legs, a coarse striped red shirt, a double cartridge-belt, and a perfect armoury in his girdle of pistols and knives. He is a wit and a rogue.

This caravanserai is only one march from Tehran, and it seemed as if all difficulties were over. Abbas Khan and the sick orderly were sent on early, with a baggage mule loaded with evening dress and other necessities of civilization . . .

It is six days since that terrible ride of ten hours and a half, and my bones ache as I recall it. I never wish to mount a horse again. It had been a very cold night, and for some time after we started it was doubtful whether snow or rain would gain the day, but after an hour of wet snow it decided on rain, and there was a steady downpour all day. The Elburz range, which the day before had looked so magnificent when fifty miles off, was blotted out. This was a great disappointment.

An ascent of low, blackish volcanic hills is made by a broad road of grey gravel, which a torrent has at some time frequented. Thorns and thistles grow there, and skeletons of animals abound. Everything is grim and grey. From these hills we descended into the Kavir, a rolling expanse of friable soil, stoneless, strongly impregnated with salt, but only needing sufficient water to wash the salt out of it and to irrigate it to become as prolific as it is now barren.

It is now a sea of mud crossed by a broad road indicated by dykes, that never-to-be-forgotten mud growing deeper as the day wore on. Hour after hour we plunged through it, sometimes trying the road, and on finding it impassable scrambling through the ditches and over the dykes to the plain, which after

offering firmer foothold for a time became such a 'slough of despond' that we had to scramble back to the road, and so on, hour after hour, meeting nothing but one ghastly caravan of corpses, and wretched asses falling in the mud.

At midday, scrambling up a hill with a little wormwood upon it, and turning my back to the heavy rain, I ate a lunch of dates and ginger, insufficient sustenance for such fatigue. On again!—the rain pouring, the mud deepening, my spine in severe pain. Ceaseless mud, ceaseless heavy rain, a plain of mud, no refuge from mud . . . Major Sawyer rode in front. Not a word was spoken.

In the evening we reached the town of Shah Abdul Azim . . . The one railroad of Persia runs from the capital to this town. As we floundered in darkness along wide roads planted with trees, there was the incongruity of a railway whistle, and with deep breathing and much glare an engine with some carriages passed near the road, taking away with its harsh Western noises that glorious freedom of the desert which outweighs all the hardship even of a winter journey.

It was nearly pitch dark when we got out of Abdul Azim and the rain still fell heavily. There was a causeway which gave foothold below the mud, but it was full of holes and broken culverts, deep in slime, and seemed to have water on each side not particular in keeping within bounds. It was necessary to get on, lest the city gates should be shut, and by lifting and spurring the jaded horses they were induced to trot and canter along that road of pitfalls. I have had many a severe ride in travelling, but never anything equal to that last two hours. The severe pain and want of food made me so faint that I was obliged to hold on to the saddle. I kept my tired horse up, but each flounder I thought would be his last. There was no guidance but an occasional flash from the hoofs of the horse in front, and the word 'spur' ringing through the darkness.

At the gate we learned that it was two miles farther to the British Legation, and

that there was no way for me to get there but on horseback. One lives through a good deal, but I all but succumbed to the pain and faintness. Inside the gate there was an open sea of liquid mud, across which, for a time, certain lights shed their broken reflections. There was a railway shriek, and then the appearance of a station with shunting operations vaguely seen in a vague glare.

Then a tramway track buried under several inches of slush came down a slope, and crowded tramway cars with great single lamps came down the narrow road on horses too tired to be frightened, and almost too tired to get out of the way. Then came a street of mean houses and meaner shops lighted with kerosene lamps, a region like the slums of a new American city, with cafés and saloons, barbers' shops, and European enormities such as gazogenes and effervescing waters in several windows. Later, there were frequent foot passengers preceded by servants carrying huge waxed cambric lanterns of a Chinese shape, then a square with barracks and artillery, a causewayed road dimly lit, then darkness and heavier rain and worse mud, through which the strange spectacle of a carriage and pair incongruously flashed.

Just as endurance was on the point of giving way, we turned from the road through a large gateway into the extensive grounds which surround the British

Legation, a large building forming three sides of a quadrangle, with a fine stone staircase leading up to the central door. Every window was lighted, light streamed from the open door, splashed carriages were dashing up and setting down people in evening dress, there were crowds of servants about, and it flashed on my dazed senses that it must be after eight, and that there was a dinner party!

Arriving from the mud of the Kavir and the slush of the streets, after riding ten hours in ceaseless rain on a worn-out horse; caked with mud from head to foot, dripping, exhausted, nearly blind from fatigue, fresh from mud hovels and the congenial barbarism of the desert, and with the rags and travel-stains of a winter journey of forty-six days upon me, light and festivity were overwhelming.

Alighting at a side door, scarcely able to stand, I sat down in a long corridor, and heard from an English steward that 'dinner is waiting'. His voice sounded very far off, and the once familiar announcement came like a memory out of the remote past. Presently a gentleman appeared in evening dress, wearing a star, which

conveyed to my fast-failing senses that it was Sir H. Drummond Wolff. It was true that there was a large dinner party, and among the guests the Minister with thoughtful kindness had invited all to whom I had letters of introduction. But it was no longer possible to make any effort, and I was taken up to a room in which the comforts of English civilization at first made no impression upon me, and removing only the mackintosh cloak, weighted with mud, which had served me so well, I lay down on the hearthrug before a great coal fire till four o'clock the next morning. And 'so the tale ended', and the winter journey with its tremendous hardships and unbounded mercies was safely accomplished.

Chapter Eight

Korea and her Neighbours, 1898

In what is now North Korea, Mrs Bishop visited the Buddhist monasteries of Keum-kang San, the Diamond Mountain, in 1894. Many of the real pleasures of this journey, however, were distinctly primitive. As she grew older, she was increasingly respected at home for her interest in the practices of other religions and for her work on behalf of medical missions. But as these extracts suggest, she found her greatest joy in the freedom of the trail.

A *mapu* is a groom. *Ku-kyöng* is sightseeing or pleasure-seeking.

The roads along which the traveller rides or trudges, at a pace, in either case, of three miles an hour, are simply infamous. Among the worst is that part of the main road from Seoul to Wön-san which we followed from Sar-pang Kori for two days to Sang-nang Dang, where we branched off for the region known as Keum-kang San, or the Diamond Mountain. The earlier part of this route was through wooded valleys, where lilies of the valley carpeted the ground, and over the very pretty pass of Chyu-pha (1300 feet), on the top of which is a large spirit shrine, containing some coarsely painted pictures of men who look like Chinese generals, the usual offerings of old shoes, rags, and infinitesimal portions of rice, and a tablet inscribed, 'I, the spirit Söng-an-chi, dwell in this place.' There, as at the various trees hung with rags, and the heaps of stones on the tops of passes, the *mapu* bowed and expectorated, as is customary at the abodes of daemons.

There is much wet rice along the route, as well as dry rice, with a double line of beans between every two rows, and in the rice revel and croak large frogs of extreme beauty, vivid green with black velvet spots, the under side of the legs and bodies being cardinal red. These appeared to be the prey of the graceful white and pink ibis, the latter in the intensified flush of his spring colouring.

On two successive days there were tremendous thunderstorms, the second succeeded, just as we were at the head of a wild glen, by a brief tornado, which nearly blew over the ponies, and snapped trees of some size as though they had been matchwood. Then came a profound calm. The clouds lay banked in pink illuminated masses on a sky of tender green, cleft by grey mountain peaks.

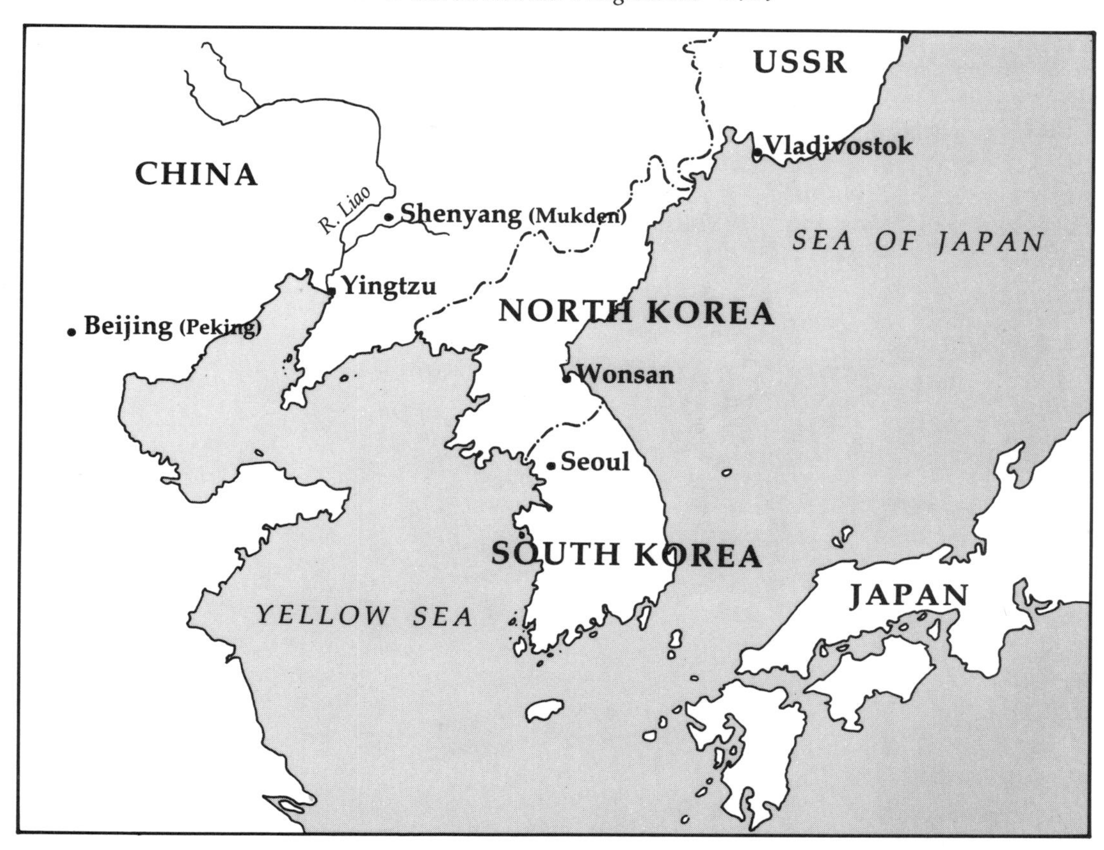

Mountain torrents boomed, crashed, sparkled, and foamed, the silent woods rejoiced the eye by the vividness of their greenery and their masses of white and yellow blossom, and sweet heavy odours enriched the evening air. On that and several other occasions, I recognized that Korea has its own special beauties, which fix themselves in the memory; but they must be sought for in spring and autumn, and off the beaten track. Dirty and squalid as the villages are, at a little distance their deep-eaved brown roofs, massed among orchards, on gentle slopes, or on the banks of sparkling streams, add colour and life to the scenery, and men in their queer white clothes and dress hats, with their firm tread, and bundled-up women, with a shoggling walk and long staffs, brought round with a semicircular swing at every step, are adjuncts which one would not willingly dispense with.

After crossing the Paik-yang Gang, there 162 yards wide and 16 feet deep, by a ferry-boat of remarkably ingenious construction, rendered necessary by the fact that the long bridge over the broad stream was in ruins, and that the appropriation for its reconstruction had been diverted by the local officials to their own enrichment, we entered the spurs or ribs of the great mountain chain which, running north and south, divides Korea into two very unequal longitudinal portions at the village of Tong-ku.

The scenery became very varied and pretty. Forests clothed many of the hills with a fair blossoming undergrowth, untouched by the fuel-gatherers' remorseless hook; torrents flashed in foam through dark, dense leafage, or bubbled and gurgled out of sight; the little patches of cultivation were boulder-strewn; there were few inhabitants, and the tracks called roads were little better than the stony beds of streams. As they become less and less obvious, and the valleys more solitary, our tergiversations were more frequent and prolonged, the *mapu* drove the ponies as fast as they could walk, the fords were many and deep, and two of the party were unhorsed in them, still we hurried on faster and faster. Not a word was spoken, but I knew that the men had *tiger on the brain*!

Blundering through the twilight, it was dark when we reached the lower village of Ma-ri Kei, where we were to halt for the night, two miles from the Pass of Tan-pa-Ryöng, which was to be crossed the next day. There the villagers could not or would not take us in. They said they had neither rice nor beans, which may have been true so late in the spring. However, it is, or then was, Korean law that if a village could not entertain travellers it must convoy them to the next halting-place.

The *mapu* were frantic. They yelled and stormed and banged at the hovels, and succeeded in turning out four sleepy peasants, who were reinforced by four more a little farther on; but the torches were too short, and after spluttering and flaring, went out one by one, and the fresh ones lighted slowly. The *mapu* lost their reason. They thrashed the torch-bearers with their heavy sticks; I lashed my *mapu* with my light whip for doing it; they yelled, they danced. Then things improved. Gloriously glared the pine knots on the leaping crystal torrents that we forded, reddening the white clothes of the men and the stony track and the warm-tinted stems of the pines; and so with shouts and yells and waving torches we passed up the wooded glen in the frosty night air, under a firmament of stars, to the mountain hamlet of upper Ma-ri Kei, consisting of five hovels, only three of which were inhabited.

It is a very forlorn place and very poor, and it was an hour before my party of eight human beings and four ponies were established in its miserable shelter, though even that was welcome after being eleven hours in the saddle.

The eastern descent of the Tan-pa Ryöng is by a series of zigzags, through woods and a profusion of varied and magnificent ferns. A long day followed of ascents and descents, deep fords of turbulent streams, valley villages with terrace cultivation of buckwheat, and glimpses of grey rock needles through pine and persimmon groves, and in the late afternoon, after struggling through a rough ford in which the water was half-way up the sides of the ponies, we entered a gorge and struck a smooth, broad, well-made road, the work of the monks, which traverses a fine forest of pines and firs above a booming torrent.

Towards evening 'the hills swung open to the light'; through the parting branches there were glimpses of granite walls and peaks reddening into glory; red stems, glowing in the slant sunbeams, lighted up the blue gloom of the coniferae; there were glints of foam from the loud-tongued torrent below; the dew fell heavily, laden with aromatic odours of pines, and as the valley narrowed again and the blue shadows fell the picture was as fair as one could hope to see. The monks, though road-makers, are not bridge-builders, and there were difficult fords to cross, through which the ponies were left to struggle by themselves, the *mapu* crossing on single logs. In the deep water I discovered that its temperature was almost icy. The worst ford is at the point where the first view of Chang-an Sa, the Temple of Eternal Rest, the oldest of the Keum-kang San monasteries, is obtained, a great pile of temple buildings with deep curved roofs, in a glorious situation, crowded upon a small grassy plateau in one of the narrowest parts of the gorge, where the mountains fall back a little and afford Buddhism a peaceful shelter, secluded from the outer world by snow for four months of the year.

Crossing the torrent and passing under a lofty *Hong-Sal-Mun*, or 'red arrow gate', significant in Korea of the patronage of royalty, we were at once among the Chang-an Sa buildings, which consist of temples large and small, a stage for religious dramas, bell and tablet houses, stables for the ponies of wayfarers, cells, dormitories, and a refectory for the abbot and monks, quarters for servants and neophytes, huge kitchens, a large guest hall, and a nunnery. Besides these there

are quarters devoted to the lame, halt, blind, infirm, and solitary; to widows, orphans, and the destitute.

The first impression of the plateau was that it was a wood-yard on a large scale. Great logs and piles of planks were heaped under the stately pines and under a superb *Salisburia adiantifolia*, 17 feet in girth, forty carpenters were sawing, planing, and hammering, and forty or fifty labourers were hauling in logs to the music of a wild chant, for mendicant effort had been resorted to energetically, with the result that the great temple was undergoing repairs, almost amounting to a reconstruction.

It was difficult for me to find accommodation, but eventually a very pleasing young priest of high rank gave up his cell to me. Unfortunately, it was next to the guests' kitchen, and the flues from the fires passing under it, I was baked in a temperature of 91°, although, in spite of warnings about tigers, the dangers from which are by no means imaginary, I kept both door and window open all night. The cell had for its furniture a shrine of Gautama and an image of Kwan-yin on a shelf, and a few books, which I learned were Buddhist classics, not volumes, as in a cell which I occupied later, full of pictures by no means inculcating holiness. In the next room, equally hot, and without a chink open for ventilation, thirty guests moaned and tossed all night, a single candle dimly lighting a picture of Buddha and the dusty and hideous ornaments on the altar below.

At 9 p.m., midnight, and again at 4 a.m., which is the hour at which the monks rise, bells were rung, cymbals and gongs were beaten, and the praises of Buddha were chanted in an unknown tongue.

It is an exercise of forbearance to abstain from writing much about the beauties of Chang-an Sa as seen in two days of perfect heavenliness. It is a calm retreat, that small, green, semicircular plateau which the receding hills have left, walling in the back and sides with rocky precipices half-clothed with forest, while the bridgeless torrent in front, raging and thundering among huge boulders of pink granite, secludes it from all but the adventurous. Alike in the rose of sunrise, in the red and gold of sunset, or gleaming steely blue in the prosaic glare of midday, the great rock peak on the left bank, one of the highest in the range, compels ceaseless admiration. The appearance of its huge vertical topmost ribs has been well compared to that of the 'pipes of an organ', this organ-pipe formation being

common in the range; seams and ledges half-way down give root-hold to a few fantastic conifers and azaleas, and lower still all suggestion of form is lost among dense masses of magnificent forest.

I left the ponies and baggage at Chang-an Sa, the *mapu*, who were bent on *ku-kyöng* accompanying me for part of the distance, and took a five days' journey . . . in unrivalled weather, in air which was elixir, crossing the range to Yu-chöm Sa (the first temple on the easterossing it by the Ki-cho, 3570 feet.

Taking two coolies to carry essentials, and a *na-myö* or mountain chair with two bearers, for the whole journey, all supplied by the monks, I walked the first stage to the monasteries of P'yo-un Sa and Chyang-yang Sa, the latter at an elevation of about 2760 feet. From it the view, which passes for the grandest in Korea, is obtained of the Twelve Thousand Peaks. There is assuredly no single view that I have seen in Japan or even in Western China which equals it for beauty and grandeur. Across the grand gorge through which the Chang-an Sa torrent thunders, and above primeval tiger-haunted forests with their infinity of green, rises the central ridge of the Keum-kang San, jagged all along its summit, each yellow granite pinnacle being counted as a peak.

On that enchanting May evening, when odours of paradise, the fragrant breath of a million flowering shrubs and trailers, of bursting buds, and unfolding ferns, rose into the cool dewy air, and the silence could be felt, I was not inclined to enter a protest against Korean exaggeration on the ground that the number of peaks is probably nearer 1200 than 12,000. Their yellow granite pinnacles, weathered into silver grey, rose up cold, stern, and steely blue from the glorious forests which drape their lower heights—winter above and summer below—then purpled into red as the sun sank, and gleamed above the twilight, till each glowing

summit died out as lamps which are extinguished one by one, and the whole took on the ashy hue of death.

The situation of P'yo-un Sa is romantic, on the right bank of the torrent, and it is approached by a bridge, and by passing under several roofed gateways. The monastery had been newly rebuilt, and is one mass of fretwork, carving, gilding, and colour, the whole decoration being the work of the monks.

The front of the Temple of the Believing Mind is a magnificent piece of bold wood-carving, the motif being the peony. Every part of the building which is not stone or tile is carved, and decorated in blue, red, white, green, and gold. It may be barbaric, but it is barbaric splendour. There too is a Temple of Judgement, with hideous representations of the Buddhist hells, one scene being the opening of the books in which the deeds of men's mortal lives are written.

The fifty monks of P'yo-un Sa were very friendly, and not impecunious. One gave up to me his oven-like cell, but repaid himself for the sacrifice by indulging in ceaseless staring. The wind bells of the establishment and the big bell have a melody in their tones such as I have rarely heard, and when at 4 a.m. bells of all sizes and tones announced that 'prayer is better than sleep', there was nothing about the sounds to jar on the pure freshness of morning. The monks are well dressed and jolly, and have a well-to-do air which clashes with any pretensions to asceticism. The rule of these monasteries is a strict vegetarianism which allows neither milk nor eggs, and in the whole region there are neither fowls nor domestic animals. Not to wound the prejudices of my hosts, I lived on tea, rice, honey water, edible pine nuts, and a most satisfying combination of pine nuts and honey. After a light breakfast on these delicacies, the sub-abbot took me to see his grandmother, a very bright pleasing woman of 80, who came from Seoul thirteen years ago and built a house within the monastery grounds, in order to die in its quiet blessedness. There I had to eat a second ethereal meal, and the hospitable hostess forced on me a pot of exquisite honey and a bag of pine nuts.

Buddhism, which, as in Japan, possesses itself of the fairest spots in Nature, fixed itself in this romantic seclusion as early as the sixth century AD, and the venerable relics of the time when for a thousand years it was the official as well as the popular cult of the country are chiefly to be found in the recesses of this mountain region, where the same faith, though now discredited, disestablished, and despised, still attracts a certain number of votaries, and a far larger number of visitors and so-called pilgrims, who resort to the shrines to indulge in *ku-kyöng*, a Korean term which covers pleasure-seeking, sight-seeing, the indulgence of curiosity, and much else. Others make the monasteries a refuge from justice or creditors, some remain desiring peaceful indolence, and not a few are vowed and tonsured who came simply to view the scenery of the Keum-kang San and were too much enchanted to leave it.

My impression of most of the monks was that their religious performances are absolutely without meaning to them, and that belief, except among a few, does not exist. The Koreans universally attribute to them gross profligacy, of the existence of which at one of the large monasteries it was impossible not to become aware; but between their romantic and venerable surroundings, the apparent order and quietness of their lives, their benevolence to the old and destitute, who find a peaceful asylum with them, and in the main their courtesy and hospitality, I am compelled to admit that they exercise a certain fascination, and that I prefer to remember their virtues rather than their faults. My sympathies go out to them for their appreciation of the beautiful, and for the way in which religious art has assisted Nature by the exceeding picturesqueness of the positions and decoration of their shrines.

The route from Chang-an Sa to Yu-chöm Sa, about eleven miles, is mainly the rough beds of two great mountain torrents.

No quadruped can travel this route. Coolies, very lightly laden, and chair-bearers carrying a *na-myö*, two long poles with a slight seat in the middle, a noose of rope for the feet, and light uprights bound together with a wistaria rope to support the back can be used, but the occupant of the chair has to walk much of the way.

Surely the beauty of that eleven miles is not much exceeded anywhere on earth. Colossal cliffs, upbearing mountains, forests, and grey gleaming peaks, rifted to give root-hold to pines and maples, oft-times contracting till the blue heaven above is narrowed to a strip, boulders of pink granite 40 and 50 feet high, pines on their crests and ferns and lilies in their crevices, round which the clear

waters swirl, before sliding down over smooth surfaces of pink granite to rest awhile in deep pink pools where they take a more brilliant than an emerald green with the flashing lustre of a diamond—rocks and ledges over which the crystal stream dashes in drifts of foam, shelving rock surfaces on which the decorative Chinese characters, the laborious work of pilgrims, afford the only foothold, slides, steeper still, made passable for determined climbers by holes, drilled by the monks, and fitted with pegs and rails, rocks with bas-reliefs, or small shrines of Buddha draped with flowering trailers, a cliff with a bas-relief of Buddha, 45 feet high on a pedestal 30 feet broad, rocks carved into lanterns and altars, whose harsh outlines are softened by mosses and lichens, and above, huge timber and fantastic peaks rising into the 'summer heaven's delicious blue'.

This route cannot be traversed in European shoes. In Korean string foot-gear, however, I never slipped once. There was much jumping from boulder to boulder, much winding round rocky projections, clinging to their irregularities with scarcely foothold, and one's back to the torrent far below, and much leaping over deep crevices and 'walking tight-rope fashion' over rails. Wherever the traveller has to leave the difficulties of the torrent-bed he encounters those of slippery sloping rocks, which he has to traverse by hanging on to tree trunks.

Our two priestly companions were most polite to me, giving me a hand at the dangerous places, and beguiling the way by legends, chiefly Buddhistic, concerning every fantastic and abnormal rock and pool.

I had hoped for rest and quiet on the following day, having had rather a hard week, but these were unattainable. Besides seventy monks and twenty nuns, there were 200 lay servitors and carpenters, and all were bent upon *ku-kyöng*, the first European woman to visit the Keum-kang San being regarded as a great sight, and from early morning till late at night there was no rest. The *kang* floor of my room being heated from the kitchen, it was too hot to exist with the paper front closed, and the crowds of monks, nuns, and servitors, finishing with the carpenters, who crowded in whenever it was opened, and hung there hour after hour, nearly suffocated me, the day being very warm. The abbot and several senior monks discussed the merits of rival creeds, saying that the only difference between Buddhists and ourselves is that they don't kill even the smallest insect, while we disregard what we call 'animal life', and that we don't look upon monasticism and

other forms of asceticism as means of salvation. They admitted that among their priests there are more who live in known sin than strivers after righteousness.

There are many bright busy boys about Yu-chöm Sa, most of whom had already had their heads shaved. To one who had not, Che on-i gave a piece of chicken, but he refused it because he was a Buddhist, on which an objectionable-looking old sneak of a priest told him that it was all right to eat it so long as no one saw him, but the boy persisted in his refusal.

At midnight, being awakened by the boom of the great bell and the disorderly and jarring clang of innumerable small ones, I went, at the request of the friendly

young priest, our fellow-traveller, to see him perform the devotions, which are taken in turn by the monks.

The great bronze bell, an elaborate piece of casting of the fourteenth century, stands in a rude, wooden, clay-floored tower by itself. A dim paper lantern on a dusty rafter barely lighted up the white-robed figure of the devotee, as he circled the bell, chanting in a most musical voice a Sanskrit litany, of whose meaning he was ignorant, striking the bosses of the bell with a knot of wood as he did so. Half an hour passed thus. Then taking a heavy mallet, and passing to another chant, he circled the bell with a greater and ever-increasing passion of devotion, beating its bosses heavily and rhythmically, faster and faster, louder and louder, ending by producing a burst of frenzied sound, which left him for a moment exhausted. Then, seizing the swinging beam, the three full tones which end the worship, and which are produced by striking the bell on the rim, which is 8 inches thick, and on the middle, which is very thin, made the tower and the ground vibrate, and boomed up and down the valley with their unforgettable music. Of that young monk's sincerity I have not one doubt.

It must be remembered however, that this easy, peaceful, luxurious life only lasts for a part of the year, and that all but a few of the monks must make an annual tramp, wallet and begging-bowl in hand, over rough, miry, or dusty Korean roads, put up with vile and dirty accommodation, beg for their living from those who scorn their tonsure and their creed, and receive 'low talk' from the lowest in the land. When we departed all the monks and labourers bade us a courteous farewell, some of the older priests accompanying us for a short distance. A severe climb up and down an irregular, broken staircase of rock took us over the Ki-cho Pass, 3700 feet in altitude, after which there is a tedious march of some hours along bare and unpicturesque mountain-sides before reaching the well-made path which leads through pine woods to the beautiful plateau of Chang-an Sa. The young priest had kept our baggage carefully, but the heat of his floor had melted the candles in the boxes and had turned candy into molasses, making havoc among photographic materials at the same time!

By now some of Mrs Bishop's journeys seem to have been undertaken for the mountaineer's compulsive reason: 'because it is there'. Certainly the object of her excursion to Mukden (now Shenyang in China) cannot have been *ku-kyöng*.

It surprised me much to find that only one foreign resident had visited Mukden, which is only 120 miles distant by a road which is traversable in winter, and is accessible by river during the summer and autumn in from eight to ten days. I left Newchwang on the 3 July, and though various circumstances were unpropitious, reached Mukden in eight days, being able to avoid many of the windings of the Liau by sailing over an inundation.

The kindly foreign community lent me necessaries for the journey, but even with these the hold of a 'pea-boat' was not luxurious. My camp-bed took up the greater part of it, and the roof was not much above my head. The descent into the hold and the ascent were difficult, and when wind and rain obliged me to close the front, it was quite dark, cockroaches swarmed, and the smell of the bilge water was horrible. I was very far from well when I started, and in two days was really ill, yet I would not have missed the special interest of that journey for anything, or its solitude, for Wong's limited English counted for nothing and involved no conversational effort.

For some distance above Newchwang or Ying-tzŭ . . . there is a complication of muddy rivers hurrying through vast reed beds, the resort of wild fowl, with here and there a mud bank with a mud hovel or two upon it. At that time reed beds and partially inundated swamps stretched away nearly to the horizon, which is limited in the far distance by the wavy blue outline of some low hills.

We ran up the river till the evening of the second day before a fair wind, and then were becalmed on a reedy expanse swarming with mosquitoes. The mercury was at 89° in the hold that night. I had severe fever, with racking pains in my head, back, and limbs, and in the morning the stamping of the junkmen to and fro, along the narrow strip of deck outside the roof, was hardly bearable. Wong had used up the ample supply of water, and there was nothing wherewith to quench thirst but the brown, thick water of the Liau, the tea made with which resembled peasoup.

On the morning of the third day it began to rain and blow, and for the next awful four days the wind and rain never ceased. The oiled paper which had been tacked over the roof of the boat was torn into strips by the violence of the winds, which forced the rain through every chink. I lay down that night with the mercury at 80°, woke feeling very cold, but, though surprised, fell asleep again. Woke again much colder, feeling as if my feet were bandaged together, extricated myself with difficulty, struck a light, and got up into six inches of a mixture of bilge water and rain water, with an overpowering stench, in or on which all things were sunk or floating. Wondered again at being so very cold, found the temperature at 84°, and that I had been sleeping under a wringing sheet in soaked clothing and on soaked sacking, under a soaked mosquito net, and that there was not a dry article in the hold. For the next three days and nights things remained in the same condition, and though I was really ill I had to live in wet clothing and drink the 'liquid cholera' of the flood, all the wells being submerged.

Telegrams later in the English papers announced 'Great floods in Manchuria', but of the magnitude of the inundation which destroyed for that season the magnificent crops of the great fertile plain of the Liau, and swept away many of its countless farming villages, only the experience of sailing over it could give any idea.

In that miserable night there were barkings of dogs, shouts of men, mewings of cats, and general noises of unrest, and in the morning, of the village of Piengdo opposite to which we had moored the evening before, only one house and a barn remained, which were shortly carried away. Many of the people had escaped in boats, and the remainder, with their fowls, dogs, and cats, were in the spreading branches of a large tree. Although the mast of my boat was considerably in the way, and it was difficult to make fast, I succeeded in rescuing the whole menagerie and in transferring it in two trips to a village on the other side, which was then 5 feet above the water.

We had reached the most prosperous region of Manchuria, a plain sixty miles in length, of deep, rich alluvial soil, bearing splendid crops, the most lucrative of which are the bean, the oil from which is the staple export of the country, the opium poppy, and tobacco. The great and small millet, wheat, barley, melons, and cucumbers cover the ground, mulberry trees for the silkworm surround the farm-houses, and the great plain is an idyll of bounteousness and fertility. Of all this not a trace remained, except in a few instances the tops of the 8-feet millet, which supplies the people not only with food, but with fuel, and fodder for their animals.

The river-bank burst during the night, and the waters were raging into the plain, from which I missed many a brown-roofed village, which the evening before stood among its willow and poplar trees. At 11 a fair wind sprang up, junks began to move, and my boatmen, who had talked of returning, untied and moved too. After an exciting scene at a bend, where the river, leaping like a rapid, thumped the junks against the opposite shore, we passed one wrecked village after another, bits of walls of houses alone standing. The people and their fowls were in the trees. The women clung to their fowls as much as to their babies. Dug-outs, scows, and a few junks, mine among them, were busy saving life, and we took three families and their fowls to Sho-wa Ku, a large junk port, where a number of houses were still standing. These families had lost all their household goods and gods, as well as mules, pigs, and dogs. On our way we sailed into a farm-yard to try to get some eggs, and the junk not replying to her helm, thumped one of the undermined walls down. It was a large farmhouse and full of refugees. The water was 3 feet deep in the rooms, naked children were floating about in tubs, and the women, looking resigned, sat on the tables. The men said that it was the last of four houses, and that they might as well be dead, for they had lost all their crops and their beasts.

A fearful sight presented itself at Sho-wa Ku. There the river, indefinite as it had previously been, disappeared altogether, and the whole country was a turbulent muddy sea, bounded on the east by a range of hills, and to the north and south limitless. Under it lay all the fruits of the tireless industry and garden cultivation of a large and prosperous population, and the remorseless waters under the influence of a gale were rolling in muddy surges, 'crested with tawny foam', over the fast dissolving homes.

On this vast flood we embarked to shorten the distance, and sailed with three reefs in the sail for thirteen miles over it, till we were brought up by an insurmountable obstacle in the shape of a tremendous rush of water where a bank had given way. There we were compelled to let go two anchors in the early afternoon. The wind had become foul, and the rain, which fell in torrents, was driven almost horizontally. Nothing that suggested human life was in sight. It might have been the Deluge, for the windows of heaven were opened. There were a muddy, rolling sea, and a black sky, dark with tremendous rain, and the foliage of trees with submerged trunks was alone suggestive of even vegetable life and of the villages which had been destroyed by the devouring waters.

In thirteen miles just one habitation remained standing, a large, handsome brick house with entrance arch, quadrangle, curved roofs, large farm buildings, and many servants' houses, some of which were toppling, and others were submerged up to their roofs. There was a look-out on the principal roof and he hailed us, but as there were several scows about, enough to save life, I disregarded him, and we sailed on into the tempestuous solitude where we anchored.

The day darkened slowly into night, the junk rolled with short plunging rolls, the rain fell more tremendously than ever, and the strong wind, sweeping through the rigging with a desolate screech, only just overpowered the clatter on the roof. I was ill. The seas we shipped drowned the charcoal, and it was impossible to make tea or arrowroot. The rain dripped everywhere through the roof. My lamp spluttered and went out and could not be relighted, bedding and clothing were soaked, my bed stood in the water, the noise was deafening.

Never in all my journeys have I felt so solitary. I realized that no other foreigner was travelling in Manchuria, that there was no help in illness, and that there was nothing to be done but lie there in saturated clothes till things took a turn for the better.

And so they did. By 8 the next morning the scene was changed. The sky was blue and cloudless, there was a cool north wind, and the waste of water dimpled and glittered, the broken sparkle of its mimic waves suggesting the ocean after a destructive storm has become a calm. After sailing over broad blue water all day, and passing 'islands' on which the luckier villages were still standing, towards evening we sailed into a village of large farm-houses and made fast to the window-bars of one of them, which, being of brick, had not suffered greatly. Eleven of the farms had disappeared, and others were in process of disappearing. The gardens, farm-yards, and open spaces were under five feet of water, the surface of which

was covered by a bubbly scum. The horses and cattle were in the rooms of the brick houses where many human beings had taken refuge. A raft made of farming implements ferried the people about.

At that farm the skipper bought a quantity of rice for his family, and by a lovely moonlight we sailed over the drowned country to his village. The flood currents were strong, and when we got there we were driven against two undermined houses and knocked them down, afterwards drifting into a road with fine trees which entangled the mast and sail, and our stern bumped down the wall of the road, and the current carried us into a square of semi-submerged houses, and eventually we got into the skipper's garden, and saw his family mounted on tables and chairs on the top of the *kang*.

Two uneventful days followed. The boatmen were in ceaseless dread of pirates, and I was so ill that I felt I would rather die than make another effort.

Arriving within three miles of Mukden, Wong engaged a passenger cart, a conveyance of the roughest description, which is only rendered tolerable by having its back, sides, and bottom padded with mattresses, and I was destitute of everything! Nothing can exaggerate the horrors of an unameliorated Chinese cart on an infamous road. Down into ruts 2 feet deep, out of which three fine mules could scarcely extricate us, over hillocks and big gnarled roots of trees, through quagmires and banked ditches, where, in dread of the awful jerk produced by the mules making a non-simultaneous jump up the farther side, I said to myself, 'This is my last hour,' getting a blow on my head which made me see a shower of sparks—so I entered the gate of the outer wall of beaten clay eleven and a half miles in circuit which surrounds the second city of the empire. Then, through a quagmire out of which we were dragged by seven mules—bruised, breathless, and in great pain, and up a bank where the cart turned over, pulling the mules over with it, and rolling down a slight declivity, I found myself in the roof with the cameras on the top of me and my right arm twisted under me, a Chinese crowd curious to see the 'foreign devil', a vague impress of disaster in my somewhat dazed brain, and Wong raging at large!

Then followed a shady compound ablaze with flowers, a hearty welcome at the house of Dr Ross, the senior missionary of the Scotch UP Church, sweet home-like rooms in a metamorphosed Chinese house, a large shady bedroom replete with comforts, the immediate arrival of Dr Christie, the medical missionary, who pronounced my arm-bone 'splintered' and the tendons severely torn, and placed the limb in splints, and a time of kind and skilled nursing by Mrs Ross, and of dreamy restfulness, in which the horrors of the hold of the 'pea-boat' and of the dark and wind-driven flood only served to emphasize the comfort and propitiousness of my surroundings.

Chapter Nine

The Yangtze Valley and Beyond, 1899

Mrs Bishop's last major journey took her through Sichuan, the richest of the Chinese provinces, in 1896 when she was 65. She travelled up the Yangtze from Yichang to Wanxian through deep gorges and notorious rapids in a flat-bottomed houseboat pulled by sixteen trackers or oarsmen. Although she still faced physical hardship with her usual equanimity, she seems to have grown rather irritable and complains more bitterly about the *lao-pan*'s (boatmaster's) howling baby than of being drenched to the skin in near-freezing weather.

We were in what looked like a mountain lake. No outlet was visible; mountains rose clear and grim against a dull grey sky. Snowflakes fell sparsely, and gently in a perfectly still atmosphere. We cast off from the shore; the oars were plied to a wild chorus; what looked like a cleft in the rock appeared, and making an abrupt turn round a high rocky point in all the thrill of novelty and expectation, we were in the Ichang Gorge, the first and one of the grandest of those gigantic clefts through which the Great River, at times a mile in breadth, there compressed into a limit of from 400 to 150 yards, has carved a passage through the mountains.

The change from a lake-like stretch, with its light and movement, to a dark and narrow gorge black with the shadows of nearly perpendicular limestone cliffs broken up into buttresses and fantastic towers of curiously splintered and weathered rock, culminating in the 'Pillar of Heaven', a limestone pinnacle rising sheer from the water to a height of 1800 feet, is so rapid as to bewilder the senses.

With a strong, fair wind our sail was set; the creak and swish of the oars was exchanged for the low music of the river as it parted under our prow; and the deep water (from 50 to 100 feet), of a striking bottle-green colour, was unbroken by a swirl or ripple, and slid past in a grand, full volume. The stillness was profound, enlivened only as some big junk with lowered mast glided past us at great speed, the fifty or sixty men at the sweeps raising a wild chant in keeping with the scene. Scuds of snow, wild, white clouds whirling round pinnacles, and desolate snow-clothed mountains, apparently blocking further progress, added to the enchantment. Crevices in the rocks were full of maidenhair fern, and on many a narrow

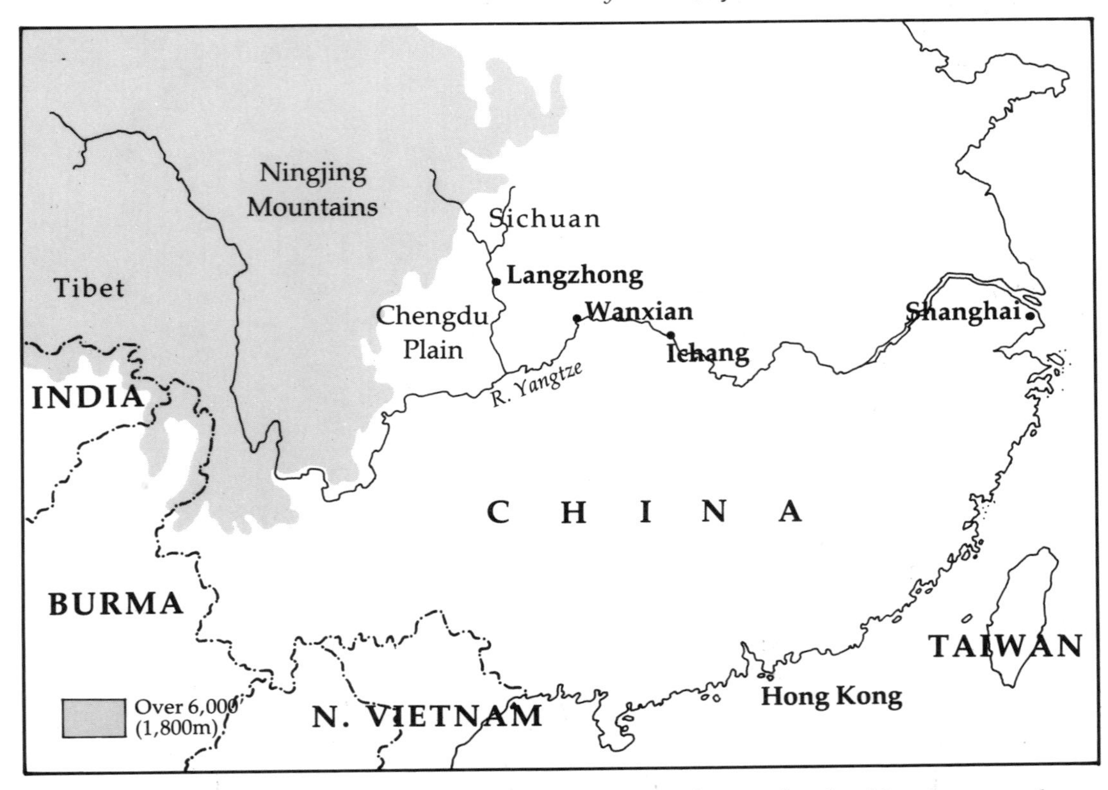

ledge clustered in profusion a delicate mauve primula, unabashed by the grandeur and the gloom. Streams tumbled over ledges at heights of 1000 feet. There are cliffs of extraordinary honeycombed rock, possibly the remains of the 'potholes' of ages since, rock carved by the action of water and weather into shrines with pillared fronts, grottoes with quaint embellishments—gigantic old women gossiping together in big hats—while groups of stalactites constantly occur as straight and thick as small pines, supporting rock canopies festooned with maidenhair. Higher yet, surmounting rock ramparts 2000 feet high, are irregular battlemented walls of rock, perhaps 20 feet thick, and everywhere above and around are lofty summits sprinkled with pines, on which the snow lay in powder only, and 'the snow clouds rolling dun' added to the sublimity of the scenery.

It was always changing, too. If it were possible to be surfeited with turrets, battlements, and cathedral spires, and to weary of rock phantasies, the work of water, of solitudes and silences, and of the majestic dark green flow of the Great River, there were besides lateral clefts, each with its wall-sided torrent, with an occasional platform green with wheat, on which a brown-roofed village nestled among fruit trees, or a mountain, bisected by a chasm, looking ready to fall into the river, as some have already done, breaking up into piles of huge angular boulders, over which even the goat-footed trackers cannot climb. Then, wherever the cliffs are less absolutely perpendicular, there are minute platforms partially sustaining houses with their backs burrowing into the rock, and their fronts extended on beams fixed in the cliff, accessible only by bolts driven into the rock, where the small children are tied to posts to prevent them from falling over, and above, below, and around these dwellings are patches of careful culture, some of them *not larger than a bath towel*, to which the cultivators lower themselves with ropes, and there are small openings occasionally, where deep-eaved houses cluster on the flat tops of rocky spurs among the exquisite plumage of groves of the golden and green bamboo, among oranges and pommeloes with their shining greenery, and straight-stemmed palms with their great fan-like leaves. Already in these sheltered places mauve primulas were blooming amidst a profusion of maidenhair, and withered clusters and tresses showed what the glory of the spring had been and was yet to be when the skirts of these spurs would be aflame with azaleas, and clematis, and great white and yellow roses, and all the wealth of flowers and trailers of which these were only the vestiges.

Another feature was boats large and small, and junks, some laboriously tracked or rowed like my own, when the wind failed, against the powerful stream, or descending, keeping the necessary steerage headway by crowds of standing men on the low deck, facing forwards, vigorously working great sweeps of *yulows*, five or ten at each, the gorge echoing all along its length to the rise and fall of the wild chants to which the rowers keep time and which are only endurable when

softened by distance. After some hours of this region of magic and mystery, near sunset we emerged into open water, with broken picturesque shores, and at dusk tied up in a pebbly bay with glorious views of mountain and woodland, not far from the beautiful village of Nan-to, and the 'needle' or 'pillar' of heaven, well known to the dwellers in Ichang.

I halted for Sunday in this lovely bay, an arrangement much approved of by the trackers, who employed the holiday in washing their clothes, smoking a double quantity of opium, and making a distracting noise, aggravated by the ceaseless yells of the boat baby, yells of an objectionable heredity and undisciplined naughtiness, which at first imposed on my ignorant sympathies. Nevertheless I luxuriated in the quiet which one can obtain when a babel is unintelligible.

On inquiring of Mr Endacott, at Ichang, his ideas of occupation on the upward voyage, his reply was, 'People have enough to do looking after their lives.' Certainly the perils of the rapids are great, and few people of whom I have heard have escaped without risks to life and loss or damage to property, either, like Consul Gardner, finding their boats disappear from under them, or like a missionary, who, coming down with his wife's coffin, came to grief, the coffin taking a lonely and ghastly voyage to a point far below. Signs of disaster abounded. Above and below every rapid, junkmen were encamped on shore under the mats of their junks, and the shore was spread with cotton drying. There were masts

above water, derelicts, partially submerged in quiet reaches, or on some sandy beach being repaired, and gaunt skeletons lay here and there on the rocks which had proved fatal to them. The danger signal is to be seen above and below all the worst rapids in the shape of lifeboats, painted a brilliant red and inscribed with characters in white: showy things, as buoyant as corks, sitting on the raging water with the vexatious complacency of ducks, or darting into the turmoil of scud and foam where the confusion is at its worst, and there poising themselves with the calm fearlessness of a perfect knowledge of every rock and eddy.

I have found that many of the deterrent perils which are arrayed before the

eyes of travellers about to begin a journey are greatly exaggerated, and often vanish altogether. Not so the perils of the Yangtze. They fully warrant the worst descriptions which have been given of them. The risks are many and serious, and cannot be provided against by any forethought. The slightest error in judging of distance on the part of the pilot, any hampering of the bow-sweep, a tow-rope breaking, a submerged boulder changing its place, and many other possibilities, and life and property are at the mercy of a raging flood, tearing downwards at the rate of from seven to eleven miles an hour. I have no personal perils to narrate. A rock twice knocked a hole in the bottom which took a day to repair, and in a

collision our bow-sweep was fractured, which led to a severe quarrel lasting half a day; this was all. I never became used to the rapids, and always felt nervous at the foot of each, and preferred the risk of fracturing my limbs among the great boulders and shining rock faces of the shores to spending hours in a turmoil, watching the fraying of the tow-ropes.

Before starting my boat's crew made offerings and vows at their favourite temples, and on the first evening they slew a fowl as an offering to the river god, and smeared its blood over the bow-sweep and the fore part of the boat. My preparations were to pack my plates, films, and general photographic outfit, journals, a few necessaries, and a few things of fictitious value, in a waterproof bag to be carried by my servant, along with my camera, at each rapid where we landed.

The night at Lao-min-tze was too cold for sleep, and before dawn I heard the wild chant of the boa. We untied at daylight. The river-bed, there 40 feet below its summer level, is an area of heaped, contorted rock-fragments, sharp-edged, through which one or more swirling streams or violent rapids pursue their course, the volume of water, even at that season, being tremendous. At its highest level these upper waters are practically non-navigable. Cliffs, mountain spurs, and noble mountains rise from this chaotic river-bed, and every sharp turn reveals some new beauty. The dark green pine is but a foil to the feathery foliage of the golden bamboo on the steep, terraced sides of tumbled heights; pleasant brown farmhouses are half seen among orange groves and orchards; grand temples, with noble specimens of the *Ficus religiosa* in their grounds, lighten hill and glen sides with their walls of imperial red. Then suddenly the scene changes into one of Tibetan grandeur and savagery, and the mountains approach the river in stupendous precipices, walling in almost fathomless water. We tied up the second night in the last crimson and violet of the sunset, where the river narrowed and progress looked impossible, and crags and pinnacles, snow-covered, rose above the dark precipices.

On that afternoon a red lifeboat suggested the first rapid, the Ta-tan, rather a *chipa* or race than a rapid, though I believe sufficiently perilous at half high water. I landed and scrambled up to the top for a three hours' wait, while three junks, each dragged up by fifty men, came up before mine, boats having to take their turn without favour. Even that ascent was an anxious sight, for sometimes the boat hung, oft-times slipped back, and several times it looked doubtful whether the crowd of men attached to the tow-rope could get her up at all. This was the first sight of the trackers' villages, which are a marked feature of the Yangtze. Each boat carries enough men to pull her up against the strong stream, but at a rapid she needs many more, and during the navigation season coolies from long distances migrate to the river and put up mat huts as close to it as possible, to which dealers in food, tobacco, *samshu*, and opium at once gravitate, along with sellers of bamboo tow-ropes. Nor are rough amusements wanting. Rough, dirty, noisy, these temporary settlements are. Their population is from forty or fifty to over 400 men. When the river rises the huts are removed, and the coolies return to other avocations. At the Hsin-tan rapid my little boat required seventy men, and some of the big junks took on 300 in addition to their crews of 120.

The following day, after being hauled up the Kwa-tung rapid and enjoying superb scenery for some hours, a turn in the river revealed walls of perpendicular rock rising to a colossal height, estimated at from 1000 to 2000 feet, the stupendous chasm of the Niu-kan gorge, to my thinking the grandest and most imposing of all, though a short one, and the same afternoon, in exquisitely brilliant sunshine, we arrived at the foot of the Hsin-tan rapid, then at its worst.

This Hsin-tan in winter is the great bugbear of the Yangtze, the crux of forthcoming steam navigation, a waterfall with a boiling cataract below, a thing of awe and majesty, where the risks, turmoil, bargaining, and noise of the Upper River are centred. This great obstacle, which I wonder that any man even thought of surmounting, was formed about two hundred and fifty years ago by the descent of a rocky mountain-side into the river. It consists of what are three definite falls in the winter-time, the first caused by a great fan-shaped mass of big boulders deposited malignantly by a small stream which enters on the left bank, and the two others by great barriers of rock which lie athwart the river, above the higher of which is a stretch of deep, calm water in peaceful contrast—the Ping-shu gorge. The cataracts extend for over a mile, and the fall is estimated at 20 feet.

Hsin-tan is a wild and beautiful village, and has an air of prosperity. Many junk owners have retired there to spend their days, and the comparative cleanliness and good repair are quite striking. One orange-embowered village on a spur has a temple with a pagoda built out over the edge of the cliff, without any obvious support. A village which might claim to be a town, at a height of fully 400 feet, is not only piled up on terraces, but the houses are built out from the cliff on timbers, and the flights of steps leading from terrace to terrace are so steep that I made no attempt to climb them. The colonnades in the street of shops and eating-houses which projects over the cliff reminded me of Varenna; indeed, there was a suggestion of Italy throughout, under an Italian sky.

I sat on a ledge for two hours, every minute expecting to see my boat move up to the foot of the cataract, but she was immovable. Then we went into a low restaurant, and got some fourth-class Chinese food, and after long bargaining

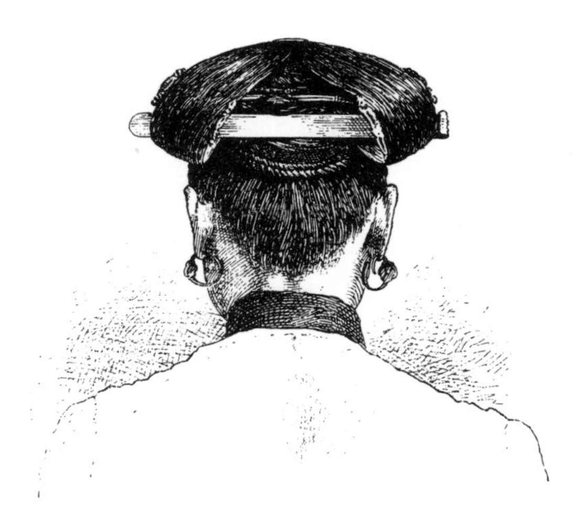

three live fowls and three eggs. Crowds, more curious than rude, pressed upon us, everywhere choking up the balconies and entrances of the eating-house, and asking no end of questions. The men asserted, as they did everywhere on the river, that with my binoculars and camera I could see the treasures of the mountains, the gold, precious stones, and golden cocks which lie deep down in the earth; that I kept a black devil in the camera, and that I liberated him at night, and that he dug up the golden cocks, and that the reason why my boat was low in the water was that it was ballasted with these auriferous fowls, and with the treasures of the hills! They further said that 'foreign devils' with blue and grey eyes could see 3 feet into the earth, and that I had been looking for the root which transmutes the base metals into gold, and this, though according to them I had the treasures of the hills at my disposal! They were quite good-natured, however. . . .

During four hours, only two junks, which had partially discharged their cargoes, effected the ascent, though each of them was dragged up by 400 men. One big junk, after getting half-way up in three hours, jibbed, and though the trackers

were stimulated by gongs and drums beaten frantically, she slowly slipped back to the point from which she started, and was there two days afterwards.

At sunset, taking a boat across the still, strong water above the fall, after having a desperate scramble over boulders of great size, we reached my boat, which was then moored at the side of the cataract in an eddy below the opposite village. The *lao-pan* said we should go up at daylight; and so we did, but it was the daylight of the third morning from that night, and I had ample opportunities for studying the Hsin-tan and its ways.

Miserable nights they were. It was as bad as being in a rough sea, for we were in the swell of the cataract and within the sound of its swish and roar. The boat rolled and pitched; the great rudder creaked and banged; we thumped our neighbours, and they thumped us; there were unholy sounds of tom-toms, the weather relapsed, the wind howled, and above all the angry yells of the boat baby were heard. The splash of a 'sea' came in at my open window and deluged my camp bed, and it was very cold.

The next two days were disagreeable, even in such majestic and exciting surroundings. The boatmen turned us and our servants out at 10 a.m., and we stood about and sat on the great boulders on the bleak mountain-side in a bitterly cold, sunless wind each day till nearly 5, deluded into the belief that our boat would move. A repulsive and ceaseless crowd of men and boys stood above, below, and behind us, though our position was strategically chosen. Mud was thrown and stuck; foul and bad names were used all day by successive crowds. I am hardened to most things, but the odour of that crowd made me uncomfortable. More than 1200 trackers, men and boys, notoriously the roughest class in China, were living in mat huts on the hillside, with all their foul and oft-times vicious accessories. The crowds were coarse and brutal. Could these people ever have come 'trailing clouds of glory'? Were they made in the image of God? Have we 'all one Father'? I asked myself.

A glorious sight the Hsin-tan is as seen from our point of vantage, half-way up the last cataract, a hill of raging water with a white waterfall at the top, sharp, black rocks pushing their vicious heads through the foam, and above, absolute calm. I never saw such exciting water scenes—the wild rush of the cataract; the great junks hauled up the channel on the north side by 400 men each, hanging trembling in the surges, or, as in one case, from a tow-rope breaking, spinning down the cataract at tremendous speed into frightful perils; while others, after a last tremendous effort, entered into the peace of the upper waters. Then there were big junks with masts lashed on their sides, bound downwards, and their passage was more exciting than all else. They come broadside on down the smooth slope of water above, then make the leap bow on, fifty, eighty, even a hundred rowers at the oars and *yulows*, standing facing forwards, and with shrieks and yells pulling for their lives. The plunge comes; the bow and fore part of the deck are lost in foam and spray, emerging but to be lost again as they flash by, then turning round and round, mere playthings of the cataract, but by skill and effort got bow on again in time to take the lesser rapid below. It is a sublime sight. *Wupans* and *sampans*, making the same plunge, were lost sight of altogether in clouds of foam and spray, but appeared again. Red lifeboats, with their smart turbaned crews, dodged in the eddies trim and alert, crowds of half-naked trackers, struggling over the boulders with their 1200 feet of tow-rope, dragged, yelled, and chanted, and from each wild shore the mountains rose black and gaunt into a cold, grey sky.

At this great cataract pilots are necessary. They are competent and respectable, licensed by the authorities, and their high charges, half a dollar for the half-hour which my small boat occupied in going up the fall, and a dollar for the five minutes taken by a big junk on the descent, enable them to live comfortably, and many of

the pretty whitewashed houses of Hsin-tan in the dense shade of orange groves are theirs. They deserve high pay, for it is a most perilous business, involving remarkable nerve and sleight of eye, for a single turn too much or too little of the great bow-sweep, and all would be lost. Every junk which took the plunge over the rock barrier into the furious billows of the cataract below looked bound for destruction. A curious functionary came on board my boat, a well-dressed man carrying a white flag, on which was written, 'Powers of the waters, give a lucky star for the journey.' He stood well forward, waving this flag regularly during the ascent to propitiate the river deities, and the cook threw rice on the billows with the same object. The pilot was a quiet, well-dressed man, giving orders by signals which were promptly obeyed. Indeed, the strict discipline to which these wild boatmen submit in perilous places is remarkable. The *lao-pan* trusted neither his life nor his money to the boat, and he even brought the less valuable possessions of wife and children on shore.

My boat had the twenty-fifth turn, and on the third day of detention she went up with seventy men at the ropes. It was an anxious half-hour of watching from the rocks, but there was no disaster, and I was glad to escape from the brutal crowd, as foul in language as in person, to the quiet of my cabin and the twilight stillness of the Ping-shu gorge. The whole ascent of the Hsin-tan rapids took my boat five hours and forty-five minutes.

No description can convey any idea of the noise and turmoil of the Hsin-tan. I realized it best by my hearing being affected for some days afterwards. The tremendous crash and roar of the cataract, above which the yells and shouts of hundreds of straining trackers are heard, mingled with the ceaseless beating of drums and gongs, some as signals, others to frighten evil spirits, make up a pandemonium which can never be forgotten.

From Wan (Wanxian) she travelled overland in an open chair with only Chinese servants to Liang-shan (Langshang) and from there across the rich Chengtu plain on her way to the high mountains bordering on Tibet—a region and a people she particularly delighted in. She had come to China to see something of the work of the

China Inland Mission, and she experienced some of the dangers to which the men and women of the Mission had exposed themselves. But she had lost much of her former elasticity and the hostility she met obviously fretted her nerves. She also refused to travel unobtrusively as the missionaries did, and continued to ride in an open chair wearing a provocative Japanese sunhat. So her last published work finds her facing that cliché of the Imperialist thriller, the 'howling of an angry Chinese mob'. But the conscientious Fellow of the Royal Geographical Society was not to be deterred from noting the customs and principal manufactures of the region she passes through.

I always objected to halt at a city, but arriving at that of Liang-shan Hsien late on the afternoon of the third day from Wan, it was necessary to get my passport copied. An imposing city it is, on a height, approached by a steep flight of stairs with a sharp turn under a deep picturesque gateway in a fine wall, about which are many picturesque and fantastic buildings. The gateway is almost a tunnel, and admits into a street fully a mile and a half long, and not more than 10 feet wide, with shops, inns, brokers, temples with highly decorated fronts, and Government buildings of sorts along its whole length.

I had scarcely time to take it in when men began to pour into the roadway from every quarter, hooting, and some ran ahead—always a bad sign. I proposed to walk, but the chairmen said it was not safe. The open chair, however, was equally an abomination. The crowd became dense and noisy; there was much hooting and yelling. I recognized many cries of '*Yang kwei-tze!*' (foreign devil) and '*Child-eater!*' swelling into a roar; the narrow street became almost impassable; my chair was struck repeatedly with sticks; mud and unsavoury missiles were thrown with excellent aim; a well-dressed man, bolder or more cowardly than the rest, hit me a smart whack across my chest, which left a weal; others from behind hit me across the shoulders; the howling was infernal: it was an angry Chinese mob. There was nothing for it but to sit up stolidly, and not to appear hurt, frightened, or annoyed, though I was all three.

Unluckily the bearers were shoved to one side, and stumbling over some wicker oil casks (empty, however), knocked them over, when there was a scrimmage, in which they were nearly knocked down. One runner dived into an inn doorway, which the innkeeper closed in a fury, saying he would not admit a foreigner; but he shut the door on the chair, and I got out on the inside, the bearers and porters squeezing in after me, one chair-pole being broken in the crush. I was hurried to the top of a large inn yard and shoved into a room, or rather a dark shed. The innkeeper tried, I was told, to shut and bar the street-door, but it was burst open, and the whole of the planking torn down. The mob surged in 1500 or 2000 strong, led by some *literati*, as I could see through the chinks.

There was then a riot in earnest; the men had armed themselves with pieces of the doorway, and were hammering at the door and wooden front of my room, surging against the door to break it down, howling and yelling. '*Yang-kwei-tze!*' had been abandoned as too mild, and the yells, as I learned afterwards, were such as 'Beat her!' 'Kill her!' 'Burn her!' The last they tried to carry into effect. My den had a second wooden wall to another street, and the mob on that side succeeded in breaking a splinter out, through which they inserted some lighted matches, which fell on some straw and lighted it. It was damp, and I easily trod it out, and dragged a board over the hole. The place was all but pitch-dark, and was full of casks, boards, and chunks of wood. The door was secured by strong wooden bars. I sat down on something in front of the door with my revolver, intending to fire at the men's legs if they got in, tried the bars every now and then, looked through the chinks, felt the position serious—darkness, no possibility of escaping, nothing of humanity to appeal to, no help, and a mob as pitiless as fiends. Indeed, the phrase 'hell let loose' applied to the howls and their inspiration.

They brought joists up wherewith to break in the door, and at every rush—and the rushes were made with a fiendish yell—I expected it to give way. At last the upper bar yielded, and the upper part of the door caved in a little. They doubled their efforts, and the door in another minute would have fallen in, when the joists were thrown down, and in the midst of a sudden silence there was the rush, like a swirl of autumn leaves, of many feet, and in a few minutes the yard was clear, and soldiers, who remained for the night, took up positions there. One of my men, after the riot had lasted for an hour, had run to the *yamen* with the news that the people were 'murdering a foreigner', and the mandarin sent soldiers with orders for the tumult to cease, which he might have sent two hours before, as it can hardly be supposed that he did not know of it.

The innkeeper, on seeing my special passport, was uneasy and apologetic, but his inn was crowded, he had no better room to give me, and I was too tired and shaken to seek another. I was half inclined to return to Wan, but, in fact, though there was much clamour and hooting in several places, I was only actually attacked once again, and am very glad that I persevered with my journey.

Knowing that my safety was assured, I examined what seemed as if it might have been a death-trap, and found it was a lumber-room, black and ruinous, with a garret above, of the floor of which little remained but the joists. My floor was in big holes, with heaps and much rubbish of wood and plaster, and became sloppy in the night from leakage from the roof. There was just clear space enough for my camp-bed. It was very cold and draughty, and after my candle was lighted rows of sloping eyes were perseveringly applied to the chinks on the street side, and two pairs to those on the other side. I should like to have done their owners some harmless mischief!

The host's wife came in to see me, and speaking apologetically of the riot, she said, 'If a foreign woman went to your country, you'd kill her, wouldn't you?' I have since quite understood what I have heard: that several foreign ladies have become 'queer' and even insane as the result of frights received in riots, and that the wife of one British consul actually died as the result. Consul-General Jamieson truly says that no one who has heard the howling of an angry Chinese mob can ever forget it.

The next morning opened in blessed quiet. There was hardly the usual crowd in the inn yard. Carpenters were busy repairing the demolished doorway. A new pole had been attached to my chair by the innkeeper. There were many soldiers in the street, through which I was carried in the rain without my hat. Not a remark was made. Hardly a head was turned. It was so perfectly quiet and orderly that after a time the *fu-tou* suggested that I might put on my hat! The events of the day before would have appeared a hideous dream but that my shoulders were very sore and aching, and that two of the coolies who had been beaten for serving a foreigner bore some ugly traces of it. My nerves were somewhat shaken, and for some weeks I never entered the low-browed gate of a city without more or less apprehension.

Liang-shan is an ancient and striking city. In the long, narrow main street, the houses turn deep-eaved gables, with great horned projections, to the roadway. There are many fine temples with their fronts profusely and elaborately decorated with dragons, divinities, and arabesques in coloured porcelain relief, or in deeply and admirably carved grey plaster, the effect of the latter closely resembling stone. The city manufactures paper from the *Brousonetia papyrifera*, both fine and coarse, printed cottons, figured silks, and large quantities of the imitation houses, horses, men, furniture, trunks, etc., which are burned to an extravagant extent at burials.

When I reached the small town of Siao-kiao I found it greatly crowded with traders, and the innkeepers so unwilling to receive a foreigner that I had to urge my treaty rights, and then was only grudgingly accommodated. There was a very ugly rush, and then a riot, which lasted an hour and a half, at the very beginning of which my *chai-jen* ran away. My door was broken down with much noise and yells of 'Foreign devil!' 'Horse-racer!' 'Child-eater!' but an official arriving in the nick of time, prevented further damage. He ought to have appeared an hour and a half before. These rows are repulsive and unbearably fatiguing after a day's journey, and always delayed my dinner unconscionably, which, as it was practically my only meal in the day, was trying. The entry in my diary for that evening was, 'Wretched evening; riotous crowd; everything anxious and odious; noises; too cold to sleep.' My lamp sputtered and went out, and my matches were too damp to strike. It is objectionable to be in the dark, you know not where, with walls absolutely precarious, and in the midst of the coarse shouts of rough men to hear a feeble accompaniment of rats eating one's few things. I object strongly to a mixed crowd blocking up my doorway or breaking in my door, for every one of the crowd knows better; even the most ignorant coolie knows well that to intrude into a woman's room or in any way violate the privacy which is hers by immemorial usage and rigid etiquette is an outrage for which there is no forgiveness, judging from a Chinese standpoint.

Chapter Ten

Postscript

The Yangtze Valley and Beyond was Mrs Bishop's last book, but not her last journey, and a more appropriate and characteristic conclusion to her career can be pieced together from letters quoted by Anna Stoddart which describe her journey to North Africa in 1901. Neither physical discomfort, nor a servant who was not only incompetent (that she was used to) but disagreeable as well, nor even the shocking condition of the local people could prevent her from once again enjoying herself thoroughly.

I left Tangier and had a severe two days' voyage to Mazagan, where the landing was so terrible, and the sea so wild, that the captain insisted on my being lowered into the boat, by the ship's crane, in a coal basket. The officers and passengers cheered my pluck as the boat mounted a huge breaking surge on her landward adventure. No cargo could be landed. I have never been in a boat in so rough a sea. Before leaving the steamer I had a return of fever; and when the camping-ground turned out to be a soaked ploughed field with water standing in the furrows, and the tent was pitched in a storm of wind and rain, and many of the tent-pegs would not hold, and when the head of my bed went down into the slush when I lay down, I thought I should die there—but I had no more illness or fever! A first night in camp is always trying, but this was chaos, for we had not expected to camp, and had not the necessaries; my servant, Mohammed, the worst I have ever had, is not only ignorant and incompetent, but most disagreeable. After an awful night — during which the heavy wet end of my tent, having broken loose, flapped constantly against my head—things mended. The rain ceased, and when a ground-sheet had native matting over it, the tent looked tolerable. We left with camel, mule, donkey, and horse, after three days, and travelled here, 126 miles, in six days, in very fine weather.

Marakesh is awful; an African city of 80,000 people, the most crowded, noisiest, vilest, filthiest, busiest city I have seen in the world. It terrifies me. It is the great Mohammedan feast, lasting a week, and several thousand tribesmen — sheiks, with their retainers—are here, all armed, mounted on their superb barbs, splendidly caparisoned—men as wild as the mountains and deserts from which they come here to do homage to the Sultan.

I have seen several grand sights—the Sultan in the midst of his brilliant army, receiving the homage of the sheiks, and on another day, similarly surrounded, killing a sheep in memory of Abraham's sacrifice of Isaac, and as an atonement for the sins of the year. I was at the last in Moorish disguise, pure white and veiled, through the good offices of Kaid Maclean [Sir Harry de Vere Maclean, for twenty-five years the generalissimo of the Sultan's army]—a Maclean of Loch Buie in Mull. I have a Moorish house to myself with a courtyard choked with orange-trees in

blossom and fruit. I also have what is a terror to me, a magnificent barb, the property of the Sultan; a most powerful black charger, a huge fellow far too much for me, equipped with crimson trappings and a peaked crimson saddle, 18 inches above his back. I have to carry a light ladder for getting on and off!

With mules, horses, and soldiers, and with Mr Summers as fellow-traveller, I left the din and devilry of Marakesh—as the Sultan's guest—and have been travelling six hours daily since, camping four nights and sleeping two in the castles of these wild tribes till tonight, when we are camped in the fastnesses of the great Atlas range at a height of 1000 feet, in as wild a region as can be imagined. This journey differs considerably from any other and it is as rough as the roughest. I never expected to do such travelling again. You would fail to recognize your infirm friend astride on a superb horse in full blue trousers and a short full skirt, with great brass spurs belonging to the generalissimo of the Moorish army, and riding down

places awful even to think of, where a rolling stone or a slip would mean destruction. In these wild mountains we are among tribes which Rome failed to conquer. It is evidently air and riding which do me good. I never realized this so vividly as now.

This is an awful country, the worst I have been in. The oppression and cruelty are hellish—no one is safe. The country is rotten to the core, eaten up by abominable vices, no one is to be trusted. Every day deepens my horror of its deplorable and unspeakable vileness. Truly Satan's seat is here.

The journey of twenty-one days is over. The last day I rode thirty miles and walked two. Is it not wonderful that even at my advanced age this life should affect me thus? It was a splendid journey; we were entertained everywhere as guests of the Sultan. The bridle tracks on the Atlas are awful—mere rock-ladders, or smooth faces of shelving rock. We lamed two horses, and one mule went over a precipice, rolling over four times before he touched the bottom. We had guides, soldiers, and *slaves* with us. The weather was dry and bracing. Today I had an interview with the Sultan through the good offices of Kaid Maclean. It was very interesting, but had to be very secretly managed, for fear of the fanatical hatred to Christians. I wish it

could have been photographed—the young Sultan on his throne on a high dais, in pure white; the minister of war also in white standing at the right below the steps of the throne; Kaid Maclean in his beautiful Zouave uniform standing on the left and interpreting for me; I was standing in front below the steps of the throne, bare-headed and in black silk, the only European woman who has ever seen an Emperor of Morocco! as I am the first who has ever entered the Atlas Mountains and who has ever visited the fierce Berber tribes. When I wished the Sultan long life and happiness at parting, he said that he hoped when his hair was as white as mine, he might have as much energy as I have! So I am not quite shelved yet! I feel much energy physically while the weather keeps as cool as now, but none mentally — even the writing of a note is a burden—so I have very reluctantly cancelled my engagements for June, and begin a northward journey of five hundred miles to live in tents and ride! I now possess a mule and a camel!

Acknowledgements for Illustrations

Jacket: Front, Mrs Bishop in Manchu dress.
Back, A prisoner in the canque. R. K. Douglas, *China*, 1887
Endpapers: *Thibet, Mongolia and Mandchouria*. Tallis map c. 1850
Frontispiece: Mrs Bishop in Manchu dress.
Title page: American Lady's Mountain Dress. Title page of *A Lady's Life in the Rocky Mountains*

Page	Description and Source
4	Mrs Bishop (Isabella Lucy Bird). Frontispiece to vol. 1 of *Journeys in Persia and Kurdistan*
9	Boroughbridge Hall, Yorkshire, where Isabella Lucy Bird was born. Anna M. Stoddart, *The Life of Isabella Bird*, 1906
10L	Mrs Edward Bird, Mrs Bishop's mother. *The Life of Isabella Bird*
10R	The Rev. Edward Bird, Mrs Bishop's father. *The Life of Isabella Bird*
13	Mrs Bishop in her travelling dress at Erzeroum, Armenia, 1890. *The Life of Isabella Bird*
18	Dr Bishop. *The Life of Isabella Bird*
19	Mrs Bishop in a Japanese straw cloak. *Unbeaten Tracks in Japan*
20T	Trackers preparing to meet Mrs Bishop at a Chinese inn, 1895. Photograph by Mrs Bishop
20B	Bridge and Inn of Shan-rang-sar, China, 1896. *The Yangtze Valley and Beyond*
23	Mrs Bishop in later life. Photograph by Elliott and Fry. Frontispiece to *The Life of Isabella Bird*
27T	Mrs Bishop about to photograph a group of Chinese at Swatow, 1895. Photograph by Mr Mackenzie
27M	Mrs Bishop (right) with her tent on her ride amongst the Bakhtiari Lurs in Persia, 1890. *The Life of Isabella Bird*
27B	Mrs Bishop's sampan on the Han River, Korea, 1894. Photograph by Mrs Bishop. *The Life of Isabella Bird*
28L	The author's trackers at dinner. *The Yangtze Valley and Beyond*
28R	The author's boat. Photograph by Mrs Bishop. *The Yangtze Valley and Beyond*
30	Mrs Bishop in Tangier, 1901, on her last trip abroad: 'I am taking for rest photography, embroidery and water-colours.' *The Life of Isabella Bird*
31	Study from life. Theodore Roosevelt, *Ranch Life and the Hunting Trail*, 1896
32T	Train motif. Henry Brainard Kent, *Graphic Sketches of the West*, 1890
32B	Wild turkeys. Grenville Mellen, *A Book of the United States*, 1839

Acknowledgements

The editor gratefully acknowledges the help and co-operation of the following Institutions and persons.

Estes Park Public Library, Estes Park, Colorado (and in particular Ms Lennie Bemiss, Local History Librarian); the Bodleian Library; the Royal Geographical Society; the Royal Scottish Geographical Society; John Murray Ltd., publishers, for permission to quote from original letters in their possession (and in particular, Mrs Murray, archivist); the Public Record Office.

To Jennifer Drake-Brockman I owe an especial debt of gratitude: without her this book would not have been written. At the Open University my thanks are due in particular to Wendy Macey for her typing, and to Ena Halmos and Angus Calder for their interest and encouragement.

And to Nick Havely my thanks are also and always due, not only for the many improvements he contributed to the manuscript, but for being the companion of so many of my own best journeys.

C.A.P.H.
The Open University, 1984

Bibliography

Works by Isabella L. Bird (Mrs Bishop)

(Dates of first editions are given)

An Englishwoman in America (John Murray, London, 1856)
Six Months in the Sandwich Islands (John Murray, London, 1875)
A Lady's Life in the Rocky Mountains (John Murray, London, 1879) [Repr. Virago Travellers 1982]
Unbeaten Tracks in Japan (John Murray, London, 1880) [Repr. Virago Travellers 1984]
The Golden Chersonese and the Way Thither (John Murray, London, 1883) [Repr. Century Travellers 1983]
Journeys in Persia and Kurdistan (John Murray, London, 1891)
Among the Tibetans (Religious Tract Society, London, 1894)
Korea and her Neighbours (John Murray, London, 1898)
The Yangtze Valley and Beyond (John Murray, London, 1899)
Chinese Pictures (Cassell, London, 1900)

Biographies

Anna M. Stoddart, *The Life of Isabella Bird (Mrs Bishop)* (John Murray, London, 1906)
Dorothy Middleton, 'Isabella Bird' in *Victorian Lady Travellers* (Routledge & Kegan Paul, London, 1965)
Pat Barr, *A Curious Life for a Lady: The Story of Isabella Bird* (Macmillan, John Murray, London, 1970) [Repr. Secker & Warburg 1984]
Luree Miller, 'English Lady Travellers: Isabella Bird Bishop' in *On Top of the World: Five Women Explorers in Tibet* (Paddington Press, London, 1976)

Index

First published in 1984
by Century Publishing Co. Ltd,
Portland House,
12–13 Greek Street, London W1V 5LE

Bird, Isabella L.
This grand beyond.
1. Bird, Isabella L. 2. Travellers——Great
Britain——Biography
I. Title II. Havely, Cicely
910.4'092'4 G246.B5

ISBN 0 7126 0392 1

Book design by Bob Hook
Picture Research by Charlotte Ward-Perkins

Photoset by Deltatype
Ellesmere Port, Cheshire
Printed in Great Britain in 1984 by
Butler & Tanner Ltd, Frome, Somerset

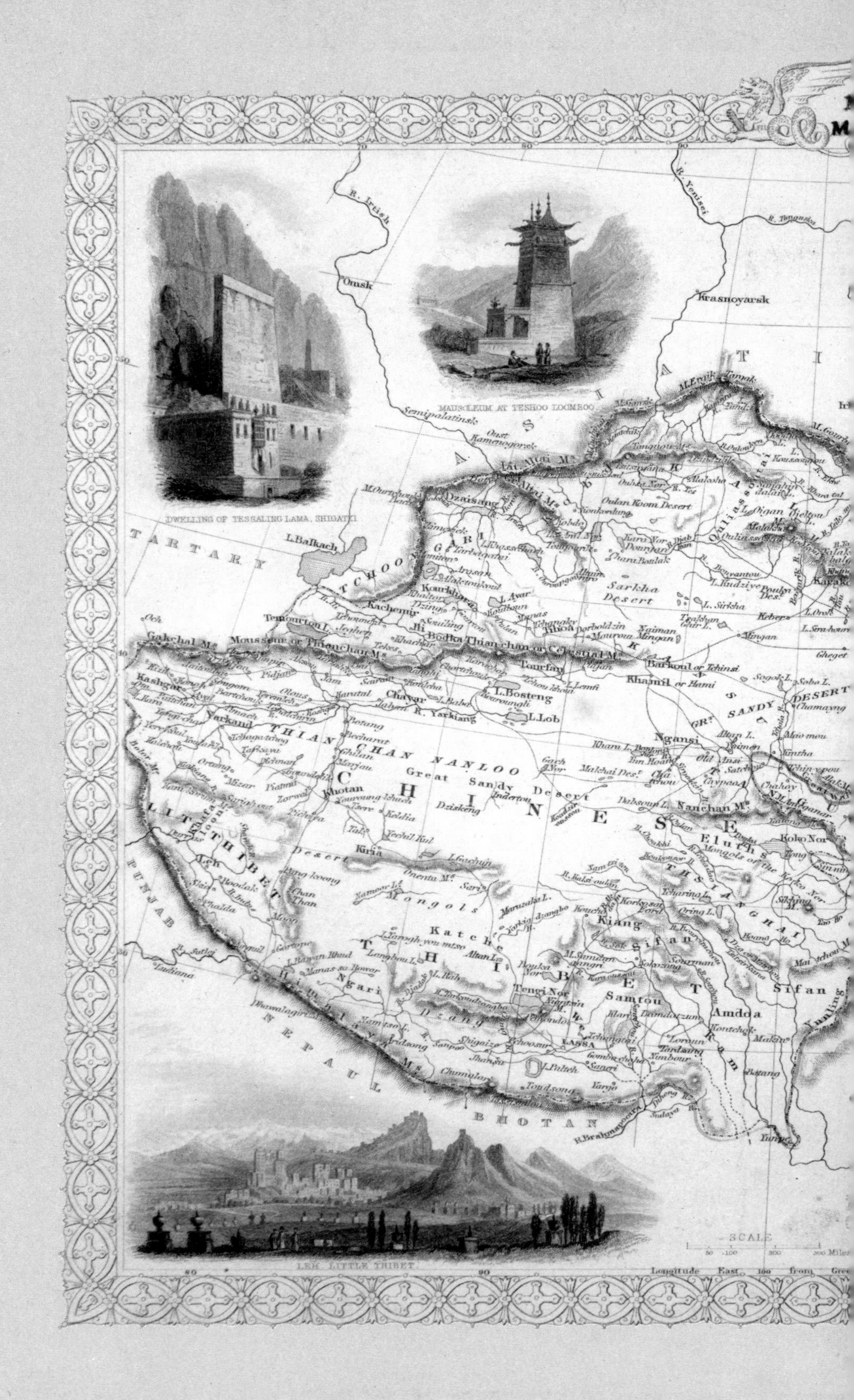

DWELLING OF TESSALING LAMA, SHIGATZI

MAUSOLEUM AT TESHOO LOOMBOO

LEH, LITTLE THIBET

Champneys Cookbook

ADAM PALMER

WITH PHOTOGRAPHS BY MARTIN BRIGDALE

BOXTREE

Acknowledgements

Thanks are due to Paula Gilbert, the Champneys dietician since 1988. Paula has coordinated the analysis of the recipes in this book and works closely with Adam and his team to advise on new dietary ideas and discuss menus.

Thanks also to Tanya and Allan Wheway, Joint Managing Directors, and to Gillie Turner, Deputy General Manager; Helena Champion, Consultant Nutritionist; Christopher McLean, Sous Chef; Ian Bamford, Chef Tournant; Jeremy Ginn, Chef de Partie; Edward Turner, Chef de Partie, and Martin Turner, for their invaluable help in producing this book.

First published in 1993
by Boxtree Limited
Broadwall House
21 Broadwall
London SE1 9PL
United Kingdom

1 3 5 7 9 10 8 6 4 2

Styling by Cherry Ramseyer
with special thanks to Villeroy & Boch Tableware Ltd
and other manufacturers for providing tableware

Designed by David Rowley Design

Edited by Anness Publishing

Colour reproduction in Hong Kong by Fotographics

Typeset by SX Composing Ltd, Rayleigh, Essex

Printed and bound in Great Britain by Butler & Tanner, Frome

A CIP catalogue record for this book is available from the British Library.

ISBN 1-85283-407-2

Contents

The Champneys Approach – a wholesome balance

WHEN Champneys started in 1925, the notion of promoting health was considered an oddity. Today, health is a word on everyone's lips, in every magazine, even on restaurant menus and the packages of many of the foods we buy. It has become an industry. Although this rise marks a vast improvement in people's eating habits, there are two risks: that we become blasé through overexposure and – an even greater danger – that we are swamped by an excess of conflicting advice.

Through all the fads and fashions, Champneys has consistently maintained and developed its straightforward approach to positive health through balanced eating. It has avoided extremes and concentrated on the gentler philosophy of moderation, common sense and enjoyment of food that anyone who has stayed at Champneys will have experienced firsthand in our restaurant.

Many people tend to think of healthy eating as a minefield of dos and don'ts, but food should be seen as something to be enjoyed as well as being good for you. Weight, shape and good health depend on what people eat and how much exercise they take. Using this book can help you to get the balance right. All the recipes have been specially created by our chef, Adam Palmer, and written in easy-to-follow stages. They cater for every occasion. Some can be made in a few minutes, while some are more complex and sophisticated dishes. There are many exciting new recipes to encourage a varied diet and also traditional favourites made with all the flavour, but using less fat and sugar.

Most of the recipes are designed to give four servings, but many can be adapted for smaller or larger quantities by decreasing or increasing all the ingredients accordingly. Calories per serving and basic nutritional information are given for each recipe, enabling you to plan a well-balanced diet. If you are on a weight-loss diet, we suggest you simply serve yourself smaller portions. Although many of the dishes are low in calories, there are also plenty for those who are not planning to lose weight. What the recipes have in common is that they are for people who want to be healthy, but who still want to enjoy their food. There is no secret to healthy eating, just the sensible application of some simple guidelines. Adopt them and you will soon start to feel better and lead a healthier, fuller life.

Ingredients

Fresh ingredients are always better than their frozen, tinned or otherwise processed counterparts. Of course, fresh foods are usually more expensive and often more trouble to prepare, but they are worth it. At Champneys, we believe the fresher the better, and many of the vegetables served in the restaurant are grown in our own kitchen garden. If you have a garden, the time and space, you may like to try growing some of your own vegetables too – it's an interesting and rewarding activity, as well as being good for you! At Champneys we use only fresh produce, but if a fresh ingredient eludes you,

Champneys health resort, set among beautiful grounds, is renowned for its elegance and style.

remember that frozen food often maintains more of its essential nutrients than other forms of processed food.

Eating a variety of foodstuffs is also important. This not only ensures a balanced intake of all the necessary nutrients, but also makes mealtimes so much more interesting. Some weight-loss diets in particular lack the variety to keep their adherents healthy and so should be avoided. If you eat properly you should not need vitamin supplements, especially if you make a point of not peeling vegetables and fruit unless it is necessary (many nutrients are in the skin or immediately beneath it). However, if you often eat vegetables that are cooked for a long time before you eat them and therefore subject to high vitamin loss, or if you smoke or drink regularly, are in ill health or pregnant, you may require a general multivitamin.

Quantities

The single biggest eating problem that we encounter at Champneys, and one that is so often ignored or overlooked, is that many of us simply eat too much. When shopping and preparing foods, gauge quantities carefully. Make serving the right quantity a part of presentation: a well-arranged plate is so much more attractive than one piled high. No meal should leave you feeling bloated: small, regular meals are better for you than large, occasional ones as they will keep your metabolic rate raised. Eat slowly. If you know you are going to eat a large meal – in a restaurant, or away from home where you are not in control of portions – try to compensate by cutting down the day before, which is much better than cutting down the day after, although this may not always be practicable.

High Fibre

Dietary fibre is essential in maintaining a healthy metabolism. It helps avoid constipation and other related Western diseases, such as haemorrhoids, varicose veins, diverticulitis and appendicitis. As well as being good for our digestive systems, fibre may also lower the amount of cholesterol in the blood. In addition, it helps us eat less calorie- or fat-rich food because its bulk fills us up. Choose wholewheat bread, flour and pasta and brown rice rather than their white counterparts. Pulses also offer high fibre and should appear regularly in your meals: lentils, split peas, kidney beans and so on. You may feel a little bloated if you eat more of these foods, but your digestion will soon adapt to the higher fibre intake. Ensure you soak and cook pulses properly, especially kidney beans, to prevent this occurring.

High Activity

Eating good, balanced meals every day is a vital step towards optimum health; regular exercise is another. However, when adding adequate exercise to your busy schedule, remember that an increase in physical activity means that you may need to increase your calorie intake to meet your additional energy expenditure. The best way to do this is to increase starch-based foods, such as bread, potatoes, pasta and rice. Do not eat a full meal immediately before or after exercising. Instead, choose a high-fibre, high-starch snack such as a banana, a slice of malt loaf, or wholewheat toast with sugar-free jam and no butter or margarine. (The fibre content controls the release of energy.) A little liquid before and after exercising is recommended. Select from tea, especially herb or fruit tea, decaffeinated coffee, skimmed milk drinks, diluted fruit juice or non-carbonated mineral water. Best of all is cool water. Remember that most people don't drink enough; aim for at least eight glasses of liquid per day.

Low Fat

Traditionally, diets have been measured by the number of calories consumed. Increasingly, however, the significance of calories is being replaced by that of fat. Too much fat – and most of us consume far too much – means an excess of calories as well as an increased risk of high blood cholesterol, high blood pressure and heart disease. Using the recipes in this book regularly should help you reduce your fat consumption, but in addition be aware of the fat content of all foods and control your fat intake carefully. Mono- and unsaturated oils are by far the best, e.g. olive, sesame and walnut. Olive-oil based margarines are actually better than poly- or saturated fat spreads and butter, and skimmed milk and low-fat cheeses are preferable to full-fat dairy products. As you will discover in this book, a wise option for making sauces is the use of low-fat yoghurt or *fromage frais* in place of the traditional cream and butter. Another good way to reduce your fat intake is to trim the skin and fat from poultry and red meat, or better still choose lower-fat options to red meat: venison and game, for example, or even the non-meat alternatives such as pulses. Remember that offal is inclined to be high in cholesterol and may have to be avoided by those suffering from high blood cholesterol. If you like gravy with your meat, add a few ice cubes before you finish cooking it. These attract the fat and can be immediately removed. When you put jam on bread or scrambled eggs on toast, the moistness of the topping means that you don't need the addition of a layer of butter or margarine. Finally, not all fats are bad for you! The oils in some fish, such as tuna, salmon and trout, have been proved to have beneficial qualities, and are believed to provide protection from coronary heart disease, as well as being a valuable source of calcium.

Low Salt

Most of us consume excessive amounts of salt in our food – this is especially true if you eat a lot of processed foods – and our palates have grown accustomed to high salt levels. Preparing our own fresh food has the additional value of allowing us to choose how much salt we add during cooking. Adding salt at the table is often no more than a habit we should curb. Too much salt is inclined to influence water retention and can be a cause of hypertension (high blood pressure).

Low Sugar

Refined sugar contains little more than calories. Honey is a more acceptable sweetener as it not only contains some useful minerals, but also fewer calories than sugar. Similarly, dried, fresh or frozen fruits make nutritious alternative sweeteners. Remember that processed drinks as well as food often contain high levels of sugar (as well as other unhealthy additives). Artificial sweeteners such as aspartame have negligible calories and are not dangerous to health in small amounts. If used in cooking, to sweeten stewed fruit, the flavour is better if added at the end.

Low Alcohol

For most of us small amounts of alcohol are a perfectly acceptable part of a healthy diet. Apart from being very enjoyable, a *little* wine can actually contribute to health by improving your circulation. However, remember that alcohol is high in calories, and that it should be treated with extreme caution if you are trying to lose weight. Although low-alcohol or alcohol-free wine is increasingly popular, it is not necessarily any lower in calories than its alcoholic equivalent. A better way of reducing both alcoholic and calorific intake is to make sure your wine glass contains a high proportion of mineral water. Don't shy away from cooking with wine: it can improve the flavour of a dish and heating to boiling point causes the alcohol and some calories to evaporate, leaving just the taste.

Appearances are important!

How food is presented is vital to its success. If a dish looks appetizing, it is far more likely to taste good! The photographs in this book will give you ideas on how to present the dishes, but do use your imagination and experiment. Bear in mind all the elements that influence the appearance of your dish: the colour, texture and shape (if any) of the food itself; the table setting, décor and flowers; the occasion; the available garnishes, and even the plate on which the dish will be served. When using flowers for garnishing, first establish that they are not poisonous and that they have not been sprayed with anything toxic. Roses, violets, nasturtiums, marigolds and borage are all fine, as long as they are washed carefully.

Special Diets

If you are taking medication or have any health concerns it is wise to consult your doctor before embarking on a diet.

Anaemia Sufferers

It is important to take a source of vitamin C with all meals to aid iron absorption. This could take the form of a glass of tomato juice, some fresh orange juice, a couple of kiwi fruits or even new potatoes cooked in their skins.

Arthritis Sufferers

To help relieve the pain associated with arthritis, it is advisable to avoid citrus fruits, red meat and raw tomatoes.

Gluten-free diets

Coeliac disease or grain allergy force some people to adopt a diet that is free of gluten, a constituent of wheat, rye, barley and oats. Wheat allergy can cause such symptoms as abdominal bloating, discomfort and weight gain. Avoiding wheat is actually quite difficult, as flour is used in a high proportion of dishes and processed foods, for example as a thickener – it can even be found in baked beans! When cooking gluten-free, remember that you should use cornflour or cornstarch, or arrowroot rather than conventional thickening agents.

As Master of Cuisine at Champneys, Adam Palmer creates a truly innovative range of delicious, exotic yet healthy dishes.

Vegetarian Diets

There has been a well-publicized move towards vegetarianism over recent years and health has been one of the main motives. From the vegan, who eats no meat, fish or dairy products, to the 'occasional' meat eater, there are many shades of vegetarianism. As a reaction against the standard Western diet many people are now lowering their meat consumption, which is definitely a move in the right direction. Animal products generally contain high proportions of saturated fats as well as protein, and we are inclined to consume too much of both of them. However, to say that vegetarianism is healthy is a dangerous generalization. It can be, so long as you ensure that your diet gives you the wide variety of nutrients that you need. Bear in mind that dairy products can contain even more saturated fat and protein than meat. If you do decide to go vegan, ensure that you eat enough protein; you need 2 sources of vegetable protein in each meal. A variety of vegetables, grains, fruit and nuts can give you all the necessary vitamins and minerals to keep you healthy, but may not give you adequate calcium, iron or vitamins D and B_{12}. Remember that lacto-vegetarian cooking is inclined to be high in calories, especially when ingredients like full-fat cheese and nuts are used in large quantities.

Most of us obtain our calcium from dairy products, but the alternative sources, although not as rich, are nuts, pulses, green leafy vegetables, figs and hard water. Vegans are recommended to drink vegetable milk fortified with calcium. Iron is abundantly present in meat and offal, but alternatives include green leafy vegetables, pulses, seeds, eggs and dried apricots. Vitamin C aids the absorption of iron, as described in the section for anaemics above. Vitamin D is obtained from sunlight, so in winter or during a typical British summer this may need to be supplemented with foods rich in the vitamin. Most of us can obtain it from oily fish, eggs and yoghurt, but vegans may have to rely on fortified foods, such as some margarines and breakfast cereals. Vitamin B_{12} is present in eggs and dairy products, so vegans should take care to have this in the form of yeast extracts, soya milk or some breakfast cereals fortified with B_{12}.

Weight-loss Diets

If your diet is for the purpose of losing weight, it is important to decide at the start how much you plan to lose over a particular period of time and to make these aims realistic. Rather than rely on charts that show what your weight should be in proportion to your height, it is sometimes better to aim for a weight suitable for your age, based on your starting weight at 18 years old if you felt happy with this weight. To lose 450 g/1 lb you will need to reduce your calorific intake by 3500 per week. A good guideline is to aim to lose 1-1.15 kg/2-2½ lb a week, which means that if your normal daily intake is 2000 calories, you will need to reduce this to 1000. It is important to remember that the more slowly you lose weight, the more likely you are to maintain the loss. Once you have reached your target weight, a good way to prevent the weight from coming back on is to maintain your special diet effectively from Monday to Thursday or Friday and then eat normally over the weekend.

Men are inclined to lose weight at a steadier and faster rate than women, due to their lower percentage of body fat and the lack of hormonal influences. Women, after losing weight steadily, will often reach a 'plateau' for 3 or 4 days when their weight remains the same. Although this is dispiriting for even the most determined dieter, it is often only a temporary halt, simply due to fluid fluctuations. Do not give up – the weight should then start to fall again.

Many of the recipes in this book can be incorporated in a weight-loss diet and the calorific value of each dish is indicated. We base our recipes on a daily energy intake of 1000 calories for women and 1200 for men. It is important to establish good eating habits at the start of your diet and to maintain them even after you have completed it and reached your target weight.

You will lose weight more easily if you cut out alcohol altogether during your diet, but many people find this difficult to do. Cut down by drinking single measures rather than doubles, or by alternating between alcohol and a low-calorie non-alcoholic alternative, and reserve at least 2 alcohol-free days a week.

A simple way to help you lose weight, as well as helping to keep you healthy, is to make sure that you drink plenty of water. Between 1-1.5 litres/1¾-2½ pints – 3¾-6½ cups is the recommended daily intake and many people fail to drink this quantity. Water taken with meals not only aids digestion but also has the effect of filling you up and limiting your appetite. Clear soup acts in much the same way, but avoid the accompanying bread roll. Also, remember to take time to enjoy your food – by eating slowly you will often satisfy your hunger before you have finished everything on your plate.

Avoiding the baddies

Many people suffer cravings for foods that are bad for them. This often occurs mid-afternoon, when a drop in blood sugar level has people reaching for fattening foods. Chocolate is among the most common of these. The craving may not only be for the obvious sugar content of the chocolate, but also for the stimulant caffeine. Caffeine contains a chemical called theobromine which gives chocoholics the buzz they seek. Giving up chocolate can be difficult and the healthy alternative of fresh fruit is rarely an acceptable substitute for serious addicts, so some self-discipline is required. Bananas may be a good 'non-fattening' alternative and each one will keep blood sugar levels up for approximately 4 hours while being only 15 calories more than an apple.

The Champneys Way
Sensible eating as part of a healthy lifestyle

In 1925, Stanley Lief, a Russian Jew who had trained in naturopathy in the United States, bought the estate of Champneys and turned it into England's first health resort. Lief had had remarkable success, treating patients suffering from ailments that traditional medicine had failed to cure. Champneys was soon discovered by British society and Lief was lionized as the new leader of alternative medicine in this country.

The secret of Lief's success may have been simpler than anyone suspected at the time. In the 1920s the rich and leisured classes who came to Champneys knew nothing of healthy eating. They consumed too much of everything, especially sugars and fats, resulting in a whole range of diseases, from depression and nervous ailments to skin diseases, asthma, colitis, peptic ulcers and coronary heart disease, and there were few of the drugs that are available today to treat these conditions. A key element of the naturopathic philosophy is fasting and today it is thought that many of Stanley Lief's 'miracle cures' of the 1920s and 1930s may have been attributable to an improvement in health brought about by simply denying patients their customary excesses.

Together with sensible eating, the Champneys way advises an overall healthy lifestyle, including having proper exercise, learning and using strategies to cope with stress and developing a positive approach to life. As well as being a wonderful experience, staying at Champneys is not an isolated holiday away from bad habits, but the start of a new, improved lifestyle for all our guests.

The first Champneys cookbook was published in 1987 in response to many requests for recipes from guests who wanted to cook dishes served in our restaurant in their own homes. Its success and enquiries about new recipes have inspired this new issue. The Champneys team, and especially chef Adam Palmer, wish you happy cooking, *bon appétit* and the very best of health.

Cold starters provide a wide range of light and healthy dishes from simple salads of Asparagus and Potato Mayonnaise to the exotic flavours of Salmon and Leek Mousse with Salmon Roe Sauce, and Chicken, Venison and Wild Mushroom Terrine. Choose colours, textures and garnishes appropriate to the meal.

Lobster and Red Pepper Mousse

4 red peppers
2 dsp olive oil
2 shallots, chopped
2 medium tomatoes, roughly chopped
2 tsp raspberry vinegar
6 sheets gelatine
550 g/1¼ lb whole cooked lobster
400 ml/14 fl oz/¾ cup natural, low-fat *fromage frais*

Vinaigrette
2 very ripe tomatoes
2 dsp white wine vinegar
75 ml/3 fl oz/⅓ cup olive oil
sea salt and freshly milled black pepper

Garnish
4 sprigs chervil (optional)

Serves 4

Chop 3 of the red peppers into rough dice. Heat a dessertspoon of the olive oil in a small frying pan (skillet) and sweat the peppers and shallots until the shallots are translucent. Add the roughly chopped tomatoes and the raspberry vinegar and reduce by half over a high heat. Remove from the heat.

Meanwhile, cover the sheet gelatine with cold water and leave to soften for approximately 5 minutes. Remove from the water with your hand and squeeze out any excess liquid, then place the gelatine in a small heatproof bowl over a pan of barely simmering water. Leave until the gelatine has melted and turned transparent.

Thoroughly stir the gelatine into the contents of the pan, then transfer the mixture to a food processor or blender and blend thoroughly. Press through a fine sieve into a clean bowl and leave to cool.

Remove the tail flesh and claw flesh from the lobster. Cut the tail meat into thin collops and reserve for garnishing. Chop up the claw meat and add the red pepper purée, then fold in the *fromage frais* and lightly season. Spoon the mixture into 4 ramekins and leave in the refrigerator for at least 2 hours to set.

To make the vinaigrette, put the tomatoes and the vinegar in a food processor or blender, lightly season and blend until smooth. Add the olive oil, pass through a fine sieve and check the seasoning. Correct the consistency with a little water if the dressing is too thick.

Peel the remaining pepper and cut into fine dice; reserve for garnishing..

To serve, place a quarter of the lobster collops in the centre of each plate to form a bed. Briefly plunge each ramekin up to the rim in hot water, invert and place a mousse on top of the collops. Spoon round diced peppers and tomato vinaigrette and top with a sprig of chervil, if liked.

Fat: high Kcals: 405 Cholesterol: medium Fibre: medium

Clockwise, from top: *Asparagus and Potato Mayonnaise, Crab, Beetroot and Apple Salad, and Lobster and Red Pepper Mousse*

Crab, Beetroot and Apple Salad

½ cooked beetroot (beet)
1 tbsp clear honey
3 tbsp cider vinegar
1 green apple
1 red apple
1 bunch chives, half finely chopped, half cut into batons
1 tbsp extra virgin olive oil
juice of 1 lime
225 g/8 oz white crab meat
3 tbsp natural, low-fat *fromage frais*
sea salt and freshly milled black pepper

Garnish
4 sprigs chervil

Serves 4

Square off the beetroot and cut into neat batons, reserving the trimmings. Purée the trimmings with the honey and cider vinegar in a food processor or blender and squeeze through a fine sieve. Reserve the juice for a dressing.

Chop the apples into small dice, leaving on the peel. Mix the puréed beetroot with half the chopped chives and half the apple then stir in a tablespoon of olive oil, the lime juice and the crab meat.

To serve, push a quarter of the crab meat mixture into a 6 cm/2½ in circular pastry cutter, pressing down firmly, and place in the centre of the plate. Carefully remove the cutter and repeat for each serving. Season the *fromage frais* and spread on top of each crab circle. Arrange beetroot batons around the crab, crisscross with chive batons, garnish with chervil. Whisk the remaining olive oil with the beetroot juice and pour over the crab.

Fat: medium Kcals: 165 Cholesterol: medium Fibre: low

Asparagus and Potato Mayonnaise

350 g/12 oz potatoes, roughly chopped
½ tsp truffle oil
3 fresh basil leaves
juice of 1 lemon
4 tbsp extra virgin olive oil
28 asparagus spears
2 truffles, sliced
sea salt and freshly milled white pepper

Serves 4

Boil the potatoes in a little salted water until soft. Drain, then place in a food processor or liquidizer with the truffle oil, basil and lemon juice and process until smooth. Slowly add the olive oil, drop by drop, with the machine turned on. Adjust the seasoning with salt and white pepper to taste. Place the mayonnaise in the refrigerator to cool.

Cut away the woody ends from the asparagus spears and trim to the same length; the stalks of older, fatter asparagus will need to be thinly peeled. Tie into 4 bundles of 7 and blanch in boiling water for 3 minutes. Refresh under cold running water, then drain. Leave to cool.

To serve, place a bundle of asparagus in the centre of each plate and discard the strings. Spoon over a little mayonnaise and top with a few slices of truffle.

Fat: high Kcals: 235 Cholesterol: low Fibre: medium

Chicken Leek Mousse with Beetroot Salad

- 10 baby leeks, blanched and cut into strips
- 2 × 170g/6 oz breasts of corn-fed chicken, skinned, boned and trimmed
- 575 ml/20 fl oz/2½ cups chicken stock (see page 138)
- 3 sheets gelatine
- 2 tbsp natural, low-fat *fromage frais*
- 1 small beetroot (beet), cooked and cut into 2.5 cm/1 in batons, reserving trimmings
- 2 tbsp cider vinegar
- 1 tbsp extra virgin olive oil
- 1 bunch chives, cut into 2.5 cm/1 in batons
- sea salt and chilli pepper

Serves 4

Line 4 ramekins with strips of leek. Poach the chicken breasts in the stock in a covered pan for 10 minutes.

Meanwhile, cover the sheet gelatine with cold water and leave to soften for approximately 5 minutes. Remove from the water with your hand and squeeze out any excess liquid, then place the gelatine in a small heatproof bowl. Put the bowl into a pan of barely simmering water and leave until the gelatine has melted and turned transparent.

Transfer the cooked chicken breasts to a food processor or blender, add the *fromage frais*, seasonings and the gelatine and process until smooth. Press through a fine sieve and spoon the mousse into the ramekins. Leave in the refrigerator for 1 hour.

To make the dressing, liquidize the beetroot trimmings with the cider vinegar and the olive oil in a liquidizer or food processor.

To serve, plunge the base of each ramekin up to the rim into hot water for 30 seconds and then turn out into the centre of each plate, arrange the beetroot (beet) batons and chives around, and spoon over the dressing.

Fat: medium Kcals: 134 Cholesterol: low Fibre: low

Sardine and Red Onion Terrine

- 900 g/2 lb fresh sardines, filleted and washed
- 2 tbsp wholemeal flour
- 2 large red onions, sliced
- 3 tbsp extra virgin olive oil
- 4 tbsp red wine vinegar

Sauce
- 1 tbsp capers
- 1 tbsp pickled gherkin slices
- 1 tbsp black olives, pitted
- sea salt and freshly milled black pepper

Serves 14

Lightly flour the sardine fillets and season with salt and pepper.

Sauté the sliced onion in a pan with 1 tablespoon of the olive oil over a low heat for 5 minutes until golden brown. Deglaze with 1 tablespoon of the vinegar. Remove the onion mixture from the pan and set aside. In the same pan, heat 2 tablespoons of the olive oil until smoking, then quickly fry the floured fillets until golden brown.

Line a 1.1 litre/2 pint/5 cup terrine with cling film or plastic wrap and place a layer of fillets on the base, followed by a layer of onions. Continue the layers until the terrine is full. Pour over the remaining vinegar, wrap cling film or plastic wrap over the top and press with a heavy weight or dish filled with cold water for at least 3 hours in the refrigerator.

Liquidize the capers, gherkin slices and olives in a liquidizer or food processor together with the remaining olive oil. Invert the terrine onto a dish or board, remove the plastic and cut into 2 cm/¾ in slices. Serve with the sauce.

Fat: medium Kcals: 135 Cholesterol: medium Fibre: low

Mackerel, Rhubarb and Mange-Tout Terrine

4 new potatoes
2 pinches saffron powder
wholemeal flour, for coating
16 × 85 g/3 oz fillets of mackerel
1 tbsp extra virgin olive oil
10 sticks rhubarb
170 g/6 oz/1 cup mange-tout (sugar snap peas), blanched
juice of 1 lemon
3 tbsp red wine vinegar
150 ml/¼ pt/⅔ cup white wine
1 tbsp clear honey
4 chives, chopped
sea salt and freshly milled black pepper

Serves 14

Preheat the oven to 150°C/300°F/gas 2. Line a 1.1 litre/2 pint/5 cup terrine with greaseproof (wax) paper. Leave the skins on the potatoes and cut into thin slices. Cook in lightly salted water with a pinch of saffron powder. Drain and leave to cool.

Season the flour, and use to coat the mackerel fillets. Heat the olive oil in a pan then fry the fillets for about 3 minutes until nearly cooked, turning once halfway through.

Cut 8 sticks of rhubarb to fit the length of the terrine and place in a roasting tray. Bake in the oven for 5 minutes until slightly softened.

Blanch the mange-tout (sugar snap peas) in lightly salted water for 1 minute, then drain and refresh under cold running water.

Layer the terrine with the mackerel fillets, baked rhubarb, mange-tout (sugar snap peas) and the slices of potato, alternating the vegetables between the layers of fish. When the terrine is full pour a little lemon juice on top and place the terrine upside on a clean tray to catch the juices. Refrigerate with a heavy weight or dish filled with cold water on top for 3–4 hours.

Cut the remaining sticks of rhubarb into 6 cm/2½ in batons and poach in the vinegar until soft. Drain and allow to cool.

When the terrine is ready, pour any juices that have run off into a pan, add the white wine, honey and a pinch of saffron powder and reduce over a high heat by half. Allow to cool.

To serve, place the terrine upside down on a serving plate and gently remove the mould, carefully peeling away the greaseproof (wax) paper. Surround with the chives and the rhubarb batons.

Fat: high Kcals: 396 Cholesterol: high Fibre: low

Wild Mushroom and Chicken Terrine

200 g/7 oz breast meat of corn-fed chicken, skinned, boned and trimmed
1 tsp extra virgin olive oil
1 onion, finely chopped
1 clove garlic, finely diced (minced)
50 g/2 oz oyster mushrooms, finely diced (minced)
100 ml/4 fl oz/½ cup white wine
1 tbsp powdered gelatine
1 sprig tarragon, roughly chopped

Chop the chicken breasts into 2.5 cm/1 in cubes. Heat the olive oil in a pan until smoking, then add the chicken, chopped onion, garlic and the oyster mushrooms. Cook for 5 minutes over a low heat until the onion is translucent.

Place the wine in a small heatproof bowl, sprinkle over the gelatine and leave it to go spongy. Place the bowl in a pan of barely simmering water and leave until the gelatine has melted and turned transparent. Stir into the pan containing the diced chicken breasts and add the tarragon. Increase the heat and reduce the liquid by two-thirds, then blend the contents of the pan in a food processor or blender together with the *fromage frais* until smooth. Spoon into a 575 ml/1 pint/2½ cup terrine mould and place in the refrigerator to set for 1 hour.

Mackerel, Rhubarb and Mange-Tout Terrine

1 tbsp natural, low-fat *fromage frais*
poppy seeds
sea salt and freshly milled black pepper

Garnish
lettuce leaves, roughly torn

Serves 10

To turn out the mould, plunge the terrine up to its rim in hot water for 30 seconds. Place a plate upside down on the mould, then turn both over and give a couple of sharp shakes. Carefully roll the terrine in the poppy seeds, then cut into 1 cm/½ in slices. Serve the sliced terrine on a serving platter garnished with torn lettuce leaves.

Fat: low Kcals: 29 Cholesterol: low Fibre: low

Melon Lime Soup

juice of 3 limes
1 tsp arrowroot
2 egg whites
2 overripe Ogen or Galia melons

Serves 4

Mix the arrowroot to a paste with a little water and stir into the lime juice. Place in a stainless steel saucepan and bring to the boil, stirring continuously. Remove from the heat.

In a clean, dry bowl, whisk the egg whites until stiff and gently fold into the thickened lime juice using a large metal spoon. Place in the freezer for 3 hours.

Halve the melons and discard the seeds. Scoop out the flesh into a food processor or blender and purée. Chill in the refrigerator for 30 minutes. Serve in chilled soup bowls with a scoop of frozen lime.

Fat: low Kcals: 86 Cholesterol: low Fibre: low

Marinated Sea Bass with Pickled Vegetables

4 × 115 g/4 oz fillets of sea bass

Marinade
½ tsp fenugreek
2 star anise
1 tsp coriander seeds
½ tsp white peppercorns
juice of 2 limes
1 tsp cider vinegar
3 tbsp white wine
6 sprigs parsley
1 bay leaf
1 small red chilli
½ tsp mustard seeds
2 dsp extra virgin olive oil

Pickled vegetables
150 ml/5 fl oz/⅔ cup cider vinegar
3 tbsp clear honey
1 pinch saffron powder
8 baby courgettes (zucchini)
32 assorted baby root vegetables
8 baby green tomatoes
sea salt and freshly milled black pepper

Serves 4

Mix all the marinade ingredients together. Place the sea bass fillets in a shallow dish and spoon over the marinade and leave for 2 hours in the refrigerator.

Meanwhile, place the cider vinegar and honey in a pan, season, and bring to the boil. Add all the baby vegetables and the saffron, and boil for one minute. Leave the vegetables to stand in the liquid until cold.

Drain the sea bass from the marinade and place under a hot grill until just cooked, 4–5 minutes.

To serve, place a sea bass fillet in the centre of each plate and surround with a selection of baby vegetables. Spoon over some of the pickling liquid onto the vegetables and a trickle of olive oil.

Fat: low Kcals: 201 Cholesterol: medium Fibre: medium

Champneys Gazpacho

100 g/3½ oz/½ cup onions, roughly chopped
100 g/3½ oz/¾ cup cucumber, roughly chopped
100 g/3½ oz/¾ cup red and green peppers, roughly chopped
575 ml/1 pt/2½ cups tomato juice
75 ml/3 fl oz/⅓ cup fresh orange juice
1 dash lemon juice
55 g/2 oz/⅓ cup fresh breadcrumbs
1 dash red wine vinegar
1 clove garlic, finely diced (minced)
sea salt and freshly milled black pepper

Garnish
4 tbsp mixed peppers, finely diced (minced)

Serves 4

Put all the ingredients, except for the diced peppers for the garnish, in a food processor or liquidizer and process until well blended. Chill in the refrigerator and serve cold, garnished with the diced peppers.

Fat: low Kcals: 88 Cholesterol: low Fibre: low

Basmati Rice Timbale with Coriander, Truffle and Pineapple Dressing

2 dsp extra virgin olive oil
170 g/6 oz wild mushrooms
1 shallot, chopped
175 ml/6 fl oz/¾ cup unsweetened apple juice
55 g/2 oz/⅓ cup pineapple, finely diced (minced), reserving stalk
½ tsp truffle oil
1 stem ginger, finely chopped
1 clove garlic, finely diced (minced)
1 fresh green chilli
1 tbsp white wine vinegar
1 egg white
1 tsp fresh coriander, chopped
juice of 1 lime
200 g/7 oz/¾ cup cooked brown basmati rice
6 tbsp natural, low-fat *fromage frais*
10 chives, finely chopped
sea salt and fresh black pepper

Serves 4

Heat half the olive oil in a small frying pan (skillet) and sweat the wild mushrooms with the shallots until the shallots are translucent. Leave to cool.

To make the dressing, place the apple juice, remaining olive oil, pineapple and stalk, truffle oil, ginger, garlic, chilli and vinegar in a separate pan and reduce over a high heat by two-thirds. Leave to cool. Strain the liquid and set aside the diced (minced) pineapple.

Whisk the egg white until stiff, gently fold into the cooled dressing, then add the coriander and lime juice.

Mix the cooked rice with the diced pineapple and add 2 tablespoons of the *fromage frais*. Season to taste, then stir in half the mushroom and shallot mixture. Divide the mixture into 4, then press each portion into a 6 cm/2½ in circular pastry cutter, pushing down firmly. Remove the cutter to leave a rice timbale.

Stir the chopped chives into the remaining *fromage frais*, season to taste, then spread a little on top of each timbale, using a flat knife. Place a timbale in the centre of each plate and garnish with the pineapple dressing and serve.

Fat: medium Kcals: 157 Cholesterol: low Fibre: low

Above: *Smoked Haddock Tartare with Artichoke Terrine and Lemon Balm Dressing;* opposite, from back: *Basmati Rice Timbale with Coriander, Truffle and Pineapple Dressing, and Salmon and Leek Mousse with Salmon Roe Sauce*

Smoked Haddock Tartare with Artichoke Terrine and Lemon Balm Dressing

350 g/12 oz Jerusalem artichokes, thinly sliced
1 dash lemon juice
1 bunch flowering thyme

Haddock Tartare
170 g/6 oz natural smoked haddock, skinned and boned
4 garlic chives, chopped
2 shallots, chopped
juice of 1 lime
1 dsp raw cane sugar
4 tbsp natural, low-fat *fromage frais*
1 pinch sea salt

Spiced sultanas
85 g/3 oz/⅓ cup sultanas
1 pinch ground ginger
1 pinch ground cumin
1 pinch ground coriander
2 cloves
1 clove garlic
1 pinch cayenne pepper

Sauce
1 lemon
1 bunch lemon balm
6 tbsp extra virgin olive oil
1 tsp clear honey
1 pinch cayenne pepper
sea salt and freshly milled black pepper

Garnish
selection of salad leaves (e.g. lollo rosso, radicchio, endive, rocket)
1 tsp extra virgin olive oil
sea salt and freshly milled black pepper

Serves 4

Line a 2.5 cm × 5 cm/1 in × 2 in terrine with cling film or plastic wrap.

To make the spiced sultanas, put all the ingredients in a pan, just cover with water and bring to the boil. Cover and continue boiling until the sultanas are plump, about 20 minutes. Add more water if the sultanas start to dry out. When plump, drain and set aside.

In a pan, cover the sliced artichokes with water, the thyme and a dash of lemon juice, bring to the boil and simmer until soft, about 15 minutes.

Arrange thin layers of artichokes and sultanas in the terrine. Cover with greaseproof (wax) paper and press with a heavy weight or dish filled with cold water for 4 hours in the refrigerator.

Cut the smoked haddock into 2 mm/⅙ in dice and place in a shallow dish. Mix together the chopped chives and shallots and mix with the lime juice, sugar, yoghurt and sea salt. Spoon over the haddock and leave to marinate for 1 hour in the refrigerator. Turn the fish over after 30 minutes.

Invert the terrine onto a dish or serving board and roll it in the thyme flowers. Cut into thin slices.

Drain the marinated fish, divide into 4 portions and push into a 4 cm/1½ in circular pastry cutter to form a round cake. Remove the cutter and spread the top of the cake with the yoghurt marinade.

Wash the salad leaves and arrange them to one side of the fish cake. Season with a little olive oil, salt and pepper and add a slice of terrine to the plate.

To make the sauce, purée a whole lemon with the lemon balm leaves, olive oil, honey, salt and cayenne pepper in a liquidizer or food processor; pass through a fine sieve and pour around the terrine.

Fat: high Kcals: 414 Cholesterol: low Fibre: low

Chicken, Venison and Wild Mushroom Terrine

veal stock (see page 139), using 1.75 l/3 pt water, 900 g/2 lb venison bones
6 medium-sized onions, finely chopped
1 medium-sized carrot, finely chopped
3 sticks celery, finely chopped
115 g /4 oz venison, minced (ground)
4 egg whites
50 ml/2 fl oz/¼ cup port
1½ heaped tsp powdered gelatine
3 × 170 g/6 oz breasts of corn-fed chicken, skinned, boned and trimmed
2 tbsp natural, low-fat *fromage frais*
2 tsp extra virgin olive oil
1 clove garlic, finely diced (minced)
225 g/8 oz mixed wild mushrooms, wiped
75 ml/3 fl oz/⅓ cup white wine
2 × 115 g/4 oz fillets of venison
1 cucumber, cut into batons, 5 cm/2 in × 3 mm/⅛ in
sea salt, freshly milled white and black pepper

Garnish
1 bunch chervil

Serves 14

Reduce the veal stock over a high heat by two-thirds, then leave to cool. Mix 4 chopped onions, the carrot and celery with the minced (ground) venison. As soon as the stock has cooled, stir in 2 egg whites and add the minced (ground) venison mixture and the port. Bring the stock to the boil, then cover and simmer for 45 minutes over a very low heat.

About 10 minutes before the end of the cooking time, sprinkle the powdered gelatine over a small amount of cold water and leave to soften for approximately 5 minutes until it has swelled. Place the gelatine in a small heatproof bowl and put the bowl into a pan of barely simmering water; leave until the gelatine has melted and become transparent.

Strain the cooked stock through fine muslin, being careful not to cloud the stock. Season with salt and freshly milled white pepper, then stir in the gelatine and cool in a dampened shallow tray in the refrigerator. When the mixture has cooled, turn out onto a piece of dampened greaseproof (wax) paper and cut into 6 mm/¼ in dice using a sharp dampened knife, and return to the refrigerator.

Meanwhile, combine the chicken breasts, the remaining egg whites and the *fromage frais* in a food processor or blender and process until smooth. Season to taste.

Heat the oil in a frying pan (skillet) and sweat the remaining onion with the garlic and the wild mushrooms until the onions are translucent. Pour in the white wine. Allow to cool, then blend with the chicken mousse and press through a fine sieve. Keep cool.

Preheat the oven to 150°C/300°F/gas 2. Grease a 1.1 litre/2 pint/5 cup terrine with olive oil and line with greaseproof (wax) paper.

Seal the venison fillets in a very hot non-stick pan for 1 minute on each side. Spread a third of the chicken mousse in the base of the terrine, then lay one of the venison fillets on top. Add another layer of chicken mousse, followed by the remaining venison fillet. Cover with the last third of chicken mousse. Bake the terrine in a *bain marie* in the oven for 25 minutes. Remove and allow to cool.

Cut carefully around the edges of the terrine using a sharp knife and plunge the base in hot water up to its rim for 30 seconds. Turn out the terrine onto an inverted plate and cut into 1 cm/½ in slices. Arrange on individual plates with a little chopped veal aspic and cucumber batons and garnish with chervil leaves.

Fat: low Kcals: 126 Cholesterol: low Fibre: low

Swiss Chard, Beetroot, Avocado and Pecan Nut Salad

170 g/6 oz beetroot (beet)
8 leaves Swiss chard, finely shredded
30 g/1 oz/¼ cup pecan nuts
1 ripe avocado, peeled, stoned and sliced

Dressing
1 red pepper, deseeded and roughly chopped
2 tbsp walnut oil
1 tbsp white wine vinegar

Serves 4

To make the dressing, purée the pepper, walnut oil and white wine vinegar in a food processor or liquidizer and pass through a fine sieve.

Cook the beetroot (beet) until soft in a little water in a non-stick pan over a high heat, approximately 30 minutes. Refresh under cold running water, peel and cut into 6 mm/¼ in squares. Mix the shredded Swiss chard and the pecan nuts with the beetroot (beet) in a large salad bowl. Toss with a quarter of the dressing. Arrange the sliced avocado on top, pour over the remaining dressing and serve.

Fat: high Kcals: 206 Cholesterol: low Fibre: medium

Above: *Chicken, Venison and Wild Mushroom Terrine;* opposite: *Marinated Sea Bass with Pickled Vegetables*

Leek, Smoked Goat's Cheese and Sesame Seed Salad

2 leeks, sliced
55 g/2 oz/1 cup smoked goat's cheese, cut into ¼ in dice
110 g/4 oz new potatoes, cooked and sliced thinly
115 g/4 oz/1 cup cherry tomatoes
1 bunch dill

Dressing
55 g/2 oz bean curd
1 tsp whole grain mustard
1 tbsp toasted sesame oil
1 tsp tahini paste
1 tbsp white wine vinegar

Garnish
1 dsp toasted sesame seeds

Serves 4

To make the dressing, place the bean curd, mustard, sesame oil, tahini paste and white wine vinegar in a food processor or blender and blend until smooth. Press through a fine sieve. Place all the other ingredients, except the sesame seeds, into a large serving bowl. Mix in the dressing, garnish with the sesame seeds and serve.

Fat: medium Kcals: 119 Cholesterol: low Fibre: low

Salmon and Leek Mousse with Salmon Roe Sauce

2 tbsp white wine vinegar
3 × 85 g/3 oz fillets of fresh salmon
20 baby leeks, cut into 7.5 cm/3 in lengths
juice of ½ lemon
2 tbsp natural, low-fat *fromage frais*
1 dsp low-fat mayonnaise
1 pinch cayenne pepper
3 sheets gelatine
2 egg whites
15 g/½ oz/¼ cup salmon roe
sea salt

Serves 4

Bring a large pan of water to the boil, add the vinegar and poach the salmon for 4 minutes. Remove from the pan and leave to cool.

Blanch the leeks in lightly salted water, refresh under cold running water and drain. Line 4 ramekins with the leeks, alternating the strips.

Reserve a little lemon juice to mix with the salmon roe later and combine the rest with the salmon, *fromage frais*, a pinch each of salt and cayenne pepper and the mayonnaise in a food processor or blender.

Cover the gelatine with cold water and leave to soften, approximately 5 minutes. Remove from the water and squeeze out any excess liquid using your hand. Put the gelatine in a small heatproof bowl over a pan of barely simmering water and leave to melt.

Whisk the egg whites until stiff and fold into the salmon mousse together with the gelatine. Pour the mousse into the lined ramekins and place in the refrigerator for 30 minutes to set.

Mix half the roe with the reserved lemon juice and press firmly through a fine sieve into a clean bowl. Add the remaining roe and mix in. Plunge the base of each ramekin into hot water for 30 seconds and turn out onto serving plates. Pour sauce around each mousse.

Fat: high Kcals: 202 Cholesterol: medium Fibre: medium

Sweet Pepper, Chicken, Pineapple and Chilli Salad

2 × 140 g/5 oz breasts of corn-fed chicken, skinned, boned and trimmed
300 ml/10 fl oz/1¼ cups chicken stock (see page 138)
¼ pineapple, cut into 6 mm/¼ in dice
1 red pepper, deseeded and finely chopped
1 yellow pepper, deseeded and finely chopped
1 green pepper, deseeded and finely chopped
55 g/2 oz/⅓ cup bean sprouts
sea salt and freshly milled black pepper

Dressing
2 tbsp low-calorie mayonnaise
juice of 1 lemon
1 pinch ground cumin
1 pinch paprika
1 pinch ground turmeric
½ clove garlic, finely diced (minced)
½ bunch fresh coriander
1 red chilli pepper, deseeded and finely diced

Serves 4

Poach the chicken breasts in the chicken stock for 10 minutes, then remove and drain on kitchen paper.

Mix together the mayonnaise and lemon juice and add a pinch of cumin, paprika and turmeric and the garlic. Stir in half the chopped coriander and then the chilli pepper. Season to taste.

Cut the chicken into strips and in a large serving bowl mix with the pineapple, peppers and bean sprouts. Stir in the dressing and garnish with the remaining coriander.

Fat: medium Kcals: 169 Cholesterol: medium Fibre: low

Hot starters offer a wide range of healthy and delicious dishes suitable for every season and taste. Warming, low-calorie soups include Celeriac, Leek and Sage, and Mexican Bean; and there are high-fibre recipes such as Tagliatelle of Mussels, and Lamb Sweetbread Ravioli and, in the selection of warm salads, Scallops with Wild Strawberry Dressing, and Marinated Pigeon with Walnuts and Grapes. For a well-balanced meal, choose a starter that complements your main course in terms of both calorie, fibre and fat content as well as flavour.

Morels stuffed with Asparagus Mousse

1 × 140 g/5 oz breast of corn-fed chicken, skinned, boned and trimmed
12 asparagus spears
175 ml/6 fl oz/¾ cup natural, low-fat *fromage frais*
32 large morels, wiped
sea salt and freshly milled black pepper

Sauce
575 ml/1 pt/2½ cups chicken stock (see page 138)
1 dsp white wine
2 tomatoes, skinned, deseeded and diced (minced)
1 sprig cheril

Serves 4

Blend the chicken breast in a food processor or blender for 1 minute, then pass twice through a fine sieve. Cut the tips off the asparagus spears and put to one side. Trim off the woody ends and blanch the stalks until tender. Drain and refresh under cold running water, then squeeze out any excess liquid. Return the chicken breast mixture to the food processor or blender, add the asparagus stalks and blend for 1 minute. Pass through a fine sieve and chill.

Reserve 1 teaspoon of the *fromage frais* and beat the rest into the chilled chicken mixture. Season. Place in a piping bag fitted with a small nozzle and pipe into the morels. Heat the chicken stock to a gentle simmer and lower in the morels. Poach for about 5 minutes, and then add the asparagus tips to the liquid and simmer for a further 7 minutes. Remove the morels and the asparagus, drain and keep warm while preparing the sauce.

To make the sauce, add the white wine to the chicken stock and reduce over a high heat by two-thirds. Add the reserved teaspoon of *fromage frais* together with the diced tomato and the chervil and remove from the heat.

To serve, arrange 8 morels and 4 asparagus tips on each plate and surround with the sauce.

Fat: low Kcals: 133 Cholesterol: low Fibre: medium

Opposite, back left: *Galantine of Smoked Quail;* back right: *Chicken and Scallop Coulibiac;* front: *Morels Stuffed with Asparagus Mousse*

Galantine of Smoked Quail

2 rashers smoked lean back bacon, fat and rind removed
115 g/4 oz tail fillet of veal
2 tbsp natural, low-fat *fromage frais*
1 egg white
1 clove garlic, skinned
55 g/2 oz/½ cup pistachio nuts, shelled
½ green pepper, finely chopped
½ red pepper, finely chopped
2 truffles, peeled and finely chopped
575 ml/20 fl oz/2½ cups chicken stock (see page 138)
1 bunch thyme
4 small quail, boned
sea salt and freshly milled black pepper

Sauce
50 ml/2 fl oz/¼ cup port
juice of 1 lemon
juice of 1 orange
2 tbsp clear honey
1 star anise

Garnish
115 g/4 oz/1 cup raspberries or redcurrants

Serves 4

Preheat the oven to 220°C/425°F/gas 7.

Place the bacon, veal fillet, *fromage frais*, egg white, garlic clove and half the pistachio nuts in a food processor or blender and process until smooth. Press through a fine sieve into a clean bowl, then stir in the chopped peppers, truffles and the remaining pistachio nuts.

Bring the chicken stock to the boil in a saucepan with the thyme. Lay the boned quails skin-side down and pipe a quarter of the veal mousse onto each quail. Season with a little salt and pepper, then wrap the quail around the mousse to form the shape of the bird once more. Place the birds into an ovenproof dish and pour over the chicken stock. Cover and cook in the oven for 14 minutes until cooked through. When the quail are cooked, leave them to cool in the stock, then transfer to the refrigerator, still in the stock.

Meanwhile, to make the sauce, place all the ingredients together in a heavy-bottomed pan and reduce over a high heat for 8-10 minutes until the liquid resembles the consistency of thin jelly. Pass through a fine sieve.

To serve, slice each quail into 4 and place in the centre of each plate. Gently warm the sauce, pour it round the quail and garnish with the redcurrants or raspberries.

Fat: high Kcals: 322 Cholesterol: medium Fibre: low

Chicken and Scallop Coulibiac

300 ml/10 fl oz/1¼ cups chicken stock (see page 138)
2 × 115 g/4 oz breasts of corn-fed chicken, skinned, boned and trimmed
2 scallops
115 g/4 oz large spinach leaves
6 sheets ready-made filo pastry
1 tbsp extra virgin olive oil

Bring the chicken stock to the boil in a pan, add the chicken breasts and poach for approximately 8 minutes until cooked through. Remove with a slotted spoon and place on a cooling tray.

Remove the scallops from the shells, cutting away any membrane and dark intestines, including the small curved muscle attached to the white meat. Wash and dry on kitchen paper. Remove the coral and reserve. Slice each piece of white meat in half and season.

In a separate pan, blanch the spinach in boiling water for 30 seconds, drain and refresh.

55 g/2 oz/¼ cup cooked wild and brown rice, mixed
sea salt and freshly milled black pepper

Sauce
2 shallots, roughly chopped
2 whole tomatoes
1 small potato, peeled and roughly chopped
1 bunch tarragon, roughly chopped
1 clove garlic, finely diced (minced)
1 dsp brandy
150 ml/5 fl oz/⅔ cup fish stock (see page 138)
1 pinch chilli pepper
juice of 1 lime

Serves 4

Preheat the oven to 180°C/350°F/gas 4.

To make each filo parcel, brush 3 sheets of pastry with a little olive oil and place one sheet on top of the other to form 3 layers. Place half the cooked rice on the top layer in the centre and season to taste with salt and freshly ground pepper.

Wrap a cooked cold chicken breast in half the blanched spinach leaves and place on top of the rice. Lay 2 pieces of scallop neatly on top of the spinach-wrapped chicken, then gather up the corners of the filo to encase the filling and twist to seal. Repeat as before with the remaining ingredients to form another parcel. Place on a greased baking sheet, and brush the tops with a little more olive oil. Bake in the oven for 12 minutes until golden brown. Remove from the oven and leave to rest for 5 minutes.

While the parcels are cooking, make the sauce. Heat a little olive oil in a pan and sweat the scallops, tomatoes, potato, tarragon and garlic for 2 minutes until the onion is translucent. Add the scallop corals and the brandy, ignite, then pour in the fish stock. Simmer for 15 minutes, then liquidize in a liquidizer or food processor and press through a fine sieve. Season with chilli pepper and lime juice. Keep in a warm place.

To serve, cut each parcel into 4 slices and place 2 slices each in the centre of 4 warm plates. Pour over a little sauce and serve immediately.

Fat: medium Kcals: 209 Cholesterol: high Fibre: low

Chickpea, Olive and Garlic Soup

170 g/6 oz/1 cup chickpeas
1 large onion, finely chopped
½ stick celery, finely chopped
4 large cloves garlic, diced (minced)
1 l/1¾ pt/4½ cups vegetable stock (see page 139)
1 bay leaf
1 sprig thyme
50 ml/2 fl oz/¼ cup extra virgin olive oil
sea salt and freshly milled white pepper
15 black olives, stoned and diced (minced)

Serves 4

Soak the chickpeas overnight, discard the soaking water, then cover with fresh water in a pan and bring to a rapid boil then simmer for approximately 1 hour until tender. Leave to cool, drain and remove the outer husks by rubbing them with a cloth.

Sweat the chopped onion, celery and garlic until soft in a covered pan. Add the vegetable stock, chickpeas, bay leaf and thyme, and simmer for 10 minutes. Blend the soup well, slowly adding the olive oil, in a food processor or blender, and then pass through a coarse sieve. Add the black olives as a garnish to finish the soup.

Fat: high Kcals: 194 Cholesterol: low Fibre: low

Carrot, Scallop and Coriander Soup

8 large king scallops
1 dsp extra virgin olive oil
6 medium-sized carrots, roughly chopped
1 large onion, roughly chopped
¼ stick celery, roughly chopped
½ clove garlic, diced (minced)
2 tsp coriander seeds, crushed
25 g/1 oz/¼ cup red lentils
1 bay leaf
1 l/1 pt 15 fl oz/4⅓ cups fish stock (see page 138)
1 bunch fresh coriander
sea salt and freshly milled black pepper

Serves 4

Remove the scallops from the shells, cutting away any membrane and dark intestines, including the small curved muscle from the white meat. Wash and dry on kitchen paper.

Heat the oil in a heavy-based saucepan, then sweat the carrots, onion, celery, garlic and crushed coriander until the onion is translucent. Carefully pick over the lentils to remove any stones. Add the lentils, bay leaf and 4 scallops, each one sliced into thirds. Pour over the fish stock and bring to the boil; cover the pan, reduce the heat and simmer for 10 minutes. Cut the stalks from the coriander (keep the leaves for garnishing), add to the pan and simmer, covered, for a further 10 minutes. Remove the soup from the heat and allow to cool slightly.

Liquidize the soup in a liquidizer or food processor, then pass through a fine sieve. Season to taste. Gently reheat the soup.

Fry the remaining 4 scallops in a hot non-stick frying pan (skillet) for 30 seconds on each side.

Place a scallop in the centre of each soup bowl, pour over the soup and garnish with coriander leaves. Serve immediately.

Fat: low Kcals: 175 Cholesterol: high Fibre: medium

Avocado and Sweetcorn Soup

1 small onion, finely chopped
1 clove garlic, diced (minced)
200 g/7 oz sweetcorn kernels, frozen or canned
2 green overripe avocados, peeled and stoned
1 tbsp light soy sauce
550 ml/20 fl oz/2½ cups chicken stock (see page 138)
1 tbsp natural, low-fat *fromage frais*
juice of ½ lemon
sea salt
cayenne pepper

Serves 8

In a non-stick saucepan, sweat the onion, garlic and 150 g/5 oz of the sweetcorn until the onion is translucent. Mash the avocado with a fork and add to the pan together with the soy sauce and chicken stock. Bring to the boil and simmer, uncovered, for 20 minutes. Remove from the heat and blend the soup in a food processor or blender. Pass through a fine sieve into a clean pan. Add the remaining sweetcorn, bring to the boil, then remove from the heat. Stir in the *fromage frais* and lemon juice, and season to taste with salt and cayenne pepper. Serve immediately with warm wholemeal bread.

Fat: medium Kcals: 88 Cholesterol: low Fibre: low

Previous page, left: *Carrot, Scallop and Coriander Soup*; right: *Chickpea, Olive and Garlic Soup*

Mexican Bean Soup

- 85 g/3 oz/½ cup dried kidney beans, soaked overnight
- 4 large tomatoes, chopped
- 2 celery sticks, chopped
- 1 medium-sized onion, chopped
- 55 g/2 oz/⅓ cup dried butter beans, soaked overnight
- 1 clove garlic, finely diced (minced)
- 1 small red chilli, deseeded
- 1 tsp fresh ginger, peeled and roughly chopped
- 850 ml/1½ pt/3¾ cups water
- 150 ml/5 fl oz/⅔ cup tomato juice
- 2 tsp paprika
- 1 tbsp fresh parsley, chopped

Serves 4

Bring a pan of water to the boil and add the kidney beans. Bring to the boil again for at least 10 minutes. At the same time, bring another pan of water to the boil, add the butter beans and cook in the same way.

Drain the beans and place in a pan with the vegetables and all the other ingredients, except for the paprika and parsley. Bring to the boil and cook for 10 minutes, skimming the surface regularly. Cover and simmer for 1½ hours until the beans are tender.

Remove the chilli pepper and liquidize the soup in a food processor or blender and then pass through a fine sieve. Pour in the tomato juice and reheat gently. Season to taste.

To serve, ladle into individual soup bowls and sprinkle with a little paprika and the chopped parsley.

Fat: low Kcals: 156 Cholesterol: low Fibre: high

Mange-Tout, Mint and Caviar Soup

- 1 large Spanish onion, chopped
- 1 clove garlic, roughly chopped
- 225 g/8 oz/1½ cups leek, roughly chopped
- 115 g/4 oz/¾ cup dried butter beans, soaked overnight
- 1.5 l/50 fl oz/6¼ cups chicken stock (see page 138)
- 1 bay leaf
- 1 sprig thyme
- 225 g/8 oz/1½ cups mange-tout (sugar snap peas)
- 1 bunch mint
- 1 tbsp natural, low-fat *fromage frais*
- 1 tbsp caviar or fish roe
- sea salt and freshly milled black pepper

Serves 4

Preheat the oven to 180°C/350°F/gas 4.

In a covered, ovenproof pan sweat the onion, garlic and leek until the onion is translucent. Add the butter beans, chicken stock, bay leaf and thyme, boil for at least 10 minutes, and transfer to the oven. Cook for 40 minutes until the beans are tender. Remove from the oven and add the mange-tout (sugar snap peas) and the mint, reserving 4 small sprigs for the garnish. Boil on top of the stove for 5 minutes, then blend in a food processor or blender until smooth. Pass through a fine sieve and check for seasoning.

Serve in individual soup bowls with a swirl of *fromage frais* and a quarter of the caviar or fish roe in each bowl. Decorate with the mint sprigs and serve immediately.

Fat: low Kcals: 169 Cholesterol: low Fibre: high

Celeriac, Leek and Sage Soup; opposite: *Mange-Tout, Mint and Caviar Soup*

Celeriac, Leek and Sage Soup

1 large head celeriac
1 medium-sized onion
2 large leeks
1 tsp extra virgin olive oil
½ clove garlic, finely chopped
1 l/1¾ pt/4½ cups chicken stock (see page 138)
1 bay leaf
1 bunch sage
sea salt and freshly milled black pepper

Serves 4

Chop the celeriac, onion and leeks into rough squares and set aside a third of a leek for garnishing. Heat the oil in a pan and sweat the vegetables with the garlic until soft. Add the chicken stock, bay leaf and sage; bring to the boil and simmer, covered, for 20 minutes.

Cut the reserved leek into fine strips and blanch in salted water. Blend the soup in a food processor or liquidizer and press through a fine sieve. Season to taste and serve with the blanched leek strips on top.

Fat: low Kcals: 85 Cholesterol: low Fibre: medium

Parsnip and Chestnut Soup

450 g/1 lb parsnips, peeled and roughly chopped
1 Spanish onion, roughly chopped
½ clove garlic
1 bay leaf
140 g/5 oz/1 cup chestnuts, roasted and peeled
1.5 l/2½ pints/6¼ cups veal stock (see page 139)
4 tbsp natural, low-fat yoghurt (see page 142)

Garnish
2 sprigs parsley, finely chopped

Serves 4

Place the parsnips, onion, garlic, bay leaf, chestnuts and veal stock in a thick-bottomed pan and bring to the boil. Simmer for 40 minutes, skimming the surface regularly to remove any scum.

Blend the soup in a food processor or liquidizer and pass through a fine sieve into a soup terrine.

Stir in the yoghurt, sprinkle with the chopped parsley and serve immediately.

Fat: high Kcals: 169 Cholesterol: low Fibre: high

Marinated Red Mullet with Pressed Leek Terrine

4 × 85 g/3 oz fillets of red mullet, boned
900 g/2 lb baby leeks
1 small yellow pepper
3 tbsp extra virgin olive oil
1 tsp raw cane sugar
8 rocket leaves
12 oakleaf lettuce leaves
sea salt and freshly milled black pepper

Marinade
1 clove garlic, roughly chopped
1 tsp walnut oil
8 white peppercorns
8 sprigs parsley
1 shallot, sliced
1 bay leaf
1 lime
2 tbsp dry white wine
8 coriander seeds, crushed

Serves 4

Mix all the marinade ingredients together. Place the red mullet fillets in a shallow dish and spoon over the marinade. Leave to marinate for 2 hours in the refrigerator.

Line 4 small pâté terrines with cling film or plastic wrap. Wash the leeks and trim to fit the length of the terrines. Blanch for 2 minutes in lightly salted water, refresh under cold running water, drain and squeeze out the excess water. Lay in the terrines, season with black pepper, cover with cling film or plastic wrap and press with a heavy weight or dish filled with cold water in the refrigerator for at least 4 hours. At the end of this time, turn out the leeks onto an inverted dish and slice into 5 cm/2 in slices. Wrap in plastic again and return to the refrigerator.

Liquidize the yellow pepper with the olive oil and sugar in a liquidizer or food processor and pass through a fine sieve. Drain the red mullet fillets and cook, skin-side up, under a hot grill for 1½ minutes. Arrange on a plate on a bed of the salad leaves. Pour on the pepper sauce and grind over some freshly milled black pepper.

Fat: high Kcals: 252 Cholesterol: high Fibre: medium

Potato and Parsley Soup

3 large potatoes, roughly chopped
1 onion, roughly chopped
1 clove garlic, diced (minced)
1 stick celery, roughly chopped
1 bay leaf
1 bunch parsley
1.5 l/2½ pt/6¼ cups chicken stock (see page 138)
sea salt and freshly milled black pepper

Serves 4

In a thick-bottomed pan sweat the potatoes, onion, garlic, celery, bay leaf and parsley stalks for 5 minutes. Add the chicken stock and boil for 20 minutes. Add the parsley heads and cook for 5 minutes, then liquidize in a food processor or blender and pass through a fine sieve. Season with salt and pepper to taste and reheat before serving.

Fat: low Kcals: 122 Cholesterol: low Fibre: high

A Salad of Marinated Pigeon with Walnuts and Grapes

2 squab pigeons
55 g/2 oz/½ cup walnut pieces
140 ml/5 fl oz/⅔ cup red wine vinegar
selection of salad leaves (e.g. lollo, rocket, radicchio, spider endive)
115 g/4 oz/1 cup green seedless grapes

Sauce
3 tbsp balsamic vinegar
1 dsp clear honey
1 tbsp walnut oil

Marinade
1 clove garlic, crushed
4 juniper berries, crushed
4 sprigs parsley
6 black peppercorns
140 ml/5 fl oz/⅔ cup balsamic vinegar
140 ml/5 fl oz/⅔ cup red wine
1 tsp walnut oil
1 pinch salt
1 bay leaf

Serves 4

Preheat oven to 220°C/425°F/gas 7.

Mix all the marinade ingredients together. Place the squab pigeon, cut in half down the breast bone, in a shallow dish and spoon over the marinade. Leave in the refrigerator for 3 hours, then drain.

Whisk together all ingredients for the sauce in a bowl.

Roast the pigeons in the oven for 8-10 minutes until pink. Leave to rest for 5 minutes in a small dish, catching the cooking juices to add to the sauce later. Slice the pigeon breasts and arrange on top of the detached leg in the centre of the plate. Place the walnuts in a saucepan and bring to the boil in the red wine vinegar for 3 minutes.

Arrange the salad leaves around the plate with the grapes and walnuts. Gently heat the sauce and pour over the pigeon and salad.

Fat: high Kcals: 386 Cholesterol: low Fibre: low

Above, left: *Lamb Sweetbread Ravioli; above, right: Tagliatelle of Mussels;* opposite, back: *Brill and Crab Soufflé;* opposite, front: *Marinated Red Mullet with Pressed Leek Terrine*

Brill and Crab Soufflé

wholemeal and wholewheat flour
270 g/9 oz raw tomato concasse (see page 137)
55 g/2 oz white crab meat, finely diced (minced)
3 tsp lobster roe
115 g/4 oz fillet of brill, skinned
110 g/4 oz brown crab meat
1 egg yolk
2 tbsp natural, low-fat *fromage frais*
15 ml/½ fl oz/3 tbsp white wine
pinch cayenne pepper
3 egg whites
sea salt and freshly milled black pepper

Serves 4

Preheat the oven to 190°C/375°F/gas 5.

Grease 4 ramekins, then dust lightly with an equal mixture of wholemeal and wholewheat flour.

Mix the tomato concasse with the diced (minced) white crab meat and place a little of the mixture in the base of each ramekin. Grind a generous sprinkling of black pepper onto each, then place some lobster roe on top.

In a food processor or blender, blend the brill fillet, brown crab meat, egg yolk, *fromage frais*, white wine and cayenne pepper and process until smooth. Pass through a fine sieve and season to taste.

Whisk the egg whites until stiff and gently fold into the fish mousse. Spoon the mousse into the ramekins and smooth the tops with a flat knife. Bake in the oven for 12 minutes until golden brown and risen. Serve immediately.

Fat: medium Kcals: 158 Cholesterol: high Fibre: low

Tagliatelle of Mussels

350 g/12 oz saffron pasta (see page 141)
1 tsp extra virgin olive oil
1 tsp white wine vinegar
2 leeks, cut into 1 cm/½ in dice
55 g/2 oz/⅓ cup each of carrot, onion, celery and fennel, roughly chopped
1 sprig thyme
4 sprigs parsley
6 white peppercorns
1 bay leaf
75 ml/3 fl oz/⅓ cup dry white wine
900 g/2 lb mussels, scrubbed and bearded
150 ml/5 fl oz/⅔ cup natural, low-fat *fromage frais*
juice of ½ lemon
sea salt and freshly milled white pepper

Garnish
4 sprigs chervil

Serves 4

Roll out the pasta as thinly as possible, either by machine or by hand, and cut into tagliatelle strips, 1 cm/½ in wide.

Heat the olive oil in a frying pan (skillet), add the leeks and the vinegar and fry until the leek is a pale golden colour. Keep in a warm place.

In a large covered pan sweat the vegetables and thyme for 2 minutes. Add the parsley, peppercorns, bay leaf and white wine and reduce over a high heat by half. Add the mussels, cover once again and cook for 4 minutes until all the shells are open, shaking the pan from time to time so that the mussels cook evenly. Remove the mussels from their shells and keep warm. Drain the cooking liquor into a separate pan and reduce over a high heat by half. Once the liquor has reduced, stir in the *fromage frais*, lightly season, return the mussels to the sauce and warm gently; do not allow to boil.

Meanwhile, bring a large pan of lightly salted water to the boil, add a little lemon juice and drop in the pasta. Cook for 2-3 minutes until *al dente*, then drain.

Pile a quarter of the pasta in the centre of each plate, and pour over the sauce and mussels. Arrange the leeks around the plate, garnish with chervil and serve immediately.

Fat: medium Kcals: 446 Cholesterol: low Fibre: high

Lamb Sweetbread Ravioli

225 g/8 oz lamb sweetbreads
100 g/4 oz fresh wholemeal pasta (see page 140)
100 g/4 oz fresh wholemeal spinach pasta (see page 141)
1 × 140 g/5 oz breast of corn-fed chicken, skinned, boned and trimmed
1 clove garlic
1 egg white
2 tbsp natural, low-fat *fromage frais*
32 baby leeks, cut into 7.5 cm/3 in pieces
1 tsp olive oil

To clean the sweetbreads, soak them in cold water for 2 hours, then use a sharp knife to cut away any discoloured parts.

To make the sauce, place the shallots, chilli and herbs in a saucepan with the cider vinegar. Bring to the boil and leave to boil until the vinegar has reduced by two-thirds. Set to one side.

Preheat the oven to 205°C/400°F/gas 6.

Roll out both pastas, either by machine or by hand into 30 cm/12 in strips. Leave to rest for 20 minutes before rolling once again on the last pasta machine setting with the green and white pastas alternating in stripes to give a colourful sheet of dough.

To blanch the sweetbreads, place them in a saucepan, cover with fresh cold water, bring to the boil and simmer, uncovered, for 4 minutes. Drain, and when cool enough to handle, pull away the connecting ducts, then remove the skin and outer pieces of membrane.

sea salt and freshly milled black pepper
20 leaves spinach, blanched

Sauce
1 shallot, finely chopped
¼ fresh red or green chilli, finely chopped, deseeded
4 basil leaves, finely chopped
2 sage leaves, finely chopped
2 tbsp cider vinegar
1 tbsp natural, low-fat yoghurt (see page 142)
1 tsp clear honey
2 tbsp natural, low-fat *fromage frais*
1 egg white
2 tbsp extra virgin olive oil
salt and freshly milled black pepper

Garnish
1 bunch chervil

Serves 4

Meanwhile, place the chicken breast in a saucepan, just cover with lightly salted water, and bring to the boil. Cover the pan, turn down the heat and poach for 5 minutes. Drain, and when cool enough to handle, remove any remaining fat. Roughly chop up.

Roast the garlic clove, skin on, for 5 minutes in a hot oven, then rinse under cold water. Remove the skin then blanch the clove 3 times in boiling water.

Put the sweetbreads, chicken and garlic clove in a blender or food processor and blend to a smooth paste. Add the egg white and *fromage frais* to the mixture in the blender and blend again briefly. Pass the mixture through a fine sieve into a bowl and season to taste.

Lay out the strips of pasta on a clean flat surface; paint the pasta lightly with water. Place the filling mixture in a piping bag fitted with a plain 1 cm/½ in nozzle and pipe small mounds of filling, each mound approximately 5 cm/2 in in diameter, onto the pasta, spacing them evenly, just over 2.5 cm/1 in apart. When a strip is completed, place another piece of pasta over the top. Seal the layers by pressing between the mounds with your fingers. With a 7.5 cm/3 in pastry cutter, cut between the mounds into ravioli pieces, crimp up the edges with your fingers. Each strip should yield 8 pieces. Continue until all the filling has been used up. Bring about 2 litres/3½ pints of lightly salted water to the boil. Add the ravioli and cook for 3½ minutes, stirring from time to time until *al dente*.

Meanwhile, lightly season the leek pieces, brush with olive oil and cook under a medium grill for 3-4 minutes until lightly browned. Keep warm in a covered dish.

To finish the sauce, place the vinegar mixture in a *bain marie*. Whisk in the yoghurt, honey, *fromage frais*, oil and egg white until the mixture is of pouring consistency. Season to taste.

Serve the ravioli on large plates on a bed of spinach with the grilled leeks to one side, and garnished with chervil leaves.

Fat: high Kcals: 452 Cholesterol: high Fibre: high

A Warm Salad of Scallops with Wild Strawberry Dressing

selection of salad leaves (e.g. rocket, endive, radicchio, corn salad)
12 king scallops
juice of 1 lemon
sea salt and freshly milled white pepper

Tear the salad leaves into 1 cm/½ in pieces, wash them, shake any excess water from the leaves and place in 4 × 7.5 cm/3 in circular pastry cutters in the centre of the plate to form a neat selection of salad. Place in the refrigerator.

Set aside 20 strawberries for garnishing and purée the rest with the balsamic vinegar and olive oil in a food processor or blender to form a thick sauce, then pass through a fine sieve or muslin cloth.

Opposite: *A Warm Salad of Scallops with Warm Strawberry Dressing;* above: *A Salad of Marinated Pigeon with Walnuts and Grapes*

Dressing
225 g/8 oz/2 cups wild strawberries
2 tbsp balsamic vinegar
50 ml/2 fl oz/¼ cup extra virgin olive oil

Garnish
3 leeks
1 tbsp extra virgin olive oil

Serves 4

Remove the scallops from the shells, cutting away any membrane and dark intestines, including the small curved muscle attached to the white meat. Wash the flesh and dry on kitchen paper. Remove and discard the coral and cut each piece of white meat in half. Season lightly with salt, pepper and lemon juice. Heat a non-stick pan over a high heat, add the scallops and cook for 20–30 seconds on each side. When cooked, divide the pieces into 4 portions and arrange on top of the salad leaves. For the garnish, discard the dark green leaves of the leeks and cut the white parts into fine strips. Heat the oil in a frying pan (skillet) and fry the leek strips for 1 minute until golden brown.

Remove the cutters and pour the strawberry dressing into a small pan and warm slightly. Pour around the scallops and a little over the salad leaves. Sprinkle with the leek strips and serve immediately.

Fat: high Kcals: 278 Cholesterol: high Fibre: low

Scallop, Bacon and Mushroom Salad with Maple Dressing

500 g/1 lb 2 oz spinach
3 small rashers lean back bacon, fat and rind removed
1 pinch ground nutmeg
8 king scallops
sea salt and freshly milled black pepper

Dressing
2 shallots, finely chopped
1 tomato, skinned, deseeded and chopped
1 tbsp maple syrup
115 g/4 oz small chanterelle mushrooms
1 tsp walnut oil
2 tbsp white wine

Serves 4

Remove and discard the stalks from the spinach, blanch the leaves in boiling water for 30 seconds, drain and refresh. In a non-stick pan, fry the strips of bacon for approximately 3-4 minutes, until golden brown. Add the blanched spinach, season with the nutmeg and salt and pepper, and cook for 3-4 minutes. Press the spinach into 4 × 5 cm/2 in round pastry cutters and place one in the centre of each of 4 large plates. Remove the cutter leaving the moulded spinach on the plate. Keep in a warm place.

Remove the scallops from the shell, cutting away any membrane and dark intestines, including the small curved muscle from the white meat. Wash briefly and dry on kitchen paper. Cut each scallop into 3, then fry over a high heat in a clean non-stick pan for 20 seconds on each side. Place on top of the circles of spinach and keep warm.

To make the dressing, in the same pan fry the chopped shallots over a high heat in a non-stick pan until translucent. Add all the other ingredients and bring to the boil. Take off the heat, pour the warm dressing over the scallops and spinach and serve immediately.

Fat: high Kcals: 231 Cholesterol: high Fibre: medium

Mushroom and Tarragon Soup

450 g/1 lb flat mushrooms
1 bay leaf
1 large onion
1 clove garlic, crushed
2 sticks celery, roughly chopped
50 ml/2 fl oz/¼ cup white wine
1 tsp clear honey
2 tsp white wine vinegar
850 ml/1½ pt/3¾ cups vegetable stock (see page 139)
1 large potato, roughly chopped
1 bunch tarragon, finely chopped
300 ml/10 fl oz/1¼ cups skimmed milk
sea salt and freshly milled white pepper

Serves 4

Sweat the mushrooms, bay leaf, onion, garlic and celery in a deep pan over a low heat for 5 minutes. Add the white wine, honey, white wine vinegar, vegetable stock, potato and three-quarters of the tarragon, and simmer for 30 minutes.

Add the milk and liquidize in a food processor or blender with the remaining tarragon until smooth, then pass through a fine sieve. Season with salt and white pepper and reheat before serving.

Fat: low Kcals: 87 Cholesterol: low Fibre: high

Mushroom Ragout with Grilled Polenta

2 bay leaves
225 g/8 oz/1½ cups polenta
450 g/1 lb wild mushrooms, roughly chopped
1 tbsp sherry vinegar
8 cloves garlic, roasted
32 shallots, roasted and roughly chopped
4 tbsp cooked tomato concasse
6 sun-dried tomatoes, finely chopped
3 tbsp parsley, finely chopped
1 bunch asparagus tips, blanched
sea salt and freshly milled black pepper

Serves 4

Add the bay leaves to 450 ml/¾ pint/2 cups water and bring to the boil. Mix in the polenta and simmer for 15 minutes, stirring constantly. Pour into a shallow bowl and leave to cool. When cool and firm spread on a clean, flat surface and cut into rounds using a 5 cm/2 in circular pastry cutter.

Season with salt and pepper and cook under a hot grill for 3 minutes until lightly browned.

In a non-stick pan, sweat the wild mushrooms over a low heat for 4 minutes. Add the sherry vinegar, increase the heat and reduce for 1 minute. Stir in the garlic, shallots, tomato concasse and the sun-dried tomatoes and cook for 2 minutes. Add the parsley and asparagus tips to the mixture. Spoon over the grilled polenta rounds and serve immediately.

Fat: high Kcals: 316 Cholesterol: low Fibre: high

Fish and seafood

Fish and seafood are high in protein and low in calories, and make wonderfully creative meals in any season. There is now a tremendous variety of fresh fish available in shops and supermarkets, ranging from red mullet and fresh tuna to salmon, sea bass and gurnard.

Turbot Steamed with Baby Spinach, Red Wine and Thyme

4 × 140 g/5 oz fillets of turbot, skinned
450 g/1 lb baby spinach, washed
1 pinch nutmeg
sea salt and freshly milled white pepper

Sauce
8 shallots, finely chopped
250 ml/8 fl oz/1 cup red wine
1 sprig thyme
300 ml/10 fl oz/1¼ cups fish stock (see page 138)

Serves 4

Preheat the oven to 205°C/400°F/gas 6.

Place the shallots, red wine and half the thyme in a pan and cook over a high heat until the shallots have absorbed all the wine. Add the fish stock and reduce by two-thirds.

Place the turbot on a steaming tray and steam over a pan of boiling water for 45 minutes.

Just before the end of the steaming time, sweat the spinach in a covered pan over a high heat for 3 minutes. Drain and season with a pinch of nutmeg, salt and white pepper. Season the wine sauce, remove the thyme and reserve for a garnish, if liked.

To serve, put a quarter of the spinach in the centre of the plate, place a turbot fillet on top and pour round the sauce.

Fat: medium Kcals: 277 Cholesterol: high Fibre: low

Opposite, from back: *Grilled Fillet of Mackerel with Apple Chutney, Gurnard Roasted with Garlic and Rosemary with Gazpacho and Turbot Steamed with Baby Spinach, Red Wine and Thyme*

Gurnard Roasted with Garlic and Rosemary with Gazpacho

4 × 225 g/8 oz gurnard, cleaned and gutted
4 cloves garlic, skinned
4 sprigs rosemary
juice of 1 lemon
sea salt and freshly milled black pepper

Sauce
1 red pepper
1 green pepper
1 yellow pepper
½ cucumber
8 tomatoes, skinned and deseeded
3 tbsp extra virgin olive oil
1 tbsp wholemeal soft breadcrumbs
1 clove garlic, finely diced (minced)
2 shallots, roughly chopped
1 tbsp balsamic vinegar
1 tsp honey
juice of ½ orange
sea salt and freshly milled white pepper

Garnish
20 cloves garlic, skinned
1 tsp olive oil
1 tsp maple syrup

Serves 4

Preheat the oven to 220°C/425°F/gas 7.

To make the garnish, peel the garlic cloves and blanch for 1 minute, drain and blanch 4 more times, using fresh water each time. Heat a roasting tray on top of the stove until smoking, then add the olive oil and syrup and brown the garlic cloves.

Stuff the cavities of each gurnard with a garlic clove and a sprig of rosemary, then trickle over a little lemon juice. Lightly season with salt and black pepper. Place on top of the garlic in the roasting tray and roast in the oven for 15–20 minutes until cooked through.

Meanwhile, make the sauce. Cut open each pepper, discard the seeds and cut the flesh into 3 mm/⅛ in dice; reserve half of each diced pepper for garnishing. Cut the cucumber in half and reserve 1 half for garnish. Cut the other half into small dice and liquidize with all the ingredients in a food processor or blender until puréed. Heat gently in a small pan.

To serve, spoon a pool of sauce onto the centre of each plate. Place a gurnard on top and garnish with diced pepper, cucumber slices and the roasted garlic.

Fat: high Kcals: 330 Cholesterol: high Fibre: medium

Grilled Fillet of Mackerel with Apple Chutney

4 tsp wholemeal flour
1 pinch cayenne pepper
1 sprig thyme
4 × 225 g/8 oz mackerel, filleted and boned
1 tbsp extra virgin olive oil

Apple chutney
1 small onion, finely chopped
1 pinch ground cumin
1 pinch ground ginger
1 pinch turmeric
1 pinch chilli pepper
1 clove garlic, finely diced (minced)
225 g/8 oz cooking apples, peeled and roughly chopped
2 tbsp sultanas
2 tbsp cider vinegar
2 tbsp clear honey
1 tsp hazelnut oil

Garnish
2 limes, cut into wedges

Serves 4

Season the flour with the cayenne pepper and thyme, then roll the mackerel fillets in the flour. Shake off any excess flour, lightly brush each fillet with olive oil and place on a grilling tray.

To make the chutney, sweat the onion with all the spices and garlic in a stainless steel pan for 2 minutes over a medium heat. Add the apples to the pan together with the rest of the chutney ingredients, and stew over a low heat for 25 minutes.

Grill the mackerel fillets under a hot grill for 8 minutes until golden brown. Serve with the warm chutney and a wedge of lime.

Fat: high Kcals: 472 Cholesterol: high Fibre: low

Salmon Baked with Samphire and Morels

4 × 110 g/4 oz fillets of salmon
2 shallots, finely chopped
1 sprig thyme
100 ml/4 fl oz/½ cup dry white wine
150 ml/5 fl oz/⅔ cup fish stock (see page 138)
170 g/6 oz samphire
285 g/10 oz/2 cups fresh morels, wiped
juice of 1 lime
2 tsp *crème fraîche*
25 g/1 oz/⅛ cup polyunsaturated spread
1 bunch chives, chopped
sea salt and freshly milled black pepper

Serves 4

Preheat the oven to 230°C/450°F/gas 8.

Heat a non-stick ovenproof pan on top of the stove over a high heat. Lightly season the pan with salt and pepper then add the salmon and cook for 30 seconds on each side. The presentation side of each fillet should now be face up. Place the pan in the oven for 8 minutes until the salmon is cooked through. Remove from the oven and place the salmon fillets on kitchen paper to drain.

In a non-stick saucepan cook the chopped shallots and the sprig of thyme until the shallots are translucent. Add the white wine and reduce over a high heat by two-thirds. Stir in the fish stock and reduce by a quarter.

In a separate non-stick pan gently cook the samphire and morels with the lime juice and a little black pepper for 3 minutes.

Remove the sauce from the stove and shake in the *crème fraîche* and the polyunsaturated spread off the heat. Season to taste and pass through a fine sieve into a warm sauce boat and stir in the chives.

Spoon a pool of sauce onto each plate, add a pile of samphire and place a salmon fillet on top with the morels arranged around the fish.

Fat: high Kcals: 297 Cholesterol: high Fibre: low

Opposite, from back: *Salmon Baked with Samphire and Morels;* above: *Cod Baked with Wild Mushrooms and Tarragon*

Cod Baked with Wild Mushrooms, Tarragon and White Wine

4 × 140 g/5 oz fillets of cod, skinned
115 g/4 oz wild mushrooms, preferably horn of plenty, wiped
1 small onion, chopped
1 bunch tarragon
100 ml/4 fl oz/½ cup white wine
115 g/4 oz/½ cup puy lentils, boiled
sea salt and freshly milled black pepper

Sauce
1 medium-sized carrot, finely chopped
4 shallots, finely chopped
2 sprigs tarragon
6 black peppercorns
1 star anise
250 ml/8 fl oz/1 cup white wine
575 ml/1 pt/2½ cups fish stock (see page 138)
85 g/3 oz/½ cup dried wild mushrooms

Serves 4

Preheat the oven to 190°C/375°F/gas 5. Put a baking sheet in the oven.

Place the cod fillets, wild mushrooms and chopped onion into an ovenproof dish with a lid. Add half the tarragon leaves (keeping the stalks for later) and cover with white wine. Season with sea salt and freshly ground black pepper. Place in the refrigerator until ready to cook.

Soak the dried mushrooms in warm water for 30 minutes, then drain. To make the sauce, in a non-stick saucepan brown the vegetables with the tarragon stalks, black peppercorns and star anise. When brown, add the white wine and reduce over a high heat by two-thirds. Add the fish stock and reduce again by two-thirds.

When the sauce has reduced, cook the cod fillets. Place the dish on the baking sheet in the oven and bake for approximately 10 minutes. Gently warm the puy lentils in a saucepan.

To serve, spoon a quarter of the lentils into the centre of each plate, place a cod fillet on top and arrange the wild mushrooms around. Check the sauce for seasoning, then pour over and garnish with the reserved tarragon.

Fat: low Kcals: 221 Cholesterol: high Fibre: low

Sea Bass Grilled with Sorrel and Chives

4 × 140 g/5 oz fillets of sea bass, scaled and boned
1 tbsp extra virgin olive oil
juice of 1 lemon
300 ml/10 fl oz/1¼ cups fish stock (see page 138)
1 tbsp dry vermouth
8 tbsp natural, low-fat yoghurt (see page 142)
1 bunch sorrel, stalks removed and chopped
1 bunch chives, finely chopped
salt and freshly milled white pepper

Serves 4

Brush the sea bass fillets with the olive oil and squeeze the lemon juice on top. Season with salt and white pepper. Refrigerate.

Add the vermouth to the fish stock and reduce over a high heat until it is of coating consistency. Leave to cool slightly and shake in the yoghurt. Keep warm in a *bain marie* on top of the stove.

Place the fish over hot charcoal or under a hot grill, skin-side down, and cook for 2 minutes. Carefully turn the fish and cook for approximately 3 minutes.

Meanwhile, in a separate non-stick pan, sweat the sorrel for 1 minute. To serve, place a quarter of the sorrel in the centre of each plate and put a sea bass fillet on top. Stir the chives into the sauce, check for seasoning and pour around the fish and sorrel.

Fat: medium Kcals: 194 Cholesterol: high Fibre: low

Red Snapper Cooked on a Bed of Aubergines with Lemon Vinaigrette

2 small aubergines (eggplants), cut into 6 mm/¼ in slices
2 lemons, roughly chopped
4 dsp extra virgin olive oil
2 tbsp white wine vinegar
1 tsp clear honey
4 × 110 g/4 oz red snapper fillets, scaled and boned
sea salt and freshly milled black pepper

Marinade
2 cloves garlic, crushed
10 black peppercorns, crushed
1 tbsp hazelnut oil
juice of ½ lemon

Garnish
1 bunch purple basil

Serves 4

Preheat the oven to 205°C/400°F/gas 6.

In a shallow dish, mix together the ingredients for the marinade together with a pinch of salt, and add the aubergine (eggplant) slices, turning to coat well. Cover and refrigerate for 1 hour.

In a liquidizer or food processor blend the chopped lemons, olive oil, vinegar and honey until smooth. Pass through a fine sieve into a small pan and put to one side.

Remove the aubergines (eggplants) from the marinade, place on a baking sheet and put the fish on top, skin-side up. Place in the oven and bake for 12 minutes until the fish is cooked through.

Drain the aubergines (eggplants) on kitchen paper, season with black pepper and arrange around one side of each plate. Warm the sauce through, taking care not to boil, and spoon a little onto the opposite side of the plate from the aubergines (eggplants). Place a fish fillet on top of the sauce and garnish with purple basil leaves.

Fat: high Kcals: 400 Cholesterol: high Fibre: low

Brill with Noodles and Clams

300 ml/10 fl oz/1¼ cups fish stock (see page 138)
juice of 4 limes
1 star anise
450 g/16 oz clams
4 × 115 g/4 oz fillets of brill
225 g/8 oz saffron pasta (see page 141)
juice of ½ lemon
2 shallots, finely chopped
45 g/1½ oz/¼ cup polyunsaturated spread
1 tbsp natural, low-fat *fromage frais*
2 tbsp raw tomato concasse (see page 137)
sea salt and freshly milled white pepper

Serves 4

Simmer the fish stock, lime juice and star anise for 10 minutes. Pick over the clams and scrub them clean. Place in a steaming compartment over the fish stock and steam for 4 minutes. Keep warm, discarding any shells that have not opened.

Poach the brill fillets in the fish stock for 3½ minutes, then drain and keep warm, reserving the fish stock.

Meanwhile, cook the noodles in a large pan filled with lightly salted boiling water to which the lemon juice has been added, 3-4 minutes.

Place the shallots in the fish stock and reduce over a high heat by two-thirds. Off the heat, shake in the cold polyunsaturated spread and the *fromage frais*. Season to taste, then press through a fine sieve.

Arrange a brill fillet, a quarter of the noodles, clams and concasse on each plate. Pour the sauce around and garnish with a sprig of chervil.

Fat: high Kcals: 510 Cholesterol: high Fibre: medium

Scallops poached in Caraway and Saffron

12 king scallops
1 shallot, finely chopped
300 ml/10 fl oz/1¼ cups fish stock (see page 138)
1 tbsp caraway seeds, crushed
2 tbsp white wine
2 courgettes (zucchini), cut into strips
1 pinch saffron threads
45 g/1½ oz/¼ cup polyunsaturated spread
2 tsps raw tomato concasse (see page 137)

Garnish
4 springs cheril

Serves 4

Remove the scallops from the shell, cutting away any membrane and dark intestines, including the small curved muscle from the white meat. Remove and discard the corals. Wash and dry on kitchen paper. Slice each scallop into 4.

Place the shallot, fish stock, caraway seeds and white wine in a pan and reduce over a high heat by two-thirds. Add the scallops, cover and gently poach for 1 minute. Remove from the liquid and keep warm.

Quickly stir-fry the courgette (zucchini) strips and arrange in the centre of each plate.

Reduce the sauce over a high heat by half and then shake in the saffron and polyunsaturated spread.

To serve, arrange the scallops around the courgette (zucchini) strips and pour a little sauce around the scallops, garnish with the tomato concasse and a sprig of chervil.

Fat: high Kcals: 228 Cholesterol: high Fibre: low

Opposite, from top: *Sea Bass Grilled with Sorrel and Chives, Red Snapper Cooked on a Bed of Aubergines with Lemon Vinaigrette, and Brill with Noodles and Clams*

Red Mullet with Salad Niçoise

2 shallots, finely chopped
75 g/2½ oz/⅓ cup mange-tout (sugar snap peas), blanched and sliced
10 black olives, stoned and chopped
4 large tomatoes, skinned, deseeded and finely chopped
1 tbsp extra virgin olive oil
2 small potatoes
4 × 225 g/8 oz fillets of red mullet, scaled
juice of ½ lime
sea salt and freshly milled black pepper

Sauce
2 tbsp cider vinegar
1 pinch saffron powder
1 tbsp extra virgin olive oil

Serves 4

To prepare the salad, mix the shallots, mange-tout (sugar snap peas), olives and two-thirds of the diced tomato in a large bowl with the olive oil and lightly season. Peel the potatoes and cut into 6 mm/¼ in dice. Boil until cooked, about 15 minutes. Allow to cool and add the potatoes to the vegetable mixture.

To make the sauce, reduce the cider vinegar and saffron over a high heat by two-thirds and stir in the olive oil.

Season the red mullet fillets with the lime juice and some black pepper and grill, skin-side up, for 4 minutes.

To serve, place a quarter of the salad niçoise in the centre of each plate, top with a red mullet fillet and pour a little sauce over the fish. Garnish with the remaining diced tomato.

Fat: high Kcals: 323 Cholesterol: high Fibre: low

Parrot Fish Cooked in an Envelope

1 tsp walnut oil
4 sprigs parsley
4 × 40 g/5 oz fillets of parrot fish, scaled, skin on
2 shallots, sliced
1 carrot, sliced
1 pinch fenugreek
4 star anise
8 black peppercorns
4 sun-dried tomatoes, roughly chopped
50 ml/2 fl oz/¼ cup dry vermouth
juice of 1 lime
sea salt and freshly milled black pepper

Serves 4

Preheat the oven to 220°C/425°F/gas 7.

Cut 4 squares of aluminium foil about 30 cm (12 in) square and fold each one in half to form a triangle. Open the foil out again to reform the square. Lightly oil one half of the foil squares and add one sprig of parsley and season with a little salt and pepper.

Place a fillet on top of each foil square and sprinkle with the shallots, carrot, spices, peppercorns and sun-dried tomatoes. Pour a little vermouth and lime juice over each fillet and fold the foil over to reform a triangle. Fold the edges double on each half to seal, fold over and seal the ends and place the packets on a baking sheet.

Bake in the oven for 8 minutes until cooked through. Serve immediately, opening the envelope at the table to enjoy the aroma as well as the flavour.

Fat: high Kcals: 236 Cholesterol: high Fibre: medium

Layers of Cabbage, Salmon and Pike Mousse with Scampi Tails

900 g/2 lb pike, filleted, boned, skinned and roughly chopped
3 tbsp natural, low-fat, *fromage frais*
1 egg white
juice of ½ lemon
1 pinch cayenne pepper
1 pinch celery salt
285 g/10 oz Savoy cabbage
900 g/2 lb side of salmon
2 shallots
75 ml/3 fl oz/⅓ cup dry white wine
150 ml/5 fl oz/⅔ cup fish stock (see page 138)
12 scampi tails, raw, peeled and cut in half lengthways
½ bunch tarragon
3 tbsp *crème fraîche*
6 tomatoes
1 bunch basil
2 tbsp extra virgin olive oil
1 tsp white wine vinegar
sea salt and freshly milled black pepper

Garnish
1 bunch chervil

Serves 4

Preheat oven to 180°C/350°F/gas 4.

To make the mousse, blend the pike, *fromage frais*, egg white, lemon juice, cayenne pepper and celery salt in a food processor or blender until smooth, then press through a fine sieve.

Using a 7.5 cm/3 in pastry cutter, cut 8 circles from the cabbage leaves. Blanch in lightly salted boiling water for 2 minutes, then refresh under running cold water.

Carefully cut the salmon through half its thickness lengthways. Use the pastry cutter to cut 8 circles out of the salmon, using a sharp knife around the outside edge of the cutter if necessary, and season. Cover 4 circles of the salmon with a cabbage circle and spread each with an eighth of the pike mousse. Place another layer of cabbage on top of the mousse, then follow with another layer of pike mousse and top with a circle of salmon. Place on a non-stick baking sheet and refrigerate until ready to cook.

Sweat the shallots in a covered non-stick pan until translucent. Add the white wine and reduce over a high heat by two-thirds. Pour in the fish stock, and reduce again by half. Bring to a gentle simmer, add the scampi tails and tarragon leaves and cook for 1½ minutes. Remove the scampi from the stock, drain and keep warm. Shake the *crème fraîche* into the stock, off the heat, and pass into a sauce boat and keep warm.

Dice (mince) one tomato and liquidize the rest of tomatoes together with the basil, olive oil and white wine vinegar in a liquidizer or food processor until smooth, then pass through a fine sieve. Warm slightly in a pan, and add just before serving. Put the salmon in the oven for 18 minutes. Remove from the oven and place in the middle of each plate and spoon both sauces around the salmon. Spoon the green sauce around the salmon, then the circle of red sauce along the edge of a green sauce. Circle the sauce with 6 scampi tails. Garnish with chervil on top of each tail.

Fat: high Kcals: 587 Cholesterol: high Fibre: medium

Grilled Tuna with Black-eyed Beans and Coriander

100 g/4 oz/1 cup black-eyed beans
2 tsp coriander seeds, crushed
2 cloves garlic, diced (minced)
1 bunch coriander, chopped
juice of 2 limes
2 tbsp extra virgin olive oil
4 × 150 g/5 oz tuna steaks, skinned and boned
1 small onion, finely chopped
4 tbsp cooked tomato concasse (see page 136)
150 ml/5 fl oz/⅔ cup tomato vinaigrette (see page 138)
sea salt and freshly milled black pepper

Serves 4

Soak the black-eyed beans in water overnight.

Make a marinade by combining the crushed coriander seeds, the garlic and a quarter of the chopped coriander in the lime juice and 1 tablespoon of the oil. Place the tuna steaks in a shallow dish and spoon over the marinade. Leave to marinate in a cool place for 2 hours.

Meanwhile, discard the soaking water from the black-eyed beans, rinse and cover with fresh cold water, lightly salted, in a non-stick saucepan. Simmer, covered, for 1 hour or until the beans are tender. Drain and reserve.

Heat the remaining oil in a large frying pan (skillet), add the onion and sweat until translucent. Stir in the tomato concasse and remove from the heat. Add the black-eyed beans, tomato vinaigrette and the rest of the chopped coriander.

Remove the fish steaks and reserve the marinade. Season the steaks, then grill, preferably over charcoal, cooking for 4 minutes on each side; brush the steaks with marinade while cooking. Warm the bean and tomato mixture, make a small mound in the centre of each plate and serve with a tuna steak placed on top.

Fat: high Kcals: 359 Cholesterol: high Fibre: medium

Opposite: *Layers of Cabbage, Salmon and Pike Mousse with Scampi Tails;* above: *Grilled Tuna with Black-eyed Beans*

Salmon Poached in Champagne served with Cucumber and Watercress Salad

4 tbsp dry champagne
4 × 110 g/4 oz fillets of salmon, skinned

Salad
4 tbsp natural, low-fat yoghurt (see page 142)
1 tsp parsley, chopped
1 tsp fresh mint, chopped
1 tsp clear honey
1 red apple, grated
1 small cucumber, cut into 4 cm/ 1½ in batons
1 bunch watercress, stalks removed
sea salt and freshly milled black pepper

Garnish
4 wedges lime

Serves 4

Bring the champagne to the boil in a shallow pan. Add the salmon and cook for 4 minutes the over a high heat. Remove from the heat and leave to cool in the champagne. Chill in the refrigerator.

To prepare the salad, mix the yoghurt, parsley, mint and honey together and season with salt and pepper. Pour over the grated apple, cucumber and watercress leaves just before serving and toss well.

To serve, place a quarter of the salad on each plate and rest a cold salmon fillet on top. Add a wedge of lime. This is delicious with a cold new potato salad.

Fat: high Kcals: 272 Cholesterol: high Fibre: low

Trout Wrapped in Chinese Leaves with Ginger and Spring Onion

4 Chinese leaves
4 × 225 g/8 oz fillets of trout, skinned
½ clove garlic, crushed
1 tsp fresh ginger, grated
2 bunches spring onions (scallions), cut into short lengths
1 piece lemon grass, cut into 4 lengthways
sea salt and freshly milled black pepper

Sauce
2 shallots, finely chopped
2 tbsp dry sherry
3 tsp light soy sauce
150 ml/5 fl oz/⅔ cup fish stock (see page 138)
juice of 1 lemon
1 pinch five spice powder

Serves 4

Blanch the Chinese leaves in boiling water for 30 seconds and refresh under cold water. Season the fish with salt and pepper, and add the garlic and the ginger. Fold the fillets into 3 and wrap in the blanched Chinese leaves.

Put the spring onions (scallions), lemon grass and wrapped fish into a bamboo steamer, and steam, covered, for 12 minutes.

To make the sauce, place the shallots, sherry and soy sauce into a non-stick pan and reduce over a high heat until all the liquid has been absorbed by the shallots. Add the fish stock, lemon juice and the five spice powder and stir well.

To serve, arrange the onions and strips of lemon grass around the fish and spoon over the sauce.

Fat: high Kcals: 243 Cholesterol: high Fibre: medium

Meat, poultry and game are extremely versatile and play an important part in a balanced diet, being an excellent source of protein. Choose from traditional roasted meats such as Venison roasted with Pistachio Mousse, Cabbage and Juniper, and Roasted Fillet of Pork with Apricot, and Onion to more exotic dishes served with fruit and vegetables. These include Duck Breast roasted with Lentils and Kumquat Marmalade and Barbecued Chicken Chilli and Pineapple wrapped in a Cornflour Pasty.

Duck Liver Mousse with Sprouting Lentils and Smoked Bacon

1 medium-sized onion, finely chopped
1 garlic clove, diced (minced)
2 tbsp brandy
150 ml/5 fl oz/⅔ cup red wine
4 sheets ready-made filo pastry
1 tbsp extra virgin olive oil
1 tbsp wholemeal flour
1 × 115 g/4 oz breast of corn-fed chicken, skinned, boned and trimmed
1 egg yolk
350 g/¾ lb fresh duck livers
1 pinch celery salt
2 dsp natural, low-fat *fromage frais*
4 egg whites
4 rashers lean smoked back bacon, fat and rind removed, cut into lardons
240 g/8 oz/1 cup sprouting lentils

Garnish
1 bunch chervil

Serves 4

Preheat the oven to 180°C/350°F/gas 4. Sweat the onion and garlic in a pan until translucent. Add the brandy and red wine, and reduce to a syrup consistency; leave to cool.

Using a 12.5 cm/5 in pastry cutter, cut out 8 circles of filo pastry. Brush each one with a little olive oil and put half of the circles on top of the others to form 4 circles and place in a small, deep round tin. Bake in the oven for 5 minutes until golden brown, leave to set and remove from the tin.

Grease 4 ramekins and lightly dust with wholemeal flour. Finely chop the chicken breast and blend with the egg yolk, onion and brandy mixture, duck livers, celery salt and *fromage frais* in a food processor or blender until smooth. Pass through a fine sieve. Whisk the egg whites until stiff and fold into the mixture. Fill the greased ramekins with the mousse and level the tops with a flat knife. Place in an ovenproof tray filled with water and cook in the oven for 20 minutes.

Meanwhile, fry the bacon lardons in a non-stick pan over a high heat until golden brown. Add the sprouting lentils, lower the heat and cook for 1 minute.

Plunge the ramekins in hot water up to their rims for 30 seconds, and turn out into the filo baskets. Place in the centre of each plate and surround with the bacon and lentils. Garnish with chervil and serve.

Fat: high Kcals: 387 Cholesterol: high Fibre: low

Opposite, from back: *Duck Liver Mousse with Sprouting Lentils and Smoked Bacon, Fillet of Beef with Mango Glaze, and Pheasant Stuffed with Truffle Mousse and Creamed Fennel*

Pheasant Stuffed with Truffle Mousse and Creamed Fennel

2 pheasants, oven-ready
115 g/4 oz tail fillet of veal
2 × 115 g/4 oz breasts of corn-fed chicken, skinned, boned and trimmed
1 clove garlic, diced (minced)
2 tbsp natural, low-fat *fromage frais*
1 egg white
4 truffles, peeled and chopped
2 tsp pink peppercorns, crushed
575 ml/1 pt/2½ cups chicken stock (see page 138)
2 bulbs fennel
100 ml/4 fl oz/½ cup white wine
4 tbsp *crème fraîche*
1 quantity Champneys bechamel (see page 141)
1 tbsp olive oil
sea salt and freshly milled black pepper

Serves 4

Preheat the oven to 220°C/425°F/gas 7.

Separate the legs and thighs from the rest of the pheasant carcass. Remove the skin and trim the leg meat from the bones and chop it roughly. Extract the breast and thigh meat whole and slice down the centre to make a cavity for stuffing. Place the chopped leg meat, veal fillet, chicken breast, garlic, *fromage frais* and egg white in a food processor or blender and mix until smooth. Pass through a fine sieve and add the truffles and pink peppercorns. Stuff the breasts and thighs with this mixture, wrap in muslin and tie at the ends. Bring the chicken stock to the boil in a large pan and lower in the muslin-wrapped pheasant. Cover and simmer gently for 5 minutes.

Remove and reserve the tops from the fennel and finely chop the bulbs. Blanch the chopped bulbs in lightly salted water for 3 minutes, refresh under cold running water and drain.

Bring the white wine to the boil in a pan, reduce over a high heat by half then add the chopped fennel. Remove the sauce from the heat and stir in the *crème fraîche* and the bechamel.

Heat the olive oil in a roasting tray on the top of the stove. Remove the pheasant from the muslin and brown for 2 minutes in the hot tray. Transfer to the oven and roast for 5 minutes until cooked and golden brown.

Chop the reserved fennel tops and add to the sauce. Warm through but do not reboil. Remove the pheasant from the oven and cut the thighs into 6 mm/¼ in slices and arrange around the breasts. Serve with a little sauce and fennel fronds.

Fat: high Kcals: 457 Cholesterol: high Fibre: low

Fillet of Beef with Mango Glaze

4 × 110 g/4 oz fillet steaks of beef, trimmed
1 large, ripe mango
1 tsp peach and lemon chutney (see page 140)
575 ml/1 pt/2½ cups veal stock (see page 139)
2 shallots, finely chopped
50 ml/2 fl oz/¼ cup madeira
2 small carrots, roughly chopped
1 large onion, roughly chopped
1 clove garlic, finely diced (minced)
1 tsp mild curry powder
1 tsp sultanas
1 pinch powdered ginger
1 egg yolk
75 ml/3 fl oz/⅓ cup extra virgin olive oil
2 large leeks
3 tbsps raw tomato concasse (see page 137)

Serves 4

Preheat the oven to 205°C/400°F/gas 6.

Tie the beef fillets with string around the centre to ensure they keep their shape while cooking.

Peel the mango then cut in half. Cut half into strips 5 cm × 3 mm/2 in × ⅛ in; reserve for the garnish. Purée the other half of the mango in a food processor or blender. Stir in the peach and lemon chutney.

Bring the veal stock to the boil and reduce over a high heat until reduced by three-quarters.

Sweat the shallots in a covered non-stick pan over a low heat until translucent. Deglaze with the madeira, reduce over a high heat by half, then pour in the veal stock. In a separate pan sweat the carrots, onions, garlic, curry powder, sultanas and ginger in a covered non-stick pan for 5 minutes over a low heat. Cover with water and cook for 30 minutes. Add to the chutney and mango mixture.

Heat a roasting tray on the top of the stove, season the beef fillets and seal on both sides in the hot tray. Roast for 12 minutes.

Meanwhile, in a large bowl whisk the egg yolk with 1 tablespoon of warm water until light and frothy. Add to the chutney mixture and mix in well. Remove the beef from the oven and spoon a little of the mango glaze over each fillet. Place under a hot grill for approximately 45 seconds.

Heat the oil in a large pan until smoking, discard the green parts of the leeks and cut the white parts into thin strips and fry until golden brown. Drain on kitchen paper.

Add the reserved mango strips and the tomato concasse to the sauce and warm slightly. Spoon a pool of sauce onto each plate and place a glazed fillet on top. Garnish with the strips of leek.

Fat: high Kcals: 464 Cholesterol: high Fibre: medium

Stuffed Breast of Chicken with a Tomato Vinaigrette

4 × 140 g/5 oz breasts of corn-fed chicken, skinned, boned and trimmed
2 large carrots, peeled and grated
1 large leek, finely chopped
16 black olives, stoned and roughly chopped
575 ml/1 pt/2½ cups chicken stock (see page 138)
sea salt and freshly milled black pepper

Vinaigrette
3 large, ripe tomatoes
2 tbsp extra virgin olive oil
1 leaf basil
1 tbsp cider vinegar

Serves 4

Make a sharp incision about 2 cm/⅔ in long into one side of each chicken breast to form a pocket.

Season the grated carrot, chopped leek and the olives with salt and pepper and stuff the chicken breasts with the mixture. Overlap the pocket openings to seal the mixture inside.

Preheat the oven to 220°C/425°F/gas 7.

In an ovenproof dish, bring the chicken stock to the boil on the top of the stove and add the chicken breasts. Place in the oven for approximately 10 minutes until poached.

Meanwhile, liquidize all the ingredients for the vinaigrette in a food processor or blender and pass through a fine sieve.

When the chicken is cooked, slice each breast diagonally into 5 pieces and place on individual plates. Spoon round the vinaigrette and serve immediately.

Fat: high Kcals: 298 Cholesterol: high Fibre: low

Roasted Baby Pigeon with Coriander and Pearl Barley Dumplings

4 squab pigeons
1 bay leaf
2 cloves garlic, finely diced (minced)
1 small onion, finely chopped
150 ml/5 fl oz/⅔ cup red wine
3 tomatoes, roughly diced
700 ml/1¼ pt/3 cups chicken stock (see page 138)
1 bunch coriander
225 g/8 oz/1 cup pearl barley
1 × 115 g/4 oz breast of corn-fed chicken, skinned, boned and trimmed
2 fresh duck livers
2 tbsp natural, low-fat *fromage frais*
1 tsp extra virgin olive oil
1 tbsp maple syrup

Preheat the oven to 205°C/400°F/gas 6.

Remove the breasts from the pigeon carcasses and leave in a cool place. Trim the wing bones and knuckles and place the bones in a non-stick pan with the bay leaf, 1 clove of garlic and onion. Cook on a high heat for approximately 4–5 minutes until brown, then add the red wine and tomatoes, 575 ml/1 pint/2½ cups of the chicken stock and the stalks from the coriander, reserving the leaves for the dumplings. Reduce over a high heat by two-thirds, then pass through a fine sieve, discarding the bones.

In a separate pan, cook the pearl barley in boiling salted water for 20 minutes, then refresh under cold running water and drain.

Combine the chicken breast, duck liver, *fromage frais* and the remaining clove of garlic in a food processor or blender and blend until smooth. Pass through a sieve and add half the coriander leaves, chopped, and half the pearl barley. Mix well and form into 20 dumplings.

Heat the olive oil and the maple syrup in a roasting tray on the top of the stove. Add the peeled shallots and cook for 1 minute. Season the

Roasted Baby Pigeon with Coriander and Pearl Barley Dumplings

20 shallots, peeled

Garnish
4 sprigs chervil

Serves 4

pigeon breasts and add to roasting tray. Cook the leg and breast meat and shallots together in the oven for 15 minutes until golden brown.

Remove from the oven and keep the pigeon and shallots warm. Strain the excess fat from the pan and place on top of the stove on a low heat. Add the remaining pearl barley, the remaining chopped coriander leaves and the sauce; warm through for 3-4 minutes.

Meanwhile, bring the remaining chicken stock to the boil in a separate pan. Drop in the chicken dumplings and simmer, with the lid on, for 3 minutes until cooked through.

To serve, heap a quarter of the warmed pearl barley and coriander mixture in the centre of each plate and place a pigeon breast on top. Surround with 5 dumplings and 5 shallots and spoon a little sauce over to cover the plate.

Fat: high Kcals: 699 Cholesterol: high Fibre: low

Duck Breast Roasted with Lentils and Kumquat Marmalade

4 × 170 g/6 oz breasts of female Barbary duck
170 g/6 oz/1 cup puy lentils
sea salt and freshly milled black pepper

Marmalade
300 ml/10 fl oz/1¼ cups fresh orange juice
225 g/8 oz/2 cups kumquats, sliced

Sauce
3 shallots, finely chopped
50 ml/2 fl oz/¼ cup port
150 ml/5 fl oz/⅔ cup red grape juice
150 ml/5 fl oz/⅔ cup chicken stock (see page 138)
2 tsp arrowroot

Garnish
4 sprigs chervil

Serves 4

Preheat the oven to 205°C/400°F/gas 6.

Remove the skin and fat from the duck breasts, reserving the fat, and season. Replace the fat on top of each breast and place in a roasting tray. Boil the lentils in salted water for 15 minutes, then refresh under cold running water.

To make the marmalade, place the orange juice in a stainless steel pan and reduce over a high heat by two-thirds, add the kumquats and cook for 10 minutes over a medium heat.

To make the sauce, sweat the shallots in a non-stick pan until translucent. Add the port and the grape juice and reduce over a high heat until the liquid reaches syrup consistency. Mix the arrowroot with a little water to form a smooth paste then stir into the syrup to thicken, still on the heat.

Roast the duck breasts for 10 minutes in the oven until pink. Remove from the roasting tray and leave to rest for 5 minutes, then slice. Drain off the excess fat from the roasting tray, add the lentils, season with salt and pepper and warm over a low heat on the top of the stove.

Put a quarter of the warmed lentils in the centre of each plate, rest the duck breast slices on top and spoon over a little kumquat marmalade. Pour the sauce around the duck and garnish with chervil.

Fat: low Kcals: 301 Cholesterol: medium Fibre: medium

Grilled Corn-Fed Chicken with Walnut and Celeriac Cakes

- 1 large head celeriac, peeled
- 1 clove garlic, finely diced (minced)
- 1 small onion, finely chopped
- 2 rashers smoked lean back bacon, cut into lardons
- 2 dsp walnuts, crushed
- 30 g/1 oz/½ cup low-fat Cheddar cheese, grated
- 1 egg white
- 1 tbsp olive oil
- 4 × 140 g/5 oz breasts of corn-fed chicken
- sea salt and freshly milled black pepper

Sauce

- 300 ml/10 fl oz/1¼ cup apple juice
- 150 ml/5 fl oz/⅔ cup chicken stock (see page 138)
- 1 cooking apple, grated

Serves 4

Preheat the oven to 220°C/425°F/gas 7.

Slice one quarter of the celeriac into thin, round slices and put to one side. Grate the rest of the celeriac and combine with the garlic, onion, bacon rashers and walnuts in a non-stick pan, put on a lid, and sweat for 5 minutes until slightly soft. Leave to cool. Add the grated cheese and egg white and mix in thoroughly. Season. Press a quarter of the mixture into a 7.5 cm/3 in circular pastry cutter onto a non-stick roasting tray, pushing down firmly with the back of the hand. Remove the cutter to leave a cake shape. Repeat 3 more times. Place in the oven and cook for 15 minutes until golden brown.

Place the celeriac slices on a grilling tray and dribble over the olive oil. Lightly season. Season the chicken breasts and place them skin-side down on top of the celeriac. Grill under a medium-hot grill for 4 minutes on one side, then turn over and cook for a further 5 minutes until cooked through.

To make the sauce, pour the apple juice and chicken stock into a stainless steel pan and reduce over a high heat by two-thirds. Add the grated apple and immediately remove from the heat.

To serve, place a cake in the centre of each plate, rest a chicken breast on top and pour a little sauce around. Drain the slices of celeriac on kitchen paper to remove any excess fat, and arrange around the plate for the garnish.

Fat: high Kcals: 382 Cholesterol: high Fibre: low

Overleaf, left: *Grilled Corn-Fed Chicken with Walnut and Celeriac Cakes;* right: *Duck Breast Roasted with Lentils and Kumquat Marmalade*

Roasted Fillet of Veal with Roasted Shallots and Garlic with a Madeira Sauce

2 cloves garlic
1 × 170 g/6 oz breast of corn-fed chicken, skinned, boned and trimmed
2 bunches watercress, stalks removed
2 tbsp natural, low-fat *fromage frais*
4 × 140 g/5 oz fillets of veal, larder trimmed and tied
1 piece caul fat
20 shallots, peeled
90 ml/3½ fl oz/⅓ cup madeira
300 ml/10 fl oz/1¼ cups reduced veal stock (see page 139)
sea salt and freshly milled black pepper

Garnish
4 sprigs chervil

Serves 4

Preheat the oven to 230°C/450°F/gas 8.

Roast the garlic, skins on, in the oven for 5 minutes, then rinse in cold water. Remove the skins, then blanch in boiling water three times. Turn the oven temperature down to 190°C/375°F/gas 5.

Combine the chicken and watercress in a food processor or blender, mix in the *fromage frais* lightly season, and process until a firm mousse is formed. Pass the mousse through a fine sieve.

Spread a layer of mousse on top of each veal fillet, then wrap each fillet in caul fat. Heat a non-stick ovenproof pan on the top of the stove, then add the veal fillets and seal for 2 minutes on each side. Remove from the pan with a slotted spoon and keep warm. Add the garlic and shallots to the pan and lightly brown. Return the veal fillets to the pan, then transfer to the oven for 15 minutes.

When the fillets are cooked, remove them from the pan together with the shallots and garlic and keep in a warm place. Place the pan on the top of the stove, deglaze the cooking juice with the madeira and reduce by half. Stir in the veal stock, reheat and season to taste.

Place a veal fillet on each plate, spoon over the sauce and surround with garlic cloves and shallots. Garnish with chervil leaves and serve immediately.

Fat: medium Kcals: 289 Cholesterol: high Fibre: low

Saddle of Venison Roasted with Pistachio Mousse, Cabbage and Juniper

450 g/1 lb saddle of venison loin
1 Savoy cabbage
1 onion, sliced
4 juniper berries
4 tbsp water
1 tbsp clear honey
1 tsp arrowroot, mixed with a little water to form a paste
sea salt and freshly milled black pepper

Mousse
2 × 140 g/5 oz breasts of corn-fed chicken, skinned and boned
1 pinch celery salt
1 pinch cayenne pepper
2 tbsp natural, low-fat *fromage frais*
1 egg
45 g/1½ oz/¼ cup pistachio nuts, shelled and roughly chopped

Herb crust
4 tbsp fresh wholemeal breadcrumbs
1 clove garlic, finely diced (minced)
2 tbsp fresh mixed herbs (e.g. tarragon, chervil, basil), chopped

Sauce
1.35 kg/3 lb venison bones
2 carrots
1 leek
2 sticks celery
2 onions
2.25 l/4 pt/10½ cups cold water
3 sprigs thyme
1 bay leaf
150 ml/5 fl oz/⅔ cup red wine
50 ml/2 fl oz/¼ cup port
450 g/1 lb/4 cups gooseberries or cranberries

Serves 4

Preheat the oven to 205°C/400°F/gas 6.

To make the sauce, place the bones and vegetables on a roasting tray and brown in the oven for 25–30 minutes. Remove from the oven and place in a pan with the cold water. Add the thyme and the bay leaf. Bring to the boil, skim the surface of the water to remove any excess fat, reduce the heat slightly and simmer for 2 hours.

Pass this stock through a fine sieve into a clean pan, discarding the bones. Reserve the thyme and add the red wine, port and gooseberries or cranberries. Reduce over a high heat by three-quarters and pass through a fine sieve once again.

To make the pistachio mousse, place the chicken breast, celery salt, cayenne pepper, *fromage frais* and the egg into a food processor or blender and mix till smooth. Pass through a fine sieve. Add the pistachios and spread a thin layer over the length of the saddle of venison.

To make the herb crust, blend the breadcrumbs, garlic and herbs in a food processor or blender till well mixed. Press onto the chicken mousse. Place the saddle of venison on top of the thyme in a roasting tray and roast for 20 minutes until cooked but still pink.

Meanwhile, shred the cabbage and add to a large pan with the onion and juniper berries. Add the water and lightly season. Cover and steam over a high heat for approximately 10 minutes until the cabbage is tender. Drain off any excess liquid.

Remove the gooseberries or cranberries from the sauce using a slotted spoon and put into a pan with the honey. Heat gently and keep in a warm place.

Serve the venison cut into 2.5 cm/1 in slices on a little of the cabbage, with the sauce around the outside, garnished with the warmed fruit.

Fat: high Kcals: 533 Cholesterol: high Fibre: high

Roasted Quail Stuffed with Chervil Mousse

1 × 140 g/5 oz breast of corn-fed chicken, skinned, boned and trimmed
1 egg
115 g/4 oz natural, low-fat *fromage frais*
1 bunch chervil, chopped
4 quails, boned (reserve the bones for the sauce)
2 rashers lean back bacon, fat and rind removed
8 baby carrots
8 baby courgettes (zucchini)
8 baby leeks
8 baby beetroot (beet)
8 shallots
8 mange-tout (sugar snap peas)

Chutney
450 g/1 lb swede, roughly diced (minced)
2 medium-sized onions, chopped
55 g/2 oz/¼ cup sultanas
2 tomatoes, roughly chopped
2 tbsp cider vinegar
1 cooking apple, diced (minced)

Sauce
4 shallots, finely chopped
10 button mushrooms
50 ml/2 fl oz/¼ cup white wine
300 ml/10 fl oz/1¼ cup chicken stock (see page 138)
6 sprigs chervil
1 bay leaf
2 black peppercorns, crushed

Serves 4

To make the chutney, cook the swede in a little water until tender, drain and mash until smooth. Sweat the chopped onions, sultanas and tomatoes in a covered non-stick pan until the onion becomes translucent. Add the cider vinegar and reduce over a high heat by half. Mix in the apple and the swede and lightly season.

To make the sauce brown the quail bones in a small, deep pan. Sweat the shallots and mushrooms in a covered non-stick pan until the shallots have softened. Add the white wine to the pan and reduce over a high heat by half. Add the chicken stock, quail bones, chervil, bay leaf and peppercorns and simmer for 20 minutes.

Preheat the oven to 205°C/400°F/gas 6.

Process the chicken breast in a food processor or blender for 2 minutes, add the egg and season, then pass through a sieve. Return the mixture to the processor or blender and beat in the *fromage frais* and chopped chervil. Fill the quail cavities with the mousse. Place half a bacon rasher on each quail breast and put the quail in a non-stick roasting tray. Roast for 10 minutes until cooked through.

Meanwhile, cook the baby vegetables in lightly salted water, simmering for about 8–10 minutes until tender.

Spoon a quarter of the chutney into a circle in the centre of each plate, place a quail on top and surround with vegetables. Spoon over the sauce and serve.

Fat: high Kcals: 500 Cholesterol: high Fibre: high

Opposite, top: *Saddle of Venison Roasted with Pistachio Mousse, Cabbage and Juniper;* bottom: *Roasted Quail Stuffed with Chervil Mousse*

marinate the prawns

chop up your ingredients

juicy, fresh mangoes

Thai-style mango salad with griddled prawns

'loads of fantastic flavours, especially the mango'

Jamie's tip

'try mangoes in both savoury and sweet dishes. They are great in spicy salsa and liven up smoothies a treat'

serves: 4
preparation time: 20 minutes
cooking time: 5-8 minutes

what you need

for the griddled prawns:
20 large, headless tiger prawns
4 skewers

for the marinade:
1 thumb-sized piece fresh ginger, grated
20g pack fresh coriander, chopped
1 red chilli, deseeded and chopped
4 tablespoons fresh lime juice
3 tablespoons olive oil
1 tablespoon sesame oil
1 tablespoon soy sauce
good pinch of brown sugar
½ clove garlic, peeled and crushed

for the salad:
1 ripe and ready-to-eat mango
2 handfuls ready-to-eat bean sprouts
3 small cucumbers, chopped
1 handful fresh coriander
1 red pepper, deseeded and cut into thin strips
1 bunch spring onions, chopped
sea salt
small handful sesame seeds
Bianconi extra virgin olive oil, to drizzle

what to do

1 Slide 5 peeled prawns onto each skewer.
2 For the marinade, mix together the ingredients and drizzle half over the prawns.
3 For the salad, peel the mango and cut flesh into thin strips. Mix with the other half of the marinade, bean sprouts, cucumber, coriander, pepper, spring onions and sea salt.
4 Heat a large frying pan and dry-fry the sesame seeds until golden. Remove and set aside. Fry the prawns over a high heat for 2 minutes until cooked through. Serve with the salad, sprinkled with sesame seeds and drizzled with the olive oil.

Sainsbury's Supermarkets Ltd, 33 Holborn, London EC1N 2HT
All items subject to availability. Some items available in larger stores only.
729/032 03/02
www.sainsburys.co.uk

get stuck in with Jamie Oliver's
Thai-style **mango** salad with
griddled prawns
Sainsbury's
making life taste better

Smoked Gammon Brochettes

1 red pepper
1 green pepper
1 courgette (zucchini)
8 mushrooms
500 g/1 lb 2 oz smoked gammon, cut into 2.5 cm/1 in dice and soaked in cold water for 4 hours
1 bay leaf
1 head celeriac
2 cooking apples
55 g/2 oz smoked goat's cheese
1 tbsp extra virgin olive oil
1 small onion, finely chopped
1 clove garlic, finely diced (minced)
1 egg
juice of 1 lemon

Marinade
6 black peppercorns
1 tbsp sesame oil
1 pinch celery salt
1 pinch cayenne pepper
1 bunch coriander
50 ml/2 fl oz/¼ cup white wine
1 tbsp soy sauce

Serves 4

Mix together all the ingredients for the marinade. Chop the peppers, courgette (zucchini) and mushrooms into 2.5 cm/1 in squares and thread them onto 8 bamboo skewers with the smoked gammon and pieces of bay leaf. Place the skewers in a shallow dish, spoon over the marinade and leave in the refrigerator for 3 hours. Turn the skewers halfway through the marinading time.

Preheat the oven to 180°C/350°F/gas 4. Grease a baking sheet.

Grate the celeriac, apples and goat's cheese into a large bowl. Heat the olive oil and fry the onion and garlic in a frying pan (skillet) until translucent. Add to the celeriac and apple mixture and stir in well. Whisk the egg, lightly season and add to the grated mixture. Divide the mixture into 4 and push each portion into a 5 cm/2 in circular pastry cutter and push down firmly. Remove the cutters and bake for 25 minutes until golden brown.

Cook the brochettes for 8 minutes under a hot grill, turning the skewers halfway through the cooking time. Serve with freshly squeezed lemon juice.

Fat: high Kcals: 434 Cholesterol: high Fibre: medium

Quail with Sweet Pepper Sauce and Autumn Vegetables

1 × 170 g/6 oz breast of corn-fed chicken, skinned, boned and trimmed
1 red pepper, deseeded
1 pinch celery salt
1 pinch cayenne pepper
1 tbsp natural, low-fat *fromage frais*
2 tbsp white wine
4 quail, boned
4 rashers lean back bacon, fat and rind removed
selection of turned root vegetables, blanched and tossed in 1 tsp clear honey
sea salt and freshly milled black pepper

Sauce
2 shallots, finely chopped
½ red pepper, diced (minced)
juice of ½ lemon
300 ml/10 fl oz/1¼ cups chicken stock (see page 138)
1 tomato
1 tbsp extra virgin olive oil

Garnish
4 sprigs chervil

Serves 4

Preheat the oven to 180°C/350°F/gas 4.

Roughly chop the chicken breast and put in a food processor or blender with the red pepper, a pinch each of celery salt and cayenne pepper, the *fromage frais* and the white wine. Process until smooth then pass through a fine sieve to produce the sweet pepper forcemeat. Season the boned quail and stuff with the forcemeat. Place a piece of bacon on top of each bird as protection against drying out. Put in a roasting tray and cook in the oven for 17 minutes until the skin is crisp and golden.

Meanwhile, make the sauce. Sweat the chopped shallots and pepper in a covered non-stick pan until the shallots become translucent. Deglaze the pan with the lemon juice, add the chicken stock and reduce over a high heat by two-thirds. Liquidize the whole tomato with the olive oil in a liquidizer or blender and pass through a fine sieve.

When the quail are cooked, slice each one into 3 and place in the centre of each plate. Shake the tomato and olive oil mixture into the hot sauce and remove from the heat. Spoon the sauce around the quail and arrange the turned vegetables around the quail. Garnish with chervil sprigs.

Fat: high Kcals: 393 Cholesterol: medium Fibre: medium

Roasted Fillet of Pork with Apricot and Onion

4 small fillets of pork
75 g/3 oz/⅓ cup dried apricots
100 ml/4 fl oz/½ cup white wine
1 tbsp extra virgin olive oil
1 large onion, finely sliced
1 tbsp potato starch mixed with a little water to form a paste

Marinade
4 tbsp light soy sauce
150 ml/5 fl oz/⅔ cup red wine
4 tbsp sake or dry sherry
1 tbsp clear honey
1 sprig fresh thyme, or a pinch dried thyme

Garnish
2 carrots

Serves 4

Combine all the marinade ingredients. Remove all excess fat from the pork fillets, place in a shallow dish and spoon over the marinade. Leave in a cool place to marinate for 2 hours.

Preheat the oven to 180°C/350°F/gas 4.

Place the apricots in a pan with the white wine. Bring to the boil, cover the pan and continue to boil for 20–30 minutes until the apricots are soft.

Meanwhile, heat a little olive oil in a frying pan (skillet), add the onion and sweat until soft.

Drain and reserve the marinade from the pork. Heat a non-stick roasting tray on the top of the stove, then seal the fillets over a high heat until golden brown. Place in the oven and roast for 20 minutes until firm but moist.

Meanwhile, in a saucepan, blanch the carrots in lightly salted water. Remove, allow to cool, then cut into strips.

Chop up the softened apricots and add the onions. In a separate saucepan, bring the marinade to the boil. Stir in the potato starch paste to thicken, and cook for a further 2 minutes, stirring continuously.

When the pork is cooked, leave to rest for 5 minutes before cutting each fillet into slices 1 cm/½ in thick. Spoon a mound of apricot and onion mixture onto individual plates. Place the sliced fillets on top, pour a little of the marinade sauce over and garnish with carrot strips.

Fat: high Kcals: 247 Cholesterol: medium Fibre: low

Poached Fillet of Veal with Broccoli Mousse and Carrot Purée

1 × 140 g/5 oz fillets of veal, trimmed of any fat and sinews
1 piece caul fat
1.75 l/3 pt/7½ cups veal stock (see page 139)
2 shallots, finely chopped
2 tbsp balsamic vinegar
6 tbsp fresh orange juice
24 baby carrots
450 g/1 lb/2½ cups carrots, roughly chopped

Mousse
2 tbsp natural, low fat *fromage frais*

To make the mousse, combine the *fromage frais*, chicken breast, egg white, broccoli florets and garlic in a food processor or blender. Lightly season, blend until smooth and pass through a fine sieve. Spread a quarter of the mousse into a dome shape on top of each veal fillet and wrap in caul fat.

Pour a third of the veal stock into a pan and reduce over a high heat by two thirds.

Sweat the shallots in a covered non-stick pan over a medium heat until translucent. Add the balsamic vinegar and 2 tablespoons of the orange juice; reduce over a high heat to syrup consistency. Add the reduced veal stock, bring to the boil and simmer for 5 minutes.

Blanch the baby carrots in a pan of lightly salted boiling water for 2 minutes. In a separate pan, reduce the remaining orange juice over a high heat by half, add the baby carrots and boil in the juice until cooked, about 12 minutes.

Poached Fillet of Veal with Broccoli Mousse and Carrot Purée

1 × 140 g/5 oz breast of corn-fed chicken, skinned, boned and trimmed
1 egg white
3 heads broccoli
1 clove garlic
sea salt and freshly milled black pepper

Serves 4

Season the remainder of the veal stock and bring to the boil. Lower in the veal fillets and simmer for 8 minutes until cooked.

Meanwhile, put the roughly chopped carrots in a separate pan, just cover with water and cook until tender. Purée in a food processor or blender.

To serve, place a quarter of the carrot purée in the centre of each plate and rest a veal fillet on top. Place the baby carrots around the purée and spoon over the sauce.

Fat: low Kcal: 205 Cholesterol: medium Fibre: medium

Marinated Fillet of Pork with Sweet Peppers

2 × 240 g/8 oz fillets of pork, fat removed
1 large green pepper, halved and deseeded
1 large yellow pepper, halved and deseeded
1 large red pepper, halved and deseeded
2 tbsp extra virgin olive oil
2 potatoes, cooked and roughly chopped
2 tbsp white wine vinegar
1 pinch chilli powder
fresh orange juice, to mix
1 tsp low-calorie granulated sweetener
1 tbsp linseeds
1 tsp sesame oil
sea salt and freshly milled black pepper

Marinade
1 stick cinnamon
2 tbsp soy sauce
2 cloves garlic, finely diced (minced)
1 tsp fresh ginger, peeled and grated
1 tbsp clear honey
1 pinch cayenne pepper
1 tsp coriander seeds, crushed
1 tsp sesame oil

Garnish
4 sprigs chervil

Serves 4

Mix all the marinade ingredients together. Place the pork fillets in a shallow dish, spoon over the marinade and leave to marinate in the refrigerator for 3 hours. Turn the fillets twice during this time.

Preheat the oven to 180°C/350°F/gas 4.

Towards the end of the marinading time, cut half of each pepper into 1 cm/½ in diamond shapes and reserve. Place each remaining pepper half separately into a liquidizer or food processor together with a third each of the olive oil, cooked potato and white wine vinegar; add a pinch of chilli powder to the red pepper mixture. Blend until smooth, then pass each sauce separately through a muslin cloth into individual bowls. Each sauce should be of the same consistency; if not, adjust with a little orange juice. Taste the sauces, and if too bitter sweeten with a little granulated sweetener, as the taste of peppers varies according to the time of year.

Heat a roasting tray, drain the meat from the marinade and sprinkle the fillets with linseeds. Seal the meat in the tray over a high heat and then roast in the oven for 18–20 minutes until golden brown.

Meanwhile, heat the pepper sauces separately. When the meat is cooked, leave to rest for 5 minutes. Heat the sesame oil in a pan and stir-fry the pepper diamonds over a very high heat for 1 minute. Cut the fillets into 6 mm/¼ in slices and divide equally between the plates, arranging them in the centre. Pour a quarter of each warmed sauce around the fillet. Sprinkle the pepper diamonds on top of the sauces and garnish the fillet with a sprig of chervil.

Fat: high Kcals: 365 Cholesterol: high Fibre: low

Veal Sweetbreads with Leeks and Watercress

150 ml/5 fl oz/⅔ cup veal stock (see page 139)
675 g/1½ lb veal sweetbreads
2 shallots, finely chopped
75 ml/3 fl oz/⅓ cup white wine
4 bunches watercress, leaves only
2 tbsp natural, low-fat *fromage frais*
4 tbsp/⅓ cup Champneys bechamel (see page 141)
2 tbsp clear honey
2 tbsp extra virgin olive oil
30 baby leeks, cut into 10 cm/4 in lengths
sea salt and freshly milled black pepper

Serves 4

Reduce the veal stock by four-fifths over a high heat. Add the sweetbreads and blanch for 8 minutes. Remove and place in a shallow dish and reserve the stock. Cover the sweetbreads with aluminium foil and press with a heavy weight or pan filled with cold water for 2 hours in the refrigerator.

To make the purée, sweat the shallots until translucent in a covered non-stick pan together with the white wine. Add the reserved stock and reduce by half over a high heat. Add the leaves from 2 bunches of watercress and purée in a food processor or blender until smooth. Season and pass through a sieve into a sauce boat.

Combine the *fromage frais* with the remaining watercress leaves, bechamel, 1 tablespoon of the honey and a little salt and pepper and mix in a food processor or blender until smooth.

Heat the olive oil in a small pan. Cut the sweetbreads into 8 rounds using a 4.5 cm/2 in circular pastry cutter, season and fry for 5 minutes until golden brown, turning once. Remove from the pan and keep warm. Add the remaining honey and 1 teaspoon of water to the pan and blanch the leeks for 3 minutes.

Pour a quarter of the wine and watercress sauce onto each plate. Sandwich a quarter of the blanched leeks between 2 sweetbread rounds and place to one side of the sauce. Serve with the watercress purée on top.

Fat: high Kcals: 429 Cholesterol: high Fibre: high

Overleaf, left: *Marinated Fillet of Pork with Sweet Peppers;* right: *Veal Sweetbreads with Leeks and Watercress*

Pheasant and Quail Stuffed with Apple and Cranberry Forcemeat

1 tbsp extra virgin olive oil
1 small onion, chopped
75 g/2½ oz veal, roughly diced
4 rashers lean smoked bacon, fat and rind removed
2 leaves sage, chopped
3 leaves basil, chopped
1 dash Worcester sauce
2 cooking apples, grated
55 g/2 oz/½ cup cranberries
1 pheasant, boned
1 quail, boned
1 clove garlic, finely diced (minced)
1 sprig of thyme
575 ml/1 pt/2½ cups chicken stock (see page 138)
sea salt and freshly milled black pepper

Serves 4

Preheat the oven to 220°C/425°F/gas 7.

Heat the olive oil in a pan, add the chopped onion, cover and sweat until translucent. Combine the onion with the veal, 2 rashers of bacon, sage, basil and a dash of Worcester sauce in a food processor or blender and blend until smooth. Transfer to a bowl, lightly season, then thoroughly mix in the grated apple and half the cranberries.

Place the pheasant between cling film or plastic wrap and lightly beat. Remove the plastic film. Repeat with the quail and lay on top of the pheasant.

Place the stuffing inside the 2 birds and roll to reform the shape of the birds. Place the remaining 2 rashers of bacon over the top of the birds and tie with string.

Spread the diced (minced) garlic on a roasting tray to form a bed for the birds and place them on top. Roast the birds in the oven for 40 minutes, basting every 10-15 minutes, until cooked; the breast should still be pink and juicy and the juices run clear when the flesh is pierced with a skewer.

When cooked, allow the birds to rest for 5-10 minutes. Meanwhile, strain the fat from the roasting tray, place the tray on top of the stove and add the thyme and the chicken stock. Reduce over a high heat by two-thirds.

Cut the birds into 6 mm/¼ in slices and arrange a quarter on each plate, together with the stuffing. Spoon over the sauce and serve.

Fat: high Kcals: 329 Cholesterol: medium Fibre: low

Barbecued Chicken Chilli and Pineapple Wrapped in a Cornflour Pasty

400 g/14 oz breast meat of corn-fed chicken, skinned, boned and trimmed
baby pineapple, skin and stalk removed, cut into chunks
¼ iceberg lettuce, finely sliced
30 g/1 oz/½ cup low-fat Cheddar cheese, grated
2 tomatoes, sliced

Marinade
1 tsp clear honey
1 fresh red or green chilli, deseeded and finely chopped
1 pinch paprika
juice of 1 lemon
1 dash Worcester sauce
1 clove garlic, crushed

Pasty dough
150 g/5½ oz/1¼ cups wholemeal flour
100 g/3½ oz/¾ cup cornflour or cornstarch
1 tsp paprika
approximately 100 ml/4 fl oz/½ cup cold water
sea salt and freshly milled black pepper

Serves 4

Cut the chicken breasts into 2 cm/¾ in cubes, or large enough so that they will not fall through the barbecue grill bars, and place in a shallow dish. Mix all the marinade ingredients together, then spoon over the cubes of chicken and leave to marinate in a cool place for 2 hours.

Meanwhile, make the pasty dough. Sift the wholemeal flour, cornflour or cornstarch, paprika and salt and pepper to taste into a large mixing bowl, then stir round to mix the flours evenly. Make a well in the centre, then gradually pour in cold water, stirring continuously and drawing in flour to make a smooth ball of dough. Transfer the dough to a lightly floured surface and knead for 2 minutes. Divide the dough into 4 equal portions and place in the refrigerator for 20 minutes. On a lightly floured surface, roll out each portion of dough to a thickness of 3 mm/⅛ in and return to the refrigerator.

Grill the chicken pieces for 5 minutes over the barbecue until almost cooked. When the chicken is nearly ready, add the rolled pasty dough portions to the barbecue and cook for 1½ minutes on each side. Place a quarter of the chicken pieces in the centre of each pasty, then fold over the sides to enclose the filling, leaving the top open. Serve with chunks of pineapple, sliced iceberg lettuce, grated Cheddar cheese and slices of tomato.

Fat: medium Kcals: 388 Cholesterol: medium Fibre: medium

Vegetable dishes provide new ideas for tasty main courses and help vegetarians obtain all the vitamins, minerals and protein necessary for a balanced diet. The exciting range of fresh vegetables now available can also be used to make delicious side dishes, always important in a meal. Fresh, uncooked foods are the healthiest of all; boost your intake of raw vegetables by mixing them with fruits, cheeses, grains, pulses and meats in a variety of irresistible salads.

Carrot and Peanut Terrine

675 g/1½ lb spinach, stalks removed
1 large courgette (zucchini)
85 g/3 oz/⅓ cup smooth peanut butter
1 tsp peanut oil
110 g/4 oz/1 cup peanuts, in husks
2 cloves garlic, finely diced (minced)
1 medium-sized Spanish onion, finely chopped
900 g/2 lb carrots, grated
1 red pepper
1 green pepper
1 yellow pepper
6 dsp orange and basil dressing (see page 137)
sea salt

Serves 14

Preheat the oven to 240°C/475°F/gas 9.

Put the spinach, 3 tablespoons of water and a little salt in a non-stick pan, cover with a lid, and sweat for 2–3 minutes until cooked. Refresh under cold running water and drain. Line a 1.1 litre/2 pint/5 cup terrine with greaseproof (wax) paper, then line with the spinach, making sure the spinach hangs well over the sides to cover the top later.

Blanch the courgette (zucchini) in boiling salted water for 1 minute, refresh under cold running water, drain and remove top and bottom parts. Spread with half of the peanut butter.

Heat the peanut oil in a large pan. Remove the peanuts from their husks, reserve a few for garnishing and sweat the rest over a low heat with the garlic, onion, carrot and remaining peanut butter, 5 minutes.

Place the peppers on a baking sheet and roast in the oven until the skins blister, 8–10 minutes. Place the peppers in sealed plastic bags for 5 minutes to loosen the skins. Remove the skins, cut each into 2 rough 5 cm/2 in squares and remove the seeds.

Divide the carrot and peanut mixture into 4, and press one quarter into the base of the spinach-lined terrine. Cover with half of the peppers, then add another layer of carrot and peanut mixture. Place the courgette (zucchini) in the centre of the terrine, followed by a layer of carrot and peanut mixture, then the remaining peppers. Top with the last quarter of carrot and peanut. Overlap the hanging spinach on top, press with a heavy weight and leave in the refrigerator until cold.

Invert the terrine onto a plate and shake hard to remove from the dish. To serve, cut the terrine into 2.5 cm/1 in slices and either reheat in a microwave for 1½ minutes or gently steam for 3 minutes. Place a few slices on each plate, spoon round a little warm orange and basil dressing and sprinkle over a few peanuts to garnish.

Fat: high Kcals: 429 Cholesterol: low Fibre: high

Bean and Pepper Lasagne

- 45 g/1½ oz/⅓ cup dried butter beans
- 45 g/1½ oz/⅓ cup dried black-eyed beans
- 45 g/1½ oz/⅓ cup dried red kidney beans
- 45 g/1½ oz/⅓ cup dried flageolet beans
- 1 red pepper
- 1 green pepper
- 1 yellow pepper
- 2 tbsp extra virgin olive oil
- 6 shallots, finely chopped
- 2 cloves garlic, finely diced (minced)
- 6 sun-dried tomatoes, roughly chopped
- 25 g/1 oz/¼ cup black olives
- 1 bunch basil, shredded
- 115 g/4 oz cooked spinach
- 1 pinch nutmeg
- 115 g/4 oz wholemeal pasta, thinly rolled (see page 140)
- 300 ml/10 fl oz/1¼ cups Champneys bechamel (see page 141)
- 55 g/2 oz low-fat Cheddar cheese, grated
- 4 tbsp cooked tomato concasse (see page 138)
- 50 ml/2 fl oz/¼ cup white wine

Garnish
- 4 sprigs chervil

Serves 4

Soak all the beans in separate bowls overnight; remove any beans that float to the surface. Discard the soaking water and place the beans in separate pans, cover with fresh water and bring to the boil. Boil for 10 minutes, then reduce the heat, put on lids, and simmer until tender, between 1-2 hours. Refresh under cold running water, then leave to drain well.

Cut the peppers into 6 mm/¼ in dice. Heat the oil in a frying pan (skillet) and sweat the peppers, shallots, 1 garlic clove, the sun-dried tomatoes, olives and shredded basil until the shallots turn translucent. Reserve a few beans for garnishing and mix the rest with the contents of the pan.

Meanwhile, place the spinach, the remaining garlic clove, a pinch of nutmeg and 3 tablespoons of water in a pan and cook over a high heat for 2-3 minutes. Refresh under cold running water, drain and chop very finely.

Preheat the oven to 180°C/350°F/gas 4.

To assemble the lasagne, using a deep 7.5 cm/3 in pastry cutter cut 16 circles of pasta and blanch in boiling water for 1½ minutes. Refresh, then place 4 circles on a greased baking sheet. Replace a pastry cutter over each circle. Use half the spinach to cover each pasta circle and place a second circle on top. Make another layer of filling with half the bean and pepper mixture and cover with a pasta circle. Repeat the layers of spinach and bean and pepper mixture as before, finishing with a pasta circle on top. Make sure there is a gap of 6 mm/¼ in between the top of the pastry cutter and the last pasta circle.

Mix the bechamel and grated cheese together and pour into the cutters to fill. Bake in the oven for 20 minutes until bubbling and golden.

Meanwhile, warm the tomato concasse with the white wine. Transfer each pastry cutter to an individual plate, using a fish slice to aid you. Run a sharp knife around the inside edge of the pastry cutters and remove from the lasagne. Spoon round the tomato concasse and reserved beans and garnish with a sprig of chervil.

Note: This dish can also be made in a deep baking sheet using the same method. Use double quantities, and cut the pasta into strips approximately 5 cm/2 in wide to fit the width or length of the tray.

Fat: high Kcals: 449 Cholesterol: low Fibre: high

Leek and Herb Sausages with Pickled Cabbage

170 g/6 oz/2 cups fresh wholemeal breadcrumbs
1 pinch celery salt
1 pinch freshly milled black pepper
85 g/3 oz/1 cup low-fat Chedder cheese, grated
½ tsp coarse grain mustard
115 g/4 oz/1 cup wholemeal flour
1 egg white
55 g/2 oz/¾ cup fine dry breadcrumbs
2 tbsp extra virgin olive oil
sea salt

Pickled cabbage
½ large red cabbage, cut into 6 mm/¼ in slices
300 ml/10 fl oz/1¼ cups red wine vinegar
1 tbsp pickling spice
2 tbsp clear honey
4 oz/115 g leeks, finely chopped
1 medium-sized onion, finely chopped
1 clove garlic, finely diced (minced)
2 tsp fresh basil, chopped
2 tsp fresh chervil, chopped
2 tsp fresh coriander leaves, chopped

Serves 4

Layer the cabbage with sea salt and leave for 4 hours. Boil the vinegar, pickling spice and honey for 5 minutes in a stainless steel saucepan. Wash the salt from the cabbage and pat the slices dry. Pour the hot vinegar mixture over the red cabbage and leave for 1 week in a sterilized pickling jar.

When the cabbage is ready, fry the leek, onion and garlic in a non-stick pan until golden brown, about 3 minutes. Add the chopped herbs and cook for another minute. Stir in the fresh breadcrumbs, celery salt, black pepper, Cheddar cheese and mustard and immediately remove from the heat. Allow to cool slightly then mould the mixture into sausage shapes and coat with the flour, egg white and finally the dry breadcrumbs.

Preheat the over to 180°C/350°F/gas 4.

Heat the olive oil in a frying pan (skillet), place the sausages in the oil and brown slightly. Remove from the pan and place on a baking sheet. Cook in the oven for 8 minutes until golden brown and then drain on kitchen paper.

Strain the vinegar from the pickled cabbage and place a mound in the centre of each plate; rest a sausage on top and serve immediately.

Fat: high Kcals: 402 Cholesterol: low Fibre: high

Lentil and Wild Mushroom Bolognese

Lentil and Wild Mushroom Bolognese

350 g/285 g/10 oz wholemeal pasta (see page 140)
2 dsp extra virgin olive oil
6 shallots, finely chopped
1 red pepper, finely diced
1 green pepper, finely diced
1 clove garlic, finely diced (minced)
170 g/6 oz wild mushrooms (e.g. girolles, morels), wiped
5 tbsp raw tomato concasse (see page 137)
55 g/2 oz/⅓ cup green lentils
55 g/2 oz/⅓ cup puy lentils

Roll out the pasta in a machine or by hand, then cut into tagliatelle.

To make the tomato sauce, sweat the onion, carrot, garlic, tomatoes, basil, parsley and bay leaf in a covered non-stick pan until the onions are translucent. Add the white wine and tomato purée and cook for 1 minute over a moderate heat. Pour in the vegetable stock, cover and gently simmer over a low heat for 20 minutes, then pass through a fine sieve and lightly season.

Heat 1 tablespoon of olive oil in a separate pan, add the shallots, peppers and garlic, cover and sweat for 2 minutes until the shallots are translucent. Add the wild mushrooms and cook for 3 minutes. Add the tomato concasse and cook for a further minute. Add half the tomato sauce to this mixture.

Meanwhile, cook the lentils in separate pans for 20 minutes each until soft. Drain and toss in the remaining olive oil.

sea salt and freshly milled black pepper

Sauce
1 onion, finely chopped
1 carrot, finely chopped
1 clove garlic, finely diced (minced)
5 tomatoes, roughly chopped
4 leaves fresh basil
4 sprigs parsley
1 bay leaf
75 ml/3 fl oz/⅓ cup dry white wine
1 tsp tomato purée
150 ml/5 fl oz/⅔ cup vegetable stock (see page 139)

Garnish
4 sprigs basil

Serves 4

Bring a large pan of lightly salted water to the boil and drop in the tagliatelle. Cook for 3 minutes until *al dente*.

To serve, pile a quarter of each of the lentils in one corner of each plate and place a quarter of the cooked tagliatelle to the side of the lentils. Spoon a quarter of the mushroom bolognese next to the tagliatelle and pour a little tomato sauce around. Garnish with a sprig of basil and grind over some black pepper.

Fat: medium Kcals: 475 Cholesterol: low Fibre: high

Aubergine Gâteau with Provençale Vegetables

Endive Salad with Balsamic Honey Dressing

2 heads of white Belgian endive
2 heads of red Belgian endive
4 peppers: 1 red, 1 yellow, 1 black, 1 orange
1 tbsp olive oil
1 bunch spring onions (scallions), roughly chopped
45 g/1½ oz/⅓ cup whole almonds, lightly roasted

Dressing
1 dsp white wine vinegar
1 dsp clear honey
4 dsp balsamic vinegar
1 tsp extra virgin olive oil
sea salt and freshly milled black pepper

Serves 4

To make the dressing, warm the white wine vinegar in a small pan and dissolve the honey in it. Add the balsamic vinegar, whisk in the oil, and season with salt and pepper.

Arrange a quarter of the endive leaves on each plate. Cut the peppers into neat dices and sauté in a little olive oil; season. Sprinkle the spring onions (scallions), peppers and the almonds onto the leaves, distributing them evenly between the plates, then sprinkle with a little of the dressing and serve.

Fat: high Kcals: 196 Cholesterol: low Fibre: medium

Salad of Smoked Salmon, Quail's Eggs and Samphire

12 quail's eggs
115 g/4 oz/¾ cup samphire
1 red oakleaf lettuce
1 head curly endive
225 g/8 oz smoked salmon
juice of 1 lime

Dressing
zest and juice of 2 lemons
½ tsp English mustard
1 egg yolk
9 dsp extra virgin olive oil

Garnish
borage flowers
4 sprigs of chervil

Serves 4

To make the dressing, place the lemon zest and juice, mustard and egg yolk in a food processor or blender and mix well. With the machine still turned on add the oil in a steady stream then pass the mixture through a muslin cloth. Season to taste.

Cook the quail's eggs for 3 minutes in boiling water, cool under running water, peel and keep in salted water in the refrigerator.

Wash the samphire and the lettuce leaves. Arrange the salad leaves around the plate, place the samphire in a 12 cm/5 in circular pastry cutter in the centre of the plate. Layer the salmon on top of the samphire, halve the quail's eggs and use to decorate the salmon and samphire layer together with the borage flowers. Squeeze some lime juice onto the salmon and serve with a spoonful of dressing and a sprig of chervil.

Fat: high Kcals: 240 Cholesterol: high Fibre: low

Aubergine Gâteau with Provençale Vegetables

1 aubergine (eggplant)
juice of 1 lemon
2 dsp garlic oil

Provençale mix
1 courgette (zucchini)
1 red pepper
1 green pepper
1 yellow pepper
1 medium-sized onion
4 cloves garlic, roughly chopped

Sauce
2 beef tomatoes
2 dsp extra virgin olive oil
1 small onion, roughly chopped
50 ml/2 fl oz/¼ cup white wine
300 ml/10 fl oz/1¼ cups vegetable stock (see page 139)
1 sprig basil, shredded
1 sprig thyme

Garnish
25 g/1 oz/1¼ cup roasted pine kernels

Serves 4-6

Cut the aubergine (eggplant) into 6 mm/¼ in slices and cover with the lemon juice to prevent discoloration.

To make the sauce, quarter the tomatoes and sauté with half the olive oil. Add the onion and cook over a high heat for 1-2 minutes. Pour in the white wine and vegetable stock and simmer until the tomato is cooked thoroughly, approximately 10 minutes. After 5 minutes add the herbs. Purée the sauce in a food processor or liquidizer, then press through a fine sieve.

Cut all the vegetables for the Provençale mix into 1 cm/½ in dice. Heat the remaining oil in a frying pan (skillet), then add the diced vegetables and garlic and sauté until just beginning to soften. Bind with a little of the tomato sauce and remove from the heat.

In a separate pan sauté the aubergine (eggplant) slices in the garlic oil. Lightly brown each side and then drain on kitchen paper. Layer the Provençale mix with the aubergine (eggplant) slices, refrigerate, cover and press with a heavy weight or dish filled with cold water for 1 hour. Cut into wedges and serve garnished with pine kernels.

Fat: high Kcals: 224 Cholesterol: low Fibre: medium

Overleaf, from top: *Endive Salad with Balsamic Honey Dressing, Smoked Salmon, Quails' Eggs and Samphire, Tomato and Olive Salad with Mango Dressing, and Wild Mushroom and Lentil Salad*

Wild Mushroom and Lentil Salad

1 tsp walnut oil
3 rashers lean smoked back bacon, cut into lardons
350 g/12 oz small girolles, wiped
selection of salad leaves (e.g. rocket, endive, lollo rosso, oakleaf lettuce)
115 g/4 oz/¾ cup sprouting lentils
55 g/2 oz/¾ cup alfalfa sprouts

Dressing

1 bunch tarragon, blanched
150 ml/5 fl oz/⅔ cup natural, low-fat yoghurt (see page 142)
1 tsp clear honey
sea salt and cayenne pepper

Serves 4

Gently heat the walnut oil in a frying pan (skillet) and sauté the bacon lardons until crispy. Drain on kitchen paper. Add the girolles to the pan, sauté until soft and drain in the same way.

Chop the blanched tarragon, mix the yoghurt and honey together and season with salt and cayenne pepper. Wash the salad leaves and dress with half the yoghurt dressing. Mix the sprouting lentils with the mushrooms and bacon. Add the alfalfa sprouts to the remaining yoghurt, mix well and place in the centre of the plate.

To serve, arrange the salad leaves on top of the alfafa and yoghurt mixture and sprinkle the mushrooms, bacon lardons and lentils around the edge.

Fat: high Kcals: 159 Cholesterol: low Fibre: low

Tomato and Olive Salad with Mango Dressing

4 plum tomatoes
4 yellow cherry tomatoes
4 red cherry tomatoes
32 black olives
1 bunch chives, cut into batons

Dressing

1 mango
2 dsp white wine vinegar
2 dsp extra virgin olive oil
4 basil leaves, shredded
sea salt and freshly milled black pepper

Garnish

4 sprigs each of purple and green basil

Serves 4

Blanch all the tomatoes together for 10 seconds, refresh under cold running water and remove the skins.

To make the dressing, peel the mango and place the flesh into a liquidizer or food processor with the vinegar. Blend until smooth, then slowly add the olive oil while the machine is running. Pass through a fine chinois and add the shredded basil. Season with a small amount of salt and black pepper, and add a little water if the dressing is too thick.

To assemble the salad, arrange the different tomatoes attractively on a plate with the olives in the centre, season with a little salt and pepper. Sprinkle the chive batons onto the salad and finish with a circle of dressing surrounding the salad. Garnish with purple and green basil.

Fat: medium Kcals: 108 Cholesterol: low Fibre: low

Onion, Fennel, Apple and Horseradish Salad

1 tsp sesame oil
2 bulbs fennel, cut into thin slices across the bulb
1 red apple, cut into 6 mm/¼ in dice
1 green apple, cut into 6 mm/¼ in dice
2 small red onions
2 tbsp sultanas
1 orange, segmented
½ head radicchio
sea salt and freshly milled black pepper

Dressing
1 tbsp clear honey
1 tsp fresh horseradish, grated
150 ml/5 fl oz/⅔ cup natural, low-fat yoghurt (see page 142)
juice of ½ lemon

Garnish
1 tbsp poppy seeds

Serves 4

Heat the sesame oil in a wok or deep frying pan (skillet) until smoking. Add the fennel and stir-fry for 1 minute. Drain on kitchen paper and leave to cool.

To make the dressing, mix the honey, horseradish and yoghurt together, add the lemon juice and season with salt and pepper.

Toss all the other ingredients together in a large bowl. Divide the radicchio between the plates, place a quarter of the salad on top, dress and garnish with poppy seeds.

Fat: low Kcals: 156 Cholesterol: low Fibre: medium

Glazed Onion and Wild Mushroom Tartlets

170 g/6 oz wholemeal pastry (see page 144)
1 tbsp extra virgin olive oil
2 Spanish onions, finely sliced
225 g/8 oz/3 cups mixed wild mushrooms, wiped
1 clove garlic, finely diced (minced)
2 tbsp balsamic vinegar
1 tbsp maple syrup
675 g/1½ lb button onions, peeled
150 ml/5 fl oz/⅔ cup vegetable stock (see page 139)
sea salt and freshly milled black pepper

Preheat the oven to 150°C/300°F/gas 2. Place a baking sheet in the oven to heat.

Grease 4 × 10 cm/4 in fluted pastry rings. On a lightly floured surface roll out the pastry and cut circles to fit the rings. Bake blind for 10 minutes and set the tartlets to one side to cool.

Heat half the oil in a pan and sweat the onions until golden brown. Spoon a quarter of the onions into each pastry case. In a non-stick pan sweat the wild mushrooms, garlic, balsamic vinegar, maple syrup and the remaining olive oil over a medium heat until cooked, approximately 5 minutes.

In a separate pan cook the button onions in the vegetable stock over a medium heat for 5 minutes. Strain both the cooking liquids for the mushrooms and the onions into another pan.

Arrange a quarter of the onions in a circle on the base of each tartlet

Garnish
1 bunch chervil

Serves 4

and pile the wild mushrooms in the centre. Season the sauce with salt and black pepper and reduce over a high heat to a sticky glaze. If necessary, add a little more maple syrup to thicken it. Pour the sauce over each tartlet, then bake in the oven for 10 minutes to warm through. Serve garnished with chervil.

Fat: high Kcals: 312 Cholesterol: low Fibre: high

Pasta, Cured Ham, Rocket, Garlic and Basil Salad

350 g/12 oz wholemeal pasta (see page 140)
1 tsp lemon juice
1 bunch rocket
30 g/1 oz Parma ham
1 medium-sized onion, finely chopped
1 clove garlic, finely diced (minced)
2 tsp fresh parsley, chopped
sea salt and freshly milled black pepper

Dressing
½ bunch basil
4 dsp extra virgin olive oil
1 tbsp cider vinegar
1 tsp Dijon mustard
juice of 1 lemon

Garnish
1 dsp Parmesan cheese, grated
4 sprigs basil

Serves 4

Roll out the pasta as thinly as possible by machine or hand. Cut into tagliatelle. Bring a large pan of water to the boil with a teaspoon of the lemon juice and drop in the pasta. Cook for 3 minutes, then drain.

Meanwhile, make the dressing. Combine three-quarters of the basil, the olive oil, cider vinegar, mustard, salt to taste and the lemon juice in a liquidizer or food processor and process until smooth, then pass through a fine sieve.

Reserve 8 whole rocket leaves and cut the rest into 5 cm/2 in pieces and place in a large bowl. Cut the Parma ham into fine strips and add to the bowl. Then add the drained pasta and all the other ingredients. Toss with the dressing. To serve, on each plate place 2 whole rocket leaves, put a quarter of the salad on top, sprinkle over a teaspoon of Parmesan and finish with a sprig of basil.

Fat: high Kcals: 322 Cholesterol: low Fibre: medium

Above: *Marinated Grilled Vegetables;* opposite, top: *Glazed Onion and Wild Mushroom Tartlet;* opposite, bottom: *Feta Cheese, Leek, Potato and Yoghurt Tartlet*

Feta Cheese, Leek, Potato and Yoghurt Tartlets

4 sheets ready-made filo pastry
1 egg white
1 small leek, finely diced (minced)
1 clove garlic, finely diced (minced)
4 small new potatoes
55 g/2 oz/1 cup feta cheese
150 ml/5 oz/⅔ cup natural, low-fat yoghurt (see page 142)
2 eggs
1 tsp walnut oil
1 bunch chives, finely chopped
a selection of salad leaves
sea salt and freshly milled black pepper

Garnish
2 pickled walnuts, cut in halves
1 bunch flowering marjoram

Serves 4

Preheat the oven to 190°C/375°F/gas 5.

Brush 2 sheets of filo pastry with a little egg white and line 4 7.5 cm/3 in tartlet moulds with 2 layers of pastry.

Sweat the leek in a non-stick pan with the garlic until it is softened. Mix the potatoes, lightly scrubbed and grated, leeks and garlic and feta cheese together and place in the pastry cases.

Mix the yoghurt with the egg, add the chives and season to taste. Pour into the pastry cases and bake for 15 minutes.

Gently ease the cases from the moulds and serve with the torn salad leaves tossed in the walnut oil. Serve garnished with marjoram flowers and the pickled walnut halves.

Fat: medium Kcals: 188 Cholesterol: high Fibre: low

Marinated Grilled Vegetables

1 large carrot
4 shallots
4 asparagus tips
1 red pepper
1 yellow pepper
1 green pepper
2 small courgettes (zucchini)
2 sticks celery
1 medium-sized leek
½ small aubergine (eggplant)
8 baby corn
1 bulb fennel
225 g/8 oz/1 cup wild rice
6 tbsp tomato vinaigrette (see page 136)
sea salt and freshly milled black pepper

Marinade
150 ml/5 fl oz/⅔ cup extra virgin olive oil
1 bunch basil, shredded
3 cloves garlic
150 ml/5 fl oz/⅔ cup dry white wine
juice of 1 lemon

Serves 4

Mix together all the marinade ingredients. Peel and chop all the vegetables into bite-sized pieces and place in a shallow dish. Spoon over the marinade and leave to marinate in a cool place for 4 hours, turning occasionally.

Thirty minutes before the end of the marinating time, rinse the wild rice in cold water. Bring a large pan of water to the boil and add the rice. Cover and simmer for 40 minutes until cooked. Drain and fluff up the grains with a fork. Keep warm.

Strain the marinade off the vegetables and place under a hot grill or on a barbecue for approximately 5 minutes until crisp and brown.

Divide the rice evenly between the plates, place the vegetables on top and pour round some tomato vinaigrette.

Fat: high Kcals: 448 Cholesterol: low Fibre: high

Vegetable and Nut Croquettes

2 tbsp hazelnut oil
1 clove garlic, finely diced (minced)
2 small courgettes (zucchini), grated
1 small carrot, grated
1 small onion, grated
1 dsp walnuts, chopped
1 dsp hazelnuts, chopped
1 bunch parsley
1 dsp smooth peanut butter
1 dsp poppy seeds
1 dsp sesame seeds

Sauce
1 red pepper
1 green pepper
2 small potatoes
1 sprig thyme
2 bay leaves
300 ml/10 fl oz/1¼ cups vegetable stock (see page 139)
1 dash chilli sauce
juice of ½ lemon
sea salt and freshly milled black pepper

Garnish
4 sprigs chervil

Serves 4

Preheat the oven to 180°C/350°F/gas 4.

Heat 1 tablespoon of the hazelnut oil in a pan and sweat the garlic and grated vegetables over a low heat until lightly cooked but still crisp. Add the chopped nuts, parsley and peanut butter and cook for 2 minutes over a low heat. Place the mixture on a clean tea towel and squeeze all the moisture from the vegetables. Roll the dry mixture into 8 croquette sausage shapes. Mix together the poppy and sesame seeds and roll the croquettes in the mixture.

To make the sauce, place the red and green peppers in separate pans with 1 potato in each. Divide all the other ingredients equally between the 2 pans and add a dash of chilli sauce to the red pepper mixture only. Bring both pans to the boil, cover and simmer for 15 minutes until the potato is cooked. Purée the 2 sauces separately in a food processor or blender and pass each through a fine sieve into individual pans. Season with lemon juice, salt and pepper.

Heat the remaining hazelnut oil in a small frying pan (skillet) and brown the croquettes. Place them on a baking sheet and cook in the oven for 12 minutes until golden brown. To serve, spoon a pool of each sauce onto a plate, place 2 croquettes on top and garnish with a sprig of chervil.

Fat: high Kcals: 214 Cholesterol: low Fibre: medium

Above: *Asparagus and Broccoli Charlotte; opposite Celeriac Spring Rolls*

Asparagus and Broccoli Charlotte

30 thin green asparagus spears
30 thin white asparagus spears
250 g/8½ oz broccoli heads
4 eggs
300 ml/10 fl oz/1¼ cups natural, low-fat *fromage frais*
sea salt and freshly milled white pepper

Sauce
1 potato, peeled and roughly chopped
575 ml/20 fl oz/2½ cups fresh orange juice
1 cardamom pod (bean), crushed
½ clove garlic, finely diced (minced)
½ bay leaf

To make the sauce, place all the ingredients except the tarragon and the *fromage frais* in a pan and reduce over a high heat by two-thirds, about 20 minutes. Stir in the *fromage frais* and pass through a fine sieve. Season to taste.

To make the charlottes, lightly grease 4 ramekins and line with greaseproof (wax) paper. Cut away the woody ends from the asparagus, then trim the tips into 4 cm/1½ in lengths; reserve the stalks for the mousse. Using string, tie the tips into bundles and blanch in plenty of salted water for 1 minute, then refresh under cold running water and drain. Discard the strings. Cut half the broccoli heads into florets and blanch as before.

To make the mousse, cook the other half of the broccoli heads with the asparagus stalks until tender. Refresh under cold running water, drain, then combine with the eggs and *fromage frais* in a liquidizer or food processor and blend until smooth. Season to taste.

Preheat the oven to 180°C/350°F/gas 4. Line the ramekins with asparagus tips, alternating green and white spears. Spoon the mousse

1 tsp fresh tarragon, chopped
2 tsp natural, low-fat *fromage frais*

Garnish
1 tomato sliced

Serves 4

mixture into the ramekins and smooth level. Place the broccoli florets around the top. Cook in a *bain marie* in the oven for 25 minutes until slightly risen. Leave to rest for 5 minutes. Meanwhile, reheat the sauce and stir in the chopped tarragon. Plunge each ramekin into hot water for 30 seconds up to the rim and turn out the charlottes onto a plate. Surround with a little of the sauce and slices of tomato. Serve immediately.

Fat: medium Kcals: 300 Cholesterol: high Fibre: high

Celeriac Spring Rolls

1 × 2.5 cm/1 in square fresh ginger, peeled
1 bunch spring onions (scallions)
2 dsp sesame oil
1 large head celeriac, cut into paper-thin strips, blanched in salted water
55 g/2 oz/½ cup bean sprouts
2 medium-sized carrots, cut into thin strips
1 small onion, sliced
1 red pepper, cut into strips
8 water chestnuts, sliced
1 clove garlic, finely diced (minced)
2 tsp light soy sauce
1 egg white

Sauce
450 g/1 lb overripe plums
1 bay leaf
1 clove garlic, finely diced (minced)
1 star anise
1 stick cinnamon
1 tsp fresh ginger, peeled and chopped
25 g/1 oz/⅓ cup fresh raspberries
1 tbsp lemon juice
1 dsp raw cane sugar
2 dsp sake or dry sherry

Makes 12 rolls

Place all the sauce ingredients in a thick-bottomed pan and cook over a high heat for 20 minutes. Cool and pass through a muslin cloth.

Cut the ginger into fine strips, blanch, then refresh 6 times under cold running water. Cut the spring onions (scallions) into 5 cm/2 in pieces, blanch separately and refresh once. Heat the sesame oil in a frying pan (skillet) and stir-fry all the vegetables until lightly cooked but still crisp. Season with soy sauce and leave to cool. Drain the celeriac slices on kitchen paper.

Place a little filling in the centre of each celeriac slice, brush the edges with a little egg white and roll up like a pancake, tucking in and securing the ends neatly.

To serve, arrange 3 rolls on each plate, spoon over the sauce, and scatter around the spring onions and ginger strips.

Fat: low Kcals: 60 Cholesterol: low Fibre: low

Celeriac and Wild Mushroom Terrine

- 1.5 kg/3½ lb courgettes (zucchini), grated
- 1.35 kg/3 lb celeriac, grated
- 2 tsp extra virgin olive oil
- 1 kg/2¼ lb onions, roughly chopped
- 1 clove garlic, finely diced (minced)
- 450 g/16 oz mixed wild mushrooms, wiped
- 1 dash Worcester sauce

Garnish

- 150 ml/5 fl oz/⅔ cup apple purée, made by boiling 3 eating apples with 2 tbsps water until soft, and then passed through a fine sieve
- 1 red pepper, finely chopped

Serves 14

Line a 1.1 litre/2 pint/5 cup terrine with cling film or plastic wrap. Sweat the grated courgette (zucchini) and celeriac in a large pan with a little salt and pepper until soft.

Heat half the olive oil in a separate pan, add the onions, garlic, wild mushrooms (reserve 8 for garnishing) and a dash of Worcester sauce and sweat until the onions become translucent.

To assemble the terrine, line the base with a thin layer of courgette (zucchini) and celeriac, then a layer of the mushroom mixture, followed by another layer of courgette (zucchini) and celeriac and so on until all the ingredients are used up.

Wrap cling film or plastic wrap over the top of the terrine, then pierce a few small holes thorugh the film to allow liquid to escape while the terrine is being pressed. Place a heavy weight or dish filled with cold water on top of the terrine and leave in the refrigerator for at least 2 hours.

To remove the terrine from the mould, invert on to a serving plate. Place a generous slice in the centre of each plate, accompanied by the apple purée, the remaining olive oil, reserved mushrooms and chopped red pepper.

Fat: low Kcals: 92 Cholesterol: low Fibre: medium

Desserts provide the perfect end to any meal. This section includes a mixture of simple sweets, old favourites, elegant desserts and special treats, such as Kiwi and Orange Slice with Sweet Vinaigrette, Poached Peaches with Cinnamon Ice Cream, and Banana and Sultana Mousse, that will leave guests feeling refreshed and satisfied.

Frozen Wild Strawberry and Yoghurt Terrine

350 g/12 oz/3 cups wild strawberries
4 sheets gelatine
300 ml/10 fl oz/1¼ cup ice cream (see page 143)
300 ml/10 fl oz/1¼ cup natural, low-fat yoghurt (see page 142)
3 egg whites

Garnish
zest of 1 lemon, cut into thin strips
1 tbsp clear honey

Serves 14

Place a third of the strawberries in a heavy-bottomed saucepan with a little water and boil until puréed.

Meanwhile, cover the sheet gelatine with cold water and leave to soften for approximately 5 minutes. Remove from the water with your hand and squeeze out any excess liquid, then place the gelatine in small heatproof bowl over a pan of barely simmering water. Leave until the gelatine has melted and turned transparent. Stir into the puréed strawberries, and strain through a muslin cloth into a 1.1 litre/2 pint/5 cup terrine. Chill in the refrigerator until set, 30 minutes.

Reserve 12 strawberries for the garnish, and liquidize the rest in a liquidizer or food processor and blend with the ice cream which has been transferred to the refrigerator half an hour beforehand to soften slightly. Stir in the yoghurt and leave to cool.

In a clean, dry bowl, whisk the egg whites until stiff and fold into the ice cream mixture, using a large metal spoon. Spoon into the terrine and transfer to the freezer for 3 hours.

To serve, slightly warm the terrine and turn it out onto a clean board. Cut into 2 cm/¾ in slices and place a slice on each plate. Heat the honey with 1 tablespoon of water and blanch the strips of lemon zest in this mixture for 4 minutes. Refresh in cold water and use as a garnish together with the reserved strawberries. Serve immediately.

Fat: low Kcals: 48 Cholesterol: low Fibre: low

Opposite, from back: *Banana and Sultana Mousse, Rhubarb Charlotte, and Frozen Wild Strawberry and Yoghurt Terrine*

Banana and Sultana Mousse

1 quantity honey tuile (see page 144)
30 g/1 oz/¼ cup carob chips
5 sheets gelatine
300 ml/10 fl oz/1¼ cups *crème anglaise* (see page 142)
2 large ripe bananas
45 g/1½ oz/¼ cup sultanas
40 ml/1½ fl oz/¼ cup dark rum
3 tbsp natural, low-fat *fromage frais*
zest of ½ lemon, finely diced and blanched in 1 tbsp honey and 1 tbsp water
1 tsp raw cane sugar

Garnish
115 g/4 oz/1 cup raspberries
½ bunch mint (optional)

Serves 4

Preheat the oven to 180°C/350°F/gas 4.

Spread the tuile on a baking sheet to form 2 rectangles, each measuring at least 13 cm × 50 cm/5 in × 20 in, and sprinkle over the carob chips. Cook in the oven for 4 minutes until golden. Remove from the oven and immediately cut the tuile into 4 rectangles 6.5 cm x 25 cm/2½ in × 10 in and wrap each rectangle around the outside of a small ramekin. Remove the honey tuile shapes from the ramekin as soon as they have cooled and hardened.

Cover the sheet gelatine with cold water and leave to soften for approximately 5 minutes. Remove from the water with your hand and squeeze out any excess liquid, then place the gelatine in a small heatproof bowl. Put the bowl into a pan of barely simmering water and leave until the gelatine has melted and turned transparent. Warm the *crème anglaise*, add the gelatine and stir thoroughly. Put half the *crème anglaise* to one side, and combine the other half with 2 of the bananas in a food processor or liquidizer and process until smooth, then press through a fine sieve. Leave to cool.

Place the sultanas with three-quarters of the rum in a pan, bring to the boil and cook for 4 minutes until the sultanas are plump and the rum absorbed. Reserve a few sultanas for garnishing and add the rest to the *crème anglaise* and banana purée, stirring in well. Stir in the *fromage frais* and the lemon zest and spoon into the 4 ramekins. Place in the refrigerator.

Thinly slice the remaining banana and sprinkle with the sugar. Place under a preheated hot grill and cook until golden brown. Leave to one side to cool.

Meanwhile, set aside 4 sprigs of mint for garnishing and finely shred the rest. Add to the reserved *crème anglaise*, stir in the rest of the rum and when cool press through a fine sieve.

Plunge the base of each ramekin into hot water for 30 seconds and turn the mousses out onto individual plates and wrap a honey tuile shape around the outside. Arrange slices of the grilled banana on top, then garnish with a few sultanas, and a sprig of mint if liked. Liquidize the raspberries in a food processor or blender, press through a fine sieve and pour round. Add a sprig of mint, if liked.

Fat: high Kcals: 472 Cholesterol: medium Fibre: low

Rhubarb Charlotte

1 dsp strawberry preserve
8 sheets gelatine
150 ml/5 fl oz/⅔ cup warm *crème anglaise*
4 dsp natural, low-fat *fromage frais*
450 g/1 lb rhubarb, chopped
1 tsp low-calorie granulated sweetener
150 ml/5 fl oz/⅔ cup red grape juice

Sponge
55 g/2 oz/¼ cup caster sugar
2 eggs
55 g/2 oz/½ cup wholemeal flour
30 g/1 oz/⅛ cup polyunsaturated margarine, melted

Serves 4

Preheat the oven to 205°C/400°F/gas 6. Line a shallow roasting tray with greaseproof (wax) paper.

To make the sponge mixture, whisk the sugar and eggs together until thick and creamy. Using a large metal spoon, fold in the flour and then the melted margarine. Spread the mixture into the lined tray, making sure it is in an even layer, approximately 6 mm/¼ in thick. Bake in the oven until golden brown and spongy to the touch. Turn out on to a wire rack and leave to cool. Peel off the greaseproof (wax) paper and cut the sponge into strips 2.5 cm/1 in thick. Spread the strawberry preserve onto the strips and sandwich together. Cut the strips widthways to leave lengths of approximately 6mm/¼ in.

Cover the gelatine with cold water for approximately 5 minutes to soften. Remove the gelatine from the water and squeeze out any excess liquid with your hand. Melt the gelatine in a *bain marie* and stir into the *crème anglaise*. Add two-thirds of the gelatine to the *fromage frais* and keep the rest liquid in the *bain marie*. Stew the chopped rhubarb in a covered pan over a low heat until soft. Add the sweetener and mix in a food processor or blender until smooth. Pass through a fine sieve, stir into the *crème anglaise* mixture and leave to cool.

In a separate pan warm the grape juice and add the remaining gelatine to it. Line 4 ramekins with this mixture to a depth of 6 mm/¼ in. Leave to set in the refrigerator, about 30 minutes. When set, line the inside of each ramekin with the sponge, placing the strips vertically. Fill the ramekins with the rhubarb mixture and leave to set in the refrigerator for at least 2 hours.

To serve, briefly plunge the base of each ramekin up to its rim in hot water. Place a plate upside down over the ramekin, smartly invert, giving a couple of sharp shakes if necessary to free the charlottes.

Fat: high Kcals: 269 Cholesterol: high Fibre: low

Apricot and Passion Fruit Water Ice

170 g/6 oz/¾ cup dried apricots
6 passion fruit
300 ml/10 fl oz/1¼ cup fresh orange juice
juice of 1 lemon

Garnish
4 sprigs fresh mint

Serves 4

Place the apricots in a pan, cover with water and bring to the boil. Simmer, covered, for 20 minutes or until the fruit is soft.

Scoop out the seeds from the passion fruit into a separate pan, add the orange juice and reduce by two-thirds over a high heat.

Drain the apricots and purée in a food processor or liquidizer. Stir in the passion fruit and orange mixture and blend again until well mixed. Press through a fine sieve into an ice cream maker or *sorbetière* and add sufficient lemon juice to reach the consistency of olive oil. Churn for 10 minutes, or until stiff. Store in a covered container in the freezer. If you do not have an ice cream maker, after adding the lemon juice, place the mixture in a container directly into the freezer. Whisk every 15-20 minutes for 3-4 hours until set. The water ice can be stored for up to 3 days in the freezer in a sealed container.

Serve in scoops garnished with sprigs of mint.

Fat: low Kcals: 105 Cholesterol: low Fibre: low

Raspberry and Strawberry Layer

1 quantity honey tuile (see page 144)
115 g/4 oz/1 cup strawberries, liquidized and strained
150 ml/5 fl oz/⅔ cup natural, low-fat *fromage frais*
1 vanilla pod
2 sheets gelatine
225 g/8 oz/2 cups raspberries

Garnish
icing (confectioner's) sugar, for dusting
85 g/3 oz/¾ cup strawberries, sliced
4 sprigs fresh mint

Serves 4

Make 15 circular honey tuile biscuits and leave to cool.

Mix the strawberry pulp with the *fromage frais* and the seeds from the vanilla pod.

Cover the gelatine with cold water and leave to soften for approximately 5 minutes. Remove from the water with your hand and squeeze out any excess liquid, then place the gelatine in a heatproof bowl. Put the bowl, in a pan of barely simmering water until the gelatine has melted and turned transparent.

Gently warm the *fromage frais* and strawberry mixture and stir in the gelatine. (You may need slightly more gelatine to set the mixture if the *fromage frais* is thin.) Place in the refrigerator to set.

Once set, place the mixture in a piping bag fitted with a medium nozzle, arrange the raspberries around a biscuit on each plate and pipe a little of the mousse in the centre of the tuile. Sandwich the biscuits together with layers of strawberry mousse and top with a plain biscuit. Dust the top of the final biscuit with icing (confectioner's) sugar, surround with sliced strawberries and decorate with a spring of mint.

Fat: high Kcals: 191 Cholesterol: low Fibre: high

Opposite: *Délice of Raspberries and Nectarine*

Bread and Fruit Pudding with Banana Sauce

12 thin slices wholemeal bread
1 tsp polyunsaturated spread
25 g/1 oz/⅓ cup fresh blueberries
1 tsp mixed spice
1 ripe banana, finely chopped
1 egg
1 tbsp clear honey
300 ml/½ pt/1¼ cups skimmed milk
½ vanilla pod

Sauce
500 ml/16 fl oz/2 cups fresh orange juice
2 small, overripe bananas, roughly chopped
½ vanilla pod, deseeded

Garnish
4 sprigs fresh mint

Serves 4

Grease 4 individual ramekins. Cut 12 circular-shaped slices of bread, using the ramekins as a template. Spread both sides of the circles of bread with the spread. Lay one circle in each ramekin.

Divide the blueberries into 4, lay on top of the bread and sprinkle with a pinch of mixed spice. Place another circle of bread on top of the fruit and press down firmly.

Divide the chopped banana into 4 and place on top of the next layer of bread. Place the third circle of bread on top and push down firmly.

Whisk the egg, honey and milk together and add the vanilla pod seeds, scraping them from the pod with the back of a knife. Carefully pour the egg custard over the puddings, waiting for the custard to soak through the layers until it reaches the rim of the ramekin. Place in the refrigerator until ready to bake.

Preheat the oven to 180°C/350°F/gas 4.

To make the sauce, put the orange juice, roughly chopped banana and vanilla pod in a pan and reduce over a high heat by two-thirds. Take off the heat, remove the vanilla pod and process in a food processor or blender until smooth. Pass through a fine sieve and keep warm.

Bake the puddings in the oven for 12 minutes until golden. Turn out into 4 individual bowls and pour over the warm sauce. Garnish with a sprig of fresh mint and serve.

Fat: low Kcals: 339 Cholesterol: medium Fibre: medium

Apricot, Fig and Coconut Terrine

4 dried figs
12 dried apricots
50 g/2 oz carob
1 passion fruit
1 tbsp clear honey
2 tbsp desiccated (shredded) coconut, toasted
icing (confectioner's) sugar, for dusting

Garnish
berry fruits

Serves 6

Roughly chop the figs, 4 of the apricots, and half the carob in a food processor or blender. Stir in the passion fruit seeds and the honey. Press into a 575 ml/1 pint/2½ cup terrine and freeze for 30 minutes.

To make the apricot purée, dice (mince) the remaining 8 dried apricots, place in a pan and just cover with water. Bring to the boil, cover and simmer for 20–30 minutes. Purée in a food processor or blender.

Melt the remaining carob in a *bain marie* and spread in a thin layer on greaseproof (wax) paper and place in the refrigerator. When set, trim with a hot knife into a 5 cm × 3 cm/2 in × 1¼ in rectangle. Remove from the paper and dip one side in the toasted coconut.

Run a sharp knife around the edge of the terrine and turn out the fruit onto a plate. Pour the apricot purée around the terrine and decorate with berry fruits as required. Dust the berry fruits with icing (confectioner's) sugar. Place the carob rectangle on top and serve.

Fat: low Kcals: 43 Cholesterol: low Fibre: low

Champneys Apple Crumble with Honey-Sweetened Fromage Frais

450 g/1 lb cooking apples, peeled, cored and roughly chopped
1 tsp ground cinnamon
45 g/1½ oz/¼ cup polyunsaturated spread
a little fresh orange juice, to mix
85 g/3 oz/¾ cup wholemeal flour
20 g/¾ oz/1½ tbsp rolled oats
20 g/¾ oz/½ tbsp raw cane caster sugar
6 tbsp natural, low-fat *fromage frais*
½ tbsp clear honey

Serves 4

Preheat the oven to 150°C/300°F/gas 2.

Place the apple, cinnamon and half of the polyunsaturated spread in a pan and cover. Gently sweat, mashing the fruit from time to time, until puréed. Add a little orange juice if the fruit begins to stick to the pan. Once cooked, keep the purée hot over a gentle heat.

Meanwhile, in a mixing bowl, rub together the flour, oats, sugar and the rest of the polyunsaturated spread until the mixture resembles breadcrumbs. Divide the mixture into 4 and lightly press into a 5 cm/2 in circular pastry cutter to form 4 circles. Lift away the cutter and place the circles on a greased baking sheet and bake in the oven for 20 minutes, until golden brown. Transfer to a wire rack.

While the pastry is cooking, whisk together the *fromage frais* and honey. Chill.

To serve, place a clean 5 cm/2 in pastry cutter onto the first plate and spoon in hot apple purée to the rim. Press down gently, then remove the cutter and place a crumble circle on top. Serve the sweetened *fromage frais* separately.

Fat: high Kcals: 248 Cholesterol: low Fibre: low

Pumpkin and Pear Pie

900 g/2 lb pumpkin
1 pinch nutmeg
1 tbsp low-calorie, granulated sweetener
225 g/8 oz wholemeal pastry (see page 144)
3 egg whites
6 tbsp low-fat, natural *fromage frais*
4 ripe pears
100 ml/4 fl oz/½ cup red wine
2 cinnamon sticks

Serves 6

Preheat the oven to 180°C/350°F/gas 4.

Peel and roughly chop the pumpkin and place in a pan with 2 tablespoons of water and the nutmeg. Cook until soft, about 20 minutes, stir in the sweetener and leave to cool.

Roll out the pastry on a clean, flat surface and line a 25 cm/10 in pie tin. Bake blind for 10 minutes until the pastry is pale gold.

Add the egg whites and *fromage frais* to the pumpkin mixture and mix in a food processor or blender until smooth, then pass through a sieve.

Peel the pears and place in a deep pan with the wine, 1 tablespoon of water and the cinnamon sticks. Poach lightly for approximately 25 minutes. Remove from the poaching liquid and set aside to cool. When cool, halve the pears and remove the core.

Place the pumpkin mixture in the pastry case, put the pears on top and bake for 30-35 minutes until golden brown.

Fat: high Kcals: 220 Cholesterol: low Fibre: high

Délice of Raspberries and Nectarine

2 eggs
55 g/2 oz/¼ cup raw cane sugar
55 g/2 oz/½ cup wholemeal flour
1 tsp cocoa powder
4 ripe nectarines
1 tsp clear honey
1 star anise
115 g/4 oz/1 cup raspberries
juice of ½ lemon
300 ml/10 fl oz/1¼ cups natural, low-fat *fromage frais*
1 vanilla pod
6 sheets gelatine
55 g/2 oz carob

Garnish
4 sprigs mint

Serves 4

Preheat the oven to 180°C/350°F/gas 4. Place a baking sheet in the oven to heat.

Whisk the eggs and sugar in a heatproof bowl placed over a pan of barely simmering water until the mixture is almost white. Remove from the heat and fold in the flour, using a large metal spoon. Halve the mixture and stir in the cocoa powder into one half. Line 2 x 450 ml/16 fl oz/2 cup terrines with the sponge mixture, one chocolate and one plain. Bake in the oven for 12 minutes until pale gold.

Reserve 1 nectarine for garnishing, and roughly chop up the rest, discarding the stones. Place the chopped nectarines in a pan with the honey and star anise and simmer for 15 minutes until the nectarines are soft. Pass through a muslin cloth and reserve 3 teaspoons of the purée for garnishing.

Reserve 12 raspberries for garnishing; in a separate pan, cook the rest with the lemon juice until a purée is formed, then pass through a muslin cloth. Reserve 4 teaspoons for garnishing.

Place the *fromage frais* and the seeds from the vanilla pod in a metal bowl, place over a pan of boiling water and heat to blood temperature, 37°C/96°F.

Cover the sheet gelatine with cold water and leave to soften for approximately 5 minutes. Remove from the water with your hand and squeeze out any excess liquid, then place the gelatine in a small heatproof bowl. Put the bowl into a pan of barely simmering water and leave until the gelatine has melted and turned transparent. Stir into the *fromage frais*, then halve and stir the raspberry purée into one half and the nectarine purée into the other.

Pour the raspberry mixture into the chocolate-lined terrine, and the nectarine mixture into the plain one. Place in the refrigerator to set.

Melt the carob in a *bain marie* and place in a piping bag. Pipe 2 circles onto a large dessert plate. Remove the terrines from the refrigerator, turn out onto a board and cut each one into 1 cm/½ in slices On each plate, fill 1 circle of carob with a quarter of the reserved nectarine purée and the other circle with a quarter of the reserved raspberry purée. Place a slice of raspberry terrine on the circle of nectarine purée, and a slice of nectarine terrine on the circle of raspberry purée. Cut the reserved nectarine into 12 slices. Garnish the plate with 3 nectarine slices and 3 raspberries, and top with a sprig of mint.

Fat: low Kcals: 277 Cholesterol: high Fibre: medium

Kiwi and Orange Slice with Sweet Vinaigrette

2 tbsp caster sugar
2 tbsp polyunsaturated spread
2 egg whites
25 g/1 oz/⅓ cup wholemeal flour
2 kiwi fruit, peeled and finely sliced
2 oranges, peeled and segmented
50 ml/2 fl oz/¼ cup *crème fraîche*, sweetened with a little honey

Vinaigrette
2 tbsp maple syrup
1 tsp white wine vinegar
2 tbsp white wine
1 strawberry, diced (minced)
4 mint leaves, finely shredded

Garnish
zest of 1 orange, blanched

Serves 6

Beat the caster sugar and polyunsaturated spread together until white and creamy. Beat in the egg whites, then stir in the flour in batches. Place the mixture in the refrigerator for 1 hour.

Preheat the oven to 175°C/325°F/gas 3 or 180°C/350°F/gas 4.

Grease a baking sheet. Using a tablespoon, drop 12 mounds of mixture onto the baking sheet, spacing them 2.5 cm/1 in apart. Spread each mound out thinly, using a flat knife, to form circles approximately 10 cm/4 in in diameter. Bake in the oven for 4 minutes, until pale gold. Transfer the biscuits to a wire rack to cool.

To make the vinaigrette, mix all the ingredients together in a serving bowl until well blended.

To assemble each serving, start with a biscuit at the base. Place a layer of kiwi and orange on top, then repeat with two more layers of biscuit and fruit, finishing with a layer of fruit. Pipe sweetened *crème fraîche* in the centre. Serve the sweet vinaigrette and blanched orange zest separately.

Fat: medium Kcals: 138 Cholesterol: low Fibre: low

Banana en Papillote

4 small, underripe bananas
1 cinnamon stick, cut into 4
4 star anise
1 vanilla pod, cut into 4
30 g/1 oz/2 tbsp carob, grated
75 ml/3 fl oz/½ cup pineapple juice

Serves 4

Preheat the oven to 230°C/450°F/gas 8.

Lightly grease a piece of aluminium foil large enough to cover 1 banana, and place a banana on top. Arrange a piece of cinnamon stick, 1 star anise and a piece of vanilla pod around the banana and sprinkle with grated carob and a quarter of the pineapple juice. Fold up the foil and seal to make an airtight pocket. Repeat the process with the other 3 bananas.

Place the sealed bananas on a baking tray and cook in the oven for 3-4 minutes. Alternatively, they can be cooked on the side of a bonfire. Serve immediately.

Fat: low Kcals: 92 Cholesterol: low Fibre: low

A Tulip of Passion Fruit and Apricot Sorbet with Fresh Fruits

100 g/3½ oz/½ cup dried apricots
150 ml/5 fl oz/⅔ cup fresh orange juice
3 passion fruit
juice of 1 lemon

Tulip basket

8 sheets ready-made filo pastry
1 tbsp clear honey

Selection of fruits

1 star fruit, sliced
4 strawberries, sliced
1 orange, segmented
1 red apple, sliced

Fruit sauce

6 strawberries
1 tsp clear honey
juice of ½ lemon

Garnish

flesh of 2 melons, scooped into small balls
zest of 1 orange, blanched and cut into strips

Serves 4

To make the sorbet, boil the apricots in the orange juice with the seeds of the passion fruit until soft, 20–30 minutes. Purée the softened fruit in a food processor or blender and then add the lemon juice. Adjust the consistency of the fruit purée with more orange juice so that it resembles thick cooking oil. Place in a large bowl and put in the freezer. Stir every hour until set, approximately 3–4 hours. Alternatively place in an ice cream maker or *sorbetière* until firm.

Preheat the oven to 180°C/350°F/gas 4. Put a baking sheet in the oven to heat.

To make the fruit sauce, place all the ingredients in a food processor or blender and mix until smooth. Pass through a sieve into a clean bowl and keep cool.

Cut the filo pastry into 8 circles, approximately 13 cm/5 in in radius. Gently heat the honey in a small pan and use half to brush 4 of the filo circles. Top each honeyed circle with another to form a double layer. Push each circle into a deep jam tart or muffin tin, making sure that the base is flat. Place on the baking sheet and bake for 5 minutes. Brush with the remaining honey, return to the oven and bake until golden brown, approximately 2 minutes. Remove from the tin and cool on a wire rack.

To serve, spoon a little of the sorbet into each tulip basket and add the sliced fruit and strawberry purée around the sorbet. Garnish with the melon balls and strips of blanched orange zest.

Fat: low Kcals: 198 Cholesterol: low Fibre: high

Pineapple and Almond Soufflé

300 ml/10 fl oz/1¼ cups skimmed milk
1 vanilla pod
2 tbsp arrowroot
2 egg yolks
2 tsp clear honey
3 tbsp natural, low-fat *fromage frais*
9 sheets gelatine
1 pineapple, peeled, stalk removed, and roughly chopped
4 egg whites
30 g/1 oz/1 cup desiccated (shredded) coconut, toasted
30 g/1 oz/¼ cup ground almonds

Garnish
1 quantity honey tuile biscuits (see page 144)
cocoa powder, for dusting
edible flowers (e.g. nasturtiums, pot marigolds, rose petals, violets)

Serves 4

Put the milk and the vanilla pod into a pan and bring to the boil. Simmer for 5 minutes. Stir a little water into the arrowroot to form a paste, then stir into the milk, mixing in thoroughly. Cook for 1 minute over a moderate heat. Remove the vanilla pod.

In a large mixing bowl, mix the egg yolks and honey together and pour on the warmed, thickened milk, stirring continuously. Pass through a fine sieve into a clean pan and cook over a low heat for 2 minutes, still stirring continuously. Do not boil. Remove from the heat and stir in the *fromage frais*.

Line 4 ramekins with greaseproof (wax) paper; the paper should be 5 cm/2 in higher than the top of each ramekin.

Cover the sheet gelatine with cold water and leave to soften, approximately 5 minutes. Remove from the water with your hand and squeeze out any excess liquid, then place the gelatine in a small heatproof bowl over a pan of barely simmering water. Leave until the gelatine has melted and turned transparent.

Meanwhile, liquidize the pineapple in a liquidizer or food processor and place in a stainless steel saucepan. Bring to the boil and boil for 3 minutes.

When the gelatine has softened, thoroughly stir into the puréed pineapple. Mix with the *fromage frais* custard. Whisk the egg whites until stiff and fold into the mixture. Divide between the ramekins, filling them to the top of the greaseproof (wax) paper. Leave to set in the refrigerator, about three-quarters of an hour.

When the soufflés have set, carefully peel away the paper. Mix the desiccated (shredded) coconut and ground almonds together on a large plate, then dip the soufflés in to coat. To serve, place a soufflé in the centre of each plate, dust with cocoa powder and garnish with flowers and accompany with a honey tuile biscuit.

Fat: high Kcals: 378 Cholesterol: high Fibre: medium

Opposite, from top: *Pineapple and Almond Soufflé, and Warm Blueberry Tartlet with Lemon and Cinnamon Ice Cream*

Warm Blueberry Tartlets with Lemon and Cinnamon Ice Cream

85 g/3 oz/¾ cup wholemeal flour
25 g/1 oz/⅛ cup raw cane sugar
45 g/1½ oz/¼ cup polyunsaturated margarine
juice of ½ lemon
icing (confectioner's) sugar, for dusting
2 dsp clear honey
2 tsp kirsch
350 g/12 oz/3 cups blueberries

Ice cream
150 ml/5 fl oz/⅔ cup ice cream (see page 143)
2 sticks cinnamon
1 vanilla pod
rind of 1 lemon, grated

Serves 4

Preheat the oven to 180°C/350°F/gas 4. Place a baking sheet in the oven to heat.

Sift the flour and add the sugar and margarine, rubbing in the fat with your fingertips until the mixture resembles coarse breadcrumbs. Add the lemon juice and enough cold water to form a dough. Knead until smooth and place in the refrigerator to rest for 20 minutes.

Roll out the dough on a lightly floured surface to a thickness of 3 mm/⅛ in. Grease 4 × 10 cm/4 in fluted pastry rings and line with the pastry. Bake blind for 5 minutes. Remove from the oven and carefully remove the pastry cases from the rings. Leave to cool on a wire rack. When cool, dust with a little icing (confectioner's) sugar.

Make the basic ice cream mixture but infuse the milk with the cinnamon sticks, vanilla pod and grated lemon rind for 20 minutes.

Warm the honey and kirsch together in a small saucepan. Add the blueberries and cook over a low heat for 3–4 minutes until soft. Spoon a quarter of the fruit into each tartlet and serve with a scoop of ice cream on top; flash under a very hot grill for 15 seconds. Serve immediately.

Fat: high Kcals: 257 Cholesterol: low Fibre: medium

Apple and Berry Strudel

2 cooking apples, grated
1 pinch cinnamon
1 tbsp clear honey
170 g/6 oz/1½ cups mixed berry fruits (e.g. strawberries, raspberries, blueberries)
2 sheets ready-made filo pastry
1 egg white
1 bunch fresh mint, finely chopped
150 ml/5 fl oz/⅔ cup Champneys *crème anglaise* (see page 142)

Garnish
4 sprigs fresh mint

Serves 4

Preheat the oven to 150°C/300°F/gas 2.

Put the grated apples, cinnamon and 1 teaspoon of the honey in a pan and sweat for 1 minute. Add the mixed berry fruits and cook gently until the fruit is soft, about 6 minutes.

Brush the filo pastry sheets with the egg white and put one sheet on top of the other. Cut the sheets into quarters and place a quarter of the fruit mixture in the centre of each pastry rectangle. Tuck in the ends of the pastry and roll up into a sausage shape.

Brush the pastry rolls with the remaining honey and bake in the oven for 15 minutes until golden brown.

Meanwhile, add the chopped mint to the *crème anglaise,* stir in well and spoon over the strudel rolls. Garnish with a sprig of mint.

Peach Consommé with Sweet Ravioli

1 vanilla pod
1 star anise
1 stick cinnamon
85 g/3 oz/1¼ cup raw cane sugar
575 ml/1 pt/2½ cups water
4 peaches

Consommé
4 overripe peaches
juice of ½ lemon

Sweet Ravioli
170 g/6 oz sweet pasta (see page 141)
1 tbsp powdered carob
1 pinch saffron powder
20 blackberries
20 raspberries
15 wild strawberries

Garnish
4 sprigs mint

Serves 4

Bring all of the ingredients, except for the peaches, to the boil and simmer for 5 minutes. Add the peaches and poach until they are just cooked. Remove the peaches with a slotted spoon, reserving the poaching liquid for the consommé, and leave to cool. Once the peaches are cool, carefully peel off the skins and put the peaches in the refrigerator.

To make the consommé, boil the peaches in the reserved poaching liquid with the lemon juice until overcooked and mushy. Remove the stones, then strain the liquid through 2 layers of muslin cloth and chill.

To make the sweet ravioli, divide the pasta ingredients into 3. Add the carob powder to one portion, the saffron to another and leave the third plain. Roll out the 3 different pastas as thinly as possible, using a machine or by hand, on one half of each sheet of pasta place 4 piles of 2 of each fruit, then fold over the pasta to enclose the fruit, pressing with your fingers to seal the layers. Set aside a few berries for garnishing and cut round the mounds of fruit with a pastry wheel or large knife to make 3 different shapes. Bring a large pan of water to the boil, drop in the ravioli and cook for 3 minutes until *al dente*. Refresh under cold running water, then place in iced water while you assemble the dish.

To serve, place a poached peach in each bowl, add 3 ravioli and pour over the chilled consommé. Garnish with a sprig of mint and the reserved berries.

Fat: medium Kcals: 297 Cholesterol: high Fibre: high

Peach Consommé with Sweet Ravioli

Iced Carob, Cherry and Pistachio Terrine

55 g/2 oz dark carob
225 g/8 oz light carob
3 sheets gelatine
300 ml/10 fl oz/1¼ cups natural, low-fat *fromage frais*
55 g/2 oz pistachio nuts, shelled
115 g/4 oz cherries, stoned and halved
115 g/4 oz/1 cup raspberries
flesh of 1 small ripe mango

Garnish
85 g/3 oz/¾ cup raspberries

Melt the dark carob in a *bain marie*. Using a palette knife, spread the melted carob onto a piece of greaseproof (wax) paper to form a rectangle approximately 15 cm × 7 cm/6 in × 3 in. Leave until nearly set, then pull a serrated pastry scraper across the centre to form a wavy line; leave to set. Melt a quarter of the light carob in a *bain marie* and use it to fill in the wavy line. Place in the refrigerator to set fully.

Cover the sheet gelatine with cold water and leave to soften for approximately 5 minutes. Remove from the water with your hand and squeeze out any excess liquid, then place the gelatine in a small heatproof bowl over a pan of barely simmering water. Leave until the gelatine has melted and turned transparent.

Mix together the remaining light carob in a bowl, then stir in the gelatine. Whisk in the *fromage frais*, then add the pistachio nuts and

Iced Carob, Cherry and Pistachio Terrine

85 g/3 oz/¾ cup blackberries
icing (confectioner's) sugar, for dusting

Serves 8

cherries. Mix in thoroughly and place in a 575 ml/1 pint/2½ cup terrine. Place in the freezer and freeze for 2 hours.

Meanwhile, purée the raspberries in a food processor or liquidizer until smooth, then pass through a muslin cloth. Repeat with the mango, passing the purée through the muslin into a separate bowl.

Cut the carob on the greaseproof (wax) paper into 4 rectangles 4 cm × 7.5 cm/1½ in × 3 in, using a knife dipped in hot water. Peel the rectangles away from the paper and return them to the refrigerator.

To serve, chill 4 dessert plates. Unmould the terrine by turning out onto a plate. Cut into 4 rectangles 4 cm × 7.5 cm/1½ × 3 in. Place a rectangle on each plate, put a slice of carob on top and spoon over the mango purée. Spoon a little raspberry purée around the outside and place a few raspberries in one corner. Garnish with the remaining raspberries and blackberries and dust with a little sugar.

Fat: low Kcals: 143 Cholesterol: low Fibre: medium

Fig, Sultana and Pecan Pie

50 g/2 oz/⅓ cup sultanas
50 ml/2 fl oz/¼ cup dark rum
285 g/10 oz/2½ cups wholemeal flour
140 g/5 oz/¾ cup polyunsaturated spread
juice of ½ lemon
2 tbsp clear honey
200 g/7 oz/1¼ cups dried figs
6 sheets gelatine
55 g/2 oz/⅓ cup pecans, halved

575 ml/1 pt/2½ cups Champneys *crème anglaise* (see page 142)

Serves 10

Soak the sultanas in the rum overnight.

To make the wholemeal pastry, sift the flour into a bowl, then, using the fingertips, rub in the polyunsaturated spread until the mixture resembles breadcrumbs. Sprinkle nearly all the lemon juice and a little water over the mixture and add the honey. Using a round-bladed knife, lightly mix in until the mixture forms large lumps; add a little more water if necessary. Form into a smooth ball, again using the fingertips, then place on a lightly floured surface. Knead until smooth and free of cracks. Form into a ball, wrap in cling film or plastic wrap and leave to rest in the refrigerator for 1 hour.

Grease a 20 cm/10 inch flan ring. On a lightly floured surface, roll out the pastry and use to line the ring. Prick the base of the pastry case, cover and return to the refrigerator for a further 30 minutes.

Preheat the oven to 175°C/325°F/gas 3. Place a baking sheet in the oven to heat.

Place the flan tin on the baking sheet and bake the pastry case blind for 12 minutes. Remove the beans and paper and leave to cool.

Put the figs in a saucepan and just cover with water; add a dash of lemon juice. Put on a lid and simmer for 30 minutes or until the figs are soft. Strain the liquid into a bowl and put the figs to one side. Return the liquid to the saucepan and reduce over a high heat until it forms a light syrup. Set to one side.

Place 3 tablespoons of water in a small heatproof bowl, sprinkle over the gelatine and leave it to go spongy, about 5 minutes. Place the bowl in a saucepan of barely simmering water and leave until the gelatine has melted and turned transparent.

Purée the figs in a blender or food processor. Add the soaked and drained sultanas to the purée, then stir in the melted gelatine. Spoon into the pastry case and place in the refrigerator to set for 1 hour. Once the mixture has set, arrange the pecans attractively on the surface. Reheat the fig syrup until it is warm and spread over the surface to glaze. Allow to cool before serving. Serve with *crème anglaise*.

Fat: high Kcals: 353 Cholesterol: low Fibre: medium

Lemon and Orange Chiffon Pie

- 170 g/6 oz/1½ cups wholemeal flour
- 2 tbsp low-calorie granulated sweetener
- 85 g/3 oz/⅓ cup polyunsaturated spread
- juice and zest of 6 oranges and 2 lemons
- 3 tsp arrowroot
- 30 g/1 oz carob
- 8 egg whites
- 1 tbsp raw cane sugar
- 1 tbsp clear honey

Serves 6

Preheat the oven to 220°C/425°F/gas 7.

In a large mixing bowl, rub together the flour, sweetener and polyunsaturated spread and bind with a little water. Roll out the dough on a lightly floured surface and use it to line a 25 cm/10 in flan ring and bake blind. Remove the beams and paper and leave to cool.

Cut the lemon and orange zest into fine strips and add to the lemon and orange juice. Bring to the boil in a small pan. Mix the arrowroot with a little water and add to the juices. Stir to thicken and remove the pan from the heat. When cool, chill in the refrigerator.

Melt the carob in a *bain marie*, spread a thin layer inside the cooled pastry case and chill in the refrigerator. When set, pour in the orange and lemon mixture.

Whisk together the egg whites, sugar and honey until the mixture forms peaks. Spread over the flan and lightly brown under a hot grill.

Fat: high Kcals: 166 Cholesterol: low Fibre: low

Fruit and Nut Slice

- 100 g/3½ oz/⅓ cup sultanas
- 75 ml/3 fl oz/⅓ cup rum
- 5 dried figs
- 300 ml/10 fl oz/1¼ cups water
- 14 sheets ready-made filo pastry
- 1 egg white
- 75 g/2½ oz/½ cup mixed walnuts and hazelnuts, crushed
- 2 cooking apples, grated
- 2 ripe bananas, diced (minced)
- icing (confectioner's) sugar, for dusting

Serves 10

Soak the sultanas in the rum overnight.

Boil the figs in the water for 20 minutes until they form a syrup.

Grease a small baking sheet and place 1 sheet of filo pastry on the base and brush with a little egg white. Sprinkle over a third of the sultanas and cover with another sheet of pastry lightly brushed with egg white. Continue to build up the slice, alternating the pastry with layers of nuts, apple and banana. Finish with a sheet of pastry and again brush with egg white.

Preheat the oven to 150°C/300°F/gas 2.

Pour the fig syrup over the pastry and bake for 20 minutes until golden brown. Remove from the oven and increase the temperature to 180°C/350°F/gas 4.

Slice the pastry into 5 cm/2 in squares, dust with icing (confectioner's) sugar and wrap each square in aluminium foil. Bake for approximately 5 minutes until warmed through. Serve immediately.
Note: Once the pastry has been wrapped in aluminium foil it can also be cooked over a hot barbecue for 5 minutes.

Fat: medium Kcals: 166 Cholesterol: low Fibre: low

Poached Peaches Served in a Honey Basket with Rosehip Tea and Fig Sorbet

2.25 l/4 pt/10½ cups fresh orange juice
2 star anise
4 ripe peaches
55 g/2 oz/¼ cup clear honey
55 g/2 oz/¼ cup raw cane sugar
30 g/1 oz/⅛ cup polyunsaturated spread
1 egg white
75 g/2½ oz/½ cup wholemeal flour
8 dried figs
1.1 l/2 pt/5 cups rosehip tea
½ lemon

Garnish
115 g/4 oz/½ cup redcurrants, removed from stems, or raspberries
icing (confectioner's) sugar, for dusting (optional)
4 sprigs mint

Serves 4

Put the orange juice and star anise in a non-stick pan and bring to the boil. Add the peaches and poach in the liquid until tender. Remove from the pan and leave to cool.

Preheat the oven to 220°C/425°F/gas 7.

Using a wooden spoon, mix the honey, sugar and polyunsaturated spread to a smooth paste in a large bowl. Slowly add the egg white and flour, stirring continuously. Spread on a baking sheet in 4 circles, each 10 cm/4 in in diameter, 3 mm/⅛ in thick. Place in the freezer for 5 minutes. Cook in the oven for 4½ minutes then immediately remove from the tray using a spatula or flat knife. Put into a deep, curved mould or rounded tea cup to form a basket shape. Leave to cool.

Boil the figs in the rosehip tea for approximately 10 minutes or until soft. Strain off a quarter of the rosehip tea and reserve. Liquidize the figs with the lemon and a little tea until it is the texture of olive oil. Pass through a sieve into a large bowl. Place in the freezer and whisk vigorously every 20 minutes; it takes about 3 hours for the ice crystals to form. Alternatively place in an ice cream maker or *sorbetière* until stiff. When the sorbet is ready place it in a sealed plastic container in the freezer.

Reduce the reserved tea to a syrup for the sauce. To serve, spoon a pool of tea syrup onto each plate, place a honey basket on top and fill with the sorbet. Add a poached peach to the basket together with small bundles of redcurrants or raspberries. If liked, dust with a little icing (confectioner's) sugar and place a small sprig of mint on top of each peach.

Fat: low Kcals: 357 Cholesterol: low Fibre: high

Opposite: *Poached Peach Served in a Honey Basket with Rosehip Tea and Fig Sorbet*

Mango Charlotte Royale

2 eggs
55 g/2 oz/¼ cup raw cane sugar
55 g/2 oz/½ cup wholemeal flour
1 tbsp reduced sugar strawberry preserve

Mousse
2 small, ripe mangos
1 tsp clear honey
8 tsp natural, low-fat *fromage frais*
3 sheets gelatine
115 g/4 oz/1 cup raspberries

Garnish
4 sprigs fresh mint

Serves 4

Preheat the oven to 180°C/350°F/gas 4. Line a Swiss roll tin with greaseproof (wax) paper, then grease the paper.

Put the eggs and sugar in a heatproof bowl, place over a pan of hot water and whisk until almost white. Remove from the heat and fold in the flour using a large metal spoon. Pour the mixture into the lined tin and bake in the oven for 12 minutes until golden. Remove from the oven, turn out of the tin onto a wire rack and leave to cool.

Reserve 2 teaspoons of chopped mango for garnishing the mousse. Remove the stone and liquidize the pulp with the honey and *fromage frais* in a food processor or blender.

Cut the cooled sponge in half lengthways, spread with the strawberry preserve and sandwich the halves together. Cut the sponge into small batons and use to line 4 ramekins.

Add the gelatine to 2 tablespoons of water and leave until it becomes spongy. Melt in a *bain marie* until transparent and stir into the mango mixture. Divide the mixture equally between the ramekins. Place in the refrigerator for 1 hour to set.

Meanwhile, place the raspberries in a food processor or blender and purée. Pass through a fine sieve or muslin cloth.

To serve, plunge the ramekins up to their rims for 30 seconds and turn out onto serving plates, if necessary giving a couple of shakes to loosen. Spoon on the raspberry purée, sprinkle over the diced mango and garnish with sprigs of mint.

Fat: low Kcals: 215 Cholesterol: high Fibre: medium

Poached Peaches with Cinnamon Ice Cream

575 ml/1 pt/2½ cups skimmed milk
1 vanilla pod, seeds removed
1 tsp cornflour or cornstarch mixed with a little water to form a paste
1 tsp ground cinnamon
2 egg yolks
1 tsp raw cane sugar
4 ripe peaches
575 ml/1 pt/2½ cups fresh orange juice
50 g/2 oz/⅓ cup fresh raspberries

Garnish
4 sprigs of mint

Serves 4

Place the milk in a pan with the vanilla pod and bring to the boil. Stir in the cornflour or cornstarch paste to thicken, then reduce the heat. Add the cinnamon and simmer, uncovered, for 2 minutes.

In a large clean, dry bowl, beat the egg yolks with the sugar until slightly thickened. Pour over the hot milk, stirring continuously. Place the milk mixture in a clean pan and cook, uncovered, over a low heat for 2 minutes taking care not to boil.

Place the milk in an ice cream maker or *sorbetière* and churn for 15 minutes, or until stiff. Store in a covered container in the freezer. If you do not have an ice cream maker, place the mixture in an uncovered container directly into the freezer. As soon as the mixture has begun to set (about 2 hours), transfer to a chilled mixing bowl and whisk thoroughly until smooth. Return the ice cream to the container and freeze, covered, for approximately 3 hours until stiff.

Place the peaches whole in a non-stick pan with the orange juice, bring to just under boiling point, then cover with a lid and poach for 3 minutes. Transfer the peaches to a plate using a slotted spoon, and as soon as they are cool enough to handle remove and discard the skins. Chill in the refrigerator.

To purée the raspberries, process them in a food processor or blender, then press through a fine sieve. Chill.

About half an hour before serving, transfer the ice cream to the refrigerator so that it will soften slightly and be easy to scoop out. To serve, spoon raspberry purée into the centre of each plate, place a peach on top and surround with quenelles of ice cream. Garnish with sprigs of mint.

Fat: low Kcals: 184 Cholesterol: high Fibre: low

Cherry and Pistachio Carob Terrine

Serves 4

To make the sponge mixture, refer to the recipe for Mango Charlotte Royale (page 132), adding 2 teaspoons of cocoa powder. Line a small square terrine with the mixture.

Make the Carob, Cherry and Pistachio Terrine (see page 126), and 1 quantity of Honey Tuile (see page 144). On removing the tuile from the oven, melt 55 g/2 oz light carob in a *bain marie* and pipe in a spiral. Pull it out with a toothpick or cocktail stick to form a web shape. Cut the tuile into halves and curve into small cone shapes and serve with the terrine.

Fat: high Kcals: 680 Cholesterol: high Fibre: high

Carob Soufflé

55 g/2 oz light carob
150 l/5 fl oz/⅔ cup *crème anglaise* (see page 142)
4 sheets gelatine
3 egg whites
3 tbsp natural, low-fat *fromage frais*
2 tbsp carob powder

Serves 4

Melt the carob in a *bain marie* and stir into the *crème anglaise*. Soak the gelatine in cold water for 5 minutes. Remove from the bowl and squeeze out the excess water using your hand. Melt in a heatproof bowl in a *bain marie* and add to the carob mixture. Line 4 small ramekins with greaseproof (wax) paper, leaving a rim 1.5 cm/½ in above the ramekin.

Whisk the egg whites until stiff and fold into the carob mixture, together with the *fromage frais*. Pour into the ramekins and chill in the refrigerator until set, about 30 minutes. When set, remove the greaseproof (wax) paper and roll the edges in carob powder.

Fat: low Kcals: 90 Cholesterol: medium Fibre: low

Carob Tears

225 g/8 oz dark carob, melted in a *bain marie*
5 sheets gelatine
150 ml/5 fl oz/⅔ cup warm *crème anglaise* (see page 142)
2 tbsp clear honey
zest of 1 orange, finely diced (minced)
3 tbsp Grand Marnier
4 tbsp *crème fraîche*

Cut 4 pieces of greaseproof (wax) paper into rectangles measuring 4 cm × 10 cm/1½ in × 8 in. Using a palette knife, spread a thin layer of melted carob on the paper. When the carob is almost set, stand the rectangles on their sides and curve round into a tear drop shape with the ends touching. Refrigerate for 5 minutes to set firm. Carefully remove the paper and place the carob tears on a flat tray in the freezer.

Cover the sheet gelatine with water and leave for 5 minutes. Remove from the bowl and squeeze out the excess water with your hand. Melt in a heatproof bowl in a *bain marie* until transparent and stir into the warm *crème anglaise*.

Add a little water to the honey, bring to the boil, drop in the orange zest and blanch for 3-4 minutes. Rinse the zest under cold running

Selection of Carob Desserts

Garnish
powdered carob, for dusting
25 g/1 oz/⅓ cup redcurrants or raspberries
25 g/1 oz dark carob

Serves 4

water and pat dry on kitchen paper. Add this to the *crème anglaise* together with the Grand Marnier and the *crème fraîche* and chill in the refrigerator. When nearly cool, but still pouring consistency, pour into a carob tear drop shape. Place in the freezer to set, about 30 minutes.

To arrange, place a 10 cm/4 in circular pastry cutter in the centre of each plate and dust the insides with carob powder. Wipe round the cutter, lift from the plate and place a soufflé on top of the powder shape. Melt the dark carob in a *bain marie* and put into a piping bag fitted with a fine nozzle. Pipe elongated fan shapes onto greaseproof (wax) paper. When set, carefully remove from the paper and use to decorate the top of the soufflé. Cut the terrine into 2.5 cm/1 in slices and arrange around the tear drop and soufflé. Add a tuile biscuit cone on one side. Garnish with redcurrants or raspberries.

Fat: medium Kcals: 287 Cholesterol: medium Fibre: medium

Basics include all the essential dressings, stocks, pasta doughs, sauces, and breads required to produce the delicious meals in this book, as well as supplementing the kitchen cupboard or refrigerator with fresh, tasty supplies.

Basic Vinaigrette

4 tbsp oil (e.g. olive, nut or herb-flavoured)
1 tbsp white wine vinegar
sea salt and freshly milled black pepper

Makes 6 portions

Mix together all the ingredients until well blended. Store in a sealed container for up to 2 weeks and use as required, mixing well before each serving.

Fat: medium Kcals: 90 Cholesterol: low Fibre: low

Tomato Vinaigrette

1 tbsp white wine vinegar
4 tbsp extra virgin olive oil
5 large, overripe tomatoes
sea salt and freshly milled black pepper

Makes 6 portions

Place the vinegar, oil and tomatoes in a food processor or liquidizer and process for 2-3 minutes until the mixture reaches a coating consistency. Season to taste with salt and black pepper. Pass through a muslin cloth into a clean container. Seal and store in the refrigerator for up to 3 days, using as required.

Fat: high Kcals: 111 Cholesterol: low Fibre: low

Cucumber and Ginger Vinaigrette

½ cucumber
2 tbsp extra virgin olive oil
2 tbsp white wine vinegar
½ tsp fresh ginger, peeled and finely chopped
sea salt and freshly milled black pepper

Makes 6 portions

Combine all the ingredients in a liquidizer or food processor. Blend vigorously, then press through a fine sieve or muslin cloth. It will keep in a sealed container in the refrigerator for up to 1 week.

Fat: medium Kcals: 48 Cholesterol: low Fibre: low

Orange and Basil Dressing

575 ml/1 pt/2½ cups fresh orange juice
1 medium-sized potato, peeled and diced (minced)
1 sprig basil

Makes 6 portions

Place the orange juice and the potato in a pan and cook over a high heat until the potato is cooked and the orange juice reduced by half.

Pour the reduced juice and the potato into a food processor or blender, add the basil and process for 1 minute. Pass the dressing through a muslin cloth and store in the refrigerator in an airtight container for up to 1 week. Use as required.

Fat: low Kcals: 49 Cholesterol: low Fibre: low

Strawberry Vinaigrette

6 strawberries
1 tbsp balsamic vinegar
3 tbsp walnut oil
sea salt and freshly milled black pepper

Makes 6 portions

Purée the strawberries in a food processor or blender, then pass them through a muslin cloth. Clean the blender or processor and return the strawberry liquor to the blender container. Gently stir in the balsamic vinegar and add the walnut oil at slow speed until it is fully blended with the strawberry juices. Season to taste.

Store in the refrigerator in a sealed container and use as required. Shake well before use.

Fat: medium Kcals: 72 Cholesterol: low Fibre: low

Tomato Concasse – Raw

Prepare quantities as required using large, ripe tomatoes

Cut each tomato into quarters, discard the seeds and excess pulp. Using a very sharp knife, carefully remove the skin from each tomato quarter. Finely chop each quarter into small dice.

Tomato Concasse – Cooked

15 large, ripe tomatoes
2 small onions, finely chopped
1 tbsp olive oil
1 tbsp white wine
1 tsp fresh mixed herbs (e.g. tarragon, thyme, basil and coriander), finely chopped

Makes approximately 6 portions

Proceed as for raw tomato concasse.

Sweat the onions in a frying pan (skillet) in the olive oil until translucent. Deglaze with 1 tablespoon of white wine, then add the tomato concasse and cook over a medium heat until soft. Add finely chopped mixed herbs as desired.

Fat: low Kcals: 94 Cholesterol: low Fibre: medium

Chicken Stock

1.35 kg/3 lb chicken carcasses
3.5 l/6 pt/15 cups cold water
2 medium-sized carrots
1 head celery
2 medium-sized leeks
3 medium-sized onions
1 bay leaf

Makes 1.75 litres/3 pints/7½ cups

Preheat the oven to 220°C/425°F/gas 7.

Roast the chicken carcasses in the oven for 20 minutes until lightly browned. When browned, place the carcasses in a deep pan and just cover with water. Roughly chop the vegetables and add them to the pan with the bay leaf. Bring to the boil, skimming the surface to remove any scum. Cover and simmer for approximately 2 hours, skimming the surface when necessary until the liquid is reduced by half.

Pass the stock through a fine sieve and discard the bones and vegetables. Leave the stock to cool, then refrigerate. Remove the fat from the surface before use. The stock can be kept for up to 3 days in the refrigerator and for up to 3 months if frozen.

Fat: low Kcals: 35 Cholesterol: low Fibre: low

Fish stock

900 g/2 lb fish bones (e.g. plaice, large sole, brill)
1 large leek
1 bulb fennel
1 large onion
1 lemon
3 sprigs parsley
6 white peppercorns
1.1 l/2 pints/5 cups water

Makes 1.1 litres/2 pints/5 cups

Place the fish bones in a pan, cover and sweat for 2-3 minutes to release the juices.

Slice the leek, fennel and onion and add to the fish bones together with all the other ingredients. Cover with 1.1 litres/2 pints/5 cups cold water, bring to the boil and simmer for 20 minutes, skimming the surface as necessary. Pass the stock through a fine sieve and discard the bones and vegetables. Leave to cool and store in a sealed container in the refrigerator for up to 3 days.

Fat: low Kcals: 35 Cholesterol: low Fibre: low

Vegetable Stock

2 large courgettes (zucchini)
4 large onions
1 bulb fennel
115 g/4 oz/½ cup celeriac
2 medium-sized leeks
2 large carrots, peeled
1 head celery
6 cloves garlic
1 tbsp olive oil
1.75 l/3 pt/7½ cups cold water
1 bunch fresh chervil
1 bunch fresh basil
1 bunch fresh thyme
1 star anise

Makes 1.75 litres/3 pints/7½ cups

Finely chop all the vegetables and the garlic. Heat the olive oil in a pan and sweat the vegetables until the onion is translucent. Add the cold water and bring to the boil, then cover and simmer for 10 minutes. Finely chop the herbs and add to the vegetable mixture together with the star anise. Simmer for a further 2 minutes. Pass through a fine sieve, discard the vegetables and leave the stock to cool.

Place the stock in an airtight container and use as required. The stock will keep for up to 3 days in the refrigerator and up to 3 months if frozen.

Fat: low Kcals: 35 Cholesterol: low Fibre: low

Veal Stock

450 g/1 lb veal bones
2 carrots, roughly chopped
1 head celery, roughly chopped
3 onions, roughly chopped
2 leeks, roughly chopped
3.5 l/6 pt/15 cups cold water
1 bouquet garni

Makes 1.75 l/3 pints/7½ cups

Preheat the oven to 220°C/425°F/gas 7.

Place the veal bones in a roasting tray and roast for 25 minutes until lightly browned. Place the roughly chopped vegetables in a deep pan and soften for approximately 15 minutes over a medium heat. Add the browned bones to the vegetables and cover with cold water. Bring to the boil, skimming off the excess fat as necessary. Add the bouquet garni, cover and simmer for 2-3 hours. Then reduce the liquid over a high heat by half.

Pass the stock through a fine sieve and discard the bones and vegetables. Leave to cool and store in an airtight container. The stock can be kept for up to 3 days in the refrigerator and up to 3 months if frozen.

Fat: low Kcals: 35 Cholesterol: low Fibre: low

Peach and Lemon Chutney

500 g/8 oz/1 cup dried peaches
500 ml/16 fl oz/2 cups water
juice and grated zest of 6 lemons
200 ml/7 fl oz/¾ cup cider vinegar
400 ml/14 fl oz/1¾ cups concentrated apple juice
2 cloves garlic
2 large green chillies
1½ tsp coriander seeds
1 tsp ground cardomom
½ tsp ground cloves
100 g/3½ oz/½ cup currants
2 apples, peeled and quartered

Makes 900 g/2 lb

Slice the peaches and soak them overnight in the water in a pan.

The next day, add the grated rind from the lemons, the lemon juice, vinegar and apple juice to the soaked fruit. Simmer, uncovered, until the peaches are soft, approximately 45 minutes, stirring gently from time to time to prevent the peaches from sticking to the pan.

Finely chop the garlic and green chillies in a food processor or blender and add to the pan together with all remaining ingredients.

Bring the mixture to the boil, cover, and reduce the heat and simmer gently for approximately 25 minutes until the apples lose their pale colour, the currants plump up and the chutney thickens. Stir occasionally to prevent sticking.

While the mixture is cooking, sterilize as many heatproof screw-top glass jars as are required for the quantity of chutney made. Wash the jars and their lids in water and detergent and then boil in water for 10 minutes. Dry upside down in a warm oven.

Allow the chutney to cool and store in the sterilized glass jars in the refrigerator for up to 1 month. The flavour improves considerably after a couple of weeks.

Fat: medium Kcals total: 2065 Cholesterol: low Fibre: high

Wholemeal Pasta

2 egg whites
150 ml/5 fl oz/⅔ cup water
100 g/3½ oz/¾ cup plain flour
200 g/7 oz/1¾ cups wholemeal flour
1 pinch salt
½ tsp truffle oil
½ tsp hazelnut oil

Makes 300 g/10½ oz dough

Whisk the egg whites and water together until well blended. Sift the plain and wholemeal flours and the salt together. Make a well in the centre and add the oils to it; stir in thoroughly. Slowly add the egg mixture to the flour and mix to a smooth dough, either by hand or in a food processor or blender.

On a lightly floured board, knead the dough until firm with the heel of your hand. The dough should be firm and elastic; if it is too sticky add a little more flour.

Roll out the pasta on a lightly floured surface until the pasta is 2 mm/⅛ in thick. Alternatively, pass through a pasta machine for a more even finish.

Cook for 3-4 minutes in salted boiling water until *al dente*. Drain and serve immediately.

Fat: high Kcals total: 1035 Cholesterol: low Fibre: high

Saffron Pasta

To add extra flavour and yellow colour to pasta soak 1 teaspoon of powdered saffron in 25 ml/1½ tablespoons of warm water for 20 minutes. Add the saffron infusion to 1 quantity of Wholemeal Pasta dough at the same time as the oils.

Spinach Pasta

To add green colour and a stronger flavour to pasta, add 55 g/2 oz/1½ cups of chopped fresh spinach to 1 quantity of Wholemeal Pasta mixture. Mix well, either by hand or in a food processor or blender until a smooth dough is formed. If the mixture seems dry, slowly add up to 3 tablespoons of cold water.

Fat: high Kcals (total): 1035 Cholesterol: low Fibre: high

Sweet Pasta

- 110 g/4 oz/1 cup flour, plain or wholemeal
- 1 small egg
- 2 tsp low-calorie granulated sweetener
- 1 dsp extra virgin olive oil

Makes 150 g/5½ oz dough

Mix all the ingredients in a food processor or blender for 1 minute. On a lightly floured surface knead to form an elastic dough. Leave to rest in the refrigerator for 1 hour before rolling as for Wholemeal Pasta.

Fat: high Kcals (total): 508 Cholesterol: high Fibre: high

Champneys Bechamel

- 575 ml/1 pt/2½ cups skimmed milk
- 1 small button onion
- 1 bay leaf
- 2 cloves garlic
- 25 g/1 oz/⅛ cup cornflour or cornstarch, mixed with a little water to form a paste

Makes 575 ml/1 pint/2½ cups

Pour the milk into a pan and add the onion, bay leaf and garlic cloves. Slowly bring to the boil, then simmer for 5 minutes. Remove and discard the onion, bay leaf and garlic and return the milk to the boil. When boiling, stir in the cornflour or cornstarch paste and continue stirring until the mixture reaches coating consistency. Cook for a further 2 minutes, then press through a fine sieve.

Fat: low Kcals: 293 Cholesterol: low Fibre: low

Champneys Muesli

575 ml/1 pt/2½ cups natural, low-fat yoghurt (see page 142)
2 dsp sultanas
1 tbsp chopped mixed nuts
3 dsp jumbo oats
1 dsp clear honey
1 large, ripe banana
115 g/4 oz/1 cup mixed berry fruits
2 red apples, grated
1 green apple, grated

Garnish
1 dsp toasted oats
1 bunch mint

Serves 6

In a large bowl, mix together thoroughly all the ingredients except the banana, berry fruits and apples. Leave the mixture overnight in the refrigerator.

Before serving, slice the banana and any large berry fruits and grate the apples, including the peel, and add to the mixture. Stir well and garnish with toasted oats and mint leaves.

Fat: low Kcals: 155 Cholesterol: low Fibre: low

Yoghurt

575 ml/1 pt/2½ cups skimmed milk
2 tsp skimmed milk powder
2 tsp live natural low-fat yoghurt

Makes 575 ml/1 pint/2½ cups

Ensure that all the utensils are clean, otherwise contamination may occur. Put all the ingredients in a small saucepan. Heat to blood temperature, 37°C/96°F. Pour into a sterilized thermos or vacuum flask. Leave for 10 hours with the lid on. Refrigerate and serve.

Fat: low Kcals: 230 Cholesterol: low Fibre: low

Champneys Crème Anglaise

575 ml/1 pt/2½ cups skimmed milk
1 vanilla pod
1 tsp arrowroot, mixed with a little water to form a paste
3 egg yolks
2 tbsp low-calorie granulated sweetener

Makes 575 ml/1 pint/2½ cups

Gently heat the milk and vanilla pod together for about 5 minutes, bring to the boil and add the arrowroot paste, stirring until slightly thickened. Cook for 2 minutes on a medium heat. Leave to cool.

Place the egg yolks and sweetener in a large mixing bowl and whisk until thick and white, 3–4 minutes. Whisk in the milk, and when thoroughly blended transfer to a clean pan and gently reheat, stirring constantly. Do not allow the custard to boil or it will curdle. Remove the vanilla pod and pass the custard through a fine sieve. It is now ready to serve but will keep for up to 3 days in the refrigerator.

Fat: high Kcals: 470 Cholesterol: high Fibre: low

Ice Cream

300 ml/10 fl oz/1¼ cups milk
1 vanilla pod
2 tsp egg replacer
1 tsp water
4 tbsp low-calorie granulated sweetener
1 tsp cornflour or cornstarch, mixed with a little water to form a paste
2 tsp *crème fraîche*

Serves 4

Pour the milk into a saucepan, add the vanilla pod and bring to the boil. Meanwhile, in a large bowl, lightly whip the egg replacer in 1 teaspoon of water. Add the sweetener and whisk until smooth.

Put the cornflour or cornstarch paste into another large bowl. As soon as the milk comes to the boil, remove from the heat, discard the vanilla pod and pour the milk onto the paste, stirring continuously, to thicken. Return the milk to the pan and simmer for 2-3 minutes to blend thoroughly, stirring from time to time. Pour the thickened milk onto the egg mixture, whisking with a fork as you pour. Leave until cool and fold in the *crème fraîche*. Pour the mixture through a fine sieve into a mixing bowl. Place in the freezer and whisk vigorously every 20 minutes (use an electric hand-whisk or a rotary whist) until the ice cream is set, about 4-5 hours. Alternatively, place the mixture in an ice cream maker or *sorbetière* and churn until firm.

When the ice cream has set, place in a freezer container with an airtight lid and use as required. The ice cream will keep in the freezer for up to 1 week.

Fat: low Kcals: 88 Cholesterol: low Fibre: low

Basic Bread

250 ml/8 fl oz/1 cup lukewarm water
30 g/1 oz/2 cakes fresh yeast
500 g/1 lb 2 oz/4½ cups strong plain flour
1 tbsp salt
1 tbsp skimmed milk powder
20 g/¾ oz/1 tsp polyunsaturated spread

Makes a 900 g/2 lb loaf, or 16 rolls

Put half the water in a small bowl, stir in the yeast and leave to ferment and froth, 5-8 minutes. Sift all the dry ingredients into a large mixing bowl, then mix in the polyunsaturated spread, using your fingertips, until the mixture resembles breadcrumbs. Make a well in the centre and add the remaining water and yeast. Mix in well, using your hand, then knead to form a soft dough, 5-8 minutes. Leave to rise for 30 minutes in a warm place, then lightly knead again for about 1 minute to knock the dough back to its original size. Leave to rise for another 30 minutes, then divide into the required portions and place on greaseproof (wax) paper on a baking sheet. Leave to prove for 15 minutes.

Preheat the oven to 190°C/375°F/gas 5.

Bake in the oven for 30 minutes until the bread is well browned and crisp on all sides. If the bread is done, it should sound hollow when tapped on the base. Transfer to a wire rack and leave to cool.

Fat: low Kcals: 119 Cholesterol: low Fibre: low

Wholemeal Pastry

115 g/4 oz/1 cup wholemeal flour
1 pinch of sea salt
55 g/2 oz/¼ cup polyunsaturated margarine
50-75 ml/2-3 fl oz/¼-⅓ cup water

Makes 1 quantity for 20 cm/8 in flan dish

Sift the flour and a pinch of salt together. Using a fork, break up the margarine in the flour and salt to achieve a crumbly texture. Mix in the water until a soft dough is formed and leave the pastry to rest in a covered container in the refrigerator. Roll out the pastry as required and use to line a greased or non-stick 20 cm/8 in circular quiche or flan dish.

Fat: high Kcals (total): 887 Cholesterol: low Fibre: high

Wholemeal Cinnamon Muffins

200 g/7 oz/1¾ cups wholemeal flour
3 tsp ground cinnamon
25 g/1 oz/⅛ cup baking powder
45 g/1½ oz/¼ cup raw cane sugar
45 g/1½ oz/¼ cup polyunsaturated spread
2 eggs
250 ml/8 fl oz/1 cup skimmed milk
icing (confectioner's) sugar, for sprinkling

Makes 12 muffins

Preheat the oven to 205°C/400°F/gas 6. Place a baking sheet in the oven to hear.

Sift the flour, cinnamon and baking powder into a mixing bowl. Add the sugar and the polyunsaturated spread and, using your fingertips, rub in well to form fine crumbs. Make a well in the centre of the flour. Gradually add the eggs and milk, mixing in with a knife to form a smooth paste; the mixture should be of dropping consistency.

Grease 12 muffin tins liberally with polyunsaturated spread. Spoon the dough a quarter of the way up each tin (the dough will rise when cooking) and bake in the oven for 15-20 minutes, until well risen and golden brown. Place on a wire rack to cool.

To serve, sprinkle with icing (confectioner's) sugar.

Fat: low Kcals: 125 Cholesterol: medium Fibre: low

Honey Tuile

30 g/1 oz/¼ cup clear honey
55 g/2 oz/¼ cup raw cane sugar
1½ oz polyunsaturated fat
85 g/3 oz/¾ cup wholemeal flour
1 egg white

Makes 20 biscuits or 10 baskets

Mix the honey, sugar and polyunsaturated fat to a smooth paste using a wooden spoon. Fold in the flour and egg white a little at a time, again to form a smooth paste. The paste should be of dropping consistency. Place in a clean bowl, cover the top of the bowl with cling film or plastic wrap and use as required, storing in the refrigerator for up to 2 days.

Fat: low Kcals: 46 Cholesterol: low Fibre: low

Champneys Fruit Loaf

- 140 g/5 oz/1¼ cups self-raising flour
- 140 g/5 oz/1¼ cups wholemeal self-raising flour
- ¼ tsp salt
- ½ tsp baking powder
- 200 g/7 oz/1¼ cups dark muscovado sugar
- 55 g/2 oz/½ cup skimmed milk powder
- 30 g/1 oz/¼ cup wheatgerm
- 55 g/2 oz/⅓ cup raisins
- 45 g/1½ oz/⅓ cup dried apricots, chopped
- 30 g/1 oz/¼ cup walnuts, chopped
- 30 g/1 oz/¼ cup hazelnuts, chopped
- 3 eggs
- 175 ml/6 fl oz/¾ cup fresh orange juice
- 75 ml/3 fl oz/⅓ cup olive oil
- 1 banana, diced (minced)

Serves 12

Preheat the oven to 175°C/325° F/gas 3. Grease a 450 g/1 lb loaf tin and line with greaseproof (wax) paper.

Mix all the dry ingredients together including the nuts and dried fruit. In a separate bowl, whisk together the eggs, orange juice, oil and bananas until frothy. Make a well in the centre of the dry ingredients and add the banana mixture, stirring until mixed. Spoon into the prepared tins and bake for about 1 hour until the loaf pulls from the sides of the tin and a skewer inserted in the centre comes out clean.

When cooked, remove from the tin and cool on a wire rack before wrapping in greaseproof (wax) paper and storing in an airtight tin for up to a week.

Fat: high Kcals: 313 Cholesterol: medium Fibre: low

Sultana, Walnut and Banana Bread

- 3 ripe bananas
- 55 g/2 oz/¼ cup polyunsaturated spread
- 1 egg, beaten
- zest of 1 orange, grated
- 255 g/9 oz/6¼ cups wholemeal flour
- 1 pinch baking powder
- 1 pinch salt
- 45 g/1½ oz/⅓ cup chopped walnuts
- 55 g/2 oz/¼ cup sultanas, soaked in cold water for 4 hours
- 4 tbsp low-calorie granulated sweetener

Preheat the oven to 180°C/350°F/gas 4. Place a baking sheet in the oven to heat.

Mash the bananas with a fork and beat in the polyunsaturated spread. Stir in the beaten egg and grated orange zest. Sieve the flour, baking powder and salt into a separate mixing bowl. Add the walnuts, sultanas and sweetener and make a well in the centre. Pour in the banana mixture and beat until smooth using a wooden spoon.

Line a 450 g/1 lb loaf tin with lightly oiled greaseproof (wax) paper. Pour the mixture into the tin, place on the baking sheet and bake for 1 hour until golden brown. Turn out onto a wire rack. Serve sliced and spread with a thin layer of polyunsaturated spread.

Fat: high Kcals (total): 2146 Cholesterol: high Fibre: high

Menus

January (Family Dinner)

A Salad of Marinated Pigeon with Walnuts and Grapes

Cod Baked with Wild Mushrooms, Tarragon and White Wine

Bread and Fruit Pudding with Banana Sauce

Above; *A Family Dinner in January;* opposite: *February's St Valentine's Day meal*

February (St Valentine's Day)

Scallop, Bacon and Mushroom Salad with Maple Dressing

Roasted Fillet of Pork with Apricot and Onion

Mango Charlotte Royale

March (Light Buffet)

Wild Mushroom and Lentil Salad

Red Mullet with Salad Niçoise

Apricot, Fig and Coconut Terrine

April (Anniversary Lunch)

Vegetable and Nut Croquettes

Stuffed Breast of Corn Chicken with a Tomato Vinaigrette

A Tulip of Passion Fruit and Apricot Sorbet with Fresh Fruits

May (Birthday Lunch)

Wild Mushroom and Chicken Terrine

Red Mullet with Salad Niçoise

Lemon and Orange Chiffon Pie

June (Barbecue)

Avocado and Sweetcorn Soup

Barbecued Chicken Chilli and Pineapple Wrapped in a Cornflour Pasty

Fruit and Nut Slice

July (Garden Party)

Champneys Gazpacho

Salmon Poached in Champagne Served with Cucumber and Watercress Salad

Warm Blueberry Tartlets with Lemon and Cinnamon Ice Cream

August (Light Lunch)

Melon Lime Soup

Celeriac and Wild Mushroom Terrine

Poached Peach with Cinnamon Ice Cream

September (Celebration Supper)

Sardine and Red Onion Terrine

Quail with Sweet Pepper Sauce and Autumn Vegetables

Champneys Apple Crumble with Honey-Sweetened Fromage Frais

October (Dinner Party)

Chicken Leek Mousse with Beetroot Salad

Roasted Fillet of Veal with Roasted Shallots and Garlic with a Madeira Sauce

Kiwi and Orange Slice with Sweet Vinaigrette

November (After Theatre Meal)

Mexican Bean Soup

Smoked Gammon Brochette with Celeriac and Apple Cakes

Banana en Papillote

December (Christmas Day)

Scallops Poached in Caraway and Saffron

Pheasant and Quail Stuffed with Apple and Cranberry Forcemeat

Apricot and Passion Fruit Water Ice

Fig, Sultana and Pecan Pie

Above: *A Light Lunch in August;* opposite: *December's Christmas Day feast*

Glossary

Al dente – an Italian term used to indicate the point at which food is perfectly cooked. It is usually used with reference to pasta which should be soft but still chewy when ready. The cooking time varies according to the type and shape of pasta used but with a little experimentation judging the *al dente* point becomes easy.

Alfalfa sprouts – these grains can be sprouted within a week. Choose whole grains free of chemicals that are sold for cooking rather than sowing. To prepare, soak overnight in warm water. Drain and place in a sterilized glass container, large enough to hold the sprouts which will expand to 5 or 6 times their original size. Cover with a small cotton or muslin square and place in a warm place, out of direct sunlight. Rinse 2 or 3 times with fresh water every day until fully sprouted. To use, drain and discard any unsprouted grains.

Arrowroot – an effective powder thickener of liquids and sauces. To avoid lumps mix to a paste with a little water before adding to the mixture to be thickened. After adding to the liquid stir in well, usually over heat.

Bain marie – cooking in a *bain marie* allows gentle and even heat distribution in the preparation of dishes using delicate ingredients which are better cooked away from direct heat or flame (e.g. sauces, carob or chocolate, and gelatine). To set up a *bain marie*, bring a large pan of water to the boil. Put a heat proof bowl or smaller pan into the first pan, resting on the boiling water. Lower the heat slightly, add the ingredients to the smaller container and simmer until cooked or melted. Make sure the larger pan does not boil dry.

Baking blind – this method of baking pastry is used where a tart of flan case needs to be partially or fully cooked for crispness before a filling is added. Roll out the pastry and use to line a flan or pie tin. Cover with greaseproof (wax) paper, leaving a small rim extending above the top of the tin. Fill the pastry case with uncooked rice, dried beans or ceramic baking 'beans' (sold at most specialist kitchen shops). To partially cook, bake for about 5 minutes in a moderate-hot oven until the pastry is golden. To cook fully, leave in the oven for approximately 15 minutes until brown. Remove the rice or beans and paper and leave to cool in the tin, then transfer to a wire rack.

Blanching – the blanching method used in these recipes refers to parboiling by blanching where ingredients are plunged into boiling water for 1 or 2 minutes (longer if specified in the recipe). This retains colour in vegetables and helps to preserve various nutrients. The food items are then usually 'refreshed' under iced or cold water to stop any further cooking from taking place.

Borage – both the leaves and small deep blue flowers of this herb are edible and can be used in salads or for garnishing. If using the leaves, pick them when young before the hairy covering thickens.

Bouquet garni – a selection of herbs, fresh or dried, which always includes thyme, bay leaf and parsley, and any others according to taste. The sprigs are tied into a bundle using string or wrapped in a small piece of muslin. The bouquet garni should be removed before serving.

Cardomom pod (bean) – this spice pod is available in 2 varieties, 'green' or white, and black. The black pods are milder and are often used in Indian dishes. For the best flavour, buy cardomom in pod rather than powder form.

Carob – similar to chocolate, carob is produced from the carob or locust bean. It is available in bars, chips or powder. Carob is lower in fat than chocolate and contains no caffeine.

Caul fat – this is the fatty membrane that lines a pig's stomach. It is often used for wrapping meat and meat terrines; it helps prevent the meat from drying out.

Chinois – a fine stainless steel sieve which allows for effective straining of liquids.

Charlotte – a custard- or cream-based dessert made in a traditional tall mould. A 'Charlotte Royale' is supported by a layer of sponge around the sides and base of the mould.

Coating consistency – a sauce of coating consistency should be thick enough to coat food evenly. To test for this, put a wooden spoon into the sauce and draw a finger across the back of the spoon. If the sauce is ready a clearly defined trail should be left.

Concasse – from the French verb *concasser*, to chop coarsely; a concasse is a dish of coarsely chopped vegetables, usually tomatoes.

Coulibiac – a layered fish dish surrounded in pastry, originating from Russia.

Crème anglaise – a light vanilla custard (see page 142).

Crème fraîche – a French cultured cream similar to soured cream. The minimum fat content of 29 per cent means that it will not separate quickly on heating. To make *crème fraîche*, use double (heavy) cream mixed with half its volume of soured cream or yoghurt. Warm the two together but do not boil. Remove from the heat, put in a clean bowl, cover with a cloth and keep in a warm place for approximately 8 hours. Then store in the fridge.

Dropping consistency – when a sauce or mixture reaches this point it should be thick enough to drip rather than pour off a wooden spoon. If the drops are allowed to fall onto a clean, flat surface they should retain their shape without flowing outwards.

Filo pastry – extremely thin sheets of pastry made from flour and water, used extensively in Greek, Turkish and Middle Eastern cooking. Buy ready-made fresh or frozen sheets of pastry. To use, brush with olive oil, or egg white for fewer calories.

Fromage frais – this unripened cheese resembles thick yoghurt. It has a very low fat content, ranging from 0 to 8 per cent. Higher fat varieties are available but the lower fat types are very useful as a replacement for cream in low-fat recipes. *Fromage frais* can be served cold in the same way as yoghurt, or in hot dishes. However, take care not to overheat or it will separate and form lumps.

Galantine – a dish of stuffed and rolled white meat served cold in jelly.

Garlic oil – this is olive oil infused with cloves of garlic to give it extra flavour. To make garlic oil, peel several cloves of garlic and place in a clean glass jar. Fill the jar with olive oil. Cover and leave to infuse for about 10 days. Use as required.

Gelatine – this is available in both powder and sheet form and is used to set dishes that are moulded or that require extra setting properties. Both types of gelatine are soaked in cold water to form a gel and are then melted to a transparent liquid in a *bain marie*. Stir well on adding the gelatine to the other ingredients to ensure even distribution. Do not attempt to add gelatine to a dish containing raw pineapple as the fruit's natural enzymes will prevent setting.

Ice cream maker or sorbetière – this machine stirs the ice cream or sorbet mixture while keeping it at a temperature below freezing point. Invaluable for regular ice cream making in large quantities, an ice cream maker reduces the amount of manual stirring that is otherwise needed.

Kumquat – this orange-coloured fruit is the smallest of the citrus family. It has a distinctive bitter-sweet flavour and both the skin and the flesh can be eaten raw, poached, candied, sliced with meat or in salads, stewed as a sauce or pickled.

Larder trimmed – to have all fat and sinew removed from a cut of meat.

Lardons – small 6 mm/⅛ in strips cut from bacon rashers, with the rind removed. Some shops sell ready-cut lardons; to cut at home, simply chop the rashers into strips, layer them on top of each other and cut again until you reach the required size.

Lentils: *puy* – these small dark green lentils are grown in the Le Puy area of France. They have a very good flavour and hold their shape during cooking.

Madeira – a fortified wine from Spain, often used in sauces. It is available in dry or sweet varieties.

Maple syrup – a sweet syrup made from the boiled sap of the maple tree. It is available in two grades: Number 1 is thinner and easier to pour and is best used as a sauce over ice cream, pancakes or waffles; Number 2 is thicker and is better for cooking. Once opened, store the syrup in the refrigerator. Be careful not to confuse maple syrup with maple-flavoured syrup, a synthetic substitute with an inferior flavour.

Mushrooms – wild mushrooms of various types are now increasingly available in shops. Two particularly delicious types are morels and chanterelles (which include girolles and horns of plenty). Morels have curiously corrugated caps and should be soaked in cold water for 5 minutes before cooking to remove any dirt or insects. Rinse under running water and drain on kitchen paper.

Girolle mushrooms are yellow in colour with slightly ragged edges, while horns of plenty are dark brown with a hollow trumpet-shaped centre; both need only a quick wipe before cooking. They can be baked, stewed or stir-fried. Both morels and chanterelles are available dried.

Note: Unless you are an expert in mushroom identification it is not advisable to gather your own crop in the countryside; many varieties of wild mushroom are highly poisonous.

Muslin cloth – a porous fine cotton cloth which is ideal for straining liquids, some fruit purées and cheese-making.

Mussels – to prepare for cooking, scrub the shells under cold running water and remove any barnacles or weeds. Throw out any with broken shells or which do not shut when knocked gently with a knife. Cut away the beard strings. To cook, follow instructions given in the recipes.

Oil: *olive* – this is a versatile oil high in monounsaturated fat made from pressing olives. Olive oil comes in various grades: the most popular are 'extra virgin', . made at the first pressing, with a stronger flavour, and the cheaper standard olive oil which is milder in taste. Olive oil is multi-purpose and can be used for shallow-frying, in salad dressings, even in baking dough.

Peanut (also known as groundnut oil) – this is a light oil with a mild flavour. It is used for frying and in salad dressings where the stronger flavour of olive oil is less suitable.

Sesame – French sesame oil and Asian toasted sesame oil are both produced from sesame seeds, yet the former is pressed from the raw seeds. The toasted seed oil has a richer taste and should be used in small quantities; it is normally added at the end of the cooking time.

Hazelnut and walnut oils – these oils are pressed from the nuts and have a very distinctive aromatic flavour. Do not heat excessively or the flavour will be considerably diminished.

Truffle oil – this is olive or sunflower oil infused with truffles; a real luxury – use sparingly.

Parma ham – ham cured using the traditional processes of the town of Parma in northern Italy. It should be served in paper-thin slices with the fatty edges removed.

Pasta machine – this machine rolls pasta dough to ever-decreasing thicknesses. Many machines have different settings or attachments for producing a variety of widths and types of strip or shape.

Provençale – a style of cooking combining garlic, tomatoes and olive oil originating from the Provence region of southern France.

Proving dough – leaving yeasted dough to rise or prove before baking, ideally in a warm place, allows fermentation to take place.

Polyunsaturated spread – a margarine made from soya or sunflower oils which are low in saturated fats and high in polyunsaturated fats. Spreads made from olive oil have similar uses and are equally suitable for greasing, baking and using in some sauces.

Quail's eggs – these tiny speckled eggs can be found in specialist stores. They are usually served hard-boiled (5 minutes) and are often presented with their shells on for visual effect.

Quenelles – these are elongated spheres made from raw fish or white poultry meat, mixed with eggs and often other ingredients for flavour or added binding qualities. Once moulded, quenelles are quickly cooked in simmering water and can be served with a sauce or in soup.

Rice: *Brown* – rice grains with the husk left on. These are chewy and have extra fibre. Brown rice takes about 40 minutes to cook but can take less time if soaked overnight.

Wild – this grain grows in lakes in North America. Although part of the crop is now cultivated, some of the harvest is still hand-picked from the wild plants. Black and shiny in appearance, the grains are boiled for approximately 40 minutes until chewy.

Ramekin – a small, round, ovenproof dish for making individual soufflés or moulds.

Refreshing – see Blanching

Saffron – the world's most expensive spice, saffron consists of the hand-picked stamens of the saffron crocus. Its distinctive flavour is brought out well in rice dishes, sweet cakes and breads and with fish. Saffron is available in either thread or powder form. To use the threads, infuse in a small amount of warm water before adding to the dish.

Sake – a Japanese wine with a high alcohol content, produced from fermented rice. It can be added to food or drunk on its own, when it is traditionally served hot.

Stir-frying – this method of frying, usually in a wok or deep frying pan (skillet) is very quick and seals in the flavour of the food as well as using the minimum of fat. To stir-fry small pieces of meat or vegetables, heat a small amount of oil in a wok until it is smoking. Add the ingredients and keep them moving by stirring them around the pan.

Sorbetière – see Ice cream maker

Tahini paste – a strongly flavoured paste made from crushed, toasted sesame seeds. The seeds and the oil tend to separate in the jar so shake well before use.

Terrine – a straight-sided ovenproof dish, usually lidded. The shape and size can vary. Small pâté terrines provide individual portions while the larger 1.1 litre/2 pint/5 cup dishes serve up to 14.

Timbale – a small moulded mound of meat, fish or vegetables, named after the ceramic dish of the same name.

Vinegar: *Red or white wine* – as the name suggests, these are made from wine; they are most commonly used in salad dressings.

Cider – this is derived from cider and is useful for preserving and pickling, although it can also be drunk on its own, diluted with water.

Balsamic – an Italian vinegar produced from grapes in a traditional and lengthy process of fermentation, often taking as long as 12 years. Although expensive, balsamic vinegar has a very rich taste and is used in small quantities.

Raspberry – this is produced by letting chopped raspberries infuse in a good quality vinegar for a few days before straining. It can be diluted and drunk alone or used in dressings or fruit salads.

Yoghurt – this is made from fermented milk and is an extremely versatile dairy product. The yoghurt with the fewest calories is made with skimmed milk. It is relatively cheap and simple to make yoghurt at home by introducing the live culture to milk (see page 142).

Greek or Greek-style – this has a creamy consistency and a fat content of at least 8 per cent. It is often made with sheep's milk.

Index

The author

ADAM PALMER is Master of Cuisine at Champneys, one of the world's finest health resorts. After working in a country house hotel in Hertfordshire and a city centre hotel in Birmingham, he joined Champneys as Sous Chef in 1987. He became Head Chef two years later.

HONOR THY MUSIC®

WESTERN EDGE

The Roots and Reverberations of Los Angeles Country-Rock

FOREWORD BY LINDA RONSTADT

COUNTRY MUSIC FOUNDATION PRESS
222 REP. JOHN LEWIS WAY S · NASHVILLE, TENNESSEE 37203

Published 2022. Printed in the United States of America.
978-0-915608-37-9
This publication was created by the staff of the Country Music Hall of Fame® and Museum.
Editor: Paul Kingsbury · Artifact photos by Bob Delevante · Printer: Lithographics, Inc., Nashville, Tennessee

PRINTED IN THE U.S.A. USING SOY-BASED INKS ON ECO-FRIENDLY PAPER

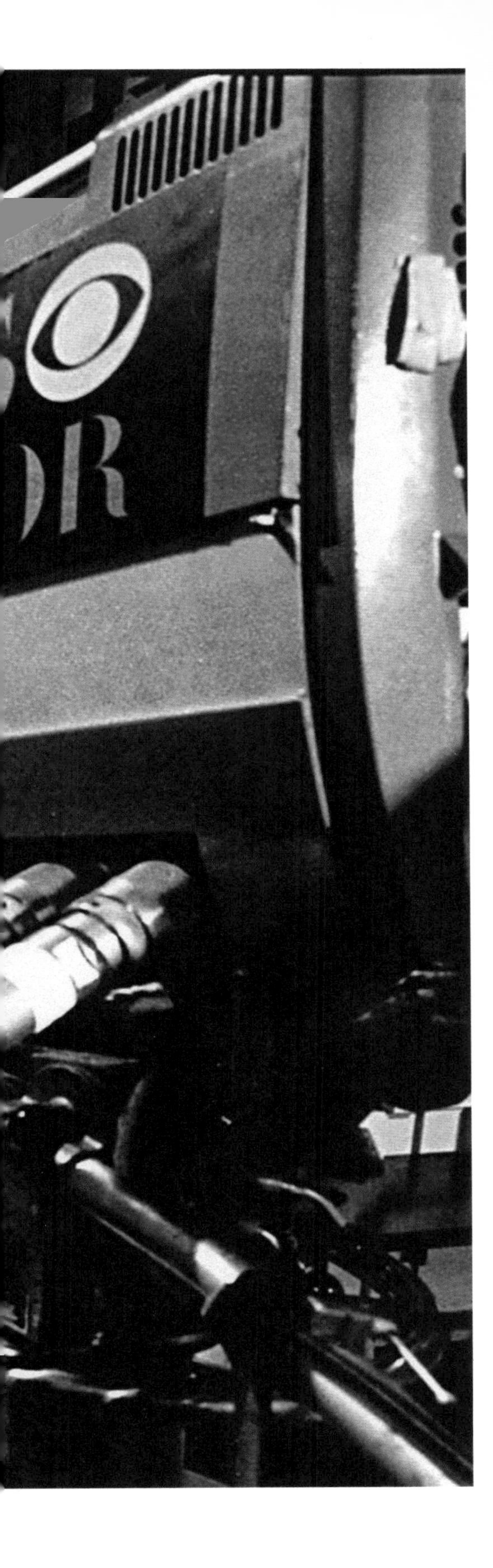

CONTENTS

Nitty Gritty Dirt Band on the set of *Playboy After Dark*, December 1968. Hosted by Hugh Hefner, the syndicated series was taped at CBS Television City in Los Angeles.
ON STAGE, FROM LEFT: Les Thompson, Jeff Hanna, Ralph Barr, Jimmie Fadden, John McEuen, and Chris Darrow

PHOTO COURTESY OF JOHN McEUEN

INSIDE FRONT AND BACK COVERS: Detail of "The American Cowboy Rodeo," the 1933 poster by California artist and cowboy Jo Mora that was the inspiration for the cover of the Byrds' *Sweetheart of the Rodeo* album

ARTIFACT COURTESY OF CHRIS HILLMAN

DEAR MUSEUM FRIEND,

Who could have predicted that banjos and steel guitars would spark a revolution in rock & roll? Or that L.A. rockers would teach their generation and those that follow to appreciate country music?

The exhibition *Western Edge: The Roots and Reverberations of Los Angeles Country-Rock* examines a time of boundary crossing and great communal creativity, from the 1960s to the 1980s. The music that emerged from that time and that place connected not just L.A.'s close-knit musical communities; it still connects us, and reminds us of the great value in crossing the boundaries that divide us too often.

When the Byrds released the pioneering album *Sweetheart of the Rodeo* in the summer of 1968, critics and the listening public alike were baffled at first. What was this? Yet groups like the Byrds, Buffalo Springfield, the Dillards, and others were on to something that would grow and gather strength. While we might debate the first true "country-rock" recording—and there are many contenders who were chasing the sound—what can't be debated is the enduring power of the phenomenon. Its sounds are still with us.

The term was fraught with natural tension. Chris Hillman described "country-rock" to us recently as "a device to sort of pigeonhole you into a more descriptive place. It's country music to me, you know. It's all country music to me—or music."

And it's country music to us. And it's rock, too. From today's vantage point, we can take in both sides of the equation and hear harmony and no contradiction.

Los Angeles has long been an ideal spot for artists and musicians who want the freedom to mix things up. There was already a long tradition of country music in the town, and country sounds were all around. It was only natural for some open-minded rock musicians to bring country into the mix and test their experiments onstage. Local clubs like the Ash Grove and the Troubadour, which feature prominently in these pages, and ultimately the Palomino and the Whisky, became temples and flashpoints for the new music and its evolution.

Soon record labels took notice. Radio took notice. Most importantly, musicians took notice, and they built new possibilities from what they heard.

Dwight Yoakam heard the sounds coming from L.A., moved there, and tapped into the energy of the local punk scene in the late 1970s and 1980s. There he found an audience for his brand of country music alongside others who understood the value of mixing tradition with raw energy and passion.

Dwight's presence within this exhibition and his support of it are crucial to our ability to tell the story. Likewise, Chris Hillman's involvement, perspective, and support have been invaluable.

As with all our major exhibitions, we have dug deep to present layers of storytelling, often taken straight from conversations with those who lived those stories. We conducted twenty-three video interviews for *Western Edge*, capturing many hours of first-hand perspective, and we've collected significant artifacts that are central to the story. Many of them are featured in this book, complementing numerous historic images.

We're thrilled that Linda Ronstadt has contributed this exhibit companion's foreword and that Randy Lewis, longtime Los Angeles music journalist, has written its main essay. We are equally honored to feature supporting pieces written by Mary Katherine Aldin, Dave Alvin, James Austin, Alison Brown, Steve Fishell, and Holly George-Warren.

This is a story of a wondrous American phenomenon, one that transported us all west, to the edge of our continent, and one that brings us today to a better appreciation of what we call, simply, country music.

Sincerely,

Kyle Young | CEO

ACKNOWLEDGEMENTS

This book, and the exhibition it accompanies, benefited from the collaborative enthusiasm we encountered among many generous people in Los Angeles and Nashville.

Planning for the project began in September 2019, when Chris Hillman and Roger McGuinn joined Marty Stuart for one of his Artist-in-Residence concerts at the Country Music Hall of Fame and Museum. Staff spent much of the afternoon with Chris and his wife, Connie Pappas Hillman, both of whom would assist us greatly throughout the development of the exhibit.

In January 2020, Chris Hillman sat down with us for an interview, filmed at the Troubadour in West Hollywood. The next day Chris and Connie welcomed us into their home to provide artifacts. On that same trip, we picked up artifacts related to the Ash Grove from Mary Katherine Aldin; conducted film interviews with musicians JayDee Maness, Larry Murray, and Herb Pedersen at the Grammy Museum; and met with James Austin, Bill Bentley, and Scott B. Bomar to enlist their help.

We were off to a good start until the pandemic necessitated the closure of the museum for six months and halted travel for *Western Edge*. Fortunately, several musicians we wanted to interview on camera either lived in Nashville or happened to be traveling through Music City. Peter Asher, Rodney Dillard, Rosie Flores, Richie Furay, Jeff Hanna, Emmylou Harris, John Jorgenson, Bernie Leadon, Taj Mahal, John McEuen, Graham Nash, Jim Ed Norman, John Sebastian, JD Souther, and Lucinda Williams generously volunteered their time and shared their stories with us.

We are also grateful to Dave Alvin, Maria McKee, Louie Pérez, and Dwight Yoakam, who spoke with our curators and film crew when we returned to Los Angeles, in 2022.

Linda Ronstadt first talked to museum staff as a special guest on our podcast series, *Voices in the Hall*, in 2019. When our writers had questions specific to *Western Edge*, she generously agreed to additional interviews. Her vivid memories and keen perspectives informed the book and the exhibit alike. Janet Stark, Linda's longtime personal assistant, was especially helpful.

Western Edge is full of wonderful stage costumes, and Michael Nesmith's Nudie suit is one we hoped to feature from the outset. He died on December 10, 2021—less than a year before the exhibit opened. We are thankful he wanted his prized outfit and other artifacts to be included. We are deeply indebted to Andrew Sandoval and Robin Campbell for arranging their shipment from California.

Likewise, we had dreamed from the beginning of reuniting the Nudie suits worn by members of the Flying Burrito Brothers on the album cover of their classic debut, *The Gilded Palace of Sin*. The Autry Museum of the American West helped us procure Chris Hillman's suit. Sneaky Pete Kleinow's stage costume was loaned to us by his daughter Anita Kleinow and shipped to us from the Rock & Roll Hall of Fame, where the suit had been on display. Gram Parsons's Nudie suit has long been on loan to the Country Music Hall of Fame and Museum from Melanie Wells and Manuel Cuevas, who created the Flying Burrito Brothers suits while head designer at Nudie's Rodeo Tailors in North Hollywood. (The whereabouts of Chris Ethridge's Nudie suit are unknown.)

Our thanks also go to David Andersen, Pete Anderson, Joel Aparicio, Fred Aronow, Sherry Raye Barnett, Diane Bouska, Gretchen Carpenter, Kai Clark, Jon Corneal, Manuel Delgado, Dan Dugmore, Ian Dunlop, Alejandro Escovedo, Marvin Etzioni, Jimmie Fadden, Pete Finney, David Glowacki, Lynne Robin Green, Sid Griffin, Ryan Hedgecock, Tom Holzen, Jimmy Ibbotson, Los Lobos, Matt Maher, Shilah Morrow, Gunnar Nelson, Matthew Nelson, Liz Norris, Polly Parsons, Dan Reeder, Laura Sáez, Nancy Sefton, Chris and Tom Skinker, Mike Smyth, Greg Sowders, Sergio Webb, and Mary Young.

Many museum staff members devoted time and talent to the book and exhibit. Space prohibits listing them all, but some deserve special mention here. Vice President of Museum Services Brenda Colladay led the exhibition team, which consisted of exhibit curators Michael McCall, Michael Gray, and Mick Buck, Shepherd Alligood, Kevin Fleming, Kathleen Campbell, Jack Clutter, Adam Iddings, Alan Stoker, Julea Thomerson, Director of Exhibitions John Sloboda, Managing Editor Paul Kingsbury, and registrars Rosemary Zlokas and Elek Horvath. Vice President of Creative Services Warren Denney and the creative team, led by Jeff Stamper and Bret Pelizzari, including Luke Wiget, Sam Farahmand, Michael Manning, Roger Blanton, Mills Hayes, Sydney Gilbert, Arlie Birket and Debbie Sanders also deserve special mention.

Music historian Colin Escott assisted us greatly by writing copy for the exhibit interactives.

Finally, we would like to thank City National Bank for its generous support of this exhibit. Likewise, we are deeply grateful to the Metro Nashville Arts Commission and the Tennessee Arts Commission, both of which provide essential operating support that underwrites museum publications, school programs, and public programs.

SIMPLE DREAMS

FOREWORD BY LINDA RONSTADT

Country music was something I grew up with. I was immersed in a wide variety of music growing up in Tucson, Arizona. My thing is eclectic mania—I like everything, but it's important to know a musical style authentically. So, I never tried to sing anything that I hadn't heard by the time I was ten years old, because I wouldn't know it authentically. I knew and loved country music.

In fact, I discovered Hank Williams when I was five. It happened on the regular trips my family made to Mexico. A high point of those drives was stopping to eat at a place called the Halfway Station between Tucson and the Mexican border. They had fantastic burritos and a killer jukebox. Half the jukebox was in Spanish and the other half was in English, and the English half included all these great Hank Williams records. I'd save up my quarters so I could hear Hank Williams and Trio Calaveras songs while we ate there.

The similarities between Mexican music and country music struck me right away. For starters, both came from an agrarian lifestyle. It's about the same old stuff. You know, the cattle are cooperating or not cooperating. The fields are cooperating or not cooperating. Your wife or girlfriend is cooperating or not cooperating.

As I grew a bit older, I listened to all these great records by Hank Williams and Elvis Presley and the Everly Brothers that my sister, Suzy, had. I would stack them up on

Linda Ronstadt at New Victoria Theatre, London, England, November 13, 1976

PHOTO BY DAVID REDFERN

the old record player with the big spindle in the middle that played 45s—in just the order I'd want them, and I'd think about it all day when I was at school. What got me through the day was knowing I would get to go home and listen to those records.

When I was in my teens, I formed the New Union Ramblers in Tucson with my brother and sister. That was another deep dive into country music, because our banjoist, Richard Saltus, turned me on to the blood harmonies of the Blue Sky Boys and bluegrass by Bill Monroe, the Stanley Brothers, and Flatt & Scruggs. These groups came out of a real country existence, and I grew up in the country myself, so I related to that. Again, the lyrics and the rich, natural-sounding harmonies reminded me of the Mexican trios I liked.

In 1964, when I was eighteen, I first visited Los Angeles, and I was hooked, so I returned during my spring break from college in ’65. The first musicians I saw live in Los Angeles were Taj Mahal and Ry Cooder—together in a band called the Rising Sons—at the Ash Grove. They had the Grove in their pocket. At that point I had never heard anything of quite that quality.

Captivated by the scene in Los Angeles, I quit college and moved there, knowing I would have more musical opportunities than I would ever have in Tucson. I didn’t have much money, but I had a burning desire to sing. Shortly after arriving in L.A., I began singing harmony with Bobby Kimmel and Kenny Edwards in our trio, the Stone Poneys. We lived in a place on the beach in Santa Monica for $80 a month, splitting the rent three ways.

Our sound evolved because of what was going on within the music scene in L.A. I heard the Byrds on the Sunset Strip, and I had known Chris Hillman from his previous

TOP RIGHT: **Linda Ronstadt, January 1968**

BOTTOM RIGHT: **Emmylou Harris and Linda Ronstadt at Universal Amphitheatre, Los Angeles, October 1, 1977**

PHOTOS BY HENRY DILTZ

OPPOSITE PAGE: **When the Stone Poneys performed at Tucson’s Palo Verdo High School, May 8, 1968, Linda Ronstadt was photographed holding a copy of Phoenix fanzine *A Closer Look*.**

PHOTO BY JOHNNY FRANKLIN

bluegrass band, the Scottsville Squirrel Barkers. I thought one day, 'Well, if he can change from mandolin to electric bass and be folk-rock, then the Stone Poneys can do that, too.' Because we were sort of a folky band when we started out. We were acoustic and would've loved to have been hired at the very traditional Ash Grove, but we weren't hip enough. The diehard folkies at the Ash Grove were playing only blues and acoustic music. So, we auditioned at the Troubadour, which was considered more commercial—and we got a gig. The Troubadour gigs led to us finding a manager, and then a record deal.

Then, in 1966, I heard a recording of "Different Drum" by John Herald's bluegrass band, the Greenbriar Boys, and discovered Michael Nesmith wrote the song. It had a country feel the way the Greenbriar Boys did it, but I told our producer at Capitol Records, Nik Venet, that I thought it could be a hit for the Stone Poneys—and with a more uptempo arrangement, it was.

When I first went solo, after the Stone Poneys disbanded, I turned to country songs I had known since childhood in part because I needed a new repertoire. I also thought they were good songs. They were beautifully written, well-constructed, and expressed a universal sentiment. I wanted to sing songs that expressed what I was going through in my own life at the time. Plus, they had simple chord progressions I could play on guitar. So, I started to work up songs like Ray Price's "Crazy Arms" and Hank Williams's "I Can't Help It (If I'm Still in Love with You)."

Like a lot of the musicians in L.A. at that time, I was trying to create hybrids. We were all just experimenting in those days. For instance, I recorded "Everybody Loves a Winner" back in those early days. The record had pedal steel guitar and bluegrass harmonies on top of an R&B rhythm section. That kind of approach came out of the routine creative exchanges we had going on in L.A. We all hung out at the Troubadour and jammed together, united by our mutual desire to weld country music songs and harmonies to an R&B—or rock & roll—rhythm section.

I had grown up listening to a lot of country in the 1950s, but after moving to Los Angeles my music gradually morphed into the Troubadour's version of country and bluegrass. And I began to look for musicians who could play songs that had come out of Nashville, but with a California twist.

The Troubadour was a special spot. I remember seeing Joni Mitchell there—every show, every night, for two weeks. JD Souther, Glenn Frey, and Don Henley were also part of the scene. You'd be sitting at the bar, and pretty soon Warren Zevon or Doug Dillard or Bernie Leadon would walk in.

The Troubadour was where everybody went to hang out and be noticed. If you wanted to make yourself known to the record community at large, you would go to the Troubadour and open mic night—the Hootenanny—on Monday night. You got three songs, and if they didn't like you, they'd boo you off stage or everybody would just talk over the music. But if it was somebody good, like Bonnie Raitt or Jackson Browne, everybody would be really quiet and listen. When the Flying Burrito Brothers came onstage wearing their Nudie suits designed by Manuel Cuevas, they blew the place away. It was really great. They sparkled and glittered.

In L.A. in those days, it felt like everyone in the music community was encouraging each other. There was a certain amount of competitiveness, of course, but it wasn't bloodthirsty. We were just trying to play music with others who understood our music. It was a special time and a special community for me, as I think it was for many people—musicians and fans alike. I hope this book and the related exhibition bring you a little closer to understanding the incredible creativity and musicianship that sprang from L.A.'s country-rock scene. And I hope it takes you back to the music we made and the freedom we felt in making it. Ω

Front and back of a Stone Poneys flyer, 1967
ARTIFACT COURTESY OF DAVID ANDERSEN

MAR 1965
Precisions

ARE YOU READY FOR THE COUNTRY?

THE MULTI-COLORED TAPESTRY OF L.A. COUNTRY-ROCK

1960s–1980s

BY RANDY LEWIS

Picture this: it's 1965. An eighteen-year-old University of Arizona freshman takes a spring-break road trip across the Sonoran and Mojave deserts from Tucson to visit a friend who'd moved to Los Angeles to chase a career in music. One night, they hit the vibrant club scene on the Sunset Strip in Hollywood to check out an exciting new band he's been hyping to her back home.

"As soon as I heard their creamy harmonies, I was mesmerized," Linda Ronstadt remembers about discovering the Byrds shortly before the band released their groundbreaking debut single, "Mr. Tambourine Man."

"It was clear to me that music was happening on a whole different level in Los Angeles," she wrote in her 2013 autobiography, *Simple Dreams: A Musical Memoir*. Although she'd been making the rounds singing in Tucson's folk clubs for some time with her brother and sister, her trip west was a light-bulb moment: "I began making plans to move to L.A. at the end of the spring semester."

The sound that upended Ronstadt's life and brought her to L.A. a few months later would soon also alter the course of music of the late 1960s and explode as a dominant force in the pop world through the 1970s: L.A. country-rock.

The Byrds onstage, March 1965, weeks after recording their debut album, *Mr. Tambourine Man*. PHOTO COURTESY OF CHRIS HILLMAN

Linda Ronstadt, c. 1965

That musical marriage resulted from a confluence of factors, unique to L.A. at the time, including geography, a hotbed of musical talent, a pervasive atmosphere of experimentation, and a rapidly changing music industry.

Although Ronstadt couldn't have known it at the time, she was present at a flash point in the emergence of a fertile scene that would come to include a number of key acts: Buffalo Springfield; Crosby, Stills & Nash; Neil Young; the Flying Burrito Brothers; Poco; Rick Nelson & the Stone Canyon Band; the Dillards; the Nitty Gritty Dirt Band; Jackson Browne; JD Souther; the Monkees; Emmylou Harris; Ronstadt herself; and, in short order upon spreading out from under her wing, the Eagles.

In the years ahead, the sound would filter into country-infused pop and rock from James Taylor, Carole King, America, Firefall, Pure Prairie League, and others.

The scene that produced so many of those acts was rejuvenated in the '80s with a new jolt of energy from brash, young mavericks such as Dwight Yoakam, Lone Justice, the Blasters, Los Lobos, Lucinda Williams, Rank and File, the Long Ryders, Rosie Flores, the Lonesome Strangers, Jim Lauderdale, and the Desert Rose Band.

The West, California historian and author J. S. Holliday once said, "is the regenerative force of America." For a period stretching across three decades, Los Angeles was a regenerative force in popular music not only nationally, but globally.

ROOTS OF A REVOLUTION: THE FIFTIES AND SIXTIES

The pioneers of what came to be known as country-rock were mostly born in the early to mid-1940s, making them preteens and teenagers at the birth of rock & roll in the mid-'50s. Not surprisingly, nearly all were enamored of the first generation of rock & rollers: Elvis Presley, Chuck Berry, Little Richard, Jerry Lee Lewis, Buddy Holly, Bo Diddley, the Everly Brothers, and others. But as the big bang of rock & roll faded at the end of the '50s, many of these fans gravitated to the folk music revival that also germinated in that decade.

First the Weavers, then the Kingston Trio, Joan Baez, and Peter, Paul & Mary grabbed listeners unmoved by pre-packaged replacements for rock's originators, i.e., "The Bobbys": Bobby Vee, Bobby Vinton, and Bobby Rydell, would-be teen idols touted to an audience in search of pop music's Next Big Thing. Their music, however, was a pale echo of that first generation. But folk music offered something meatier to a generation of aspiring musicians.

The Kentucky Colonels at Newport Folk Festival, July 26, 1964
FROM LEFT: Roland White, Billy Ray Latham, Clarence White, and Roger Bush
PHOTO BY JIM MARSHALL / COURTESY OF DIANE BOUSKA

The young folksinger who generated the most excitement once his music began seeping out of New York's Greenwich Village was Bob Dylan. The folk revival resurrected narrative storytelling in song and brought it to a new generation. Most media attention focused on the folk scene in and around New York, but a tight-knit community raised on rock but also well-versed in folk, bluegrass, and country music was simultaneously taking root in Southern California.

One of the earliest acts that would figure crucially in L.A. country-rock was the Three Little Country Boys, started in 1954 by transplanted Maine siblings Clarence, Roland,

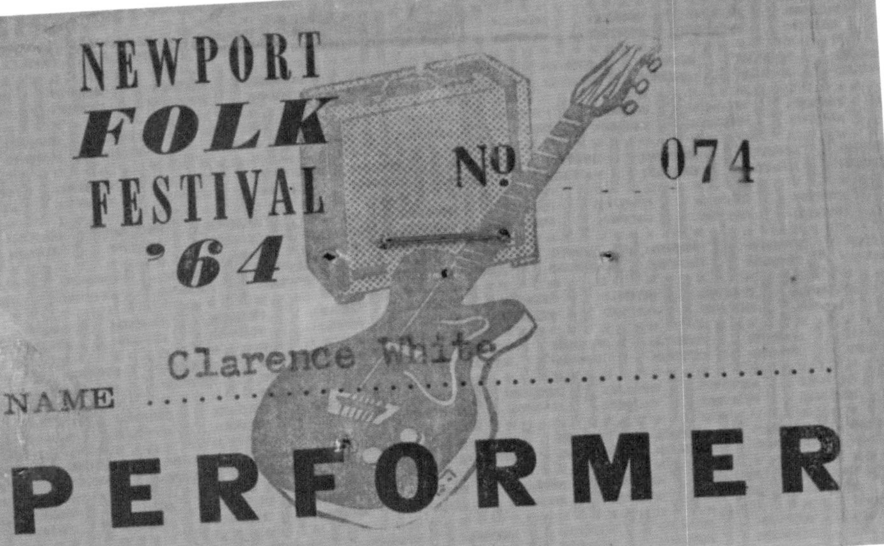

ABOVE: Clarence White's pass from the 1964 Newport Folk Festival
ARTIFACT COURTESY OF TOM HOLZEN

and Eric White Jr. Their group became the Kentucky Colonels and realigned the traditional bluegrass lineup of fiddle, banjo, mandolin, and guitar through Clarence White's acoustic guitar mastery, pushing the instrument front and center, and out of its traditional rhythm accompaniment role.

Meanwhile, Missouri brothers Doug and Rodney Dillard, along with bandmembers Mitch Jayne and Dean Webb, moved to L.A. in search of the Ash Grove, the fabled epicenter for blues, folk, and gospel music. Almost miraculously, within a few days of arriving, the Dillards landed a performance slot at the Hollywood club that led to a recording contract and a featured role on *The Andy Griffith Show* portraying local family band the Darlings and winning the Dillards national television exposure.

Vern and Rex Gosdin, who hailed from Alabama, helped form the Golden State Boys, a skilled young Southern California bluegrass group. The ensemble soon recruited a hotshot young mandolinist named Chris Hillman.

Hillman had made a name for himself in the Scottsville Squirrel Barkers, a San Diego-based bluegrass ensemble formed in the early 1960s by guitarist Larry Murray and bassist Ed Douglas out of their music store, the Blue Guitar, home to a thriving folk-bluegrass-country music scene one hundred miles south of L.A.

RIGHT: Faux-buckskin shirt worn by Rodney Dillard onstage with the Dillards, c. 1964

ARTIFACT COURTESY OF RODNEY DILLARD

ABOVE: The Dillards with actor Andy Griffith, c.1964. The Dillards portrayed the Darlings, a bluegrass-picking family, in six episodes of *The Andy Griffith Show*, 1963–66. FROM LEFT: Rodney Dillard, Doug Dillard, Griffith, Mitch Jayne, and Dean Webb

PHOTO COURTESY OF RODNEY DILLARD

OPPOSITE PAGE: Rodney Dillard played this 1963 Martin D-28 with the Dillards on *The Andy Griffith Show* and on most of their albums.

ARTIFACT COURTESY OF RODNEY DILLARD

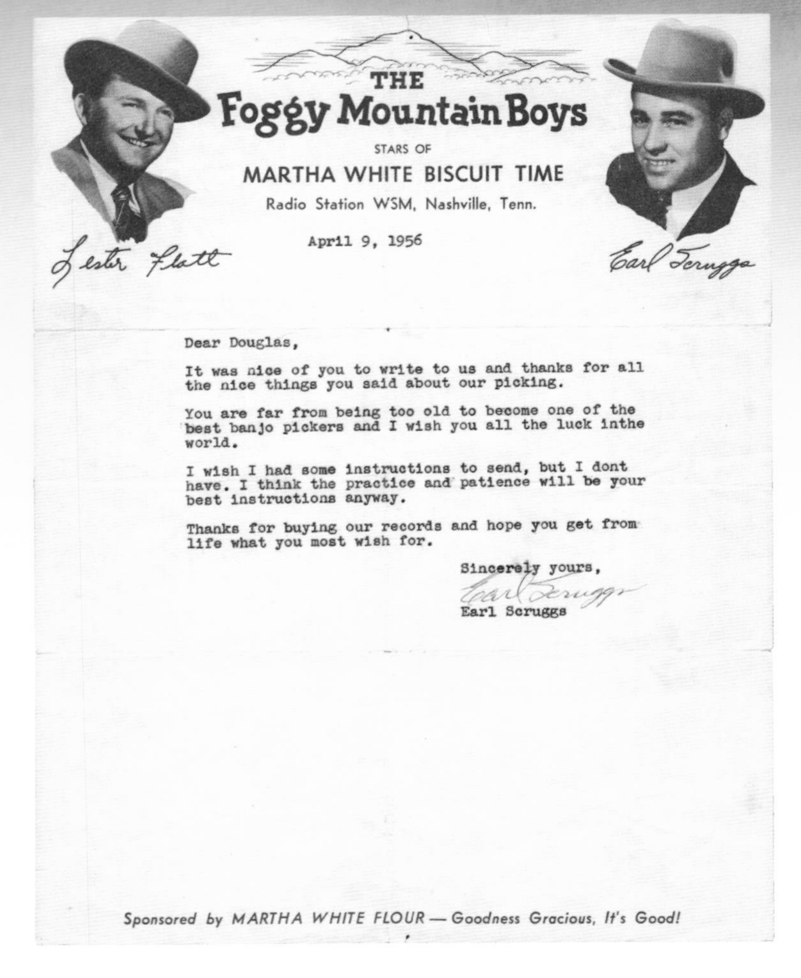
THE
Foggy Mountain Boys
STARS OF
MARTHA WHITE BISCUIT TIME
Radio Station WSM, Nashville, Tenn.

Lester Flatt Earl Scruggs

April 9, 1956

Dear Douglas,

It was nice of you to write to us and thanks for all the nice things you said about our picking.

You are far from being too old to become one of the best banjo pickers and I wish you all the luck inthe world.

I wish I had some instructions to send, but I dont have. I think the practice and patience will be your best instructions anyway.

Thanks for buying our records and hope you get from life what you most wish for.

Sincerely yours,

Earl Scruggs
Earl Scruggs

Sponsored by MARTHA WHITE FLOUR — Goodness Gracious, It's Good!

To the north in Berkeley, the Pine Valley Boys took note of what was happening down L.A. way, and some of its members soon moved south—among them guitarist-singer Herb Pedersen, who struck up a lifelong friendship and musical collaboration with Hillman.

By 1965, with Dylan rapidly morphing from acoustic folksinger to electric rocker, folk-minded L.A. players also began plugging instruments in and bringing more driving rhythms to bear. The Dillards, the Whites, Hillman, and others found a more welcoming attitude in L.A. toward new ideas, approaches, and instrumental adventurousness.

Dazzling instrumental proficiency among younger players like Doug Dillard, Clarence White, and Hillman brought new energy to bluegrass. Rich harmony singing, also a staple of folk and bluegrass, became a signature

CONTINUED ON PAGE 29

Artist Earl Newman created this silk-screened poster for the Blue Guitar, the San Diego instrument and repair shop where the Scottsville Squirrel Barkers rehearsed and first performed, c. 1962.

ARTIFACT COURTESY OF CHRIS HILLMAN

OPPOSITE PAGE, FROM LEFT:
This advertisement ran in *Billboard*'s "Music on Campus" issue, March 1965.

Banjo virtuoso Earl Scruggs of bluegrass pioneers Flatt & Scruggs sent this letter of encouragement to nineteen-year-old Doug Dillard in 1956.

ARTIFACTS COURTESY OF LYNNE ROBIN GREEN

FOUNDATIONS OF A MOVEMENT

BY HOLLY GEORGE-WARREN

The country-rock scene that emerged in Southern California in the 1960s and 1970s had origins that reached back decades earlier. Los Angeles had been steadily growing as a key entertainment center since the 1910s, when the film industry took root in Hollywood. The town's movie industry was already in full flower in 1934, when Texan Gene Autry, a handsome, twenty-six-year-old recording artist, came west for a cameo in his first motion picture, *In Old Santa Fe*—a milestone in the rise of country music culture in Southern California.

Country Music Hall of Fame member Gene Autry, 1935

OPPOSITE PAGE: Western-wear designer Nathan Turk made this cowgirl costume for Rose Maddox of the Maddox Brothers & Rose.

Autry did not star in that movie, but he stole the picture with his singing, and within a year he sparked a fifteen-year boom of "musical westerns"—also known as singing cowboy movies—in Hollywood. From 1935 until he enlisted in the Army Air Corps in 1942, Autry would

regularly appear high on the list of Hollywood's biggest stars at the box office. He also made records that sold in the millions, including "South of the Border," "Mexicali Rose," and his theme song, "Back in the Saddle Again."

Autry's broad appeal enticed nearly every Hollywood studio to try singing cowboy movies, and a number of charismatic cowboys followed in his bootsteps, including Roy Rogers and Tex Ritter. Women also made inroads: Rogers's co-star Dale Evans, a Texan who had begun her career as a big band singer, married her leading man and became the "Queen of the West" alongside America's "King of the Cowboys" in movies and on television. In the process, country & western music (as it was then known) was heard and seen across the U.S.

Both the allure of working in singing cowboy movies and the scourge of the 1930s Dust Bowl droughts spurred many rural southwestern and southern musicians to relocate to California in search of riches and stardom. Among them was a destitute farming family from Boaz, Alabama, who hitchhiked to California. In 1937, they traded their migrant produce-pickers' sacks for musical instruments and became a family band known as the Maddox Brothers & Rose, featuring young sister Rose on full-throated vocals. They were trendsetters in two key ways: they wore wildly decorative stage costumes made by Nathan Turk (inspiring their nickname "the Most

Colorful Hillbilly Band in America"), and they played a raucous, rhythmic blend of country music, western songs, and hillbilly boogie that pointed the way to rock & roll.

World War II brought yet more transplants to California, including those stationed there in the armed forces or working in munitions plants. Taking advantage of this young, transplanted audience hungry for country sounds, competitive western swing bandleaders Spade Cooley and Bob Wills each led big bands that packed the popular Venice Pier Ballroom and San Fernando Valley dance halls. Near Griffith Park in L.A., the massive Riverside Rancho (with a 10,000-square-foot dance floor) opened in the early 1940s, hosting regular Spade Cooley shows and, later, a fifteen-year residency by Cooley's former vocalist Tex Williams.

When Capitol Records opened for business in Hollywood in 1942, the label took note of the burgeoning demand and signed top country & western acts alongside their pop artists. These included Tex Ritter, Tex Williams, Merle Travis, Jimmy Wakely, Hank Thompson, and Tennessee Ernie Ford. When producer Ken Nelson assumed A&R duties at Capitol in 1951, he recruited several talented Bakersfield-based artists—Buck Owens, Merle Haggard, Jean Shepard, and Tommy Collins among them—to the Capitol label. The hard-country edge and broad musical range of such performers planted seeds of influence for

The Country Boys at the Riverside Rancho dance hall, Glendale, California, 1954. From left: Eric White Jr., Roland White, Joanne White, and Clarence White. PHOTO COURTESY OF DIANE BOUSKA

TOP, FROM LEFT: Fred Maddox, Rose Maddox, and Cal Maddox of the Maddox Brothers & Rose in the 1940s

country-rockers. During the 1950s and early 1960s, California continued to broadcast a wealth of country music via popular 1950s television programs. Based in Compton's Town Hall auditorium, the locally broadcast *Town Hall Party* offered a colorful cast of seasoned players from 1953 to 1961, including master guitarist Joe Maphis and his wife, Rose Lee; proto-rockabilly Skeets McDonald; and young rockabilly siblings the Collins Kids. Meanwhile, on ABC-TV *The Adventures of Ozzie and Harriet* introduced all of America to young Ricky Nelson, who went from singing on the program to making appealing rockabilly as well as pop-rock records ("Poor Little Fool," "Travelin' Man") that topped the national pop charts and featured the hot guitar work of Joe Maphis and James Burton.

These musical styles, and the musical ambience they shared, had a far-reaching impact on musicians in Southern California. The smooth harmonies of the singing cowboys; the keening pedal steel parts of Ralph Mooney on records by Buck Owens and Merle Haggard; the stunning guitar work of Merle Travis, Joe Maphis, and James Burton; the rocking energy of the Maddox Brothers & Rose and the Collins Kids—all of these elements had their effect on the musicians who made country-rock sing in Southern California and paved the way for their experiments. Ω

This double-neck Mosrite electric guitar was built for Joe Maphis, a virtuoso musician and *Town Hall Party* cast member.

CONTINUED FROM PAGE 22

for several L.A. groups—as Ronstadt's first impression of the Byrds attests, and as subsequent music from Poco, Crosby, Stills & Nash, and the Eagles proved throughout the '70s and beyond.

THE LINCHPIN: CHRIS HILLMAN

If there's a linchpin figure in the story of L.A. country-rock, it's hard to think of anyone more critical than Chris Hillman.

"Yeah, we all know how great he was in the Byrds, but his contributions go well beyond that," said the late Tom Petty, the lifelong Byrds fan who produced Hillman's 2017 solo album, *Bidin' My Time*. "Chris was a true innovator—the man who invented country-rock. Every time the Eagles board their private jet, Chris at least paid for the fuel."

Growing up in north San Diego County's rural enclave of Rancho Santa Margarita, Hillman was mesmerized, as so many of his contemporaries were, by Elvis Presley's 1956 appearance on *The Ed Sullivan Show*. But he wasn't motivated to start playing until the folk revival hit, his interest fueled largely by his older sister's record collection.

Chris Hillman, c.1965. PHOTO COURTESY OF CHRIS HILLMAN

The Golden State Boys, 1963. FROM LEFT: Chris Hillman, Don Parmley, Rex Gosdin, and Vern Gosdin

Upon discovering the music of bluegrass, Hillman fell in love with the mandolin and started playing bluegrass with like-minded San Diego pals: banjo player Kenny Wertz and guitarist Gary Carr, who soon invited him to sit in with them, Larry Murray, and Ed Douglas in the Squirrel Barkers.

"Just getting up to play was a thrill," Hillman wrote in his 2020 autobiography, *Time Between: My Life As a Byrd, Burrito Brother, and Beyond*. "If we made any money, that was an extra treat."

In addition to his direct impact across the 1960s, '70s, and '80s as a founding member of the Byrds; the Flying Burrito Brothers; Stephen Stills's Manassas; the Souther-Hillman-Furay Band; McGuinn, Clark & Hillman; and the Desert Rose Band, he was a catalyst for many others' careers.

Not the least among those were Buffalo Springfield, whose career took off after Hillman persuaded Whisky a Go-Go co-owner Elmer Valentine to hire the band. He also brought Gram Parsons into the Byrds, then started the Flying Burrito Brothers with him, en route to introducing Parsons to a female singer with whom he would make music history: Emmylou Harris. When Hillman and McGuinn fired David Crosby from the Byrds, it opened the door for Crosby to join Buffalo Springfield alum Stephen Stills and the Hollies' Graham Nash in one of rock's first supergroups, Crosby, Stills & Nash.

"Nobody really knew who [Chris] was when he was in the Byrds," Crosby told the *Los Angeles Times* in 2017. "At the beginning he was just standing there playing bass. But as soon as he started writing and singing, people figured out, 'Oh, I get it.' Then when he did . . . the Desert Rose Band, it was plain he was excelling as a singer and a songwriter. He was the whole package."

Dwight Yoakam takes it a step farther: "Without Chris Hillman acting as the connective tissue between West Coast country music traditions, and the rock & roll generations, from Buck Owens to the Byrds," he once wrote, "there would be no modern country music."

This 1958 Martin D-28 belonged to Chris Hillman's first musical mentor, Bill Smith. A custodian at Hillman's San Diego high school, Smith gave the teenager what Hillman later called "the start of my formal education" in country and bluegrass music.

ARTIFACT COURTESY OF CHRIS HILLMAN

THE BYRDS TAKE FLIGHT

Historian J. S. Holliday's idea about the West's regenerative powers manifested frequently in '60s L.A., not just musically but also in the national fascination with Southern California surf culture, fashion, custom hot rods, and an aerospace industry feverishly working to help put human beings on the moon before the decade ended. In music circles, tradition was understood and respected, but new frontiers beckoned. "Back east, most of the great bands were from the Carolinas or Kentucky or

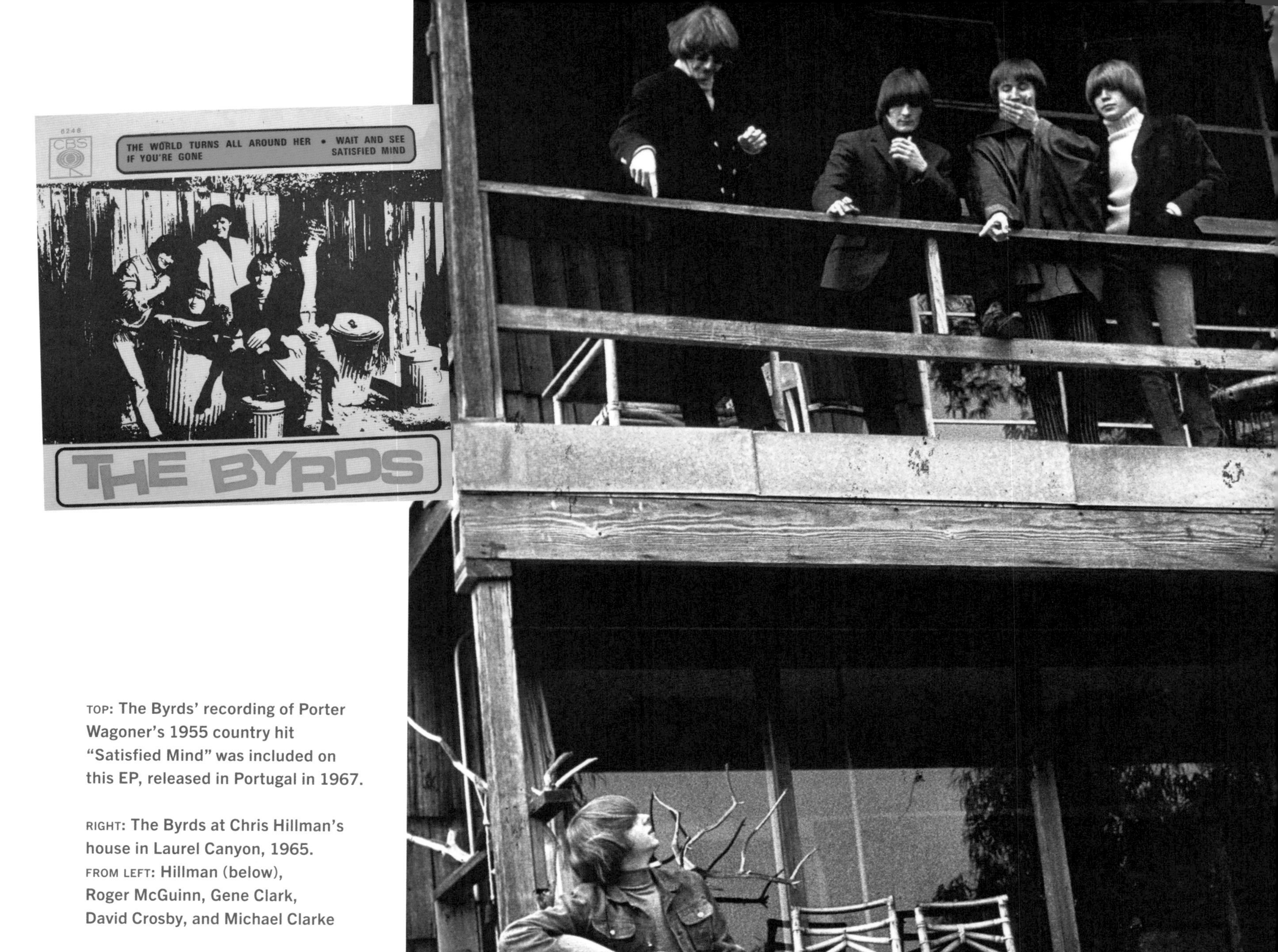

TOP: The Byrds' recording of Porter Wagoner's 1955 country hit "Satisfied Mind" was included on this EP, released in Portugal in 1967.

RIGHT: The Byrds at Chris Hillman's house in Laurel Canyon, 1965. FROM LEFT: Hillman (below), Roger McGuinn, Gene Clark, David Crosby, and Michael Clarke

OPPOSITE PAGE: The Byrds sign autographs in England during their first European tour, 1965. FROM LEFT: David Crosby, Chris Hillman, Gene Clark, Roger McGuinn, and Michael Clarke

ARTIFACT AND PHOTOS COURTESY OF CHRIS HILLMAN

FROM LEFT: **The Byrds at Columbia Studios in Hollywood, January 1965. From left: Roger McGuinn, Chris Hillman, Gene Clark, David Crosby, and Michael Clarke**

This gold foil flyer promoted the Byrds's concert at the Earl Warren Showgrounds, Santa Barbara, California, April 15, 1967.

ARTIFACT COURTESY OF CHRIS HILLMAN

Tennessee, and they all would play at the same places, so their sound was pretty similar," recalled Pedersen, who briefly subbed for banjo master Earl Scruggs while the latter underwent hip surgery, affording him the chance to apprentice with Lester Flatt—and to experience first-hand the difference between the eastern bluegrass world and what he was part of out west.

"They were a little stricter back in the Southeast," he said. "They wanted to stay really close to the traditional sound."

Not so in L.A., where winds of change were as forceful as the gusting Santa Anas blowing hot from the north. The Beefeaters started in 1964 as yet another folk trio, but quickly shifted gears. The powerhouse trio of singers

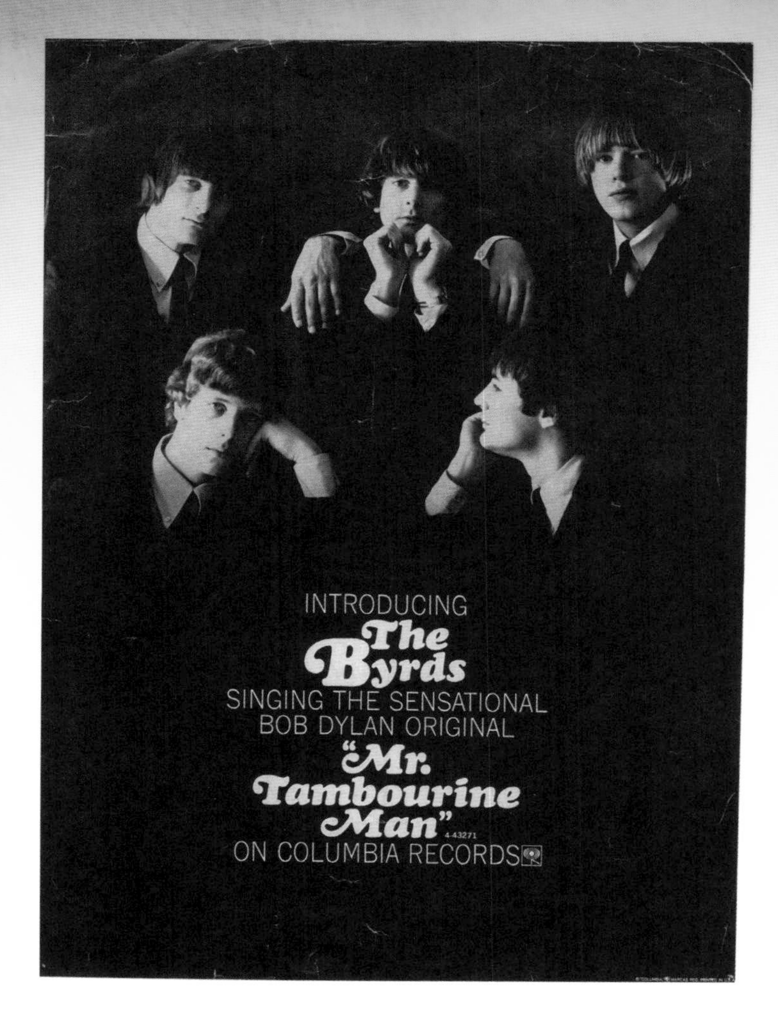

Advertisement for the Byrds' groundbreaking debut single, "Mr. Tambourine Man," released April 12, 1965

ARTIFACT COURTESY OF CHRIS HILLMAN

—Roger McGuinn, Gene Clark, and David Crosby—added drummer Michael Clarke and started veering more toward rock, prompting manager Jim Dickson to invite Hillman to a rehearsal.

"They thought they had their lineup, but Crosby wasn't comfortable playing bass and wanted to switch to guitar," Hillman wrote. "Then Dickson asked me a question that would change the course of my life: 'Can you play bass?'

"I had never held a bass, let alone played one," Hillman recalled. "I replied, 'Sure I can handle it'." His mandolin skills translated quickly, and he soon became one of the most melodically inventive bassists in rock. Before the Byrds recorded their first single—Dylan's "Mr. Tambourine Man," which almost single-handedly ushered in "folk-rock"—Dickson offered his young charges a priceless bit of advice: "You guys need to go for substance and depth. Make records you can be proud of—records that can hold up for all time. Are we making an artistic statement or just going for a quick buck?"

That attitude dovetailed with Hillman's, and many others in L.A.'s creative community. But it was unusual coming from a talent manager. Pop music was still largely considered disposable, and the guiding principle on the business side was, in essence, get it while you can, however you can.

The quantum leap the Byrds made from folk to rock, from acoustic instruments to those enlivened by alternating current, was set to music by McGuinn and Hillman in what became one of the Byrds' cornerstone songs: "So you want to be a rock & roll star?/Then listen now to what I say/Just get an electric guitar/Then take some time and learn how to play."

CONTINUED ON PAGE 41

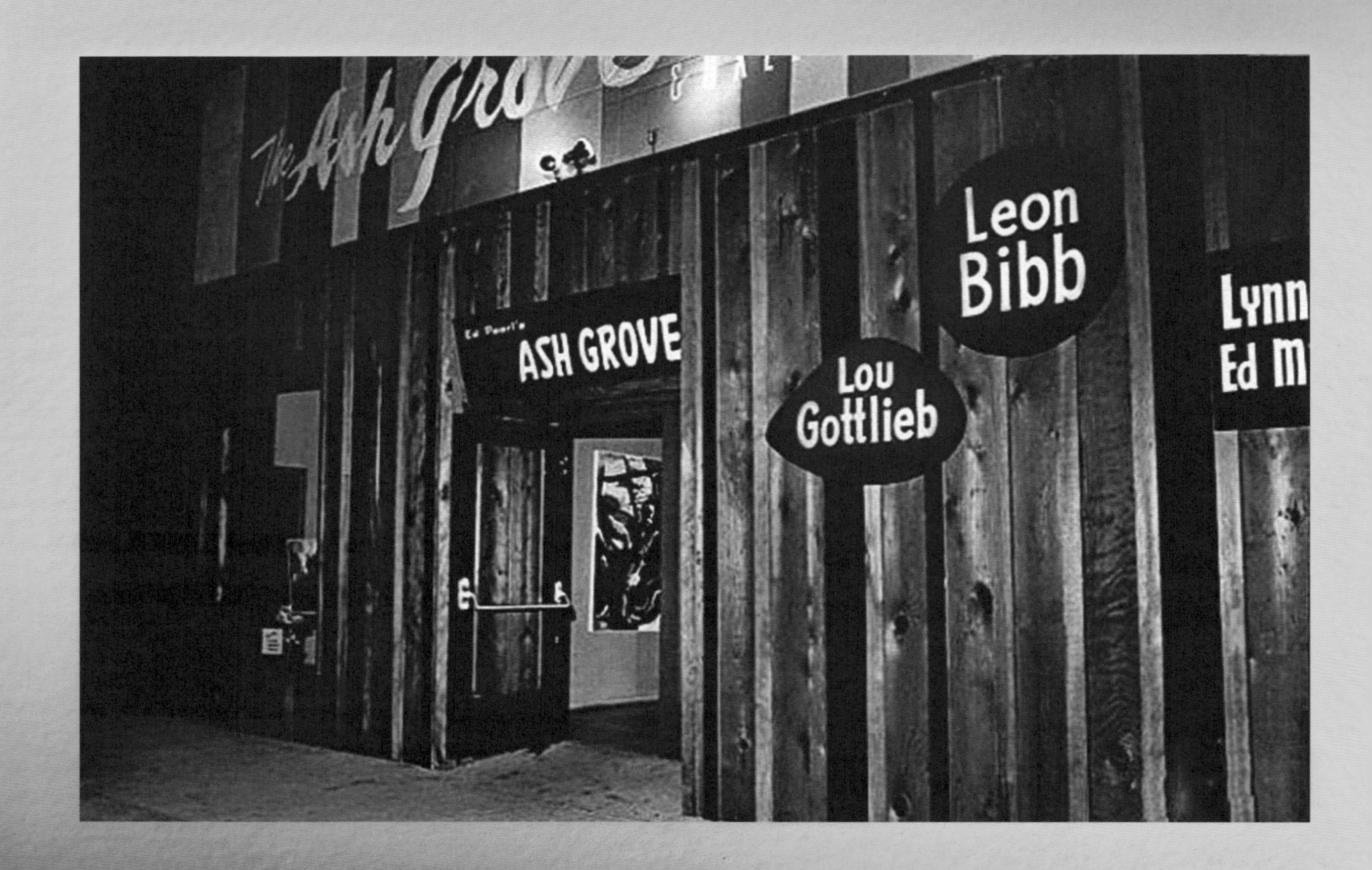

L.A.'S ROOTS MUSIC JUNCTION: THE ASH GROVE

BY MARY KATHERINE ALDIN

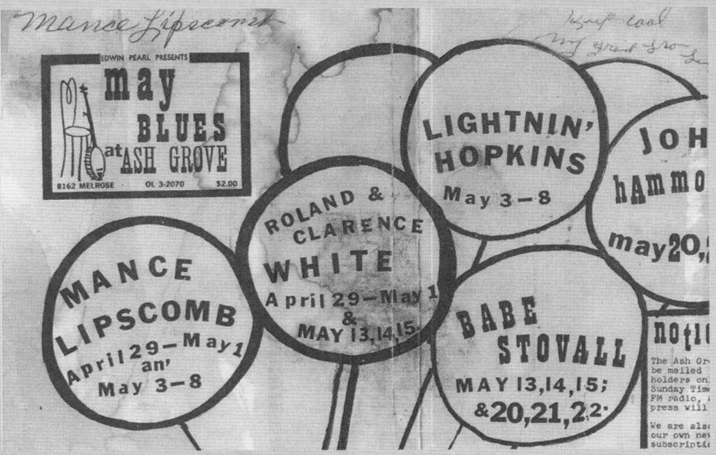

Advertisements for blues, bluegrass, and R&B acts appearing at the Ash Grove in the 1960s

ARTIFACTS COURTESY OF DAVID ANDERSEN AND FRED ARONOW

OPPOSITE PAGE: The Ash Grove, 1959

In 1958, folk music in the United States was on the cusp of something huge. That year, the Kingston Trio released their first album and their million-selling hit song, "Tom Dooley." College kids from California to Maine bought guitars and banjos and learned their first three chords, sowing the seeds of the folk music boom of the mid-1960s. Cafe and club owners across the country, sensing the surge of interest, capitalized on it, and in 1958, three major folk music clubs opened for business: the Gaslight Cafe in New York's Greenwich Village, Club 47 in Cambridge, Massachusetts, and the Ash Grove in Los Angeles.

Unlike the two East Coast venues, which presented primarily contemporary folk sounds, the Ash Grove was strong on tradition. Owner Ed Pearl was knowledgeable about traditional music, having taken guitar lessons from Bess Lomax Hawes and presented Pete Seeger in concert. So when, on July 11, 1958, at age twenty-six, he opened the Ash Grove at 8162 Melrose Avenue, on the former site of a furniture factory, it was with the intention of showcasing traditional folk, blues, and country music. Before long, the 200-seat club was booking such giants as Howlin' Wolf, Muddy Waters, Doc Watson, and Bill Monroe, and eventually their acolytes—the Byrds, the Flying Burrito Brothers, the Nitty Gritty Dirt Band, and Jackson Browne.

I worked at the Ash Grove from approximately 1962 through 1972. For the princely sum of $25 a week (later raised to $50), I worked with Ed Pearl in the club's office during the day, handling a variety of clerical chores. At night, I absorbed the different styles and sounds in the front concert room while I acted as part-time cashier, my office having been commandeered for a dressing room.

The music in that front room attracted many young musicians who would form the nucleus of country-rock. It started with bluegrass. In late 1962, Ed Pearl heard of a family band called the Country Boys and offered them a job. Brothers Clarence, Roland, and Eric White fronted the band, and by the time they changed their name to the Kentucky Colonels they were becoming widely recognized for Clarence's unparalleled lead guitar work and Roland's mandolin expertise. In the audience at various times to hear them were Bernie Leadon, Jerry Garcia, and Chris Hillman, who met Clarence there; in later years, Chris would bring Clarence into the Byrds as their lead guitarist.

Another bluegrass band that pioneered country-rock and got off to a running start at the Ash Grove was the Dillards, whom Ed first heard playing informally in the lobby. At their first paid gig at the club, producer Jim Dickson signed them to make an album, and a television producer (who just happened to be in the audience) tapped them for *The Andy Griffith Show,* to appear as

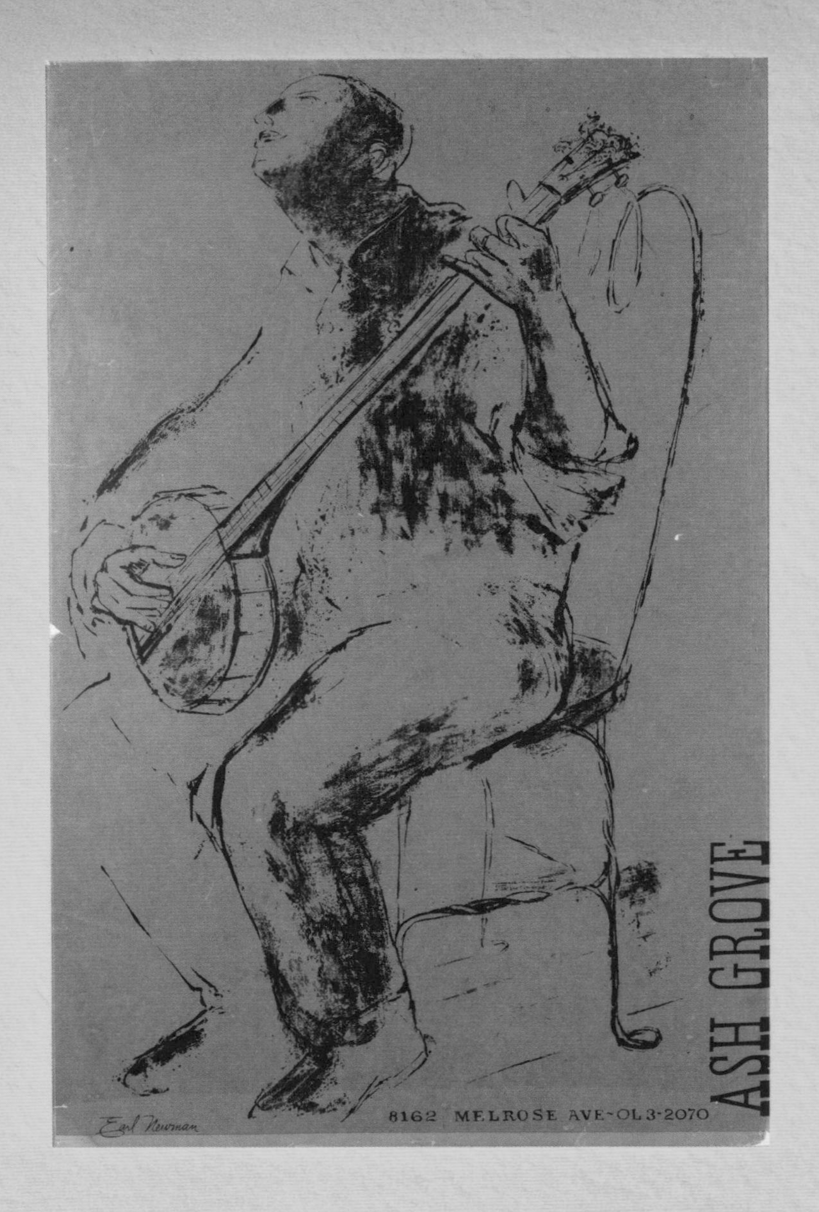

Earl Newman designed this silk-screened poster for the Ash Grove.

ARTIFACT COURTESY OF MARY KATHERINE ALDIN

OPPOSITE PAGE: Flyer for appearances by guitarist Doc Watson and the band Kaleidoscope at the Ash Grove, 1967

ARTIFACT COURTESY OF DAVID ANDERSEN

Ash Grove owner Ed Pearl in front of his club, 1969

COURTESY OF FRED ARONOW

the Darlings, a stereotypical family of hillbilly musicians. Coincidentally, the Kentucky Colonels would also make two appearances on the *Griffith* show.

Blues music also drew in many younger musicians. Because the Ash Grove did not serve hard liquor and therefore had no age limit, two teenage brothers from Downey, Dave and Phil Alvin, spent many nights at the club, soaking up the sounds of everyone from T-Bone Walker to Big Joe Turner. Since they were too young to drive, their patient mother brought books and knitting and waited outside the club in her car, giving them a musical education that was put to good use later when they formed their own group, the Blasters. Similarly, Ry Cooder started playing at the Ash Grove at sixteen, first backing singer Pamela Polland and, soon after, singer-songwriter Jackie DeShannon.

The Ash Grove employees and musicians formed a kind of family circle. In later years, whenever the club needed a benefit, particularly after one of several fire bombings (likely motivated by antagonism to Ed's liberal politics), many bands came back to play for free as a tribute to Ed, including the Byrds, the Flying Burrito Brothers, the Chambers Brothers, Spirit, and Canned Heat. The first generation of Ash Grove musicians, who were in their sixties and seventies then, are all gone now, but many of the younger ones, senior citizens themselves now, are still recording and performing, carrying the spirit of the Ash Grove into the future. Ω

Buffalo Springfield rehearsing at their house in Malibu, California, October 30, 1967
FROM LEFT: Bruce Palmer, Stephen Stills, Neil Young, Dewey Martin, and Richie Furay

CONTINUED FROM PAGE 35

The group soon revealed an affinity for country music with an authentic reading of Porter Wagoner's 1955 hit "Satisfied Mind," on their 1965 album *Turn! Turn! Turn!* It wasn't a big leap to country-rock the following year in "Mr. Spaceman," with its bouncy country beat and twangy guitar licks.

In England, the Beatles demonstrated their love for the sound of country music in their 1965 reworking of Buck Owens's 1963 hit "Act Naturally," built on a honky-tonk bounce familiar to two-stepping country fans, but powered by drummer and singer Ringo Starr's forceful rock backbeat. Other Beatles tracks circa 1964-66 revealed noticeable country leanings: "I Don't Want to Spoil the Party" (Rosanne Cash logged a hit country version in 1989), "What Goes On," "I'm Looking Through You," and "I've Just Seen a Face" (covered by the Dillards on their influential 1968 album, *Wheatstraw Suite*).

THE FIRST FLOWERING OF COUNTRY-ROCK

Other acts began to venture forth with this hybrid: Lovin' Spoonful's "Fishin' Blues" from their 1965 album, *Do You Believe in Magic?*, evidenced country and rock compatibility, although the exaggerated country framing made the track come across almost as a novelty record.

In L.A., however, country-rock was quickly becoming a viable musical force, emerging organically from a vibrant and diverse community established in and around Hollywood clubs such as the Ash Grove (a blues-folk-gospel mecca) and the rock-friendlier Troubadour and Whisky a Go-Go. And barely a dozen miles north, but a world away culturally, was the most important country honky-tonk in the West: the Palomino Club in North Hollywood.

The newly formed Buffalo Springfield flashed country credibility in a couple of Stephen Stills's songs from their 1966 debut album: "Go and Say Goodbye" and "Pay the Price." On their third album, *Last Time Around* (1968), Richie Furay's song "Kind Woman" prominently featured Rusty Young's pedal steel guitar, marking it as one of the first L.A. country-rock songs to do so.

Canadians Neil Young and Bruce Palmer and drummer Dewey Martin joined up with Stills and Furay following Stills and Furay's stint in New York with the Au Go Go Singers, another large-contingent folk ensemble à la the New Christy Minstrels. Furay also had crossed paths during that period with Gram Parsons, a Florida native who was then testing the New York folk scene before heading west to give L.A. a shot.

One of the Troubadour's regulars was Texas singer-songwriter Mike Nesmith, who had first recorded under the

TOP: Doug Dillard and Gene Clark of Dillard & Clark, 1968

The Stone Poneys at the Bitter End, New York, 1968
FROM LEFT: Shep Cooke, Linda Ronstadt, and John Keski

PHOTO BY CHARLIE GILLETT

OPPOSITE PAGE: The International Submarine Band, 1966
CLOCKWISE FROM LEFT: Ian Dunlop, Mickey Gauvin, John Nuese, and Gram Parsons

PHOTO COURTESY OF IAN DUNLOP

pseudonym Michael Blessing, with little impact. But after he was cast to act, and possibly sing, in NBC-TV's new sitcom about the hijinks of a fictional rock group called the Monkees, his songs regularly surfaced on their albums, alongside tunes from songwriting pros such as Tommy Boyce and Bobby Hart, Carole King and Gerry Goffin, and Neil Diamond.

Two of Nesmith's contributions to the group's 1966 debut album—"Papa Gene's Blues" and "Sweet Young Thing" (the latter written with Goffin and King)—revealed his country roots. Session musician James Burton's stinging, countrified Telecaster electric guitar work stood out on "Papa Gene's Blues," while a phalanx of raucous country fiddles defined "Sweet Young Thing."

One Nesmith song that producers of the Monkees nixed for the TV show came to Ronstadt's attention. She and the Stone Poneys released "Different Drum" in 1967 using a rocked-up arrangement by Capitol Records staff producer Nick Venet, then watched it soar to #13 on *Billboard*'s Hot 100 chart. Thus, Ronstadt's mighty voice was introduced to the music world.

Even in the early going of an emerging style and sound, a couple of key differences from Nashville country music were apparent. Whereas the dominant recordings coming out of Music City in the mid-'60s were driven, as they long

had been, by individual singers, in L.A. the momentum tilted toward bands: the Byrds, Buffalo Springfield, Poco, and the Flying Burrito Brothers.

This reflected the dual influence on the Southern California community of the British Invasion and the underlying impact on so many musicians working in L.A. of the cornerstone bluegrass groups: Bill Monroe & the Blue Grass Boys, the Stanley Brothers, and Flatt & Scruggs. Such acts emphasized the interplay among multiple musicians rather than the star power of a single performer.

Many of those Southern California groups consisted of several accomplished singers and instrumentalists: in the Byrds, Roger McGuinn had been a session player in New York before coming to California; Hillman had earned respect as a mandolin player of great dexterity, a skill he translated promptly to electric bass; and David Crosby and Gene Clark brought distinctive voices and the ability to blend exquisitely with other singers.

Roger McGuinn performs with the Byrds at New York's Central Park, July 20, 1970.

PHOTO BY RAEANNE RUBENSTEIN

OPPOSITE PAGE: This stage costume—decorated with rhinestones and embroidered peacocks, orchids, and stars—was designed for the Monkees' Michael Nesmith by Nudie's Rodeo Tailors, 1967.

ARTIFACT COURTESY OF MICHAEL NESMITH

CONTINUED ON PAGE 51

The Byrds inside the Colosseum, Rome, Italy, May 8, 1968, on a European tour that included Doug Dillard on electric banjo
FROM LEFT: **Dillard, Chris Hillman, Roger McGuinn, Kevin Kelley, and Gram Parsons.** PHOTO COURTESY OF CHRIS HILLMAN

WHAT WAS THE FIRST COUNTRY-ROCK RECORD?

BY RANDY LEWIS

The term "country-rock" has long been associated with a music scene that had its genesis in the mid-1960s in Los Angeles and came into high relief through acts such as the Eagles, Linda Ronstadt, the Flying Burrito Brothers, and numerous others.

"Country-rock was nothing more than country song sensibilities with a rock rhythm section," said Eagles founding member, banjo player, guitarist, and songwriter Bernie Leadon. When country-rock emerged in the mid-sixties, he said, "The volume of a country band was still—at that time in the fifties and sixties—moderate. But the rock groups got louder and louder.

"Fender made bigger and bigger amplifiers," Leadon said. "The PA [public address] system couldn't keep up with the volume of the guitar amps. So, then the PA systems grew, and the whole thing grew into this much, much louder thing, and country-rock was nothing more than the kids violating the norms of country music in their elders. It's like, 'Let's turn up. Come on, man.'"

By that measure, a bona fide country-rock recording wouldn't necessarily need to feature steel guitar, banjo, fiddles, dobro, or harmonica.

So, who did get there first? Let's work backward.

The Byrds' *Sweetheart of the Rodeo* album, released in August 1968, is widely regarded as the Big Bang for country-rock. The Byrds, however, confessed they had no intention of concocting a new musical hybrid; they simply wanted to make a make a country record.

In any case, the Byrds weren't operating in a vacuum. By 1968, numerous L.A. rock artists were exploring the intersection of that music with country. Before joining the Byrds, Gram Parsons and the International Submarine Band pointed the way toward country-rock with their one and only album, released in March 1968. But it failed to make *Billboard*'s album chart and had little impact until after Parsons's death in 1973, when fans began to seek out his earlier recordings.

The impact factor also mitigates balloting for other pre-*Sweetheart* releases, both from 1967, that balanced country and rock effectively. *Gene Clark with the Gosdin Brothers*, Clark's first solo effort after quitting the Byrds, and *Now Is the Time for Hearts and Flowers* from the band Hearts and Flowers (featuring Scottsville Squirrel Barkers founding member Larry Murray) were both innovative mixtures of country and rock but heard by few outside of Los Angeles.

Rick Nelson released a pair of albums in 1966 and 1967, well before he started the influential Stone Canyon Band, but both skewed heavily country, with little feel of rock in the grooves.

Earlier yet, however, other artists were testing the waters in individual tracks. Consider, for example, Linda Ronstadt & the Stone Poneys' hit version of "Different Drum" in 1967; two Stephen Stills songs on Buffalo Springfield's 1966 debut album, "Go and Say Goodbye"

Nudie's Rodeo Tailors designed this rhinestone-accented jacket, with embroidered submarines and torpedoes, for Gram Parsons of the International Submarine Band. Parsons later gave it to drummer Jon Corneal, his friend and bandmate.

ARTIFACT COURTESY OF JON CORNEAL

and "Pay the Price"; and the Byrds' 1966 single "Mr. Spaceman." All brought rock and country elements together, as did two Mike Nesmith songs, "Papa Gene's Blues" and "Sweet Young Thing" (written with Gerry Goffin and Carole King), that appeared on the Monkees' 1966 debut album.

Are we any closer to identifying the earliest record deserving to be called country-rock?

On a recent episode on Dwight Yoakam's SiriusXM satellite radio show, *The Bakersfield Beat,* Yoakam told guest Chris Hillman that his song "Time Between," from the Byrds' 1967 album, *Younger Than Yesterday,* deserved the title.

Hillman said no, that the honor belonged to a record that had appeared six years earlier, one both musicians ultimately agreed included everything that would eventually constitute the L.A. country-rock sound: twangy Fender Telecaster guitar (courtesy of Louisiana transplant James Burton), a rollicking rhythm foundation from electric bassist Joe Osborne, and a signature percussive pulse provided by that most rock & roll of instruments: cowbell.

The first country-rock song according to Hillman and Yoakam? Rick Nelson's 1961 hit "Hello Mary Lou." Let the counter-arguments begin. Ω

James Burton and Rick Nelson, early 1960s

TOP: Hearts and Flowers, 1968
FROM LEFT: Larry Murray, Dave Dawson (seated), and Bernie Leadon

The Flying Burrito Brothers, 1969. FROM LEFT: Chris Ethridge, Gram Parsons, Chris Hillman, Sneaky Pete Kleinow, and Michael Clarke. PHOTO BY JIM McCRARY

CONTINUED FROM PAGE 45

Of course, McGuinn's adoption of the Rickenbacker twelve-string electric guitar, which he had been inspired to pick up after seeing the Beatles using a Rickenbacker, became a hallmark of the group's sound throughout the Byrds' career.

Similarly, Neil Young and Stills became enthusiastic electric guitarists as teenage players and brought that energy and volume into even the country-skewed material in Buffalo Springfield's repertoire.

Additionally, L.A. country-rock had a wider thematic range than the mainstream country acts, whether it was the sci-fi whimsy of the Byrds' "Mr. Spaceman," the proto-feminism Ronstadt brought to "Different Drum," or the marriage of '60s counterculture fatalism and abiding religious faith captured in the Flying Burrito Brothers' "Wheels."

GRAM PARSONS AND *SWEETHEART OF THE RODEO*

In other corners, rock music was getting harder, heavier, and more psychedelicized as the '60s unfurled. L.A. contributed too—Arthur Lee & Love, the Doors—but also remained a cauldron for rock's fascination with country.

This 1963 Martin 00-21 was used extensively by Gram Parsons and later acquired by Emmylou Harris.

ARTIFACT COURTESY OF EMMYLOU HARRIS

Squirrel Barkers co-founder Larry Murray teamed with Rick Cunha and Dave Dawson in Hearts and Flowers. Their 1967 album, *Now Is the Time for Hearts and Flowers,* influenced many with a full album's worth of countrified rock, though it had negligible commercial impact.

Exiting the Byrds, Gene Clark assembled his first solo album, *Gene Clark with the Gosdin Brothers*, another important full-on country-rock session that arrived in 1967. But it was overshadowed by the Byrds' *Younger Than Yesterday,* released almost simultaneously. *Younger Than Yesterday* included "Time Between," the first song of import written by Hillman and considered a textbook example of L.A. country-rock.

At the time, however, McGuinn and Hillman were seeking new blood following the departures of Clark and Crosby. Hillman had recently met Parsons while both were in line at a bank, and they quickly bonded over shared musical passions. He invited Parsons to a Byrds rehearsal;

Parsons's undeniable charisma and vocal and songwriting talent moved the band to hire him as an adjunct player. Just months earlier, Parsons had recorded his first album fronting and writing songs for the International Submarine Band, notable for the presence of steel guitarist JayDee Maness, pianist Earl Ball, and bassist-songwriter Chris Ethridge, the latter also part of the first Burrito Brothers lineup.

But it was because of his new association with the Byrds that Parsons's star began to rise. He was the one (with strong support from Hillman) who catalyzed their move toward blending country and rock sensibilities on their watershed *Sweetheart of the Rodeo* album. Parsons was also the only bandmember who contributed new compositions, bringing two songs he had written to the 1968 album: "Hickory Wind" (written with Bob Buchanan) and "One Hundred Years from Now." Parsons's roots in the Deep South often surfaced in his laid-back drawl, which was distinct from most of the twang-free L.A. singers who were blending country with rock in the '60s.

Nudie's Rodeo Tailors designed this leather suit for guitarist Clarence White of the Byrds, c. 1969.
ARTIFACT COURTESY OF MARTY STUART

OPPOSITE PAGE: **Chris Hillman and Gram Parsons, Topanga Canyon, California, 1969.** PHOTO BY JIM McCRARY / COURTESY OF CHRIS HILLMAN

COSMIC COWBOY COUTURE

In late 1968, the Flying Burrito Brothers went to Nudie's Rodeo Tailors in North Hollywood to order extravagantly embroidered, rhinestone-embellished stage costumes, which they associated with authentic country music. Collaborating with Nudie Cohn's head designer, Manuel Cuevas, each musician selected colors, fabric, and embroidery to reflect his personal style and taste.

For the cover of their 1969 debut album, *The Gilded Palace of Sin*, A&M Records art director Tom Wilkes took the Flying Burrito Brothers and several models to Joshua Tree National Park, where the band posed in their Nudie suits for photographer Barry Feinstein. Featured here are three of the four suits from the album cover. The whereabouts of Chris Ethridge's white suit with embroidered roses are unknown.

"Nobody before Gram Parsons went into country bars with suits with marijuana on them and long hair and rhinestone belts." — JD Souther

FROM LEFT: Steel guitarist Sneaky Pete Kleinow's black velvet suit features embroidered dinosaurs on the front and back. Gram Parsons's suit has embroidered marijuana leaves, opium poppies, pills, cartoonish pinup girls, hellfire, and a shining cross. Chris Hillman's blue velvet suit is embellished with peacocks, seahorses, the Greek god Poseidon, and the face of an Aztec-style sun.

Artifacts courtesy of the Autry Museum of Western Heritage, Manuel Cuevas, Melanie Wells, Anita Kleinow, and the Rock and Roll Hall of Fame and Museum

FROM LEFT: Sneaky Pete Kleinow, Gram Parsons, Chris Ethridge, and Chris Hillman

PHOTO BY: JIM McCRARY

It's widely lauded as the inception of country-rock, even though albums from Clark and Hearts and Flowers preceded it. Yet *Sweetheart of the Rodeo* didn't catch fire with the public either, peaking at #77 on *Billboard*'s pop album chart.

Still, country-rock continued to proliferate as groups reconfigured or disbanded. From the ashes of Buffalo Springfield, which imploded after barely eighteen months, came Poco (featuring Furay and Jim Messina), Crosby, Stills & Nash (and, occasionally, Young), and Neil Young as a solo act. The Nitty Gritty Dirt Band, which formed in 1966 and briefly included Jackson Browne before he went solo, reached #45 in *Billboard* with the first single, "Buy for Me the Rain," from their self-titled 1967 debut album.

Ronstadt & the Stone Poneys released three albums before disbanding. She briefly drafted the Corvettes, which included Bernie Leadon, the Dirt Band's Jeff Hanna, future Kaleidoscope front man Chris Darrow, bassist John London, and drummer John Ware.

Ronstadt subsequently assembled another group with players from L.A.'s Longbranch/Pennywhistle, Texas rock band Shiloh, Poco, and Rick Nelson's Stone Canyon Band, only to then set her stellar new conglomeration free to pursue music of their own as the Eagles.

Richie Furay used this 1959 Gibson ES-355, with custom white finish, with Poco, the Souther-Hillman-Furay Band, and as a solo artist.

ARTIFACT COURTESY OF RICHIE FURAY

A key development in the continuing evolution of country-rock by 1968 was the addition of steel guitar as a full-time component in the Flying Burrito Brothers and Poco. Taking their cues both from Maness's role in the International Submarine Band and the central part Maness and Nashville steel ace Lloyd Green played in the Byrds' *Sweetheart of the Rodeo*, the Burrito Brothers brought in steel player Sneaky Pete Kleinow, and Poco drafted Colorado steel guitarist Rusty Young into their original lineups, cementing their kinship to traditional country while still relying on the rhythmic drive of electric bass and drums and prominent roles for electric guitars.

Decorated with rhinestones, leather fringe, and embroidered motifs inspired by Native American art, this stage costume was designed for Poco's Richie Furay by Nudie's Rodeo Tailors, c. 1969.

ARTIFACT COURTESY OF RICHIE FURAY

TOP: **Poco at the Newport Pop Festival at Devonshire Downs racetrack, Northridge, California, June 22, 1969. From left: Rusty Young, Richie Furay, and Jim Messina.** PHOTO COURTESY OF RICHIE FURAY

CONTINUED ON PAGE 65

doug weston's
Troubadour
presents
doug
weston's
Troubadou

Doug Weston's Troubadour,
9081 Santa Monica Boulevard

PHOTO BY JOEY TRANCHINA

WHERE THE ACTION WAS: THE TROUBADOUR

BY JAMES AUSTIN

"I liked the Ash Grove because the artists were very traditional. I liked the Troubadour because they had both traditional music and pop music, plus comedy acts. They had a bar in the front, so you had to walk through the room where the stage was in order to get to the bathrooms in the back. That way you got to see part of the show, and everyone that played there for free. We all got to see each other's work that way. Managers and record label executives were there every night looking for talent."
—Linda Ronstadt, May 2022

"The Troubadour was the launch pad to stardom for the Byrds, the Flying Burrito Brothers, Elton John, Joni Mitchell, Jackson Browne, the Eagles, and many more. The open mike Hoot-Nights were classic and an opportunity to take that first step. Grand memories indeed!"
—Chris Hillman, April 2022

Linda Ronstadt and Chris Hillman are typical of the musicians who came of age in the 1960s in Southern California, shared ideas about country and rock music, collaborated, and went on to perform at a nightclub called the Troubadour, founded by Doug Weston. It was a crucial gathering place for musicians who would blend elements of country and rock music, forming potent new combinations.

Doug Weston, owner of the Troubadour

"Doug Weston was arguably the godfather of the Southern California singer-songwriter movement in the late sixties and early seventies," said *Los Angeles Times* music critic Robert Hilburn. "[He was] someone whose unshakable belief in the inspirational power of music made his club both a showcase and meeting hall for much of the best young talent of a generation."

He was born Alexander Douglas Weston in New York in 1926—a time when "talking pictures" were on the horizon and the Model T was a common mode of transportation. Weston entered the Los Angeles nightclub scene with the ambition of putting Los Angeles on the music map, starting with a focus on folk music. He opened the first incarnation of the Troubadour, located on La Cienega Boulevard, in 1957, when folk music was not generally heard on pop radio.

The original Troubadour was a small, narrow club with a bar and a few tables in an opposite corner. In 1961, Weston had earned enough money to move the club to 9081 Santa Monica Boulevard. At the new location, which would become permanent, the business sign ran the entire length of the venue and read: Doug Weston's Troubadour. Nestled close to the Hollywood Hills and the Sunset Strip, it was accessible to many and was *the* place to hang out.

When he was asked who played his club, Weston stated, "We won't book someone just because he will draw a crowd. We have to believe he has something to say." By "he," Weston also meant women, a mixture of ethnicities, and bands. The acts who played the Troubadour

were, as Weston put it, "like a hall of fame": Bo Diddley, Lenny Bruce (arrested at the club for saying "schmuck"), the Byrds, Waylon Jennings, Kris Kristofferson, Gordon Lightfoot, Roger Miller, Laura Nyro, Linda Ronstadt, and Nina Simone. Weston liked to think of the acts who played his club as "modern day troubadours."

The success of Weston's club did not occur in a vacuum. By 1968, underground FM rock stations KPPC and KMET ran live ads for the Troubadour, blanketing Southern California. The new hybrid of country and rock gained traction at the Troubadour, with performers like Buffalo Springfield, the Flying Burrito Brothers (both Hillman and Parsons), Michael Nesmith, the Nitty Gritty Dirt Band,

Michael Nesmith at the Troubadour, 1970. Also pictured is the Nudie's Rodeo Tailors shirt he wore that night. The shirt is embellished with rhinestones and embroidered cacti.

PHOTO BY HENRY DILTZ / ARTIFACT COURTESY OF MICHAEL NESMITH

and, eventually, the Eagles taking flight. The club helped launch an exciting new subgenre with country twang, steel guitars, harmonies, and a distinctive backbeat. Blissed-out hippies borrowed elements of the stripped-down sound of Bakersfield country and fused it with a rock panache. The country-rock genre grew and became profitable because of the Troubadour—a worldwide beacon for the new sounds.

Larry Murray, singer and guitarist for the country-rock group Hearts and Flowers, described Weston as a charismatic entrepreneur. “He loved to talk with musicians. He was a guy who could sniff out talent in a variety of genres,” said Murray. Murray should know, as he convinced Weston to let him organize and manage the Monday open-mike hootenanny (aka “Hoot Night”) in the early 1960s. It gave the club a feeling of community for musicians and patrons. “The Troubadour was a place where everyone went to hang out and get noticed,” recalled Ronstadt. “If you wanted to make yourself known, you’d go to the open-mike.”

Sadly, Weston grew frustrated with the music business. Robert Hilburn told me that “Doug became tormented by the fact that everyone—the musicians and record companies—was making so much more money than he was.” Weston also became increasingly involved with drugs, which affected his management of the club.

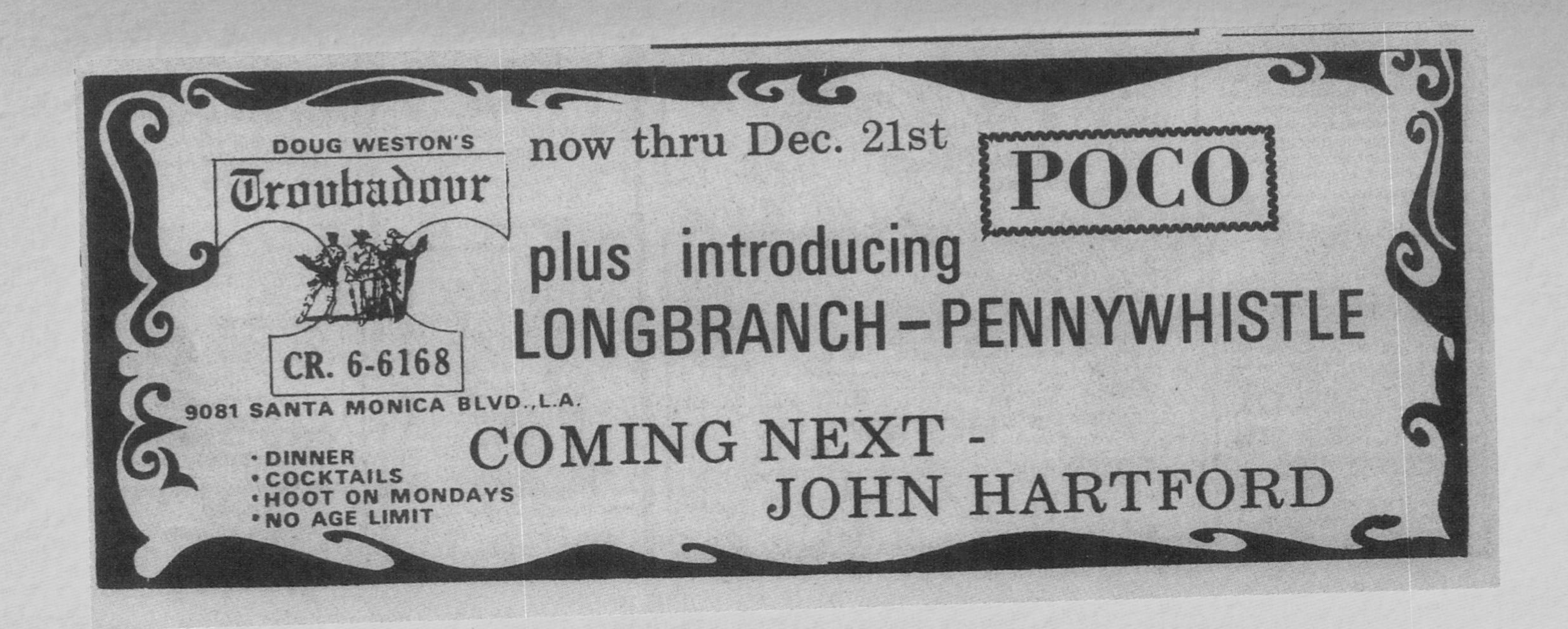

"Sad because Doug was such an invaluable part of the rich L.A. music scene," said Hilburn.

Weston tried to update the musical menu over time, booking punk bands and power-pop groups, but the central role the Troubadour played in the city's musical subculture slipped away. "The Sad Café," from the Eagles' album *The Long Run,* pays homage to the Troubadour. Written by JD Souther and members of the Eagles, the lyrics describe the club's heyday ("it seemed like a holy place, protected by amazing grace").

The Troubadour remains a monument to a special era in music and has showcased some of the great acts from all over the world. I saw Elton John prove that on August 25, 1970, playing a six-night electrifying engagement that launched his career and solidified the legacy of the venue. Doug Weston died of pneumonia on February 14, 1999. Through the Troubadour, he made an impact. His vision for a community venue became a melting pot and in turn helped nurture the country-rock fusions that continue to entertain and inspire today. Ω

TOP: Managed by Doug Weston, Glenn Frey and JD Souther's duo, Longbranch/Pennywhistle, opened for Poco at the Troubadour in December 1968.

OPPOSITE PAGE, FROM TOP: The Byrds at the Troubadour, spring 1968 FROM LEFT: Gram Parsons, Chris Hillman, Kevin Kelley, and Roger McGuinn

PHOTO COURTESY OF CHRIS HILLMAN

Linda Ronstadt at the Troubadour, 1971

PHOTO BY SHERRY RAYNE BARNETT

Elton John at the Troubadour, August 1970

PHOTO BY ED CARAEFF

CONTINUED FROM PAGE 57

Clearly, country-rock was coming together as a bona fide pop music genre, though it still showed up only sporadically on the charts as the 1960s drew to a close. That was about to change dramatically.

THE SEVENTIES: L.A. SOUND EXPLOSION

At the dawn of a new decade, years of civil and political unrest, the divisiveness of the Vietnam War, social tensions that had erupted during the Civil Rights era, and the blossoming sexual revolution that all played out dramatically in the '60s left millions of Americans emotionally reeling.

The biggest hits of 1970 played to societal exhaustion, offering emotional comfort and, often, spiritual solace. The likes of Simon & Garfunkel's "Bridge Over Troubled Water," the Beatles' "Let It Be," the Jackson 5's "I'll Be There," and George Harrison's "My Sweet Lord" reined in the sonic volume and calmed the frenetic energy from the *music in extremis* heights reached in the age of Woodstock, Jimi Hendrix, Janis Joplin, and the Doors.

Michael Nesmith & the First National Band, c.1970
FROM LEFT: **John London, Red Rhodes, Nesmith, and John Ware**

Michael Nesmith used this Gibson J-200 with the First National Band.
ARTIFACT COURTESY OF MICHAEL NESMITH

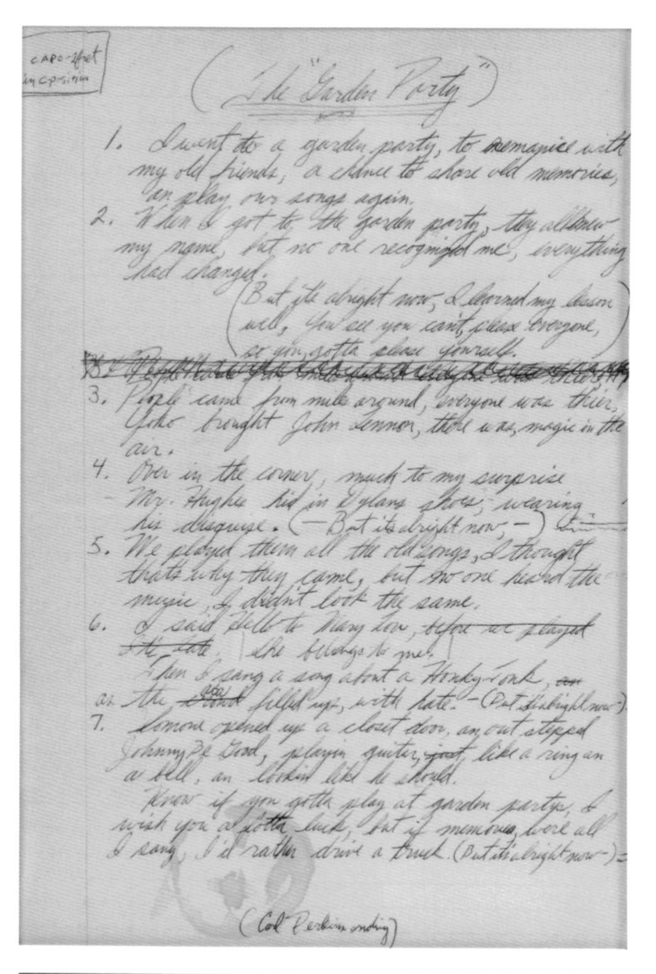

CAPO-2fret in C position

("The Garden Party")

1. I went to a garden party, to reminisce with my old friends, a chance to share old memories, an play our songs again.
2. When I got to the garden party, they all knew my name, but no one recognized me, everything had changed.
(But its alright now, I learned my lesson well, You see you can't please everyone, so you gotta please yourself.)
3. People came from miles around, everyone was there, Yoko brought John Lennon, there was magic in the air.
4. Over in the corner, much to my surprise Mr. Hughes hid in Dylans shoes, wearing his disguise. (—But its alright now,—)
5. We played them all the old songs, I thought thats why they came, but no one heard the music, I didn't look the same.
6. I said hello to Mary Lou, ~~before we played the date.~~ she belongs to me.
Then I sang a song about a Honky-tonk, an the crowd filled up, with hate. —(But its alright now).
7. Someone opened up a closet door, an out stepped Johnny Be Good, playin guitar, ~~just~~ like a ring an a bell, an lookin like he should.
Know if you gotta play at garden partys, I wish you a lotta luck, but if memories were all I sang, I'd rather drive a truck. (But its alright now—)

(Col Perkins ending)

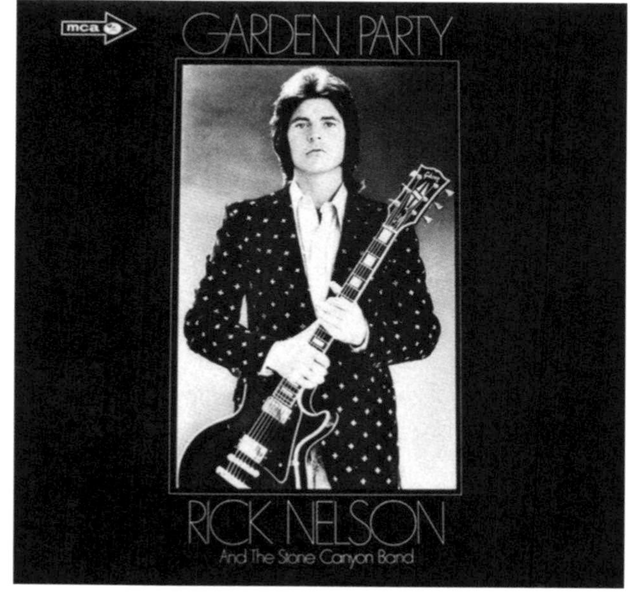

Rick Nelson and the Stone Canyon Band at the Troubadour, October 1969, recording the live album *Rick Nelson in Concert*
FROM LEFT: Randy Meisner, Nelson, Pat Shanahan (on drums), Allen Kemp, and Tom Brumley

OPPOSITE PAGE: Rick Nelson's handwritten lyrics to his 1972 hit, "Garden Party"

Rick Nelson used this 1969 Gibson Les Paul Custom while fronting the Stone Canyon Band. He is pictured with it on the cover of their 1972 album, *Garden Party*.

ARTIFACTS COURTESY OF GUNNAR AND MATTHEW NELSON

Millions found solace in the soothing music of Carole King, James Taylor, and others, much of it rooted in folk and country music. Softer sounds dovetailed with the merging of country and rock that had been incubating for years in Los Angeles and increasingly found its way onto radio airwaves and national sales charts.

Country-rock provided an appealing alternative to the amped-up rock of Led Zeppelin, Black Sabbath, Grand Funk Railroad, and Alice Cooper with music built on tradition yet alive with new lyrical sophistication and emotional expressivity.

Ronstadt continued exploring the connection between country and rock, old and new, in her eclectic 1970 album, *Silk Purse*, which included Hank Williams's "Lovesick Blues," Gene Clark and Bernie Leadon's "He Dark the Sun," and the album's Top Thirty single, Gary White's "Long Long Time."

Ronstadt's voice could break with the best female singers Nashville had to offer, but with her immersion in Mexican music, opera, and pop standards growing up, she never developed the kind of twang that would make listeners mistake hers for a traditional country voice. Instead, her dual hallmarks were sheer power and an innate capacity for great nuance in sculpting the songs she chose.

Another secret weapon Ronstadt brought to bear, both early on and throughout her career, was her ability to recognize great material. Singers who were not also songwriters often were discounted as mere instruments of producers or record company executives. But Peter Asher, the singer, songwriter, producer, and talent manager who oversaw her breakthrough 1974 album, *Heart Like a Wheel*, is one of many who happily testify to the strong hand she always exerted, whether choosing and arranging songs in the recording studio or for public performances.

Almost simultaneously as Ronstadt was coming into her own as a solo act, Nesmith quit the Monkees and released his first solo album: *Magnetic South*, a full-on country-rock adventure generously showcasing innovative steel guitarist Red Rhodes, along with ex-Corvettes London and Ware in Nesmith's First National Band.

His first single, "Joanne," made the pop Top Thirty, but the album peaked at only #143 in *Billboard*. Too country for rock radio, and too rock for country radio, many said. *Rolling Stone* later deemed it "the greatest music you never heard."

It was also in 1970 that the Nitty Gritty Dirt Band released *Uncle Charlie and His Dog Teddy*, an album that yielded the group's first Top Ten single: Jerry Jeff Walker's poignant waltz, "Mr. Bojangles." After a Shreveport,

Gene Clark, early 1970s

Nitty Gritty Dirt Band, c. 1971. FROM LEFT: Jimmie Fadden, Jeff Hanna, Jimmy Ibbotson, John McEuen, and Les Thompson

PHOTO BY CHRIS WALTER

TOP LEFT: The Nitty Gritty Dirt Band performed at the Paradox, a coffeehouse in Orange, California, May 1966. Brief member Jackson Browne appears in the photo.

ARTIFACT COURTESY OF DAVID ANDERSEN

ABOVE: John McEuen played this 1967 Gibson Style 800 five-string banjo on the Nitty Gritty Dirt Band's landmark 1972 album, *Will the Circle Be Unbroken*.

ARTIFACT COURTESY OF JOHN McEUEN
AND THE ROCK AND ROLL HALL OF FAME AND MUSEUM

LEFT: Hand-painted bass drumhead, c.1970

Clarence White onstage with the Byrds at Schaefer Music Festival, Central Park, New York, July 20, 1970

PHOTO BY RAEANNE RUBENSTEIN

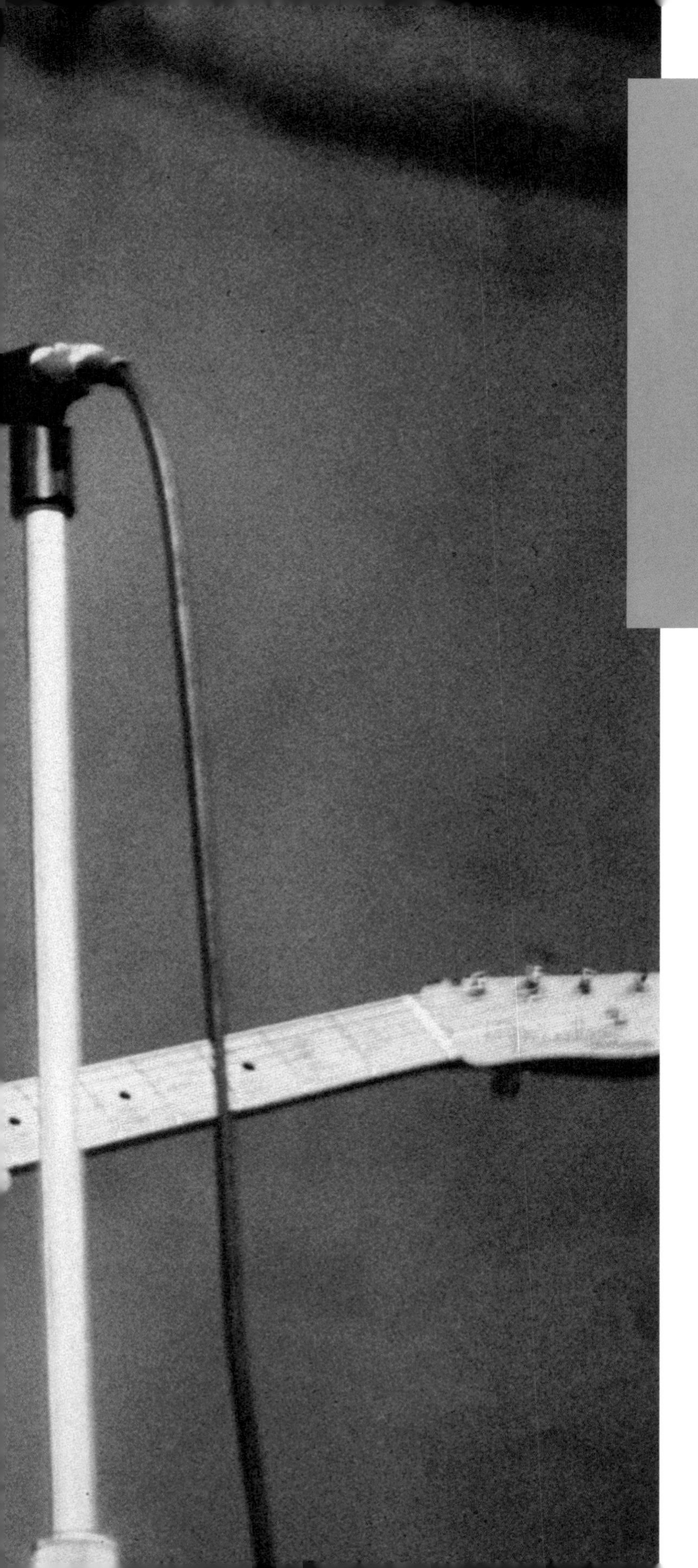

New Era Follies Presents

"A WEEKEND OF GOOD TIME MUSIC"

Some Former Byrds, Burrito Bros. & Friends
Playing Together Again for 3 Nights

CLARENCE WHITE GRAM PARSONS EMMY LOU HARRIS
GENE PARSONS RICK ROBERTS BYRON BERLINE
CHRIS ETHERIDGE KEN WIRTZ ROGER BUSH ALLEN MUNDE

ALSO 'GOOD-TIMING' WITH THE GANG ARE:

FRIDAY 6·15
8:00PM—2:00AM
TRACY NELSON/Mother Earth
ERIC WEISBERG/Deliverence
NEW GRASS REVIVAL

SATURDAY 6·16
2:00PM—2:00AM
TRACY NELSON/Mother Earth
CHARLES RIVER VALLEY BOYS
CHRIS SMITHER TOWNES VAN ZANDT
NORMAN BLAKE/Grant Boatright
NEW ENGLAND BLUE GRASS BOYS
RUSS KIRKPATRICK N·R·B·Q

SUNDAY 6·17
2:00PM—2:00AM
TRACY NELSON/Mother Earth
JONATHAN EDWARDS N·R·B·Q
NORMAN BLAKE/Grant Boatright
ORPHAN HOOKFOOT
LIZ MEYER BRIAN BOWERS

THE GREAT MC GONIGLE'S SEASIDE PARK
Annapolis, Md.
No Camping Available Free Parking

ADVANCE SALES $4 a Day $10·3 Days Tickets are available at all Ticketron locations GATE SALES $5 per Day
TECHNICAL PRODUCTION BY YORKTOWN LIGHTS & NATIONAL SOUND
For Directions See The Washington Post or Woodwind/For Information Call (202) 965·9650

Louisiana, station started playing the track, a record company rep called to tell the band the label wanted to issue it as a single.

"We were like, 'Oh, we love "Mr. Bojangles," but it's almost four minutes long,'" Jeff Hanna remembered recently. "'And it's a waltz about an old guy and a dog. They'll never play it on Top Forty radio.' And of course, us having our elbow on the pulse of America, we were totally wrong. And thank goodness. . . . It also became a pivotal part of the story of how *Will the Circle Be Unbroken* came to be."

In June 1973, Gram Parsons, Emmylou Harris, the New Kentucky Colonels, and Country Gazette headlined a weekend of concerts at Carr's Beach, Annapolis, Maryland. They shared a backing band that included Clarence White, Sneaky Pete Kleinow, and Chris Ethridge. These were among the final performances by White, who was killed by a drunk driver on July 15, 1973, and Parsons, who died in September.
ARTIFACT COURTESY OF STEVE FISHELL

CONTINUED ON PAGE 79

SPLENDOR IN THE GRASS: AN INSIDER'S VIEW OF WEST COAST BLUEGRASS

BY ALISON BROWN

I came of age in the Southern California bluegrass scene of the mid-1970s, some thirty years and 2,000 miles from the Ryman Auditorium stage, where bluegrass music first ignited in 1945. While bluegrass arose in the rural Southeast, the music found a completely different home, and personality, on the West Coast in the 1960s and 1970s. Although bluegrass was an anomaly in the surf culture of my hometown of La Jolla, just north of San Diego, it was ubiquitous in the pizza palaces, folk clubs, and theme parks around Southern California.

None of the bluegrass musicians I learned from, or played with, were farmers, although some were descendants of Dust Bowl migrants who had made a new life in California a generation earlier. Others were migrants of a different kind—legendary players like fiddler Byron

Stuart Duncan, Steve Libbea, Vince Gill, and Alison Brown at Knott's Berry Farm, 1978

OPPOSITE PAGE, FROM LEFT: Alison Brown at a banjo contest. Santa Maria, California, 1976

Stuart Duncan and Alison Brown at Knott's Berry Farm, Buena Park, California, 1979

Stuart Duncan and Alison Brown at the Canadian National Banjo Championship, 1978

PHOTOS COURTESY OF ALISON BROWN

Berline and Vince Gill—who headed west for the musical opportunities afforded by the film industry and recording scene in Los Angeles. But mostly, the Southern California pickers I knew were white-collar, college-educated folks, who discovered bluegrass as a result of the "great folk scare" of the 1960s.

As they played it, bluegrass took on a new hue. The grit, the blues edge, and hard-driving groove that characterized the sound of the music's founding fathers—to my mind, the musical expression of the hard times of their shared Depression-era youths—became more laid back and relaxed under California's endlessly sunny skies. The repertoire expanded too, with grassed-up covers of country-rock radio fare alongside the nostalgic "cabin" songs of the music's creators. It wasn't until I'd spent time in the South, with its tacitly acknowledged rules of what is and isn't bluegrass, that I fully appreciated how musically liberal the West Coast scene was by comparison. That openness was to my benefit, too. As a girl playing the banjo, the most masculine bluegrass instrument of them all, I'm not sure I would have found the same measure of encouragement in southern Appalachia.

My first live experience with California bluegrass was in 1974. I was twelve years old, an aspiring banjo player and a recent arrival from New England. My parents took me to a monthly meeting of the San Diego Bluegrass Club,

which was, perhaps not surprisingly, held at a Shakey's Pizza Parlor. That night I watched ten-year-old Stuart Duncan burn down Paul Warren's fiddle solo on "Earl's Breakdown" (a Flatt & Scruggs classic), and I knew I'd found my people.

For the rest of the decade, Stuart and I played together at folk clubs around L.A., which had gained their reputations in the burgeoning folk scene a decade earlier. These were legendary rooms like the Troubadour, the Ice House, McCabe's, and the Palomino Club, where, because they served alcohol, we kids had to stand in the bathroom between sets. (California child labor laws were no-nonsense back then.) At shows and jams around L.A., we hung on every note played by masters like Byron Berline, Larry McNeely, and John Hickman.

One afternoon in 1978, on a lark, Stuart and I joined forces with Vince Gill and the Libbea Brothers and won the Knott's Berry Farm bluegrass band contest.

Coming up in Southern California, I followed a bluegrass path cut by West Coast trailblazers a generation ahead of me. In L.A., the Kentucky Colonels began reimagining the possibilities for bluegrass instrumentation in the sixties, with Clarence White building on Doc Watson's legacy and expanding the role of the acoustic guitar as

The Scottsville Squirrel Barkers at Disneyland, Anaheim, California, 1963. FROM LEFT: Kenny Wertz, Chris Hillman, Larry Murray, Ed Douglas, and Gary Carr
PHOTO COURTESY OF CHRIS HILLMAN

The Hillmen performed at Disneyland, c. 1964.
ARTIFACT COURTESY OF CHRIS HILLMAN

both a lead and rhythm instrument in a bluegrass setting. In the Bay Area in the early seventies, Old & In the Way, with the Grateful Dead's Jerry Garcia on banjo, was stretching out on vibey instrumental interludes that foreshadowed eighties jamgrass. In 1977, the David Grisman Quintet, based in San Francisco, released their debut album; with its intoxicating blend of swing, gypsy jazz, and bluegrass as well as occasional odd time-signatures and extended solos, the quintet obliterated any idea of musical limitations for traditional bluegrass instruments.

The Dillards recorded the album *Pickin' and Fiddlin'* with Byron Berline in 1965. FROM LEFT: Dean Webb, Berline, Doug Dillard, Rodney Dillard, and Mitch Jayne

Byrone Berline and Doug Dillard at a bluegrass festival, 1973

These musical mavericks helped open the door to a galaxy of new possibilities, and it was impossible for me not to fall under their sway. In the summer of 1978, Stuart's dad drove us back east on a weeks-long road trip to do the bluegrass festival circuit. Inspired by miles of repeated listening to a cassette of the Grisman Quintet's album, Stuart and I ventured to play "Nick's Noodle," a tune we had learned from Grisman collaborator and Seatrain's fiddler Richard Greene at a bluegrass festival in Hugo, Oklahoma. After our set, we were shocked and amused to be scolded by a festival goer for "mocking the music." The thought just hadn't occurred to us; that kind of instrumental experimentation was part and parcel of the bluegrass music we had been steeped in.

Eventually I found my way to Nashville, following behind some of my California bluegrass heroes and compadres, including Roland White, Vince Gill, and my old pal Stuart Duncan. With our shared love for the music's roots, coupled with a drive to incorporate contemporary influences, I think that each of us brought part of the West Coast scene's legacy with us to Music City. As for me, I've never lost my appetite for pushing the musical envelope for the banjo and challenging the preconceived notions about an instrument that has struggled to shed its hillbilly image. For that, I'm indebted to my California bluegrass roots. Ω

CONTINUED FROM PAGE 73

Indeed, two years later the group headed to Nashville to collaborate with some of the most significant figures in country music history for what would become a career-defining triple album. West met South in the groundbreaking union between the long-haired California hippies and so many country tradition standard-bearers: Mother Maybelle Carter, Roy Acuff, Earl Scruggs, Doc Watson, and Merle Travis, among the highlights.

The country-rock sound was rapidly reaching beyond Southern California. It had appeared in 1969 in Dylan's *Nashville Skyline* album and the hit single "Lay Lady Lay." It was there in hits from John Fogerty's group Creedence Clearwater Revival ("Lookin' Out My Back Door" even name-checked Buck Owens). It was felt in Top Ten pop singles such as Janis Joplin's rendition of Kris Kristofferson's "Me and Bobby McGee," John Denver's "Take Me Home, Country Roads" and "Rocky Mountain High," America's Neil Young-esque "A Horse with No Name," and Danny O'Keefe's "Good Time Charlie's Got the Blues."

None of this was lost on Johnny Cash, who in addition to being one of the titans of country music, also was a connoisseur of great songs, singers, and songwriters. When ABC gave him his own TV show in 1969, Cash insisted on choosing his own guests, and landed no less than Bob Dylan for the premiere episode.

He also drew on some of the brightest lights of the L.A. music community, inviting Linda Ronstadt, James Taylor, Joni Mitchell, and Neil Young to Nashville for guest spots on the show that took place in the historic Ryman Auditorium. The experience was especially pivotal for Young, who decided to book some recording sessions while he was in the country capital, as Dylan had done in recent years for his *Blonde on Blonde*, *John Wesley Harding*, and *Nashville Skyline* albums.

Chris Hillman and Stephen Stills onstage with Manassas, 1972

Chris Hillman's backstage pass and tour briefcase

PHOTO AND ARTIFACTS COURTESY OF CHRIS HILLMAN

Detail of the 1968 Gibson Dove guitar JD Souther bought at his father's music store in Amarillo, Texas, and used when performing with Glenn Frey as Longbranch/Pennywhistle

ARTIFACT COURTESY OF JD SOUTHER

OPPOSITE PAGE: Chris Hillman, Richie Furay, and JD Souther of the Souther-Hillman-Furay Band, c. 1974

PHOTO BY HENRY DILTZ / COURTESY OF CHRIS HILLMAN

JD Souther used this modified 1963 Fender Duo-Sonic guitar with the Souther-Hillman-Furay Band.

ARTIFACT COURTESY OF JD SOUTHER

Those 1971 sessions yielded the most successful album of Young's career, *Harvest,* which reached #1 early the following year and gave him his first, and only, *Billboard* Hot 100 #1 hit single in "Heart of Gold." More important to Young, it introduced him to steel guitarist Ben Keith, who became a key collaborator of Young's until Keith's death in 2010.

"I love every sound he makes—no matter what the [heck] it is," Young said when introducing Keith onstage in 1973.

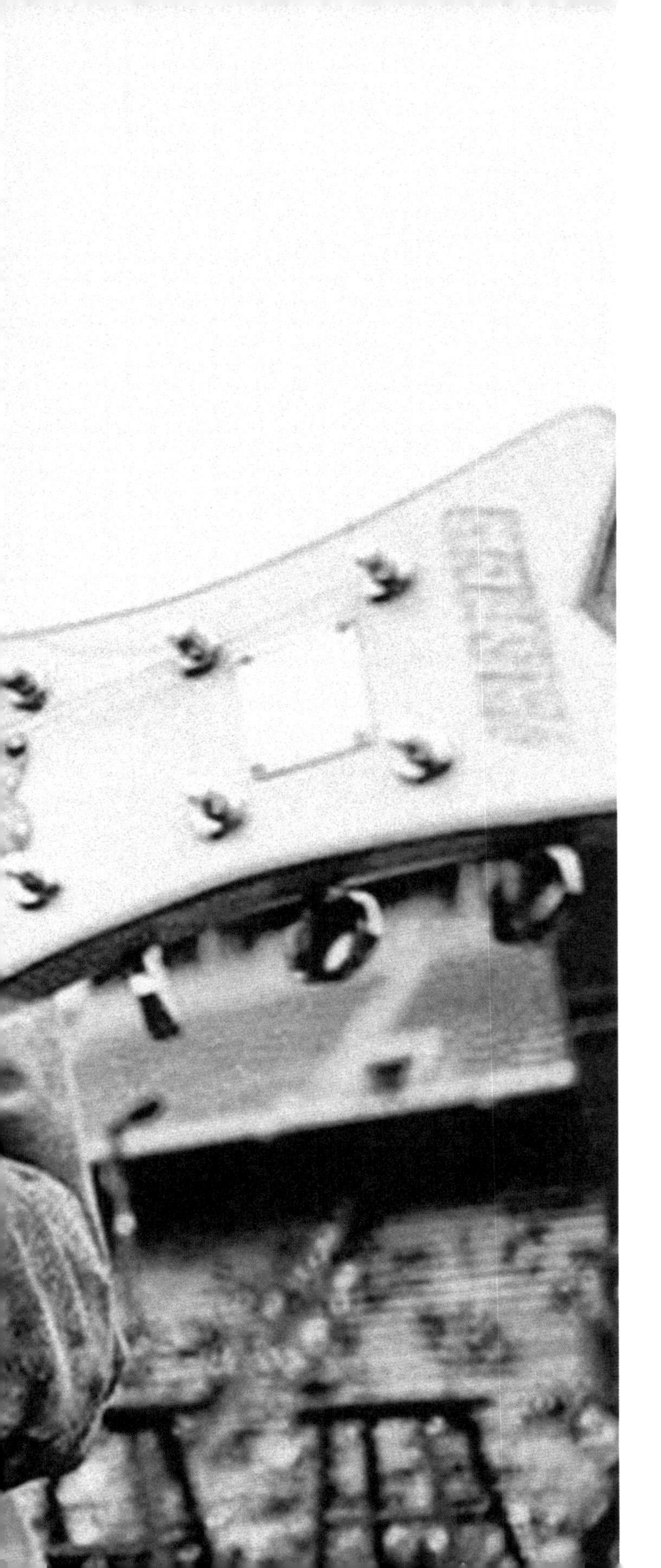

It was also in Nashville that Young first teamed with producer Elliot Mazer and ace studio musicians including bassist Tim Drummond and drummer Kenny Buttrey, part of an ad hoc group nicknamed the Stray Gators, who would join Young on several tours and records.

The efficiency of the Nashville recording process appealed to Young's penchant for spontaneity. "*Harvest* was just easy," he told author Jimmy McDonough in his 2002 biography, *Shakey*. "I liked it because it happened *fast*, kind of an accidental thing—I wasn't looking for the Nashville Sound, they were the musicians that were there. They got my stuff down and we did it. Just come in, go out—that's the way they do it in Nashville."

It wasn't to last, of course, given Young's restless desire to stay out of any comfort zones. "This song put me in the middle of the road," Young wrote of "Heart of Gold" in the liner notes for his 1977 career retrospective album, *Decade*. "Traveling there soon became a bore, so I headed for the ditch."

Before heading out on that rockier road, however, Young had shepherded the marriage of L.A. rock and country music to the top of the pop charts.

Neil Young at the soundcheck for Crosby, Stills, Nash & Young's concert at Balboa Stadium, San Diego, December 21, 1969

PHOTO BY HENRY DILTZ

CONTINUED ON PAGE 89

PEDAL TO THE METAL: THE TRANSFORMATIVE POWER OF STEEL GUITAR IN COUNTRY-ROCK

BY STEVE FISHELL

JayDee Maness used this 1969 Emmons D-10 pedal steel guitar when he was in the house band at the Palomino Club (1970–1974) and on hundreds of recordings.

ARTIFACT COURTESY OF JAYDEE MANESS

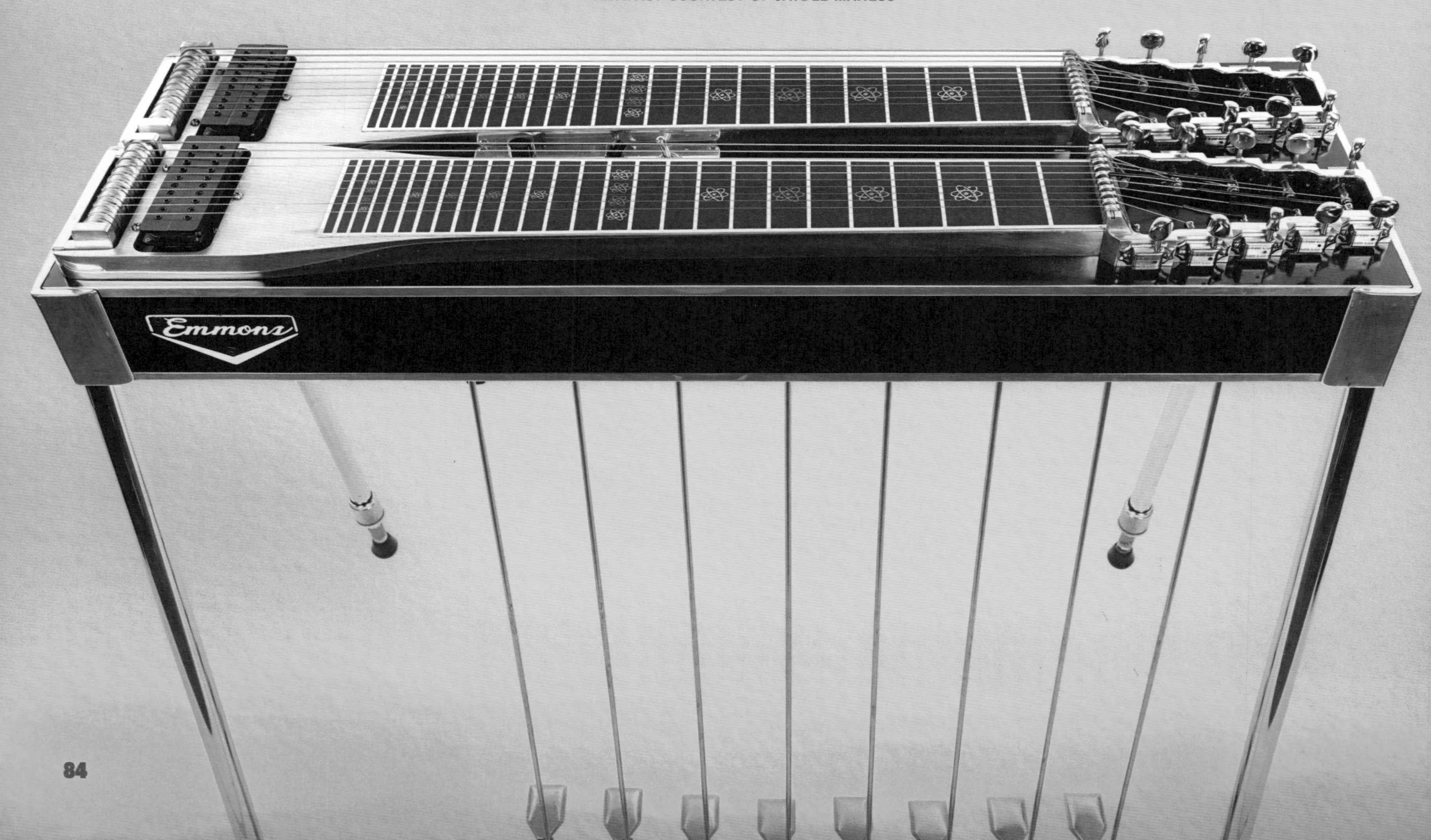

When the Byrds journeyed to Nashville in March 1968 to make their next album, they traded in their twelve-string, folk-rock style for country songs played on banjos, fiddles, and pedal steel guitars. At his first session, famed Nashville steel guitarist Lloyd Green asked the Byrds where he should play in the songs. “Everywhere!” they said.

Green responded with a rousing intro for Bob Dylan’s “You Ain’t Goin’ Nowhere,” and sessions for the Byrds’ trailblazing *Sweetheart of the Rodeo* album took flight. “They had no preconceptions about how they were going to cut the record or how the steel should fit in,” remembered Green. “I was free to do what I wanted.”

During later sessions for the album in L.A., the band wanted even more steel. “After hearing what I’d played on his International Submarine Band project, Gram Parsons called me for the *Sweetheart* sessions,” recalled steel master JayDee Maness. “I didn’t know much about their history. I was there to do a good job and play country music.”

Initially, *Sweetheart of the Rodeo* was a musical departure that alienated many Byrds fans. “Even though it wasn’t a commercial success, *Sweetheart* was the Big Bang,” said Jeff Hanna, co-founder of the Nitty Gritty Dirt Band. “Everyone I knew who bought it went out and started a country-rock band.”

The pedal steel was a big part of that album’s influential sound. The instrument’s distinctive tone and ever-moving chordal voicings added a sweet, colorful backdrop beneath the soaring vocal harmonies of Southern California’s new hybrid “country-rock” sound. For new listeners, steel offered a stark, exotic contrast to the power-chord rock of Jimi Hendrix, Cream, and Led Zeppelin.

JayDee Maness with Buck Owens & the Buckaroos, 1969
FROM LEFT: Doyle Holly, Don Rich, Buck Owens, Jerry Wiggins, and Maness

Steve Fishell (foreground) jams with Emmylou Harris, bass player Michael Bowden, and guitarist Albert Lee at a club in Camarillo, California, c. 1982.
PHOTO BY RANDALL LAMB / COURTESY OF STEVE FISHELL

In 1968, around the same time the Byrds were taking off with *Sweetheart*, another watershed moment for West Coast pedal steel came when twenty-two-year-old virtuoso Rusty Young added tasteful fills to Buffalo Springfield's "Kind Woman," written by Richie Furay. Rock fans were captivated by the new sound. Buffalo Springfield soon disbanded, but bandmates Furay and Jim Messina, along with Young, embraced the new hybrid sound and reconfigured as a country-rock band, Poco.

L.A.-based steel players represented diverse styles and backgrounds. All shared a common vision: to move pedal steel beyond traditional country music into genres like rock, pop, and folk. Many players were inspired by Nashville legend Buddy Emmons, whose unequaled musical and engineering gifts made an enormous impact on modern steel's development. Early West Coast innovators like Joaquin Murphey, Speedy West, and Ralph Mooney influenced steel players everywhere, especially in California. Mooney's soulful, driving, honky-tonk style—with showers of sharply picked, rolling notes—distinguished early hits by Wynn Stewart, Buck Owens, and Merle Haggard.

Emmons—himself a fan of Murphey, West, and Mooney—moved from Nashville to Southern California in 1968. He graced Judy Collins's gorgeous rendition of Ian Tyson's "Someday Soon" (1969) and became one of L.A.'s first-call session players.

Rusty Young wore this Nudie's Rodeo Tailors jacket with Poco, c. 1969.
ARTIFACT COURTESY OF MARY YOUNG

Chris Hillman and Sneaky Pete Kleinow of the Flying Burrito Brothers at San Francisco's Fillmore West, 1969
PHOTO COURTESY OF CHRIS HILLMAN

Other country-rooted steel veterans like Red Rhodes (James Taylor's "Sweet Baby James"), Tom Brumley (Rick Nelson's "Garden Party"), Ben Keith (Neil Young's "Heart of Gold"), and JayDee Maness made indelible, influential contributions to the West Coast steel sound.

Inspired by steel's uncanny ability to mimic the human voice, folk, bluegrass, and rock musicians adopted the instrument. Multi-instrumentalist David Lindley pioneered a heart-stopping lap steel style, overdriving his vintage instruments through customized amplifiers cranked up to eleven on Jackson Browne songs like "Running on Empty." Jerry Garcia's bouncing steel licks added playful color to Crosby, Stills, Nash & Young's "Teach Your Children." Texan Al Perkins recorded with the Flying Burrito Brothers and the Rolling Stones, then joined Stephen Stills's Manassas with former Byrds and Burrito Brothers co-founder Chris Hillman. Bernie Leadon, another ex-Burrito Brother, took up steel and, when not playing lead electric guitar, contributed appealing fills to songs like "Best of My Love" with his new band, the Eagles.

Few players made as many inroads into rock and pop as Flying Burrito Brothers co-founder Sneaky Pete Kleinow. A pioneering stylist, Kleinow employed his own unique eight-string tuning on a vintage Fender steel, creating adventurous, careening, symphonic sounds unlike anything heard before. He became the player of choice for a diverse range of artists including Joni Mitchell, Joe Cocker, Fleetwood Mac, and Stevie Wonder. California's progressive atmosphere encouraged experimentation. Pedal steel proved to be a great driver for special effects like phase shifting, distortion, and tape echo. Poco's Rusty Young even played through a Leslie cabinet, emulating a Hammond B-3 organ.

L.A.'s country-rock inspired an entirely new generation of steel guitarists. Scores took the plunge: Dan Dugmore, Ed Black, Greg Leisz, Hank DeVito, and I were transfixed by the sound, learned how to play, and went on to enjoy fulfilling professional careers. Southern California proved to be very fertile ground for the pedal steel guitar. Players there turned the instrument's traditional conventions upside down, helped expand its popularity, and dispelled any notion that all roads for steel guitar led to Nashville. Ω

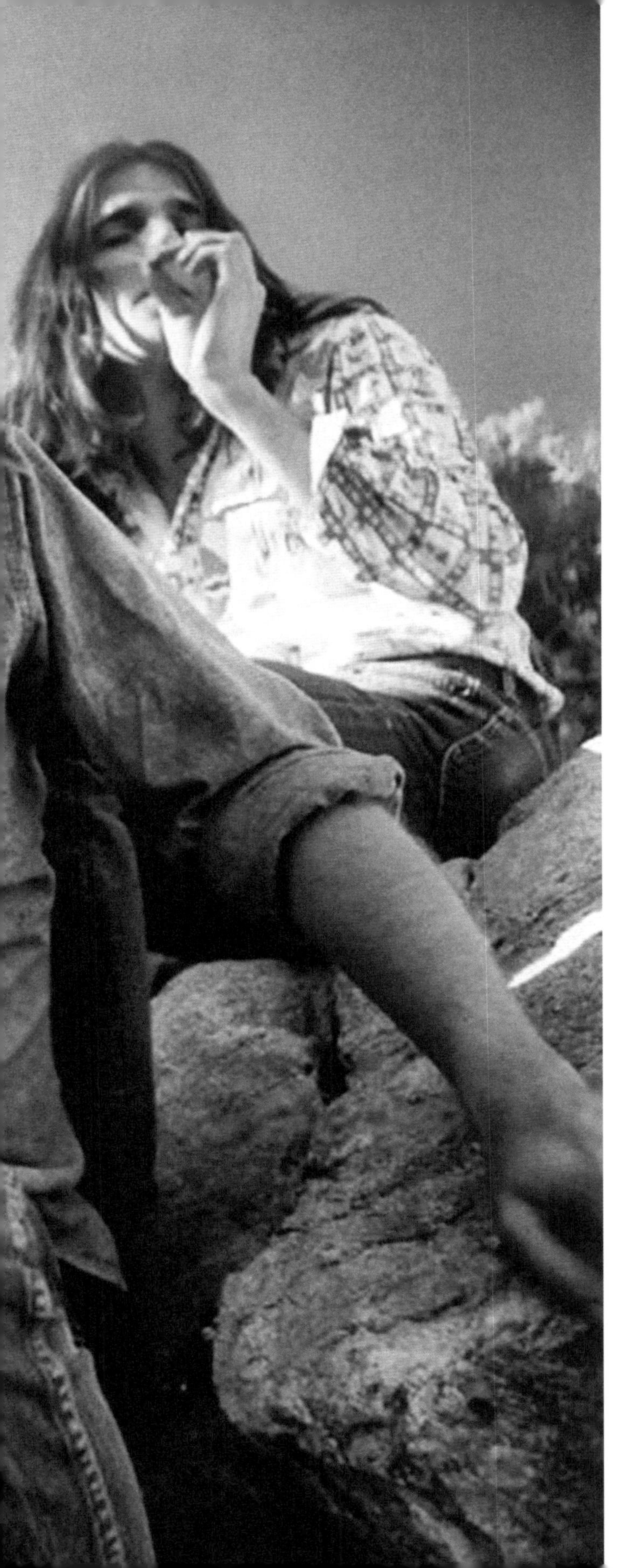

CONTINUED FROM PAGE 83

BREAKTHROUGHS: THE EAGLES, LINDA RONSTADT, AND EMMYLOU HARRIS

But the sound of country-rock would soon reach its zenith with the Eagles. When Ronstadt and manager John Boylan brought Longbranch/Pennywhistle singer and songwriter Glenn Frey together with Shiloh drummer Don Henley to back her, they midwifed the birth of one of the most successful songwriting teams in rock music history. Ronstadt quickly recognized the potential in their scintillating vocal harmony blend and gave them her blessing to branch out on their own.

Coincidentally, Hillman, Parsons, and the Flying Burrito Brothers had already made an important impression on the future Eagles too, but not in the way they might have wished. Leadon had seen the Burritos deliver a sloppy show at the Troubadour one night, one that served as an object lesson for the Eagles.

"Here come the Burrito Brothers, they got all their [Nudie] suits on, they get up [and I think] 'Well, this is going to be something!' Right? They sucked, they were horrible," he said. "They were so undisciplined; they couldn't start a song together."

Eagles at Joshua Tree National Park, 1972
FROM LEFT: Randy Meisner, Don Henley, Bernie Leadon, and Glenn Frey
PHOTO BY HENRY DILTZ

Bernie Leadon played this extensively modified 1962 Fender Telecaster onstage and in the studio with the Eagles, including on "Take It Easy," "Peaceful Easy Feeling," and "Tequila Sunrise." Inside the guitar's hollowed-out body is the B-bender mechanism Leadon used to replicate the twang of a pedal steel guitar by bending and raising the pitch of the B string.

ARTIFACT COURTESY OF BERNIE LEADON

His new compatriots vowed not to make that mistake. "All the Eagle guys were really motivated," Leadon said. "We really wanted to succeed. We wanted to be so rehearsed, so tight, that [even] if everybody's exhausted, two guys have the flu, and two other guys aren't speaking, that we could go out and do a really professional show where you're not going to know any of that stuff's going on. . . . So, we never did a bad show."

The quartet's 1972 debut album, *Eagles*, put the group's inviting country-rock instrumental blend and meticulous, layered vocal harmonies onto the charts right away. The single "Take It Easy," which Frey helped Jackson Browne finish, reached #12 on the *Billboard* pop chart. ("Glenn came up with the song's best line," Browne said recently, crediting him for the line *It's a girl, my Lord, in a flatbed Ford, slowin' down to take a look at me*.) It was followed quickly by the group's first Top Ten song, "Witchy Woman," written by Henley and Leadon.

The group's two primary voices—Frey's clean, rock-rooted tenor and Henley's dusky, high baritone that was as much Memphis soul as Texas drawl—combined exquisitely, and blended seamlessly with the upper-register high harmonies and occasional leads served up first by bass player Randy Meisner and then by his replacement, Timothy B. Schmit.

Bernie Leadon played this Vega Tubaphone #3 model five-string banjo on Eagles' recordings, including "Midnight Flyer" from their 1974 album, *On the Border*.

ARTIFACT COURTESY OF BERNIE LEADON

The talk in the street
sounds so familiar
Great Expectations
everybody's watchin you
The people you meet
they all seem to know you
Even your old friends
treat you like you're somethin new

Johnny come lately
New kid in town
Everybody loves you
you can't let them down

She looks in your eyes
the music begins to play
Hopeless romantics
dancing
(desperation
desperate to try again
(desperation
have we go again
After a while
dancing the night away
Restless Hearts
that never mend

I hate to say it but I got so bad
sometimes I think I never have enough
but you were just tryin
to give me the best of your love

[2]

BEAUTIFUL FACES LOUD EMPTY PLACES
LOOK AT THE WAY THAT WE LIVE
BURN IN THE HOT LIGHTS
LATER IT'S NOT QUITE
THEY BURN BRIGHT
GOOD NIGHTS
IF IT'S a good night
you burn in the bright lights

HOTEL CALIFORNIA
OUTLAW MAN
DOOLIN DALTON
7 BRIDGES ROAD
LYIN EYES
WASTED TIME (STRINGS)
TAKE IT TO THE LIMIT (STRINGS)
NEW KID
DESPERADO (STRINGS)
DESPERADO INTERLUDE (STRGS)
MIDNIGHT FLYER
TURN TO STONE
ALREADY GONE
WASTED TIME INTERLUDE
ONE OF THESE NIGHTS
FUNK 49
GOOD DAY IN HELL
R.M.W.
WITCHY
JAMES DEAN
BEST OF MY LOVE
WALK AWAY
TEQUILA
TAKE IT EASY

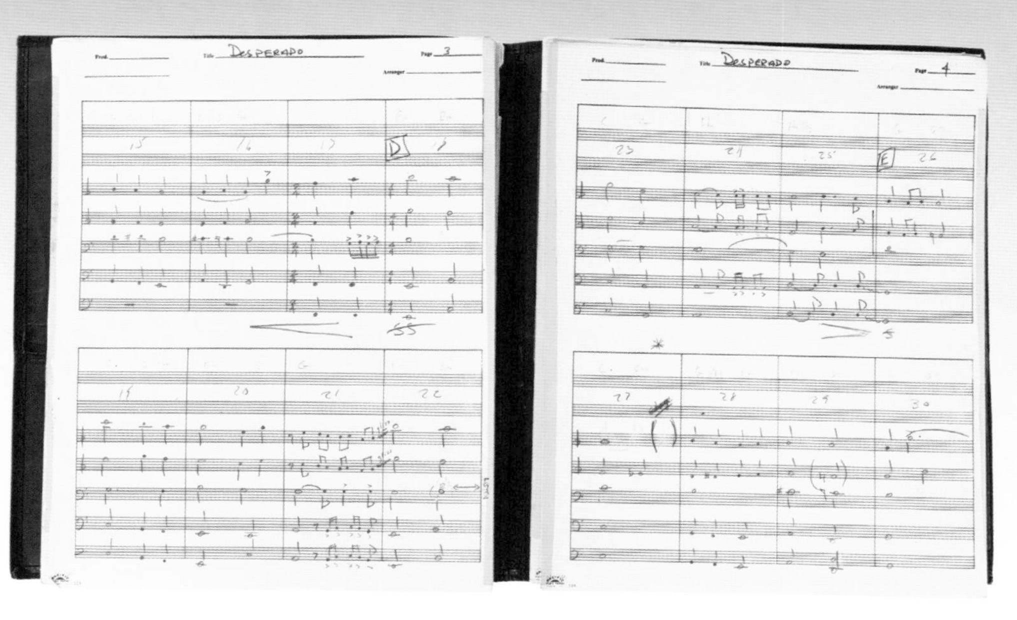

The Eagles, like Ronstadt, also made way for material from the community out of which they sprang, writing and/or recording songs not only with Browne but other Southern California figures including Jack Tempchin ("Already Gone"), Gene Clark ("Train Leaves Here This Morning," written with Leadon), and JD Souther ("Doolin-Dalton"). Tapping the L.A. singer-songwriter talent pool took their songs thematically beyond the typical livin', lovin', losin' songs that had long dominated mainstream country music.

Browne was beginning to have chart success of his own with a Top Ten single, "Doctor My Eyes," from his 1972 debut album, *Jackson Browne* (aka *Saturate Before Using*). Several more singles kept the Eagles on radio airwaves and made them an increasingly popular concert attraction. It took until their third album, *On the Border*, however, for Frey, Henley, and the band to score their first #1 single, "Best of My Love," which the group's leaders had written with Frey's Longbranch/Pennywhistle bandmate Souther.

TOP: **Jim Ed Norman composed this score and conducted London's Philharmonic Orchestra when the Eagles recorded "Desperado" at London's Island Studios in 1973.**

ARTIFACT COURTESY OF JIM ED NORMAN

OPPOSITE PAGE, LEFT: **JD Souther's handwritten lyrics to "New Kid in Town" and "Best of My Love." Co-written with Glenn Frey and Don Henley, both songs were #1 hits for the Eagles.**

ARTIFACTS COURTESY OF JD SOUTHER

Set list used by the Eagles in concert, c. 1977

ARTIFACT COURTESY OF JIM ED NORMAN

It helped push the album into the Top Twenty, paving the way for the Eagles' massive breakthrough in 1975 with *One of These Nights*, a commercial blockbuster that spent five weeks at #1. It produced another #1 hit—the title track—plus two more that made the pop Top Five: "Lyin' Eyes" (#2) and "Take It to the Limit." Whereas a few years earlier these guys were schmoozing in the Troubadour's bar, now they were headlining stadiums.

Meanwhile, Ronstadt continued her own steady rise, spotlighting talented new songwriters on her way up. She landed a Top 100 single in 1972 with her version of Browne's "Rock Me on the Water" and reached #51 with Eric Kaz and Libby Titus's "Love Has No Pride." She finally scored her first #1 single in 1974, with Clint Ballard Jr.'s "You're No Good," which propelled the *Heart Like a Wheel* album that contained it to the top of the charts as well.

The pieces came together for Ronstadt after she tapped Peter Asher to produce *Heart Like a Wheel*. A string of Top Ten albums followed through the '70s and into the '80s, among them *Simple Dreams*, which held the top spot on *Billboard*'s pop album rankings for five weeks in 1977.

Also taking over as her manager, Asher, half of the '60s British folk-rock duo Peter & Gordon, had come to L.A. to manage James Taylor, whom he'd originally signed to the Beatles' Apple Records in 1968.

Glenn Frey and Linda Ronstadt, 1977. PHOTO BY JAMES FORTUNE

TOP: Jackson Browne, 1978. PHOTO BY BILL STRAUS

OPPOSITE PAGE: JD Souther joins Linda Ronstadt on stage at Universal Amphitheatre, Los Angeles, October 1, 1977. PHOTO BY HENRY DILTZ / COURTESY OF JD SOUTHER

Steel guitarist Dan Dugmore onstage with Linda Ronstadt, 1977

OPPOSITE PAGE: Dan Dugmore used this 1973 Sho-Bud Pro-II pedal steel guitar onstage and in the studio with Linda Ronstadt, including on her 1977 country and pop hit, "Blue Bayou."

ARTIFACT COURTESY OF DAN DUGMORE

"I was [in New York] for a few months altogether, and then moved to L.A.," Asher said recently, "because it was clear that L.A. was where the action was in regard to the kind of music that James was making."

After having produced Taylor's self-titled debut album for Apple, Asher then produced Taylor's 1970 follow-up, *Sweet Baby James*, and his next two albums for Burbank-based Warner Bros. Records using several musicians from L.A.'s music community. Although Taylor hailed from Boston, he grew up in North Carolina, and he framed many of his songs in country-rock settings, notably the waltzing, steel guitar-drenched "Sweet Baby James." Others showed his fondness for folk, R&B, soul, and blues styles, helping lift the 1970 album to #3 in *Billboard*.

L.A. country-rock was becoming a powerhouse force in pop music. But it was not all smooth sailing. After being fired by Hillman from the Flying Burrito Brothers for his increasingly erratic escapades, Gram Parsons signed a solo deal in 1972 with A&M Records. Hillman still considered him a friend, if no longer a musical collaborator; when Parsons said he was seeking a female singer for duets he wanted to record, Hillman instantly thought of Emmylou Harris, whom he'd encountered recently in a Washington, D.C., folk club.

"Meeting Gram, for me, it's kind of like that: the Big Bang, the huge turning point," Harris said recently. "I didn't quite get country music for the first bit of time I was with him. But I had a chance to go on the road and

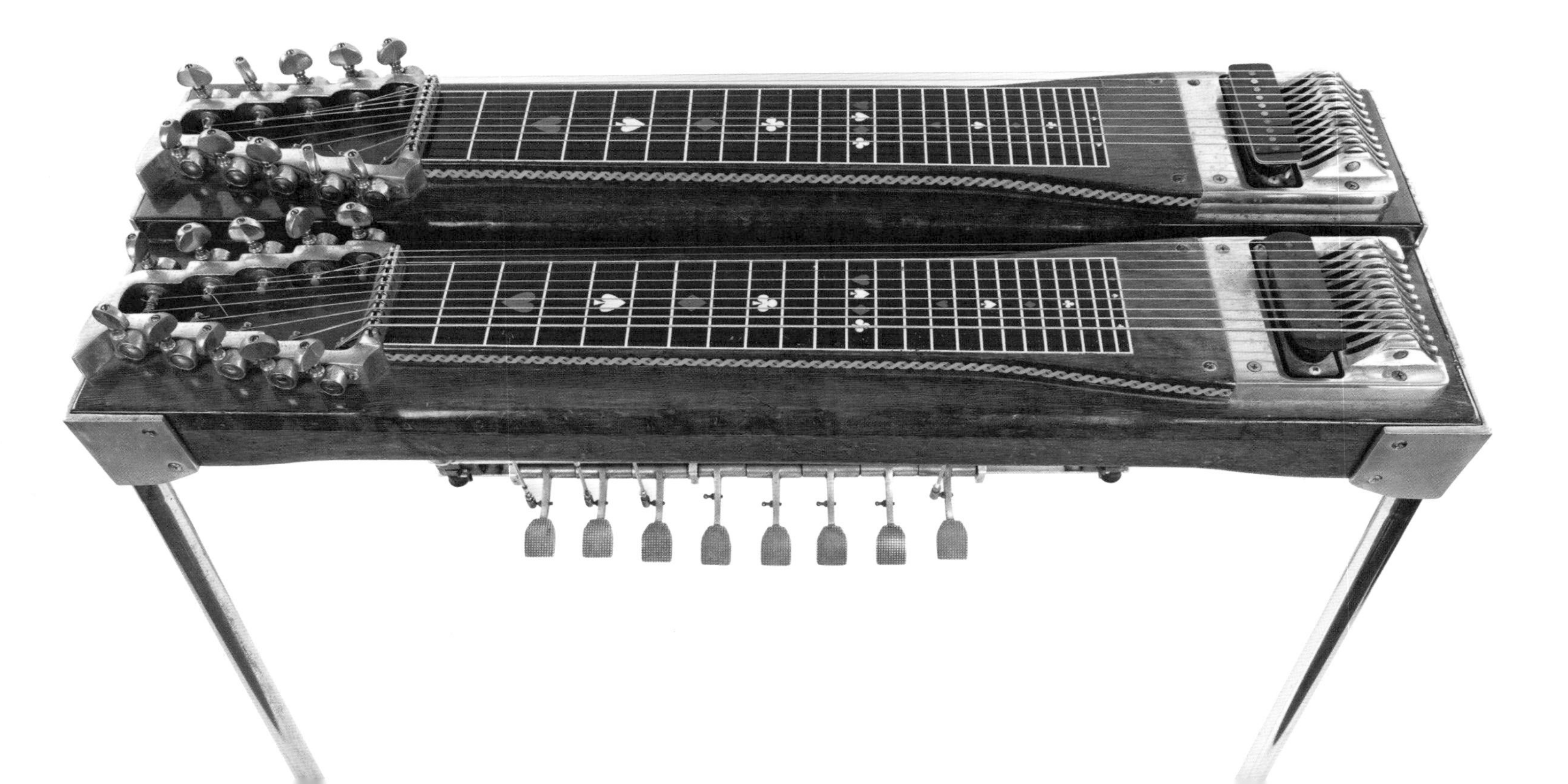

GRAM PARSON
THE

Gram Parsons and Emmylou Harris onstage, 1973

OPPOSITE PAGE: Gram Parsons in Los Angeles, June 1973
PHOTO BY GINNY WINN

make some money, and it's the first time I ever played in front of a band with drums and the electric instruments, everything. . . . As a folk singer you just didn't do that. But I discovered there was a real joy to it."

As much as Harris and Parsons clicked musically and personally while working on his 1973 debut solo album, *GP*, Parsons's downward spiral was accelerating as he descended further into addiction. He died September 19, 1973, at age twenty-six, from a drug overdose. His second album, *Grievous Angel*, was released posthumously in 1974, and reached only #195 in *Billboard*.

Harris was devastated but pushed ahead as a solo act. Her major-label debut in 1975, *Pieces of the Sky*, featured many of the L.A. musicians who'd been working in and around Parsons: Ronstadt, Leadon, Pedersen, guitarist Burton, pianist Glen D. Hardin, and fiddler Byron Berline.

Through her first four albums following the death of Parsons—*Pieces of the Sky*, *Elite Hotel*, *Luxury Liner*, and *Quarter Moon in a Ten Cent Town*, all recorded chiefly in Los Angeles—Harris almost single-handedly created a new template for progressive country music. She found a way to honor tradition and celebrate innovation

Emmylou Harris acquired this 1955 Gibson J-200 with custom black finish in the 1970s. The rose inlay and three-segment saddle on the moustache bridge were added by luthier Danny Ferrington.

simultaneously, bringing new life to vintage material by such standard-bearers as the Louvin Brothers, Dolly Parton, George Jones, and Merle Haggard while introducing many listeners to powerful emerging writers, including Rodney Crowell, Susanna Clark, Townes Van Zandt, Guy Clark, and Jesse Winchester, and continuing to champion songs from Burrito Brothers members Parsons, Hillman, and Chris Ethridge.

Harris transplanted her artistic vision to Nashville when she moved east in the early '80s to further explore the intersectional possibilities between acoustic bluegrass, country, rock & roll, folk, and gospel in a string of acclaimed albums that burnished her reputation as a tastemaker through the '80s and beyond.

Following the massive success of "One of These Nights," the Eagles headed further into rock, in part a reflection of Frey's background as a rock dude from Detroit. Leadon left, and was replaced by James Gang guitar hero Joe Walsh. Randy Meisner's 1977 exit opened the door for Timothy B. Schmit—the singer-bassist who had taken Meisner's place in Poco when he joined the Eagles.

Emmylou Harris wore this Nudie's Rodeo Tailors cowgirl outfit onstage with Gram Parsons and during her solo career. Designed for actress Gail Davis, star of the popular 1950s TV Western series *Annie Oakley*, the costume was never retrieved from Nudie's shop, where Harris purchased it in the early 1970s.

The group soared higher yet with *Hotel California*, creating one of the best-selling studio albums in pop music history. It held the #1 spot for eight weeks in 1976 and generated two #1 hit singles: "New Kid in Town" and the title track, plus "Life in the Fast Lane," which reached #11.

The group soon became one of the most critically acclaimed bands of the '70s as well as one of the most commercially successful. *Los Angeles Times* pop music critic Robert Hilburn lauded *Hotel California* as "a legitimate rock masterpiece," one that unflinchingly examined the price that fame and fortune can exact from those who find their way to the upper reaches of pop culture success.

In 1979, the Eagles released *The Long Run,* which topped *Hotel California* by logging nine weeks atop the nation's album chart. Three more Top Ten singles emerged, including the #1 "Heartache Tonight," a quintessential demonstration of the group's picture-perfect harmonies.

But the pressure of chasing perfection for a decade combined with tensions among members, and the Eagles called it quits in 1980. The acrimony was such that Henley, answering a question about when the group might reunite, said, "When hell freezes over." The phrase came back to haunt, and advertise, their eventual resurrection

Emmylou Harris & the Hot Band opening for Elton John at Dodger Stadium, Los Angeles, October 25, 1975. PHOTO BY DAN REEDER

BLASTERS

Whisky a Go Go
BLASTERS
LOS LOBOS
Whisky a Go Go
FEB 3
MIDDLE CLAS
TRAGIC DAN
SHADOW
MINSTRELS
5-6
DICKIES

more than a decade later. And in a musical twist of fate, much as the Flying Burrito Brothers' erratic show a decade earlier had inspired the Eagles toward a committedly professional performance ethic, in the decade ahead, the Eagles' own mega-success pushed some of their country-rock progeny toward a new, more down-to-earth version of the sound they had perfected.

THE EIGHTIES: BACK TO BASICS

The Eagles' multiplatinum success represented, for some, a dark side of the music industry's phenomenal growth during the '70s. Albums took increasingly long to create as groups spent more and more time—and money—aiming for perfection in the studio. This put record-making beyond the reach of many aspiring young players. A do-it-yourself ethos emerged in the mid- and late-'70s, in the form of garage rock and punk music. In London, New York, Detroit, Los Angeles, and other metropolitan areas, a new wave of bands emphasized brash attitude and outsized emotion over instrumental and vocal proficiency.

This battered 1964 Fender Mustang was Dave Alvin's primary guitar with the Blasters and the Knitters.
ARTIFACT COURTESY OF DAVE ALVIN

OPPOSITE PAGE, TOP: **The Blasters at Fitzgerald's, Houston, Texas, 1984** FROM LEFT: **Dave Alvin, John Bazz, and Bill Bateman.** PHOTO BY BEN DESOTO, *HOUSTON CHRONICLE*

The Blasters and Los Lobos shared the bill at the Whisky a Go Go, West Hollywood, January 1982. PHOTO BY JOEL APARICIO

In L.A., as elsewhere, what started as a liberating break from the status quo rapidly developed its own rigid set of rules: eardrum-busting volume, runaway locomotive tempos, mohawk haircuts, and music reeking of rage.

Musicians who had grown up with some exposure to the vast realms of American music that included early rock & roll, country, folk, blues, and/or jazz soon bridled at this new set of limitations and began rebelling against the punk rebellion—or at least pushing at its boundaries.

Seeded in part by a reaction to punk, a roots-music revival sprouted in England and New York as well as L.A. Perhaps the most commercially successful act to emerge from this trend was the Stray Cats neo-rockabilly trio from New York, whose significant record sales helped bring record company support to the movement.

Among the handful of L.A. venues that were willing to host combative punk rock shows, some also started to welcome scrappy, homegrown rockabilly, country-rock, and roots acts such as the Blasters, Los Lobos, Lone Justice, the Knitters, Rank and File, and the Long Ryders. As in previous decades, L.A.'s open-minded musical sensibility also continued to draw outsiders. Kentucky country maverick Dwight Yoakam; Louisiana-bred singer-songwriter Lucinda Williams; Indiana singer-songwriter John Hiatt; San Antonio singer, guitarist,

and songwriter Rosie Flores; and North Carolina's Jim Lauderdale all found enthusiastic audiences in L.A. Many admired what Emmylou Harris had been doing in Southern California, first with Gram Parsons, then on her own and with the Hot Band, so they packed up and headed to L.A. "I used to always say, born in Kentucky,

TOP: Pete Anderson and Dwight Yoakam, 1986
PHOTOS BY ALAN L. MAYOR

RIGHT: This bolero jacket with rhinestones and embroidery was designed for Dwight Yoakam by Manuel Cuevas, c. 1986.

OPPOSITE PAGE: Dwight Yoakam wore this Stetson hat and Mex Tex brand jacket in the 1986 music video for "Honky Tonk Man."
ARTIFACTS COURTESY OF DWIGHT YOAKAM

raised in Ohio, but I grew up in California," Yoakam told a PBS interviewer in 2019, outlining the elements he fused in his California country-drenched music. "Emmylou Harris actually was a great influence on me moving to L.A., as was the connection to the previous California country music generation, like [Buck Owens's band] the Buckaroos and Merle Haggard, that kind of Bakersfield honky-tonk sound. That intrigued me."

A remarkably rich and inclusive scene developed, spanning punk, vintage rock, introspective folk, edgy

Dwight Yoakam's 1989 Martin HD-28P
ARTIFACT COURTESY OF DWIGHT YOAKAM

TOP: Dwight Yoakam performs at Fan Fair at Nashville's Fairgrounds, June 1986. PHOTO BY ALAN L. MAYOR

Los Lobos, Dwight Yoakam, and his band at The Keystone, Palo Alto, California, 1984. FROM LEFT: **Steve Berlin, Louie Pérez, David Hidalgo, Cesar Rosas, Conrad Lozano (kneeling), Dwight Yoakam, Pete Anderson, Jeff Donovan (kneeling), and JD Foster.** PHOTO BY JOEL APARICIO

country, down-and-dirty blues, and Mexican music that had long thrived in and around L.A.

"When we discovered the Blasters, we said, 'Wow, here is a scene-within-a-scene that we might fit into,'" Los Lobos' songwriter Louie Pérez told journalist Chris Morris in his 2015 biography, *Los Lobos: Dream in Blue*. "What we're doing with the Tex-Mex and the Ritchie Valens stuff, it fits. Now people are listening to different things." It inspired members of seminal L.A. punk group X to start a side project, the Knitters, exploring their passion for country and folk music. X lead singer Exene Cervenka, bassist-singer John Doe, and drummer D.J. Bonebrake teamed with Blasters lead guitarist Dave Alvin and Red Devils bassist Jonny Ray Bartel in 1982, and landed a record deal of their own. The Knitters released an

L
P
PANTHER

AN EAST L.A. WOLF CAN SURVIVE

Los Lobos (which translates to "the Wolves") combined Mexican music with blues, country, rhythm & blues, and zydeco, and were a key band to emerge on the L.A. roots-music scene. They found a new audience when embraced by the L.A. punk-rock community, sharing bills with the Blasters and X. The band came together in 1973 when David Hidalgo and Louie Pérez bonded over their eclectic musical tastes as students at Garfield High School in East Los Angeles and recruited fellow students Francisco Gonzales, Conrad Lozano, and Cesar Rosas to join them. Gonzales left in 1976, and saxophonist Steve Berlin joined in 1984. They are still going strong today.

These instruments have been extensively used by Los Lobos.

OPPOSITE PAGE, FROM LEFT:
Conrad Lozano's 1973 Fender Telecaster bass

Cesar Rosas's bajo sexto, a traditional Mexican twelve-string guitar

Delgado jarana jarocha custom built for Louie Pérez by Candelario "Candelas" Delgado in the 1970s. The eight-string, guitar-shaped instrument originated in Veracruz, Mexico.

David Hidalgo's Hohner Panther accordion

RIGHT: Steve Berlin's Unison S400 tenor saxophone and sticker-covered case

ARTIFACTS COURTESY OF LOS LOBOS

through THE CHILL OF WINTER
RUNNING ACROSS A FROZEN LAKE
HUNTERS HOT ON HIS TRAIL (TRACKS)
ALL ODDS are AGAINST HIM
With A FAMILY TO PROVIDE FOR
WILL HE OUT SMART THEM
WILL THE WOLF SURVIVE

Drifting by the roadside
lines etched on an aging face
wants to make some honest pay
Losing to the Range wa[illegible]
with two strong legs to guide him
two strong arms keep him alive
will the wolf survive

Sounds across the nation
coming from young hearts and minds
battered drums and old guitars
singing songs of passion
its the truth that they all look for
the one thing we must keep alive

Los Lobos at Cathay De Grande, Los Angeles, 1982
FROM LEFT: Cesar Rosas, Conrad Lozano, Louie Pérez, Steve Berlin, and David Hidalgo. PHOTO BY JOEL APARICIO

Ray-Ban sunglasses worn by Cesar Rosas

Louie Pérez's handwritten lyrics to the title track of Los Lobos' 1984 album, *How Will the Wolf Survive?*

ARTIFACTS COURTESY OF LOS LOBOS

OPPOSITE PAGE: Rank and File at Tuts nightclub, Chicago, Illinois, May 7, 1983. FROM LEFT: Tony Kinman, Chip Kinman, Alejandro Escovedo, and Slim Evans

PHOTO BY PAUL NATKIN

Lone Justice's first drummer, Don Willens, designed this flyer promoting the band's show with Rank and File at the Music Machine, Los Angeles, April 9, 1983.

ARTIFACT COURTESY OF RYAN HEDGECOCK

energetically charged acoustic album, *Poor Little Critter in the Road,* in 1985, recording songs by Merle Haggard, Helen Carter, Alton Delmore, and Leadbelly alongside several original numbers. Two decades, later they reunited for a follow-up, *The Modern Sounds of the Knitters,* with another eclectic and earthy batch of performances.

The Dils, a punk group out of San Diego, was another act whose members quickly outgrew the stylistic limitations of punk rock. "There were louder and faster bands who were pushing even farther into punk," said singer and bassist Tony Kinman, who plied Hollywood clubs before defecting to Austin to form pioneering cowpunk band Rank and File with his brother, Chip. "That wasn't the kind of music we were interested in anymore. It was frustrating to write songs for a punk audience that didn't like them."

Another audience, however, loved them. When the long-estranged Everly Brothers reunited in the 1980s, their Dave Edmunds–produced album *Born Yesterday* opened with Rank and File's "Amanda Ruth."

For a time, it appeared that the Next Big Thing out of L.A. might be roots-rock band Lone Justice, fronted by charismatic singer-songwriter Maria McKee. They signed

CONTINUED ON PAGE 120

1980s ROOTS-ROCK: HOW I GOT TO THE MIDDLE OF IT ALL

BY DAVE ALVIN

In 1977, I was a twenty-one-year-old fry cook who had concluded that music and whatever dreams I may have once had about a life playing music were dead and gone. Rock & roll had dumped the roll from its name and moved into soulless, corporate sports arenas. Due to tight and bland programming formats, neither AM nor even FM radio were the exciting, pioneering forces they had once been. Worst of all for me was that the Ash Grove nightclub—where my older brother Phil and I had been blessed to see countless blues, folk, and bluegrass giants perform when we were teenagers—had burned down four years earlier.

The closing of the Ash Grove crippled the once vibrant, eclectic roots music scene in Southern California, and I had never really gotten over that loss. But then one night in 1977, I saw a national TV news program about this new band in England called the Sex Pistols and this new music called punk rock. After that, my life was never the same.

Suddenly rock music was exciting, wild, and a bit dangerous again. For some time, I'd been feeling like a defeated old man who would probably remain a fry cook forever, but then I heard the news reporter say that Johnny Rotten, the brash, young, loudmouth leader of the Sex Pistols, was twenty-one years old. I felt like a bucket of ice-cold water had been thrown in my face. Johnny Rotten and I were exactly the same age!

There was also the liberating fact that the Sex Pistols weren't very proficient on their instruments because, at that time, neither was I. Their disregard for musical virtuosity got me thinking that I should get over my shyness about my often-clumsy guitar playing and get out in the world and make some loud, glorious noise.

There was one problem, however. I grew up listening to and loving blues, folk, country, old rock & roll, and early jazz, but none of those roots music styles were represented much at that time in the British punk/new wave sounds. There were touches of raw rockabilly in early punk rock, though. I knew rockabilly was a wild mixture of blues and country that valued emotion over technique, so I figured that was where I could start trying to reconcile my love of roots music with the energy and abandon of punk rock.

In those days, I sported a scraggly beard and a nondescript 1970s haircut, but neither of those fit the tough,

The Blasters in action, early 1980s
FROM LEFT: Dave Alvin, Bill Bazz, and Phil Alvin

OPPOSITE PAGE: Leather jacket worn by Dave Alvin onstage with the Blasters in the early 1980s
ARTIFACT COURTESY OF DAVE ALVIN

in-your-face style of punk rock, so I'd have to change my look somehow. I soon shaved my patchy beard, donned a beat-up leather jacket, started combing my hair into a tall pompadour, and quit my job as a fry cook. I have never looked back.

Fortunately for me, my brother Phil was feeling the same way. He and I had always shared a passion for old American music, but I had never been good enough to be a member of the excellent blues and R&B bands that he'd been leading since he was fifteen years old. This time, though, seemed like the right moment for us to finally start a band together.

Phil and I had a common background in music. Growing up in 1950s-1960s California, he and I could soak up just about every kind of American music anyone could desire. Around our parents' house, we were exposed to Bing Crosby, Nat King Cole, and swing-era big bands, plus my father's favorite, polka music, while on the

This sticker-covered road case for Dave Alvin's 1964 Fender Mustang reflects his love of old blues, country, and other roots music.

ARTIFACT COURTESY OF DAVE ALVIN

rock & roll radio stations, we were thrilled by Elvis, Fats Domino, doo-wop, and Chuck Berry.

On local TV, we watched West Coast country music shows like *Melody Ranch* (hosted by Billy Mize and Johnny Bond), *Town Hall Party* (which featured greats like Joe Maphis, Merle Travis, Marty Robbins, and Johnny Cash as well as rockabilly legends like Eddie Cochran and Gene Vincent), and the early *Buck Owens Show*, which showcased young Bakersfield performers like Buck, Merle Haggard, and Wynn Stewart.

Late at night after bedtime, we'd lie in bed and surreptitiously tune our transistor radio to the powerful border radio stations that played doo-wop, norteño, blues, gospel, and country through the wee hours across western North America. Thanks to the influence of our older cousins' taste in music, my brother and I became obsessed with rhythm & blues, folk, honky-tonk songs, vintage jazz, surf, western swing, garage rock, and underground rock before we were even teenagers. By the time I was thirteen, Phil and I were sneaking into local blues dives and nightclubs like the Ash Grove to see,

TOP: Dave Alvin with Cesar Rosas of Los Lobos at Club 88, Los Angeles, 1981

BOTTOM: Phil Alvin with David Hidalgo of Los Lobos, 1981

PHOTOS BY JOEL APARICIO

Dave Alvin (center), the Long Ryders' Greg Sowders (left) and Sid Griffin, with some of their favorite albums, c. 1984

PHOTO BY ROBBIN KOHN / COURTESY OF GREG SOWDERS

follow around, pester, and learn from legendary blues artists like Big Joe Turner, T-Bone Walker, and Lightnin' Hopkins. Because of all these influences, we decided our band, the Blasters, would mix all those music styles together with the fierce energy of punk rock and see what we came up with. To us, no matter the style or genre, it was all just American music.

I can't lie and say the Blasters were lovingly embraced by everyone when we finally started getting gigs in the punk joints. My old Fender Mustang guitar still has shattered glass imbedded in it from beer bottles thrown by disgruntled punk audience members who didn't think we belonged there. We were, however, warmly welcomed to the party by many of the local, popular cutting-edge bands, like X, the Go-Gos, and the Plimsouls, who helped us score important shows in big-time clubs like the Starwood and the Whiskey.

I was also pleasantly surprised to find more than a few folks like me who had grown up at the Ash Grove. Even though most of the music in this punk and roots scene was very different than what we grew up with, through it we rediscovered the kind of bohemian music community that the Ash Grove had once given us. With that sense of community in mind, once we were selling out shows on our own and had a record deal on Slash/Warner Brothers, we would help up-and-coming bands and artists who were trying to break into the scene and who shared similar musical roots—such as Los Lobos, Dwight Yoakam, Lone Justice, and Rank and File—by getting them on shows with us or enthusiastically pitching them to our record label. As I was to learn the hard way later in my career, the Los Angeles music scene was unusual in that, unlike a lot of the outside music world, the musicians on that scene actually looked out for and took care of each other.

It was a wild, intense, and strange time. A lot of very talented roots and rock musicians and singers came out of that scene who have since gone on to great acclaim and have made some of the best music of the past forty years. For me, I'm just happy that I didn't spend my whole life as a fry cook. Ω

Ash Grove flyer promoting shows by blues, folk, and bluegrass artists that Dave and Phil Alvin might have seen in the late 1960s
ARTIFACT COURTESY OF FRED ARONOW

Cowboy-print bandana worn by Dave Alvin with the Blasters
ARTIFACT COURTESY OF DAVE ALVIN

CONTINUED FROM PAGE 113

to red-hot Geffen Records and were shepherded by superstar producer Jimmy Iovine. But the group's 1985 major-label debut album failed to put across the band's live energy and stalled at #56 in *Billboard*; the follow-up, *Shelter*, only reached #65, and before long, the disillusioned group disbanded.

But in a sign of the changing times, Yoakam became a top album seller, and Williams, Flores, Hiatt, and Lauderdale eventually moved to Nashville. Several landed record deals during a window of receptivity to innovative music that critically acclaimed Texas singer-songwriter Steve Earle, another beneficiary, has called Music City's "Great Credibility Scare of the '80s." They were joined in Nashville by other émigrés from L.A.—like Rosanne Cash, Rodney Crowell, Vince Gill, the Sweethearts of the Rodeo, and Emmylou Harris—who believed at that time they belonged in mainstream country music.

Lone Justice, 1984. FROM LEFT: Ryan Hedgecock, Maria McKee, Don Heffington, and Marvin Etzioni

PHOTO BY DENNIS KEELEY / COURTESY OF RYAN HEDGECOCK

The Long Ryders with Gene Clark, backstage at McCabe's Guitar Shop, Santa Monica, August 10, 1984. FROM LEFT: Stephen McCarthy, Tom Stevens, Clark, Sid Griffin, and Greg Sowders

PHOTO BY GARY NICHAMIN / COURTESY OF GREG SOWDERS

Lucinda Williams at the Palomino Club, North Hollywood, 1985

PHOTO BY JASPER DAILEY

THE KNITTERS AT THE PALACE 11.17.84 HOLLYWOOD, CA

The Knitters backstage at the Palace, Los Angeles, November 1984
FROM LEFT: Dave Alvin, John Doe, Jonny Ray Bartel, Exene Cervenka, and D.J. Bonebrake. PHOTO BY GARY LEONARD

Chris Hillman, meanwhile, finally stepped front and center in the Desert Rose Band, which emerged out of a call from Dan Fogelberg. He had recorded a bluegrass album, *High Country Snows*, in 1985, and invited Hillman, Pedersen, multi-instrumentalist John Jorgenson, and bassist Bill Bryson to open for him and back him during his own show for a segment spotlighting the material. Jorgenson began lobbying Hillman to start a new electric country band with the same musicians. With the addition of steel player JayDee Maness and drummer Steve Duncan, the Desert Rose Band was born. A stream of DRB hits helped brighten country radio playlists over the next half-dozen years. All the while, Hillman rejected urgings to move to Nashville, preferring to remain based in L.A.

Rosie Flores, c. 1987

PHOTO COURTESY OF ROSIE FLORES

Rosie Flores used this 1985 Fender Telecaster, with a Bigsby tailpiece, when she was in the Screamin' Sirens, an all-female band based in Los Angeles in the 1980s.

ARTIFACT COURTESY OF ROSIE FLORES

OPPOSITE PAGE: The Desert Rose Band, 1988
FROM LEFT: John Jorgenson, Steve Duncan, Bill Bryson, Chris Hillman, JayDee Maness, and Herb Pedersen

PHOTO BY BARRY FEINSTEIN / COURTESY OF CHRIS HILLMAN

"I'll never forget a compliment I got from Jimmy Capps, who was a staff guitar player at the [Opry]," Pedersen said recently, recalling an incident from decades earlier. "He said to me, 'When you and Chris came down here and played the Opry a few nights ago, [he said,] 'It's funny that it would take two guys from California to show Nashville what country music is supposed to sound like.' And I thought, 'Wow, high praise indeed.' "

Yet while this energetic musical microclimate was flourishing in L.A., pop music in general was moving away from the country-rock sound that flourished in the '70s. The popularity of computer programmed, beat-driven dance music by English acts such as Duran Duran, Wham!, and others surged. Prince, Michael Jackson, and Madonna led a stateside migration away from softer textures of L.A. country-rock toward music targeting discos.

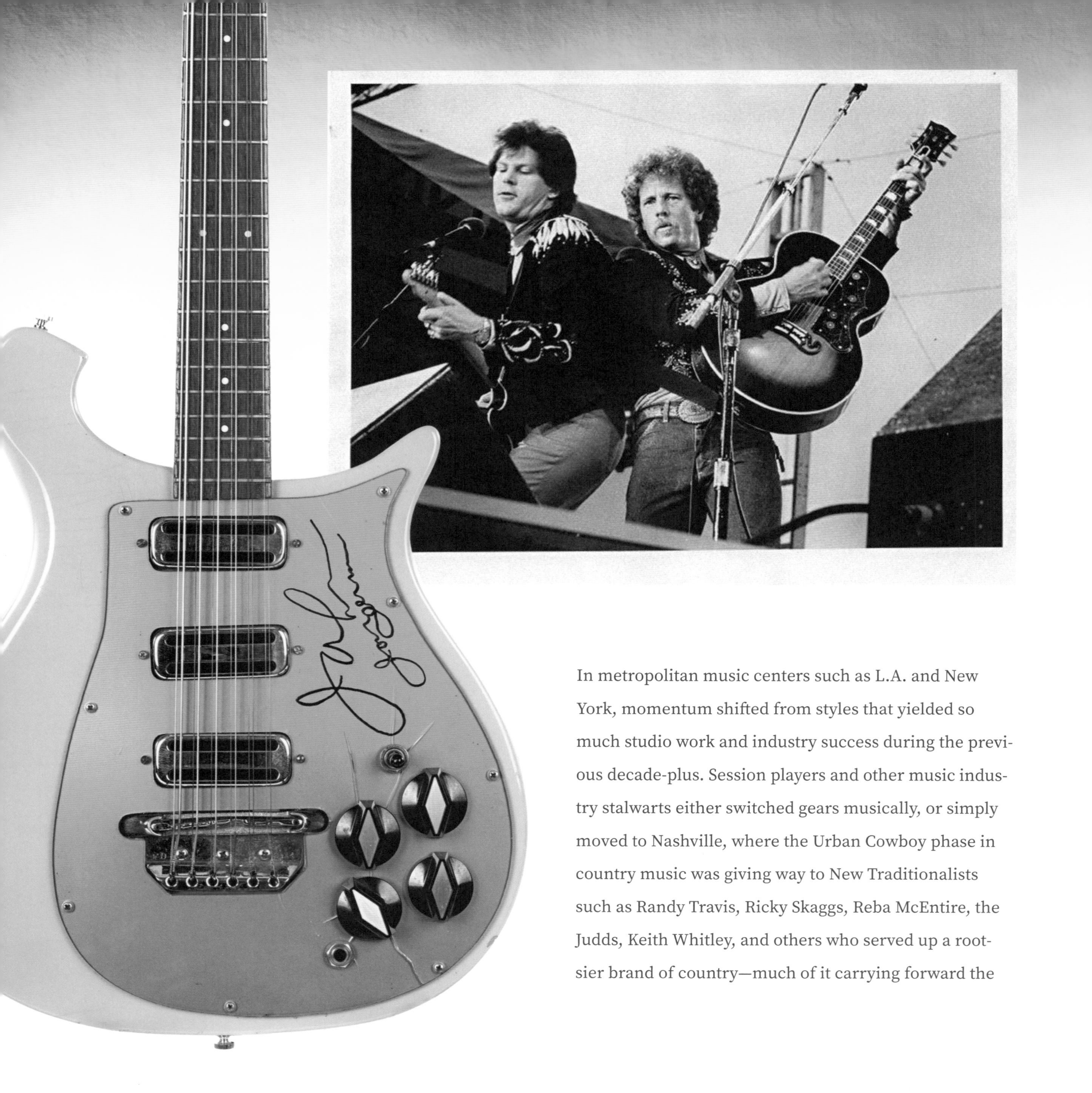

In metropolitan music centers such as L.A. and New York, momentum shifted from styles that yielded so much studio work and industry success during the previous decade-plus. Session players and other music industry stalwarts either switched gears musically, or simply moved to Nashville, where the Urban Cowboy phase in country music was giving way to New Traditionalists such as Randy Travis, Ricky Skaggs, Reba McEntire, the Judds, Keith Whitley, and others who served up a rootsier brand of country—much of it carrying forward the sounds introduced to rock listeners by the Eagles, Ronstadt, the Byrds, and the Flying Burrito Brothers.

Soon, yet another generation of country stars including Vince Gill, Diamond Rio, Martina McBride, Trisha Yearwood, Faith Hill, Pam Tillis, Patty Loveless, and Kathy Mattea began to rise, influenced as much or more by '70s acts such as the Eagles and Linda Ronstadt as they may have been by Merle Haggard, Dolly Parton, Johnny Cash, and Hank Williams. Likewise, several successful country bands also emerged in the '80s that showed more influence from the Eagles and country-rock than from traditional country harmony groups like the Statler Brothers and the Oak Ridge Boys. These bands included Alabama, Exile, Restless Heart, and Highway 101. Alabama became one of mainstream country's powerhouses in the '80s and '90s largely using a vocal and instrumental template created by the Byrds, the Burritos, and the Eagles.

Garth Brooks, the biggest country star of the '90s, has always acknowledged his debt to the music of James Taylor, the Eagles, Jackson Browne, and others who personified Southern California music of the '70s.

In one more ironic twist, as a new century approached, the sound that once helped define Los Angeles became central to the music out of Nashville for the next couple of decades. Ω

Chris Hillman's Manuel jacket with rhinestones and embroidered roses
ARTIFACT COURTESY OF CHRIS HILLMAN

OPPOSITE PAGE: **John Jorgenson played this 1967 Rickenbacker 450-12 twelve-string electric guitar, with custom turquoise finish and gold anodized pickguard, with the Desert Rose Band.**
ARTIFACT COURTESY OF JOHN JORGENSON

John Jorgenson and Chris Hillman of the Desert Rose Band, 1987
PHOTO BY DIANE CURRY / COURTESY OF CHRIS HILLMAN

CONTRIBUTORS

LINDA RONSTADT has received twelve Grammy Awards, two Academy of Country Music Awards, and one Emmy Award, as well as several Tony and Golden Globe nominations. Her autobiography, *Simple Dreams: A Musical Memoir,* was published in 2013.

RANDY LEWIS covered popular music, with an emphasis on country music and roots-rock, for the *Los Angeles Times* from 1981 to 2020. He was named entertainment journalist of the year at the 2016 National Arts & Entertainment Journalism Awards and 2019 print journalist of the year by the Los Angeles Press Club.

HOLLY GEORGE-WARREN is the award-winning author of sixteen books, including *Janis: Her Life and Music,* a biography of Janis Joplin, and *Public Cowboy No. 1: The Life and Times of Gene Autry*.

MARY KATHERINE ALDIN is a reissue record producer and annotator. For the past forty-five years, she has hosted traditional music radio shows on KPFK-Los Angeles. She is a member of the Folk DJ Hall of Fame and the Blues Hall of Fame.

JAMES AUSTIN is a former producer and former vice president of A&R at Rhino Records. He won a Grammy in 2005 for the movie soundtrack *Ray*. He specializes in projects documenting the roots of American music.

ALISON BROWN is a Grammy-winning banjo player and co-founder of the Nashville-based roots label Compass Records. She was the first woman ever to receive an Instrumentalist of the Year award from the International Bluegrass Music Association.

STEVE FISHELL, a pedal steel guitarist and Grammy-winning record producer, is the author of *Buddy Emmons: Steel Guitar Icon,* a biography of the pedal steel innovator.

DAVE ALVIN is a Grammy-winning singer, songwriter, guitarist, and producer. He was a founding member of the Blasters and also performed as a member of X and the Knitters. He is the author of the recently released collection of poems, essays, and lyrics titled *New Highway*.

OPPOSITE PAGE: This Nudie suit was designed for Jon Corneal, the drummer with the Flying Burrito Brothers when they went to Nudie's Rodeo Tailors in late 1968 to order flashy stage wear. Corneal played on the group's debut album, *The Gilded Palace of Sin*, but left the band before the photoshoot for the LP cover. The embroidered motifs on the suit represent Corneal's home state of Florida.

ARTIFACT COURTESY OF JON CORNEAL

RECOMMENDED READING

Worn onstage by Emmylou Harris, Linda Ronstadt, and Rosie Flores, this sequined vest was designed by Nudie's Rodeo Tailors for actress Gail Davis. She never retrieved it from Nudie's shop, where Harris purchased the vest in the early 1970s, and later gave it to Flores. ARTIFACT COURTESY OF ROSIE FLORES

Browne, David. *Crosby, Stills, Nash & Young: The Wild, Definitive Saga of Rock's Greatest Supergroup.* New York: Hachette Book Group, 2020.

Doe, John, with Tom DeSavia and friends. *Under the Big Black Sun: A Personal History of L.A. Punk.* New York: Hachette Book Group, 2017.

Doe, John, with Tom DeSavia and friends. *More Fun in the New World: The Unmaking and Legacy of L.A. Punk.* New York: Hachette Book Group, 2021.

Einarson, John, with Richie Furay. *For What It's Worth: The Story of Buffalo Springfield.* New York: Cooper Square Press, 2004. First published in 1997.

Einarson, John. *Desperados: The Roots of Country Rock.* New York: Cooper Square Press, 2001.

Einarson, John, with Chris Hillman. *Hot Burritos: The True Story of the Flying Burrito Brothers.* London: Jawbone Press, 2008.

Fong-Torres, Ben. *Hickory Wind: The Life and Times of Gram Parsons.* New York: St. Martin's Press, 1998. First published in 1991.

Furay, Richie, with Michael Roberts. *Pickin' Up the Pieces: The Heart and Soul of Country Rock Pioneer Richie Furay.* New York: Crown Publishing Group, 2012.

Grant, Lee. *Everybody on the Truck! The Story of the Dillards.* Nashville: Eggman Publishing, 1995.

Griffin, Sid. *Gram Parsons: A Music Biography.* Etiwanda, California: Sierra Books, 1994. First published in 1985.

Hillman, Chris. *Time Between: My Life as a Byrd, Burrito Brother, and Beyond.* Nashville: BMG Books, 2021.

Hoskyns, Barney. *Waiting for the Sun: A Rock 'n' Roll History of Los Angeles.* Milwaukee: Backbeat Books, 2009. First published in 1996.

Hoskyns, Barney. *Hotel California: The True-Life Adventures of Crosby, Stills, Nash, Young, Mitchell, Taylor, Browne, Ronstadt, Geffen, the Eagles, and Their Many Friends.* Hoboken: John Wiley & Sons, 2007.

McDonough, Jimmy. *Shakey: Neil Young's Biography.* New York: Random House, 2013. First published in 2002.

McEuen, John. *The Life I've Picked: A Banjo Player's Nitty Gritty Journey.* Chicago: Chicago Review Press, 2018.

McLeese, Don. *Dwight Yoakam: A Thousand Miles from Nowhere.* Austin: University of Texas Press, 2012.

Meyer, David. *Twenty Thousand Roads: The Ballad of Gram Parsons and His Cosmic American Music.* New York: Bloomsbury Publishing, 2009.

Morris, Chris. *Los Lobos: Dream in Blue.* Austin: University of Texas Press, 2015.

Nash, Graham. *Wild Tales: A Rock & Roll Life.* New York: Three Rivers Press, 2014.

Nesmith, Michael. *Infinite Tuesday: An Autobiographical Riff.* New York: Three Rivers Press, 2018.

Rogan, Johnny. *The Byrds: Timeless Flight Revisited: The Sequel.* London: Rogan House, 1997.

Ronstadt, Linda. *Simple Dreams: A Musical Memoir.* New York: Simon & Schuster, 2013.

Selvin, Joel. *Ricky Nelson: Idol for a Generation.* New York: Random House Value Publishing, 1992.

Walker, Michael. *Laurel Canyon: The Inside Story of Rock-and-Roll's Legendary Neighborhood.* New York: Farrar, Straus and Giroux, 2010.

2022 BOARD OF OFFICERS AND TRUSTEES

CIRCLE GUARD

The Country Music Hall of Fame and Museum Circle Guard unites and celebrates individuals who have given their time, talent, and treasure to safeguard the integrity of country music and make it accessible to a global audience through the Museum. The Circle Guard designation ranks as the grandest distinction afforded to those whose unwavering commitment to the Museum protects the legacies of the members of the Country Music Hall of Fame, and, by extension, the time-honored achievements of all who are part of the country music story.

2022 GUARD

Steve Turner, Founder
Kyle Young, Commander General
David Conrad
Bill Denny
Ken Levitan
Mary Ann McCready
Mike Milom
Kenneth Roberts
Seab Tuck
Jerry B. Williams

In 1985, Lone Justice visited the Country Music Hall of Fame and Museum at its original location on Nashville's Music Row.
FROM LEFT: Don Heffington, Ryan Hedgecock, Maria McKee, Tony Gilkyson, and Marvin Etzioni

PHOTO BY ALAN L. MAYOR